# Praise for *Agile Ga*[illegible]



"Clinton Keith has written an excellent boo[illegible]s. He combines an in-depth analysis of the chall[illegible] scale game development with hands-on advice on the use of Scrum. His often funny anecdotes illustrate that this guy has really experienced the heat of large computer games projects."

—*Bendik Bygstad, Professor in Informatics, University of Oslo*

"This book is an *essential* guide for developing creative projects, in an Agile format. There are so many misunderstandings of what 'Agile' truly is, and Clint explains it in a way that anyone can understand. If you are managing creative teams, this is a must-read."

—*Brian Graham, VP Product Development*

"I had the great fortune to complete my Scrum Master Certification training from Clint just before he published the first edition of *Agile Game Development*. I've still got the copy I bought in 2010, when it was first released. We've stayed in touch and learned and shared a lot over the past 10 years. I love Clint's writing style and hope that the new edition of the book inspires many more, like myself, to continuously learn and grow as Agile practitioners."

—*Erik Byron, Game Developer and Consultant*

"I wish Clinton Keith could go back and write this book 15 years ago—it would have helped me see things a lot differently. *Agile Game Development* is a one-stop-shop for game teams interested in using Scrum techniques."

—*CJ Connoy, Sr. Producer*

"Clinton Keith combines his experience as both video game developer and Agile practitioner to apply Scrum philosophy to the unique challenges of video game development. Clint clearly explains the philosophy behind Scrum, going beyond theory and sharing his experiences and stories about its successful application at living, breathing development studios."

—*Erik Theisz, Certified Scrum Professional – ScrumMaster*

"By the time you wake up and realize that you really need this book, your project will probably be too far gone. Dive into Agile before it's too late and let Clinton be your guide. Tested under the fires of true game production, everyone involved in game development will gain from reading Clinton's wisdom."

*—Jason Della Rocca, Co-Founder, Execution Labs, and former Executive Director of the International Game Developers Association*

"If you've ever felt that gaps exist between 'traditional' software development using Scrum and video game development using Scrum, this book is for you. Clinton effectively bridges those gaps by covering the adjustments necessary for disciplines, individual roles, and processes and project phases unique to game development, thoroughly supporting it with explicit examples and practical advice. Simply put, a must-read for game developers who are currently using or plan to implement Scrum or other Agile processes within their company."

*—Jeff Lindsey, Organizational Coach*

"It is not just problem solving that Agile helps—it also creates an environment of creating value that would not otherwise be created if the direct communication between developers was not there. An example is a programmer exposing some unrequested values of a feature of their own volition (and communicating this) because they better understood what the designer was trying to do—making a better product for it. This is some of the 'magic' that happens with the top game teams in the business."

*—Scott Blinn, Creative Director, Greyborn Studios*

"Too many developers spend months working on the technology for their next game before starting the game itself. Sometimes, they never make it to developing the game! The most pragmatic solution to this is using preexisting technology; however, if custom technology is required, then only create what is needed as you go.

"A trap many developers fall into is thinking 'We'll be using this feature in the next five games, so it's worth putting a lot of time into it now.' If this is done for all features, the first game will never be finished, let alone the next five. My rule of thumb is that until I've solved a problem at least a couple of times, I don't have enough information to make a generalized solution.

"A great way of achieving these goals is adopting an Agile development practice. We are using Scrum for our current game, keeping us focused on creating just enough infrastructure to reach our current sprint/milestone."

*—Alistair Doulin, CTO, Bane Games*

# Agile Game Development

# Pearson Addison-Wesley Signature Series

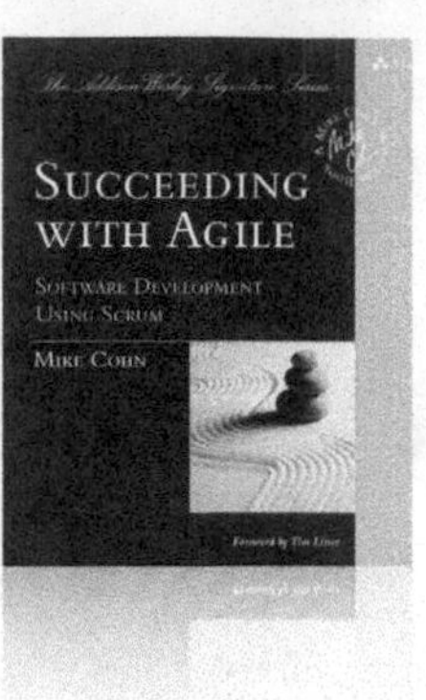


**Visit informit.com/awss/cohn for a complete list of available publications.**

---

The Pearson Addison-Wesley Signature Series provides readers with practical and authoritative information on the latest trends in modern technology for computer professionals. The series is based on one simple premise: great books come from great authors.

Books in the Mike Cohn Signature series are personally chosen by Cohn, a founder of the Agile Alliance and highly regarded Agile expert and author. Mike's signature ensures that he has worked closely with authors to define topic coverage, book scope, critical content, and overall uniqueness. The expert signatures also symbolize a promise to our readers: you are reading a future classic.

Make sure to connect with us!
informit.com/socialconnect

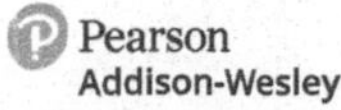

# Agile Game Development

## Build, Play, Repeat

*Second Edition*

Clinton Keith

Addison-Wesley

New York • Boston • San Francisco
Toronto • Montreal • London • Munich • Paris • Madrid
Capetown • Sydney • Tokyo • Singapore • Mexico City

For information about buying this title in bulk quantities, or for special sales opportunities (which may include electronic versions; custom cover designs; and content particular to your business, training goals, marketing focus, or branding interests), please contact our corporate sales department at corpsales@pearson.com or (800) 382-3419.

For government sales inquiries, please contact governmentsales@pearson.com.

For questions about sales outside the U.S., please contact intlcs@pearson.com.

Visit us on the Web: informit.com/aw

Library of Congress Control Number: 2020937216



Published by Pearson Eduction, Inc.



ISBN-13: 978-0-13-652781-7
ISBN-10: 0-13-652781-7

10 2023

**Editor-in-Chief**
Mark Taub

**Acquisitions Editor**
Haze Humbert

**Managing Editor**
Sandra Schroeder

**Senior Project Editor**
Lori Lyons

**Cover Designer**
Chuti Prasertsith

**Copy Editor**
Paula Lowell

**Production Manager**
Aswini Kumar/codeMantra

**Indexer**
Erika Millen

**Proofreader**
Abigail Manheim

**Compositor**
codeMantra

*Dedicated to John Rowe, the leader who inspired, encouraged, and trusted us to find new ways to make games.*

# Contents at a Glance

# Contents

# Foreword

The insight that game development and Agile approaches like Scrum were a near-perfect match was no surprise to Clinton Keith. As the CTO of his studio, he was a pioneer in the pairing of Agile and game development. Though some were skeptical, Clint saw the possibilities, and as a result, he not only created the first game developed using Scrum but also helped his teams put the fun back into game development.

And why shouldn't game development be fun as well as profitable? It's true that the game industry is well known for aggressive deadlines and that teams are working with ambiguous requirements in a very fluid marketplace, but that is exactly the kind of environment where Agile can help the most. Because Agile is iterative and incremental and forces a team to put the game into a playable state at least every one to four weeks, the team members can see new features and scenarios develop right before their eyes.

In *Agile Game Development: Build, Play, Repeat*, Clint shares his experience and insights with us. He tells us everything we need to know to successfully use Agile in the challenging field of game development. In this new, expanded second edition there is additional coverage on live and mobile games. There's also new material on scaling Agile to large projects and the extra complexity of "AAA" console games.

The subtitle of this book—*Build, Play, Repeat*—is apt. It refers to both how a video game is developed and how a good game team should take ownership of its development process. That, too, must be built, played with, and the cycle repeated endlessly as a team seeks continually to improve. What better way to seek continual improvement than to hear stories and get advice from the pioneer who first merged Agile and game development?

Throughout the book, Clint offers invaluable guidance on getting all the specialists who are necessary on a game project to work together in an Agile manner. He even delves into how to use Scrum when working with a publisher. In providing all of this guidance, Clint doesn't shy away from the challenges, including the hard ones of creating an Agile-friendly culture. Instead, he generously shares his advice so that we can perhaps avoid common and dangerous pitfalls.

There is little doubt in my mind that the book you are holding can have a profound effect on any game project and studio. After being introduced to and accustomed to Agile, team members will not want to work any other way. They will have learned what Clint knew long ago—that Scrum is the best way to handle the complexity and uncertainty of game development.

*—Mike Cohn*
*Cofounder, Scrum Alliance and Agile Alliance*

# Preface

This book is for game developers who either are using Agile and Lean methodologies or are curious about what it all means. It condenses much information from many fields of Agile product development and applies it to the game industry's unique ecosystem. This book relies on the experiences of more than 200 studios that have developed games using Agile since 2003.

If you are not in the game industry but curious about it or Agile, you should enjoy this book. Because it needs to communicate to every discipline, it doesn't get bogged down in the specifics of any one of them because, for example, artists need to understand the challenges and solutions faced by programmers for cross-discipline teams to work well.

Although this book is titled *Agile Game Development*, it doesn't focus exclusively on Agile frameworks like Scrum. It draws from Lean practices as well as methods and experiences from studios around the world.

The last decade of game development has seen more change and upheaval than any other decade in its short history. Mobile devices, digital game marketplaces, eSports, cloud gaming, Games as a Service, and so on have all challenged our assumptions about how to make games. Although I cannot say most studios have perfectly adopted Agile, it has given us some benefit to deal with this past decade.

How did Agile and game development meet? For me, it started in 2002 at Sammy Studios. Like many studios, our path to Agile came by way of impending disaster. Sammy Studios was founded in 2002 by a Japanese Pachinko manufacturing company. Its goal was to rapidly establish a dominant presence in the Western game industry. To that end, Sammy Studios was funded and authorized to do whatever was needed to achieve that goal.

As seasoned project managers, we quickly established a project management structure that included a license of Microsoft Project Server to help us manage all the necessary details for our flagship game project called *Darkwatch*.

The plan for *Darkwatch* was ambitious. It was to rival *Halo* as the preeminent first-person console shooter. At the time, we thought that as long as we had the resources and planning software, little could go wrong that we couldn't manage.

It didn't take long for many things to go wrong. Within a year, we were six months behind schedule and slipping further every day. How was this happening?

- **Disciplines were working on separate plans:** Each discipline had goals that permitted team members to work separately much of the time. For example, the animation technology was developed according to a plan that called for many unique features to be completed before any were proven. This resulted in the animation programmer working on limbs that could be severed while the animators were still trying to make simple transitions work. Correcting these problems required major overhauls of the schedule on a regular basis.
- **The build was always broken:** Getting the latest version of the game working took exceptional effort. The Electronic Entertainment Expo (E3) demos took more than a month of debugging and hacking to produce a build that was acceptable. Even then, the game had to be run by a developer who had to reboot the demo machine frequently.
- **Estimates and schedules were always too optimistic:** Every scheduled item, from small tasks to major milestone deliverables, seemed to be late. Unanticipated work was either completed on personal time or put off for the future. This led to many nights and weekends of overtime work.
- **Management was constantly "putting out fires" and never had time to address the larger picture:** We managers selected one of the many problems to fix each week and organized large meetings that lasted most of a day in an attempt to solve it. Our list of problems grew faster than our ability to solve them. We never had the time to look to the future and guide the project.

The list goes on, and the problems continued to grow. Most problems were caused by our inability to foresee many of the project details necessary to justify our comprehensive plan's assumptions beyond even a month. The bottom line was that our planning methodology was wrong.

Eventually, our Japanese parent company interceded with major staff changes. The message was clear: Because management was given every possible resource we wanted, any problems were our own fault, and we were given short notice to correct them. Not only our jobs but also the existence of the studio hung in the balance. Our CEO, John Rowe, gave us the firm mandate and authority to implement any change we needed to make.

It was in these desperate times that I began researching alternative project management methods. Agile practices such as Scrum and Extreme Programming (XP) were not unknown to us. The original CTO of Sammy had us try XP, and a project lead was experimenting with some Scrum practices. After reading a book about Scrum (Schwaber and Beedle, 2002), I became convinced that it could be used in our environment.

Upon discovering Scrum, we felt that we had found a framework to leverage the talent and passion of game development teams. It was challenging. The rules of Scrum were biased toward teams of programmers creating IT projects. Some things didn't work.

This began an endless series of discoveries about what *Agile* meant and what worked for game developers. I began speaking about Agile game development in 2005. This was around the time that studios were developing titles for Xbox 360 and PlayStation 3. Teams of more than 100 people were becoming the norm, and project failures cost in the tens of millions. Unfortunately, many studios took the Agile message too far and perceived it as a silver bullet.

In 2008, after speaking with hundreds of developers at dozens of studios, I decided that I enjoyed helping game developers adopt Agile enough to become a full-time independent coach. I now coach and train 10 to 20 studio teams a year and teach developers how to be Scrum Masters in public classes. My experiences working with and learning from these developers have led to this book.

## The Second Edition

This edition adds 50 percent more content to the first. It also revises much of the existing content based on what we've learned over the past decade. For example, Scrum and Kanban have expanded to the point where it is the most used framework in the world, but it hasn't remained static. Using the "inspect-and-adapt" principle, millions of teams have run many experiments and have grown our learning about how people best work together and make better products.

Since the publication of the first edition in 2010, there have been many changes to how Agile and Lean have been adopted, interpreted, and sold. As with most innovations, the early adopters saw success, but that was followed by a "gold rush." Studios bought into adoption seeking a "quick fix" to their problems, and there emerged many coaches and trainers with little understanding of the challenges of game development willing to sell them those fixes. As a result, there were a lot of bad adoptions and backlash in the game industry.

Fortunately, a more pragmatic view of Agile and Lean has emerged. Studios now see that these practices and values can be a part of a process that they define and own. That continual experimentation and engagement is a necessary part of a successful approach to making games, without the necessary packaged labels.

This edition reflects that pragmatic view. It dives deeper into the industry experience that I've been privileged and lucky to have found myself participate in. It places games and their developers above all else.

## Organization

Part I, "The Problem and the Solution," begins with the history of the game industry. How have the industry's products and methodologies for development changed? What has led us to bloated budgets, schedules that are never met, and project overtime death marches? It concludes with an overview of Agile and Lean and how the problems of managing the development of games can benefit from their values.

Part II, "Scrum and Kanban," describes Scrum and Kanban roles and practices, and how and why they apply to game development. It explains how a game's vision, features, content, and progress are communicated, planned, and iterated over the short and long term.

Part III, "Agile Game Development," describes practices used over a full game development project. It shows how practices used for short iterations can be expanded for entire games to manage not only how features are developed but how content creation can be planned, scheduled, and continually refined and improved throughout a game's development.

Part IV, "Agile Disciplines," explains how each of the widely diverse disciplines work together on an Agile team. It describes the role of leadership for each discipline and how each one maps to Scrum roles.

Part V, "Getting Started," details the challenges and solutions of introducing these practices to your studio and publisher. This section describes how studios, over the past decade, have overcome cultural inertia to improve their development environment by avoiding typical pitfalls and transforming team interactions.

Part VI, "Growing Beyond," takes you beyond the fundamental practices and dives deeper into the depths of coaching and leading Agile development teams and studios. It shares lessons of pushing the boundaries of scaling up and using distributed teams for large AAA games, and how Agile and Lean practices have been applied to live games. It explores how the new platforms, technologies, and ideas are best maneuvered through agility.

Although this is a starting place for Agile game development, it is by no means the end. There are great books about Scrum, Extreme Programming, Lean, Kanban, user stories, Agile planning, and game development. These books can provide all the detail you desire on the path of continual improvement.

Developers for iPhone, PC, and massively multiplayer online games use the practices described in this book. I share many stories based on my technical background, and indeed there are more existing practices for the Agile programmer, but the book applies to the entire industry. There are stories and experiences shared by many people from every discipline, genre, and platform.

## Register Your Book

Register your copy of Agile Game Development at informit.com for convenient access to downloads, updates, and corrections as they become available. To start the registration process, go to informit.com/register and log in or create an account. Enter the product ISBN 9780136527817 and click Submit. Once the process is complete, you will find any available bonus content under "Registered Products."

*Be sure to check the box that you would like to hear from us to receive exclusive discounts on future editions of this product.

# Acknowledgments

Since the first edition of this book came out, I've been traveling around the world, training and coaching teams on what you find in this book. It has been an illuminating privilege and honor to visit around 20 studios per year. None are the same, but everyone making games seems to be part of an amazing single tribe. The tribe is composed of creative, passionate humans who, in my opinion, form the most exciting tribe in the world. They have shared stories, struggles, and innovations. I thank them the most.

This book took a year from start to finish. During this time, I received much feedback and advice from those who downloaded draft chapters and helped steer the direction the book took. Thanks to Bruce Rennie, James Birchler, James Everett, David West, and Justin Woodward for reviewing chapters and contributing ideas.

This edition was made far easier with the contributions and reviews from Andie Nordgren, Brian Graham, Bruce Rennie, Caroline Esmurdoc, Dante Falcone, David West, Erik Theisz, Grant Shonkwiler, Greg Broadmore, James Birchler, James Everett, Justin Woodward, Kalle Kaivola, Michael Riccio, Rory McGuire, Shelly Warmuth, and Tim Morton.

Many thanks to everyone from Pearson, including Haze Humbert, for her persistence, vision, and support seeing this book through; and Tracy Brown, Lori Lyons, and Paula Lowell for their patient editing.

To everyone at the studios I've visited, for allowing me to work with and learn from them. Finally, thanks to the great people at Magnopus for the photos on the cover.

I would like to acknowledge the inestimable debt to my mentor and friend, Mike Cohn. Mike visited High Moon Studios as a coach. Seeing the impact of his teaching inspired me to want to do the same. I couldn't have taken this major step without his support and encouragement.

# About the Author

Over the course of 35 years, **Clinton Keith** has gone from programming avionics for advanced fighter jets and underwater robots to developing and leading on hit video game titles such as *Midtown Madness*, *Midnight Club*, and *Darkwatch*, among a dozen others as a CTO and Director of Product Development. He introduced the video game industry to Agile practices in 2003 and now trains and coaches video game teams. Clinton is the author of the first edition of this book, *Agile Game Development with Scrum*, and co-author of *Gear Up! Advanced Game Practices*.

His website is www.ClintonKeith.com.

# PART I

# The Problem and the Solution

Chapter 1

# The Crisis Facing Game Development

The pioneer days of video game development have all but disappeared. Apart from the indie scene, sole developers—who designed, programmed, and rendered the art on their own—have been replaced by armies of specialists. An industry that sold its goods in Ziploc bags now rakes in more cash than the Hollywood box office. As an industry, we've matured a bit.

However, in our rush to grow up, we've made some mistakes. We've inherited some discredited methodologies for making games from other industries. Like children wearing their parents' old clothes, we've frocked ourselves in ill-fitting practices. We've met uncertainty and complexity of our projects with planning tools and prescriptive practices that are more likely to leave a "pretty corpse" at the end of the project than a hit game on the shelves or the online store. We've created a monster that has removed much of the fun from making fun products. This monster eats the enthusiasm of extremely talented people who enter the game development industry with hopes of entertaining millions. Projects capped with months of overtime (also known as **crunch**) feed it. A high proportion of developers are leaving the industry and taking years of experience with them. It doesn't need to be this way.

## The Solutions in This Chapter

Solutions start with clearly seeing the problems and how they arose.

This chapter reviews the history of game development and how it has evolved from individuals making games every few months to multiyear projects that require more than 100 developers. It will show how the development model, adopted from

Industrial Revolution thinking, has created a crisis for game development, where innovation and creativity suffer and the pressure to follow ill-conceived plans leads to poor working environments.

The chapter sets the stage for Agile/Lean solutions in the rest of the book with the goal of ensuring that game development remains a viable business and to ensure that the creation of games is as fun as it should be.

**Note**

This chapter will use "AAA" arcade or console games as the main examples of cost, because they've been around the longest.

## A Brief History of Game Development

In the beginning, video game development didn't require artists, designers, or even programmers. In the early seventies, games were dedicated boxes of components that were hardwired together by electrical engineers for a specific game. These games first showed up in arcades and later in home television consoles that played only one game, such as Pong.

As the technology progressed, game manufacturers discovered that new low-cost microprocessors offered a way to create more sophisticated games; programmable hardware platforms could run a variety of games rather than being hardwired for just one. This led to common motherboards for arcade machines and eventually to popular home consoles with cartridges.[1] The specific logic of each game moved from hardware to software. With this change, the game developers turned to programmers to implement games. Back then, a single programmer could create a game in a few months.

In 1965, Gordon Moore, the cofounder of Intel, defined a law that predicted that the number of transistors that could fit on a chip would continue to double every two years. His law has persevered for the past four decades (see Figure 1.1).

The home computer and console market have been driven by this law. Every several years a new generation of processors rolls off the fabrication lines, the performance of which dwarfs that of the previous generation. Consumers have an insatiable thirst for the features[2] this power provides, while developers rush to quench

1. Circa 1977 with the release of the Atari 2600 console

2. Realistic physics, graphics, audio, and so on

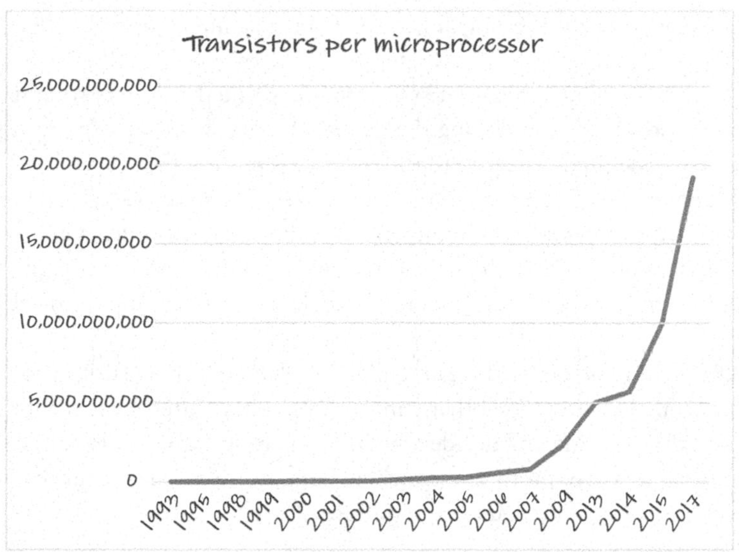


**Figure 1.1** *The number of transistors in PC microprocessors*

*Source:* Based on https://ourworldindata.org

those thirsts with power-hungry applications. To game developers, the power and capability of home game consoles were doubling every two years—processor speeds increased, graphics power increased, and memory size increased—all at the pace predicted by Moore.

Each generation of hardware brought new capabilities and capacities. 3D rendering, CD-quality sound, and high-definition graphics bring greater realism and cost to each game. Memory and storage have increased as fast. Thirty years ago, the Atari 2600 had less than 1,000 bytes of memory and 4,000 bytes of cartridge space. Today's PlayStation has 8,000,000 times the memory and 125,000,000 times the storage! Processor speeds and capabilities have grown just as dramatically.

## Iterating on Arcade Games

The model first used to develop games was a good match for the hardware's capabilities and the market. In the golden age of the video arcade, during the late seventies and early eighties, games like *Pac-Man*, *Asteroids*, *Space Invaders*, and *Defender* were gold mines. A single $3,000 arcade machine could collect more than $1,000 in quarters per weekend. This new gold rush attracted quite a few prospectors. Many of these "wanna-be" arcade game creators went bankrupt in their rush to release games. A manufacturing run of 1,000 arcade machines required a considerable investment—an investment that was easily destroyed if the machines shipped with a poor game.

With millions of dollars of investment at stake, arcade game developers sought the best possible game software. Developing the game software was a tiny fraction of the overall cost, so it was highly effective to throw bad games out and try again—and again—before committing to manufacturing hardware dedicated to a game. As a result, game software development was highly iterative. Executives funded a game idea for a month of development. At the end of the month, they played the game and decided whether to fund another month, move to field-testing, or simply cancel the game.

Companies such as Atari field-tested a game idea by placing a mocked-up production machine in an arcade alongside other games. Several days later Atari would count the quarters in the machine and decide whether to mass-produce it, tweak it, or cancel it outright. Some early prototypes, such as Pong, were so successful that their coin collection boxes overflowed and led to failure of the hardware even before the end of the field-test (Kent, 2001)!

This iterative approach helped fuel the release of consistently high-quality games from companies like Atari. The market decline in the mid-eighties was caused by the increased proportion of inferior games released because of falling hardware costs. The cartridge-based home consoles allowed almost anyone to create and mass-produce games cheaply. The financial barrier of high-distribution cost disappeared, as did much of the disciplined iteration, which previously ensured only better games were released. When the market became flooded with poor-quality games, consumers spent their money elsewhere.

## Early Methodologies

In the dawn of video game development, a single person working on a game didn't have much in the way of a "development methodology." A game could be quickly developed in mere months. As the video game hardware became more complex, the cost to create games rose. A lone programmer could no longer write a game that leveraged the full power of evolving consoles. Those lone programmers needed help. This help came increasingly from bigger project teams and specialists. For example, the increase in power in the graphics hardware allowed more detailed and colorful images on the screen; it created a canvas that needed true artists to exploit. Software and art production became the greater part of the cost of releasing a game to market.

**Note**

If you're an indie game developer, keep reading. Many of the practices used by larger teams still apply to you. Chapter 23, "There Are No Best Practices," explores Agile indie development practices.

Within a decade, instead of taking three or four people months to create a game, a game might take thirty or forty people months.

To reduce the increasing risk, many companies adopted **waterfall**-style methodologies used by other industries. Waterfall is forever associated with a famous 1970 paper by Winston Royce.[3] The waterfall methodology employed the idea of developing a large software project through a series of phases. Each phase led to a subsequent phase more expensive than the previous. The initial phases consisted of writing plans about how to build the software. The software was written in the middle phase. The final phase was integrating all the software components and testing the software. Each phase was intended to reduce risk before moving on to more expensive phases.

Many game development projects use a waterfall approach to development. Figure 1.2 shows typical waterfall phases for a game project.

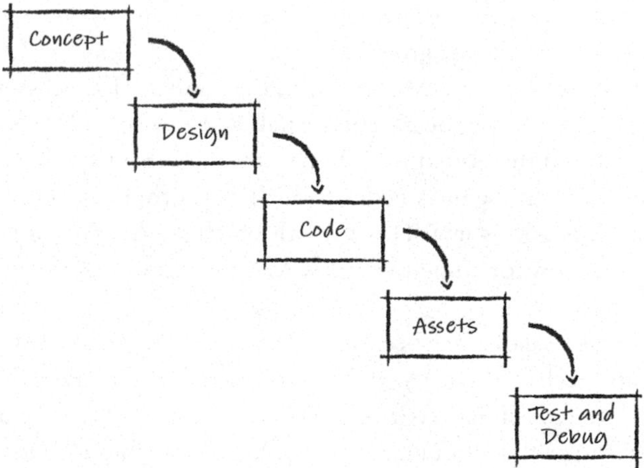


**Figure 1.2** *Waterfall game development*

3. http://www-scf.usc.edu/~csci201/lectures/Lecture11/royce1970.pdf

Waterfall describes a flow of phases; once design is done, a project moves to the analysis phase and so on. Royce described an iterative behavior in waterfall development, which allowed earlier phases to be revisited. Game development projects also employ this behavior, often returning to redesign a feature later in development when testing shows a problem. However, on a waterfall project, a majority of design is performed early in the project, and a majority of testing is performed late.

Ironically, Royce's famous paper illustrated how this process leads to project failure. In fact, he never used the term *waterfall*; unfortunately, the association stuck.

## The Death of the Hit-or-Miss Model

In the early days of the game industry, a hit game could pull in tens of millions of dollars for a game maker. This was a fantastic return on investment for a few months of effort. Profits like these created a gold rush. Many people tried their hand at creating games with dreams of making millions. Unfortunately, a very small percentage of games made such profits. With the minimal cost of making games, however, game developers could afford to gamble on many new innovative titles in hopes of hitting the big time. One hit could pay for many failures. This is called the *hit-or-miss* publishing model.

Sales have continued to grow steadily over the 30 years of the industry's existence.[4] Figure 1.3 shows the sales growth for the total video game market from 1996 to 2020 (projected). This represents a steady growth of about 10 percent a year. Few markets can boast such consistent and steady growth.

Although hardware capabilities followed Moore's law, the tools and processes employed to create the games did not. By the nineties, small teams of people were now required to create games, and they often took longer than several months to finish. This raised the cost of creating games proportionally, and they've continued to rise, roughly following Moore's law. This growth of effort (measured in people-years) has continued to grow for all platforms, with some games approaching $250 million in cost.

The growth in effort to create a game has been much greater than the market's growth. The number of games released each year hasn't diminished significantly, and the price of a game for the consumer has risen only 25 percent (adjusted for inflation).[5] This has greatly reduced the profit margin of the hit-or-miss model. Now a hit pays for fewer misses, because the misses cost hundreds of times more than they did 30 years ago. If the trend continues, soon every major title released will have to be a hit just for a publisher to break even.

4. Except for the occasional market crashes every decade!

5. Electronic Entertainment Design and Research

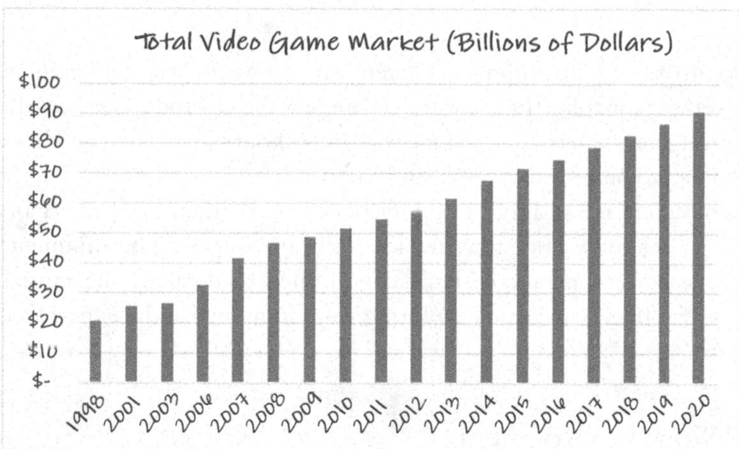


**Figure 1.3** *Market sales for video games*

*Source:* Based on statistics from multiple sources: M2R, NPD, CEA, DFC

## The Crisis

Projects with more than 100 developers, with costs exceeding many tens of millions of dollars to develop, are now common. Many of these projects go over budget and/or fail to stay on schedule. Most games developed are not profitable. The rising cost of game development and the impending death of the hit-or-miss model has created a crisis for game development in three main areas: less innovation, less game value, and a deteriorating work environment for developers.

### Less Innovation

We will never create hit games every time, so we need to find ways to reduce the cost of making games and to catch big "misses" long before they hit the market. One unfortunate trend today is to attempt to avoid failure by taking less risk. Taking less risk means pursuing less innovation. A larger proportion of games are now sequels and license-based "safe bets" that attempt to ride on the success of previous titles or popular movies.

Innovation is the engine of the game industry. We cannot afford to "throw out the baby with the bath water."

## Less Value

Reducing cost has also led to providing less content for games. This reveals itself in the reduction in average gameplay time consumers are provided by today's games. In the eighties, a typical game often provided more than 40 hours of gameplay. These days, games can often be completed in less than 10 hours.

This reduction in value has had a significant impact on the market. Consumers are far less willing to pay $60 for a game that provides only 10 hours of entertainment. Mobile or live game players are increasingly conditioned to demand substantial entertainment value for free, with teams exploring ways to monetize the experience over time.

## Deteriorating Work Environment

With predictability in schedules slipping and development costs skyrocketing, developers are bearing a greater burden. They are asked to work extended overtime hours in an effort to offset poor game development methods. Developers often work 12 hours a day, seven days a week, for months at a time to hit a critical date; lawsuits concerning excessive overtime are not uncommon (for example, see http://en.wikipedia.org/wiki/Ea_Spouse).

Talented developers are leaving the industry because they are faced with choosing between making games or having a life outside of work. The average developer leaves the industry before their 10-year anniversary.[6] This prevents the industry from building the experience and leadership necessary to provide innovative new methods to manage game development.

## Mobile/Live Challenges

The explosion of the mobile and live game markets over the past decade has created incredible pressure on development teams in a whole new way. Teams now have to respond to competitive pressures in weeks instead of years. Live games with millions of users release new versions almost weekly. Major defects that slip through testing can lose many of those players.

Additionally, the need to collect information and respond to how players use the game is incorporated into the daily development cycle. Mobile game teams often release many slightly different versions of the game to test various ways to engage the player (A/B testing). Responding quickly to changing player needs is now a matter of survival.

6. https://igda.org/resources-archive/quality-of-life-in-the-game-industry-challenges-and-best-practices-2004/

Mobile teams not only face the same challenges that AAA games face, but they have to optimize the entire pipeline of development from idea to deployment. On the positive side, because the concept-to-deployment iteration is so short, introducing and measuring the benefits of improved Agile practices is far easier.

**Note**

According to one study, making money on a mobile app is not common: "A quarter of the respondents said they had made less than $200 in lifetime revenue from Apple. A quarter had made more than $30,000, and 4 percent had made over $1 million."[7]

## What Good Looks Like

There is a silver lining. The market is forcing us to face reality. Other industries have faced a similar crisis and improved themselves.

We need to transition as well. The game market is healthy. New gaming platforms such as virtual and augmented reality are always launching, and as the past decade has shown, new markets can emerge quickly and grow our industry beyond our expectations. It is still a young industry and because of the continual change may never get old.

This book is about different ways to develop games. It's about ways people work together in environments that focus talent, creativity, and commitment in small teams. It's about "finding the fun" in our games every month—throwing out what isn't fun and doubling down on what is. It's not about avoiding plans but about creating flexible plans that react to what is on the screen.

This book applies Agile and Lean methodologies, such as Scrum and Kanban, to game development. It shows how to apply such practices to the unique environment of game development; these are practices that have been proven in numerous game studios. In doing this, we are setting the clock back to a time when making a game was more a passionate hobby than a job. We are also setting the clock forward to be ready for the new markets we are starting to see now, such as the iPhone and more downloadable content.

7. https://www.pulitzer.org/files/2013/explanatory-reporting/09ieconomy11-18.pdf

## Summary

Despite the growth of the video market, rising costs, complexity, and the rate of change in markets have continued to put pressure on studios to explore ways to find better practices. Agile and Lean mindsets and practices, used for more than a decade, have been shown to provide those improvements.

## Additional Reading

Bagnall, B. 2005. *On the Edge: The Spectacular Rise and Fall of Commodore*. Winnipeg, Manitoba: Variant Press.

Cohen, S. 1984. *Zap: The Rise and Fall of Atari*. New York: McGraw-Hill.

Chapter 2

# Agile and Lean Development

In the eighties, the backlash against waterfall methodologies was growing. Large defense and IT projects were failing with growing frequency. This led to numerous books and articles defining better practices. Some of these methodologies, such as evolutionary delivery, promoted incremental development of products using iterations. Each iteration contained a slice of all the phases of development instead of development being spread out over an entire waterfall cycle. The iterations could be as short as a week but included analysis, design, coding, integration, and testing within that time frame rather than spreading each of them out over years as they could be on a waterfall project.

## The Solutions in This Chapter

This chapter will describe, in general terms, what Agile and Lean thinking are and how they address the enumerated problems in game development. It outlines the principles and values of that thinking and connects it with the challenges facing the industry as a whole.

We'll look at some of the typical problems that face game development projects, as illustrated by a hypothetical game postmortem. We'll see how Agile and Lean thinking help meet the challenges faced by this game.

## What Is Agile?

Many emerging iterative and incremental methodologies were referred to as **lightweight methods** until 2001 when a group of experts gathered and decided to refer to them as **Agile** methodologies. The result of this gathering was to create the "Agile Manifesto,"[1] which summarizes the values and principles of these lightweight methods.

The Agile Manifesto reads as follows:

> We are uncovering better ways of developing software by doing it and helping others do it.
>
> Through this work we have come to value:
>
> - **Individuals and interactions** over processes and tools
> - **Working software** over comprehensive documentation
> - **Customer collaboration** over contract negotiation
> - **Responding to change** over following a plan
>
> That is, while there is value in the items on the right, we value the items on the left more.

These simple values have enabled Agile frameworks such as Scrum and XP to share a common philosophy and principles. This book describes how to apply these frameworks to game development.

## What Is Lean?

Game development has more challenges than most other software products. We explore and add features that our players might like, but we also have to mass-produce a lot of content that will tell stories or provide many hours of online entertainment.

The mass production of content can benefit from the lessons learned from manufacturing industries that have adopted Lean practices and principles that outperform the "assembly line" approach that is mirrored in waterfall methodologies.

The origins of "Lean thinking" precede World War II. Large-scale manufacturing industries began to understand that the greatest untapped resource was the brains of the assembly-line worker; encouraging them to take more ownership for improving workflow and quality resulted in huge improvements.

Since then, Lean thinking has found its way into every industry. It helps teams focus on continual improvement, fast delivery, and improving the entire flow of product creation.

1. http://www.AgileManifesto.org

Lean thinking lends itself to the challenges of production. Its practices are a good complement to Scrum practices. They help teams create transparency within asset production workflows and wring out the highest amount of quality and efficiency.

Lean thinking also applies to live support. Teams that need to respond to issues with the games they support or the urgent needs of players have to streamline how they work and prioritize their work daily. The transparency and tools that Lean practices such as Kanban provide help them do that.

**A Lean Thinking Metaphor**

"Lean thinking is a proven system that applies to product development and production, as evidenced by Toyota and others. And although most often applied to products, it is also used in service areas—both within Toyota and in domains such as health care. The image and metaphor we like to convey a key thinking mistake—and opportunity—is the sport of relay racing.

"Consider the relay racers standing around waiting for the baton from their running colleague. The accountant in the finance department, looking aghast at this terrible underutilization 'waste' indicated in some report, would probably mandate a policy goal of "95% utilization of resources" to ensure all the racers are busy and 'productive.' Maybe—he suggests—the runners could run three races at the same time to increase 'resource utilization' or run up a mountain while waiting. Funny...but this kind of thinking lies behind much of traditional management and processes in development and other domains. Of course, in contrast, here is a central idea in Lean thinking:

"'Watch the baton, not the runners.'" (Larman, Vodde, 2014)

Lean approaches benefit various aspects of game development by

- Eliminating wasteful practices such as rebuilding assets that weren't ready to be built because we committed to specific start dates too early
- Building quality into production rather than testing it at the end of development
- Treating developers not as cogs in a machine, but as craftspeople who can improve the production process by applying skill and knowledge
- Optimizing the entire production pipeline by moving work quickly through it so that we can frequently iterate on improving the workflow

This book describes how Kanban, a set of tools for implementing these Lean principles, is used for game development.

**Definition: Is Agile Lean or is Lean Agile?**

Many of the practices and principles of Agile and Lean are similar to one another. There are arguments about which came first or which is the foundation of the other. In practice I find blending the principles and practices most useful, so when the book uses the word "Agile" here it means "Agile and Lean."

## Why Game Development Is Hard

Beyond the technical and creative challenges, game development presents studio cultural, team, and management challenges, which are overwhelming. We'll begin by looking at a hypothetical but typical postmortem, and then extrapolate from it the three most typical areas into which game project problems fall.

### Learning from Postmortems

I've been a fan of *Game Developer Magazine* and Gamasutra.com since they started publishing. My favorite articles are the postmortems of game projects. Not only do they show how different studios work, but they also show that none of us are facing such challenges alone. Some postmortems are brutally honest about the overwhelming challenges developers face. Reading these postmortems feels like passing a car wreck; you shouldn't look, but you do anyway.

These postmortems are a good starting place to reveal the reasons for adopting an Agile framework for game development, so I've concocted a short postmortem based on a hypothetical game called *Quintessential*. It encompasses the more common issues seen in published postmortems and my own project experiences.

**The *Quintessential* Postmortem**

*Quintessential* is a sci-fi shooter released by Hypothetical Studios. Although the project tested the endurance of everyone—from quality assurance (QA) to publisher—it shipped to critical acclaim. This postmortem describes what went right with the development of the game and what went wrong.

**What Went Right?**

The things that went right had to do with the studio's culture and employees, the prototypes, and the license.

**Studio Culture**

Hypothetical Studios is a great place to work. The studio was founded by game development veterans who wanted to create the best possible environment in which to develop games. Everyone has their own office, a convenience for those late nights when you need a little peace and quiet. The kitchen is stocked with free beverages and snacks. Our game room has pool tables, foosball tables, and classic arcade machines for blowing off steam. No one works late alone. The entire team commits to working hard together. Hypothetical promotes teamwork. We're all "in it" together.

**Talented Employees**

Hypothetical Studios hires the best people for every discipline. Our programmers are top-notch; they are constantly exploring new areas of technology. Hypothetical doesn't rely on any middleware; we exert full control over every aspect of our engine. Our creative group has lofty goals and the talent to match.

**Great Prototypes**

The early prototypes of *Quintessential* demonstrated a great deal of promise for the game, and we were able to develop them very quickly. For example, we demonstrated a system that allowed every part of the visible world to be destroyed. Although this feature wasn't shipped with the game, it showed the capabilities of the technology early on.

**Great License**

*Quintessential* was based on the popular movie that was a summer blockbuster six months before the game shipped. This drove considerable interest in the game.

**What Went Wrong?**

The things that went wrong had to do with the ship date, the timing of going into production, when people were added to the project, and the technical challenges.

### Unachievable Ship Date

*Quintessential* was supposed to ship simultaneously with the movie. Hypothetical, a small studio with only two projects, was under a great deal of pressure to meet the original ship date, but in the end, we were unable to do so. Part of the reason was that the game's features continued to change during development. These changes were not accounted for in the schedule, and they added time.

### Going into Production Too Soon

The project was originally scheduled to start level production 12 months before the release date. Unfortunately, when the time arrived, we weren't far enough along with the game mechanics to lay out the levels properly. For example, the player was given a jet pack that allowed them to fly through the air after production started. This required us to add more vertical spaces than we had planned. Nonetheless, the schedule forced us into production on the originally scheduled date; launching the game on the same date as the movie was considered very important. As a result, many of the levels had to be reworked when the game mechanics were figured out.

### Adding People Late to the Project

As we fell behind in production, the studio brought more people over from the other project to increase the pace. These new additions to the project team needed a lot of handholding to come up to speed, however. When they did come up to speed, they merely created more assets that had to be reworked later. In the final tally, merging the two project teams actually slowed us down.

### Underestimating the Technical Challenges

The original destructible prototype showed so much promise that it was added to the design with few questions asked. It was going to be the killer feature that would make the game a hit. Unfortunately, the programmers discovered—too late—that the destructible system didn't work on a large majority of smartphones. We were forced to make the painful decision to drop the feature and replace all the destructible geometry in the production levels with the static geometry as originally planned.

### Ignoring Monetization Until It Was Too Late

As a free-to-play game, we were counting on making money by monetizing the game through in-game purchases of advanced armament, shielding, and spaceship enhancements. Unfortunately, because we didn't add and test the integration of such add-ons early, we had to throw out and rebuild many of the systems to accommodate add-ons and to rebalance the game after its initial release. Many players didn't like this and bailed on the game.

**Conclusion**

We are proud of our efforts to produce a good game that is worthy of the license. Although we had some challenging times, that's the nature of making games. The lesson we learned is to plan a little better at the start of the project. Had we explored the monetization system a bit earlier, we could have had it ready for the initial deployment of the game.

## The Problems

This postmortem tells a story familiar to many experienced developers. Why do projects start out so full of hope and end up in a spirit-numbing crunch of overtime and wasted effort? Is this the best way to make games? I hope not.

So, why do projects run into trouble? There are three major reasons: feature creep, overoptimistic schedules, and the challenges of production.

### *Feature Creep*

**Feature creep** is the term given to features being added to a project after the original scope is defined. There are two main reasons for feature creep; the first is when the stakeholders see the game in progress and request new features. This is referred to as **emergent requirements**. The second is when the feature doesn't live up to its expectations so more work is added.

Feature creep isn't a bad thing unless the budget and/or schedule remain unchanged as work is added. It happens so gradually that management accepts it without much question. Why do they allow this? It's usually because they have little choice; troubled projects often agree to changes that the stakeholder requests to avoid cancellation.

Opportunities to add value to the game are identified throughout the project, but with a tight schedule and workload, they either have to be ignored or have to be added at great peril to the deadline. Unfortunately, swapping out planned features for new ones that require the same amount of effort is not an option. Feature creep tends to expand the total scope.

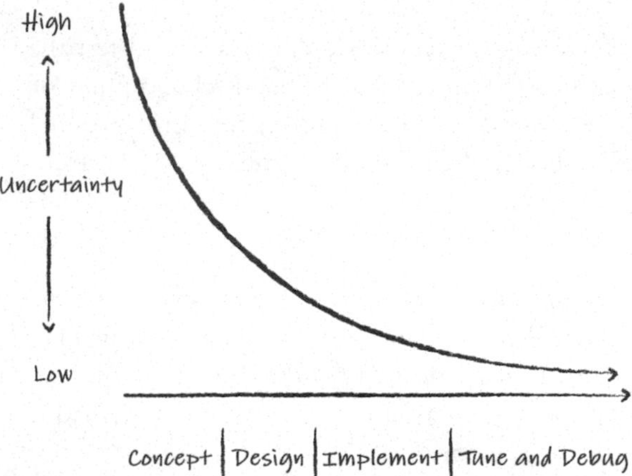


**Figure 2.1** *Reducing uncertainty*

Feature creep and change are inevitable. Have you ever gone back and read the original game design document for a game you just shipped? Often it seems that the title page is the only thing that doesn't change.

This is often the main problem with writing "Big Designs Up Front" (BDUF): The goal is to answer all questions about the game. In reality, we can't really know everything about a game at the start. Knowledge comes only when we have the controller in hand and are playing the game at a decent frame rate on the target machine. The only way to recognize fun is to play the game.

In the early stages of the game, we have the greatest range of uncertainty. We may be certain that we're making a first-person shooter, but knowledge of exactly what types of weapons are best is lacking. We learn more when we can shoot characters in the game.

Figure 2.1 demonstrates how uncertainty diminishes over the phases of a game or feature's development. Uncertainty is highest at concept definition and slowly drops as a product or feature set is testable on the target machine.

A waterfall project carries hundreds of uncertain features forward to the testing phases—called **alpha** and **beta**—just before shipping. An Agile project eliminates the uncertainty in small iterations that include every part of development.

### *Overoptimistic Schedules*

Task estimation is not an exact science. Even when we estimate simple things in daily life, such as running an errand at the store, unanticipated problems crop up and throw off our estimates. Traffic will jam, or the lines at the store will be long. The accuracy of estimates drops when more complex tasks are estimated, such as those for making games. Many things throw off the estimated time to complete a task:

- The difference in experience and productivity between two people who have a task assigned to them. Studies have shown that the range of productivity will vary by a factor of ten.
- How many other tasks a person is working on at a single time (multitasking).
- The stability of the build and tools used to complete the task.
- The iterative nature of a task: It's never certain how many iterations are going to be necessary for tuning and polishing a feature to "find the fun."

**Terminology**

Studios use the words "deploy" or "ship" when a game is released into the market, and this book uses both. Commonly, live digitally distributed games use "deploy." and disc-based games use "ship."

### *The Challenge of Production*

The challenges for pre-production and production are quite different. **Pre-production** is the exploration of what the game is. The challenge of pre-production is to find the fun of the game that drives the goals of production. **Production** is the stage where the team builds a dozen or so hours of content, such as characters and levels. Production fleshes out the story and surroundings to leverage the mechanics created in pre-production. The challenge of production is to maximize efficiency, minimize waste, and create predictability.

Predictability is more important and more plausible during production. Production represents a great deal of work. Dozens of characters and levels have to be built before a game is shipped. Production often accompanies a major staffing increase or engagement of an outsource company. Mass-producing assets such as characters and levels shouldn't start early. The game mechanics and asset budgets must be established to create proper assets on the first pass to avoid expensive rework.

Production should begin when the uncertainty about the game mechanics and the uncertainty of the technology and tools to make the game have been greatly reduced. Figure 2.2 shows how a project should pass through the prototype, pre-production, and production phases based on the level of certainty about technical solutions, asset budgets, and quality and design knowledge.

Most game projects cannot afford the luxury of entering production when they are ready, but pre-production is difficult to predict. The exploration of what is fun and the range of mechanics to mass-produce are difficult to schedule. When pre-production takes longer than expected, projects are often forced to enter production by the demands of a schedule. Figure 2.3 shows how the transition from pre-production to production should happen.

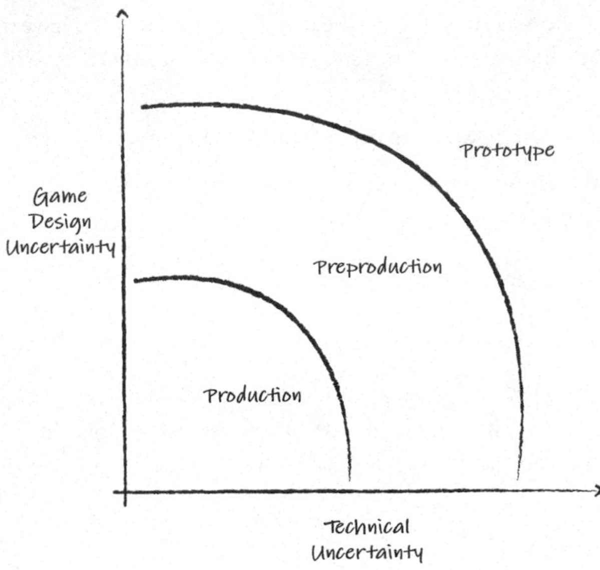


**Figure 2.2** *Uncertainty of design and technology*

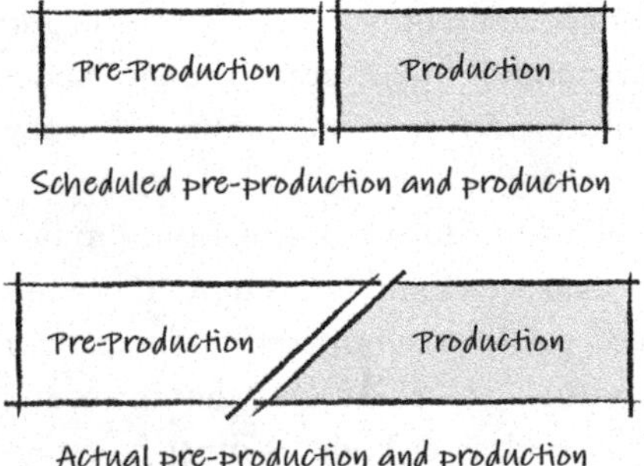


**Figure 2.3** *Scheduled vs. actual production transition*

Some assets are ready for production earlier than others. Our knowledge of the budgets and quality of how the game should ship determines the timing of when an asset enters production. If these things are unknown, the asset should not be in production.

When teams enter production too soon, they do so without the proper knowledge of what to build. By the time the team discovers the true requirements, they may have created a good chunk of production assets based on false assumptions. If the requirements have changed—for example, removing the destructible geometry or adding the jet pack in *Quintessential*—then those assets need to be reworked. This creates a lot of wasted effort and time.

### *Responding Quickly to Players*

Many, if not most, games being played are continually being updated. These games are monetized not only from an initial sale, but also from adding content or selling upgrades and other things that players want.

As a result of this, the increased competition in online marketplaces, and the lower initial purchase costs,[2] today's players are much more fickle and likely to "jump ship" to a competing game that offers a desired feature sooner.

Live game developers who take months to design, plan, develop, test, and deploy versions of their games can be upstaged by competitors who deploy every few weeks.

**Experience**

I was hired to work with a team that was supporting a popular agriculture-simulation social network game that had been around for years. They had been seeing their daily active user counts declining steadily since a competing game, developed by a startup after three months of initial development, had appeared and was deploying new versions of their game weekly. Despite the clear evidence to the contrary, this established game team didn't see the benefit of increasing their cadence of deployments.

## Applying Both Agile and Lean

Just as carpenters wouldn't settle on just using a hammer or a saw for their work, game developers can't settle on one set of tools for all development. The most successful teams will continually explore and refine practices on a regular basis.

Figure 2.2 shows the areas of uncertainty for pre-production and production. Game developers find that when they are exploring ideas and core mechanics for games, using the time-boxed approach of Scrum, where cross-discipline teams "swarm" on a problem and deal with emergent issues daily, works best. However, when the uncertainty of what is fun is reduced and the vocabulary of the mechanics is refined, then producing the content for the game is best served by using Kanban practices. Similarly, when a game is deployed, then a combination of Scrum and Kanban practices often serves the team well. Chapter 22, "Live Game Development," explores this in detail

Agile and Lean are complementary and overlapping in principle.

2. Such as the free-to-play games

**Agile vs. Lean**

This book's primary focus is to help game developers make great games and enjoy doing it. The first edition of this book received criticism from Scrum and Kanban purists who said it "broke the rules" of their favorite brand.

It doesn't make sense to me to adhere to some strict rules of a framework that promotes exploration and ownership. Process doesn't determine which games are great. People, talent, and creativity have more impact.

## Why Use Agile and Lean for Game Development?

What has driven the industry towards Agile and Lean? Primarily, market forces for higher quality, lower cost, and faster cadences are driving us. As discussed in Chapter 1, "The Crisis Facing Game Development," the cost of creating games continues to grow. While the market expands and diversifies, the long-term stability of any studio or team has diminished. Competition has increased, and the news is filled with announcements of studio closures or large-scale layoffs.

### Cost and Quality

Let's take a quick look at the economics of the game market for "AAA" console or PC games. With a retail cost of $60, a game that sells half a million copies grosses $30 million. After licensing, distribution, marketing, and publishing costs are subtracted, about one-fourth of the gross sales, or $7.5 million, is left to pay for the development of a game. Many game development projects cost more than $7.5 million, and the largest majority of games don't approach sales of half a million units. Most games fail to break even!

Developers are trying to keep costs down on development by doing the following:

- Seeking opportunities to outsource asset creation and code development
- Relying on middleware[3] solutions
- Reducing the amount of content (releasing a game with 8 hours of gameplay rather than 16)

3. **Middleware** is technology purchased from a vendor or another developer.

Publishers are also trying to reduce the number of games that lose money for them by doing the following:

- Relying on a greater proportion of licensed properties, such as movie-based games
- Relying more on sequels and older franchises that have been successful in the past
- Seeking to monetize games in questionable ways
- Taking fewer chances on new ideas

These steps can reduce the quality of games on the market and discourage players from buying games.

Now let's look at how Agile addresses quality and cost issues. We'll see how Agile helps us "find the fun" and eliminate some of the most notorious sources of wasted work common to game development.

## Finding the Fun First

A benefit of iterative development is to develop a product in small steps and incrementally add features that satisfy the player in the fastest and most economical way. A fun game is more appealing to players and results in more sales. "Find the fun" is the mantra of any iterative and incremental game development project. Fun is only found with the controller in your hand.

Figure 2.4 shows a notional representation of when the fun or value was discovered during a waterfall-developed game. Waterfall projects typically show minimal progress in finding the fun in the first two-thirds of the project. Except for occasional prototype or The Electronic Entertainment Expo (E3) demos, much of the work is spent executing to a plan and not demonstrating value. It's not until the end of the project—when all the pieces come together and the game is being tuned and debugged—that the project team has a clear idea of what the game is and can identify improvements. Unfortunately, the end of the project is the worst time for this to occur. The project is facing an impending deadline, and any significant change for the sake of increased value is often rejected out of consideration for the schedule.

### Question

How many times have you been in alpha or beta and wished for a few extra months to improve the game?

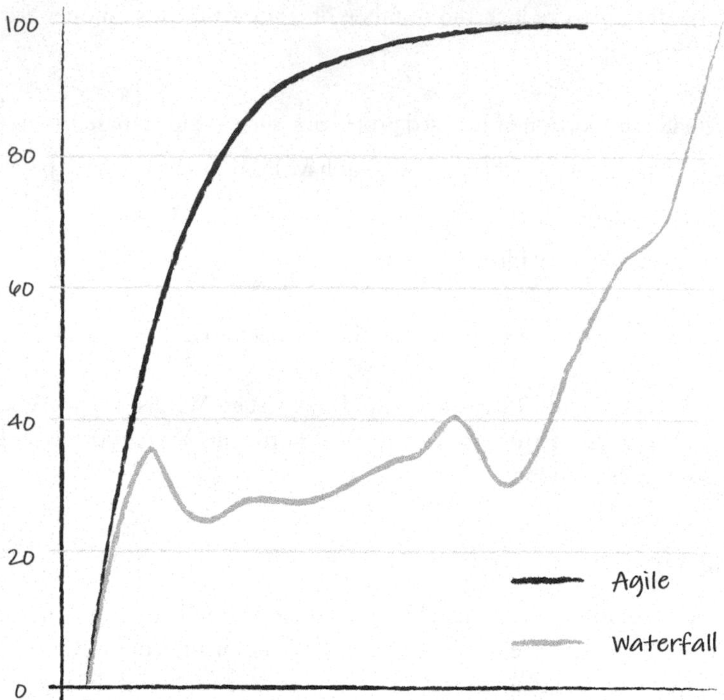


**Figure 2.4** *Finding the fun*

The Agile project value curve approaches development in a value-first approach. This happens when the project iterates on bringing features to a near-shippable state in a value-prioritized order. The publisher expects value to be demonstrated early unless the core idea is not good or the developers are not up to the task of making a great game. This enables the stakeholders and project team to avoid wasting years of effort and cost on projects that won't be fun. The "find the fun" mantra forces us to focus our efforts on making the game better every iteration. A game that is not fun must be questioned at every step.

## Iterate More, Fail Fast

Simple iteration enables game developers to explore more ideas. By delivering working software iteratively, a project can prove whether an idea is viable earlier in development. This makes it possible to enact the kill-gate model where a dozen ideas are launched and narrowed down until the best remain.

**Note**

A **kill-gate** model of development is where a number of prototypes are started with the intention of funding only one to completion. The prototypes are narrowed down as they demonstrate their value. The ones that are not proving their value are stopped at the "gate" and are "killed" rather than allowed to continue. This is different from the stage-gate model, which is discussed in Chapter 17, "Working with Stakeholders."

## Agile Values Applied to Game Development

Let's look at the Agile values from the Agile Manifesto and see how they apply to video game development.

### *Individuals and Interactions Over Processes and Tools*

Our processes and tools to manage ever-growing projects have grown dramatically. Large teams have driven the creation of management hierarchies. Project schedules and design documents—which attempt to predict every requirement and task necessary to make a fun game—require expensive databases to manage. All of these are considered necessary to tackle the complexity that arises from having upward of 100 people working on a multiyear project.

Game development requires developers from widely different disciplines. Take, for example, a cutting-edge AI character who needs to walk around an environment and challenge the player in the game. The creation of this character requires the participation of animators, designers, character modelers, texture artists, programmers, and audio composers, among others.

It's important that these disciplines collaborate as much as possible to be effective. For example, it is important for an animator who discovers a bug in the animation technology to work with an animation programmer as quickly as possible. Processes and organization can add delay. In this example, the programmer may be working on a series of tasks that were assigned by a lead. This may prevent that programmer from helping the animator without permission from their lead. This leads to a chain of communication, as shown in Figure 2.5.

The animator has to pass the request up through the chain of command; the request then has to make it back down to a programmer who can solve the problem. In this example, the request involves five people and four requests! This flow is prone to failure and delay.

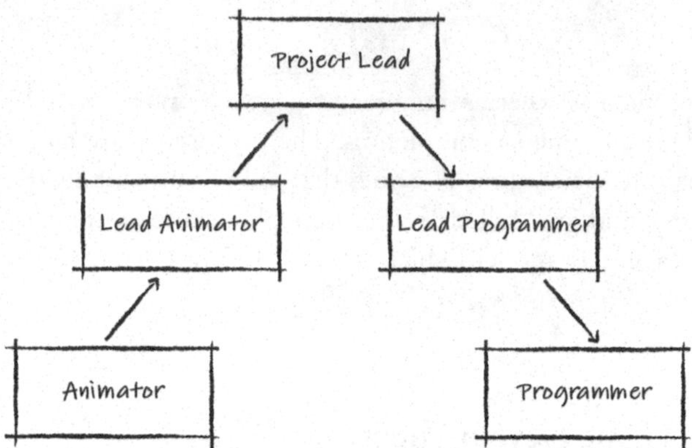


**Figure 2.5** *A chain of communication*

So, what is happening in the big picture?

- More than 100 people from various disciplines on one team
- Thousands of unpredictable problems that can introduce wasted time and effort
- Inflexible plans and tools to manage people who can't predict and quickly react to these problems
- Hierarchies of management that can lead to further waste

Agile methodologies address these issues from the bottom up. One way is by promoting teams able to solve many of these problems on their own. They manage the smallest level of details but not the highest levels. They unburden leadership of the role of managing minor details. They enable leadership to focus on the big picture.

Teams start taking on larger problems as they discover they can take a small amount of ownership to solve the smallest problems. They begin asking for more ownership in other areas:

- In creating better team structures that can solve more problems by reducing external dependencies and improving focus on problem solving
- By identifying risks early and addressing them before they become problems
- By identifying and growing leaders among themselves

Agile values are preferences and not binary decisions. We still need processes and tools to support the Agile team, but having individuals solving problems with their colleagues on a daily basis is more valuable.

**Creating Value**

"It is not just problem solving that Agile helps—it also creates an environment of creating value that would not otherwise be created if the direct communication between developers was not there. An example is a programmer exposing some unrequested values of a feature of their own volition (and communicating this) because they better understood what the designer was trying to do—making a better product for it. This is some of the 'magic' that happens with the top game teams in the business."

—Scott Blinn, Vexigon, Inc.

### *Working Software Over Comprehensive Documentation*

For game development, we'll use the following redefinition for the second value:

> Working game over comprehensive design

I've substituted *game* for *software* because a game is more than software.

Some form of design documentation is necessary. Publishers, licensors, and other stakeholders want a clear idea of the project goals and vision. Portfolio planning and franchise or licensing requirements may create constraints on the project. Communicating what is known about the project up front has great value.

**Note**

I've seen a game design document for a fantasy shooter game that contained details such as the number of bullets per magazine! How can we really know how many bullets per clip we should have in the design phase? Why do we need to plan for that detail before we have the knowledge of what we need? This is an example of the problem that detailed plans can create: They can create work that is not necessary. If all the assumptions about the weapon system were implemented before discovering what was fun about it, much of that work is wasted. If the project sticks to the detailed plan, then it won't be the best game possible.

### *Customer Collaboration over Contract Negotiation*

Our ultimate customer for games is the player. They decide where they spend their time and money. For live games, we find ways to communicate with them and measure what they do to help guide what we develop.

Another type of customer to an agile team is the stakeholder. Stakeholders have a "stake" in the game, such as money invested in its development and outcome, or even their jobs. Examples of stakeholders are:

- Publishers
- Studio leads and executives
- Franchise owners

Often, the stakeholders of a game will insist on having the team produce a game as defined in a contract, which includes design, schedule, and cost goals.

Agile teams address work differently. Instead of following the specifications of a contract to the letter, they work with stakeholders to adjust the goals of the game as the game emerges and they learn more about its value. Chapter 17, "Working with Stakeholders," explores this topic in more detail.

### *Responding to Change over Following a Plan*

Was there a detailed schedule on your last project? Did development follow that schedule? If development departed from the plan, was the detailed schedule updated to reflect the changes? The Agile approach is to plan for what is known and to iterate against what is not known.

Expanding project teams and ever-increasing feature and hardware complexities have driven managers to turn to increasingly detailed planning. As we saw in Figure 2.1, defined processes are best applied when we have certainty about the technology required by a project and well-understood requirements that we know will develop into a hit game. These two criteria are rarely seen. Not only do our platforms change frequently, but creating a fun, innovative game is always challenging.

## Lean Principles Applied to Game Development

Lean has a number of underlying principles that apply to game development.

### *Eliminate Waste*

Lean practices focus on finding and eliminating waste everywhere. This is especially useful in content creation where many games generate two to three times the number of assets. They eventually ship due to either creating the assets before the mechanics and technology they depend upon are known or the costs for creating them are fully known.

### *Build In Quality*

Don't fix it at the end. Build in quality as you create features. Many games postpone creating a quality experience until the end when they throw large numbers of testers at games filled with bugs and performance problems. A lean approach addresses these issues throughout development.

### *Create Knowledge*

Imagine that after two years of effort, you have just shipped the gold master version of your game. The project was challenging; it was a genre new to the studio, so a lot of technology had to be created. It was the first title that the studio has shipped on a PlayStation. There were a lot of false starts and dead ends.

Now imagine that you and the entire project team could go back in time to the beginning of the project and start all over again. Would you do anything differently? Of course, you would! You wouldn't repeat all the mistakes you made the first time. You would work far more effectively to reimplement code you knew would work and rebuild levels you know are fun. With this increased knowledge, you would ship a better game far earlier.

This thought experiment demonstrates four things about knowledge:

- Its creation is something that occurs during the project.
- It has a great deal of value.
- Creating knowledge has a high cost.
- Knowledge is the greatest asset your studio can create.

A fundamental problem with the waterfall approach to games is that our crystal ball BDUFs are not entirely clear. As we develop a game, we are learning. We learn what plays well with the controller, what looks good on the target platform, and how to make the game run fast enough with enough AI characters to make it challenging. We create knowledge every day.

This knowledge is impossible to fully embed in a BDUF or schedule. Game development is primarily about learning what to make and how to make it. It's about reducing uncertainty over time. Agile development focuses on building knowledge about value, cost, and schedule, and adjusting the plan to match reality.

### *Defer Commitment*

Make irreversible decisions as late as you can responsibly make them.[4] Keep your options open. If you defer making such decisions until you have more knowledge, you'll make better decisions. Examples:

- Defer specifying level and character polygon budgets until your renderer can demonstrate the necessary performance.

4. Deferring an engine choice for half the game's development would be irresponsible.

- Defer creating a camera management architecture until you have built up a number of cameras that work in the game.
- Defer story design until you have the core mechanics in place that the "story beats" require.

**"We Don't Know"**

Saying, "We don't know enough yet to make a decision" can be challenging in some studio cultures.

### *Deliver Fast*

Give your customers something quickly. Continually iterate. In these time of highly competitive live game updates, beating a competitor to the market with better features is measured in days. Lean encourages an optimized pipeline to streamline the time it takes from concept to delivery. Chapter 22, "Live Game Development," explores this topic in detail.

### *Respect People*

The people building the product know best how to improve the process. Create a culture where continual improvement comes from everyone. The people closest to the work will come up with the best ideas about how to improve that work. That doesn't come from telling them to do it. It comes from empowering them to be more than "task monkeys."

Game development requires craftspeople. Craftspeople grow their skills over time, which requires continual learning and practice. Lean organizations invest in their people and protect that investment by creating cultures that make people want to stay.

### *Optimize the Whole*

Local optimization actually makes the whole less effective. Use tools such as "Value Stream Maps" to visualize how everything flows and optimize there. A development pipeline that very quickly iterates on a design that's been sitting in a queue for months and months isn't very effective. Lean examines where the "pile-ups" are occurring and streamlines the whole (see Chapters 10 and 22).

**Reminder**

The use of the word *Agile* in this book refers to both *Agile* and *Lean* values and principles.

## What an Agile Project Looks Like

An Agile project is composed of a series of iterations of development. Iterations are short intervals of time, usually one to three weeks, during which the game makes progress. Developers implement individual features that have value to customers every iteration. These features are called **user stories**. Iterations include every element of game development that takes place in an entire game project:

- Concept
- Design
- Coding
- Asset creation
- Debugging
- Optimizing
- Tuning and polishing

The game is reviewed at the end of every iteration, and the results influence the goals of future iterations. This is an example of using the "inspect and adapt" principle. Every four to eight iterations, the game is brought to a **release** state, which means that major goals are accomplished (like online gameplay) and the game is brought to a near-shippable level.

### Note

Some studios use the term *release* to mean the game is released into the market. In this book, releases mean "potentially deployable or shippable." Releases are described in more detail in Chapter 3, "Scrum." User stories are described in Chapter 8, "User Stories."

The "inspect and adapt" principle is the cornerstone of Agile practices. Teams and stakeholders inspect the progress of a game every iteration and adapt the plan to address what is valuable and what is not. Teams inspect how they are working together every iteration and adapt their practices to improve their effectiveness.

**Note**

The first iterations of a project will often focus on building the minimum necessary infrastructure, if one does not exist, before any valuable gameplay is seen.

Agile projects don't avoid planning. They adopt planning practices that allow for change as the project is developed. In most waterfall projects, milestones lead the project toward the goal defined in the BDUF, as illustrated in Figure 2.6.

After the project has achieved the goals foreseen in the BDUF, everyone realizes that they really want to be somewhere else. Unfortunately, as we've seen, the project is usually out of time and money here.

Agile projects also make steps toward a goal. However, using the "inspect and adapt" cycle, they achieve better results sooner through the ability to steer the plan toward a more desirable goal, as shown in Figure 2.7.

The constraints on the project sets limits on how much the goal can change. A driving game won't slowly morph into a golf game over time.

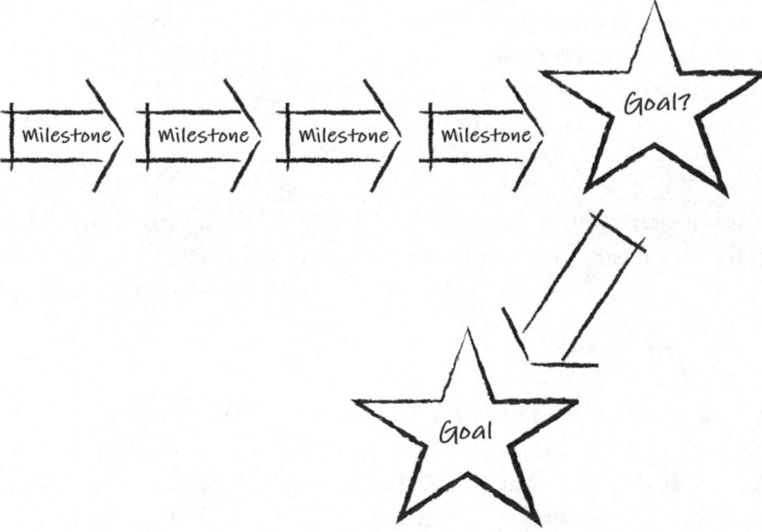


**Figure 2.6** *Milestone steps toward a goal*

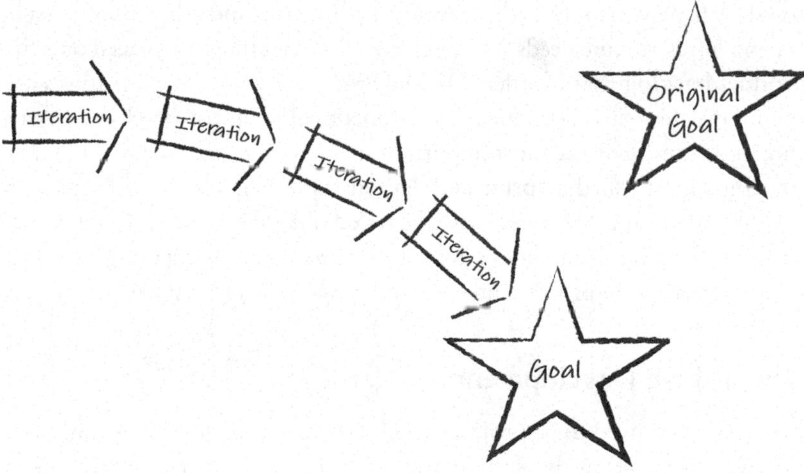


**Figure 2.7** *Iterations toward a goal*

## Agile Development

Figure 2.8 shows the high-level flow of an Agile game project.

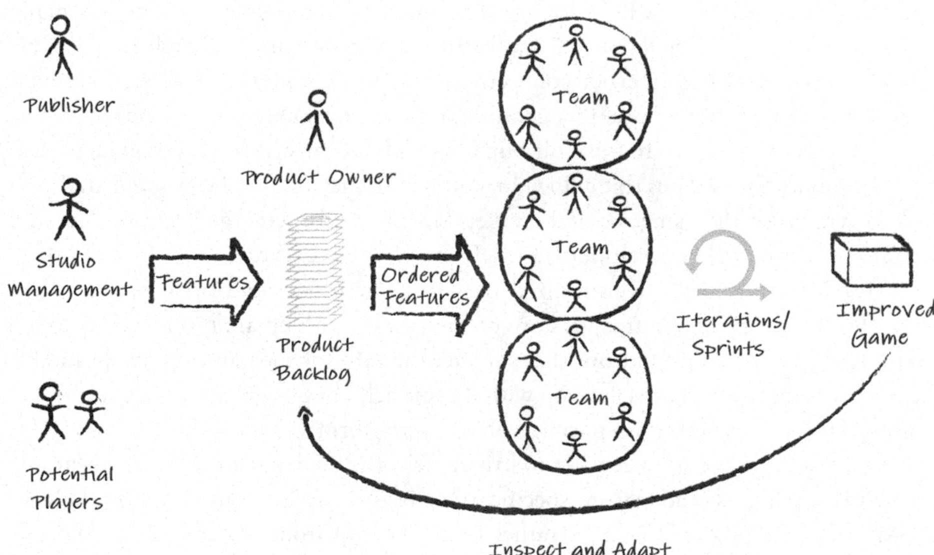


**Figure 2.8** *Agile development flow*

Starting on the left, players and stakeholders identify features and other requirements (such as tools and infrastructure needs) for the game. These features are placed on a list called the **product backlog** that is ordered by the Product Owner. These features are written to communicate their value. Small cross-functional teams of developers focus on completing one or more of the most important features from the Product Backlog in a time-boxed iteration called a **sprint** and demonstrate their progress through an improved version of the game in a review with the stakeholders. A Scrum Master assists each Scrum team by helping them remove impediments to progress, ensuring that they are following the agreed-upon process and exploring ways to improve that process.

## Projects Versus Live Development

Most game development used to be project-based. Projects have discrete beginnings, middles, and endings aimed at developing a game to be shipped. Following this, a team would then move on to another project. As a developer, I always felt a bit of sadness at leaving a game I had worked on for many months.

With the spread of the Internet in the '90s, PC games had the advantage of allowing upgrades and expansions after a release, and a few developers stayed with a game for its entire life. Some popular massively multiplayer online games (MMOs) have support crews fixing bugs or making sure the games keep up with the latest operating system changes a decade after their initial release! Digital distribution platforms such as Steam have built on the PC's strength of connectivity and openness to allow many developers access to popular online marketplaces with incrementally released games.

As consoles gained Internet connectivity and local storage, we started seeing a similar pattern. Often, it wasn't a good thing for players. Day-one patches became a way for game developers to push off bug fixes and optimizations. This forced players to wait hours for updates to be downloaded before they could play a stable and polished version of the game. Digital marketplaces have also emerged on consoles and offer a way for smaller developers to reach console players directly.

Mobile games have revolutionized the live game model and open marketplaces by offering cheap or even free versions of their games, which are monetized through advertising or by selling add-ons that enhance the value of the game. Console and PC games have been slower to catch up with this model, but players are becoming accustomed to these monetization patterns on every platform.

As games and teams transition to live models, the term *project* has less meaning. Schedules, budgets, and feature specifications become more fluid based on the day-to-day key performance metrics rather than fixed up-front profit and cost projections (also known as guesses) from a marketing group. Rather than the approach of

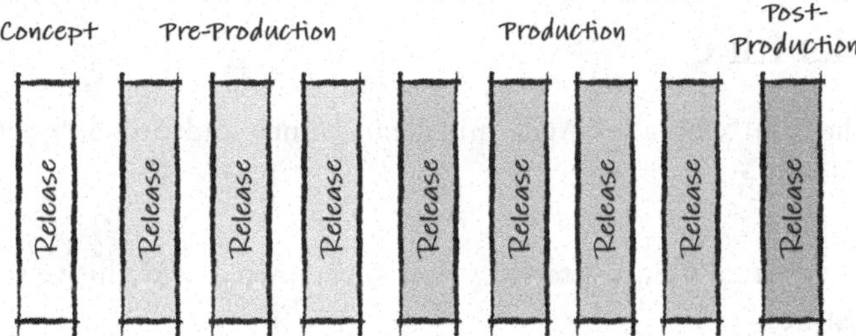


**Figure 2.9** *Agile project flow*

stuffing every conceivable feature into a single shipped version and hoping that some of those features will drive sales, many AAA game developers are approaching a "Games as a Service" (GAAS) model of releasing a minimally playable game (MPG, a variation of the minimally viable product approach) and keeping teams together to release add-on features based on how the market reacts.

### Pre-Deployment Releases

Many live games deploy a version of their game on a frequent basis. Before the first deployment, Agile games use **releases**, which are sets of sprints, to produce deployable versions of their products, as described in Chapter 9, "Agile Release Planning." For them, releases are like milestone deliverables that bring the game to a "near-shippable" state (see Chapter 9).

Most larger-scale Agile game projects execute a series of releases through concept, pre-production, production, and post-production stages of development, as shown in Figure 2.9. The need for these stages and how Agile practices are modified for them are described in Chapter 10, "Video Game Project Management."

## The Challenge of Agile and Lean

The challenge of applying Agile isn't in merely adopting the practices. The practices are simple. The real challenge arises in the collision between the culture of a studio, their publisher, and Agile. Agile and Lean approaches such as Scrum and Kanban create transparency. Every deficiency that obstructs the best flow of work is singled out for examination. Rather than putting faith in a design document, a game needs to stand on its own merit every iteration.

## What Good Looks Like

Whenever I visit a studio that embodies Agile and Lean values and principles, I always experience the following:

- **Discovery:** They've created unique practices that solve problems exclusive to their process and games.
- **Engagement:** Developers are engaged in evolving the process and are able to contribute to their games in a creative way.
- **Challenging:** They don't accept anything as gospel, but question every new practice.
- **Safe:** There is safety in running experiments that often fail without blame. Developers are able to point out the problems in their process or studio without fearing retribution.

## Summary

Acting with transparency is the key to the success when applying Agile and Lean practices. These methodologies will merely show where and what the problems are. It is up to the individuals, teams, and leaders to solve those problems and thereby realize the benefits of Scrum. The remainder of this book addresses how Agile is applied to game development. The next chapter provides an overview of Scrum, which is the core set of practices for an Agile game team.

## Additional Reading

DeMarco, T., and T. Lister. 1985. Programmer performance and the effects of the workplace. *Proceedings of the 8th International Conference on Software Engineering in Washington, D.C.* Los Alamitos, CA: IEEE Computer Society Press.

Larman C., and B. Vodde 2017. *Large-Scale Scrum: More with LeSS.* Boston, MA: Addison-Wesley.

Taylor, F. W. 1911. *The Principles of Scientific Management.* New York: Harper Bros.

# Part II

# Scrum and Kanban

# Chapter 3

# Scrum

In 1990, I was a member of the team developing the avionics testbed for an experimental fighter jet called the YF-23. This work required me to stay at a McDonnell Douglas facility in St. Louis, Missouri, for almost a year. Members of the team had gathered from all around the company to prepare the avionics for demonstration to the Air Force. We faced many imposing challenges—most caused because the various components of hardware and software had been separately developed, and they were resisting integration. The avionics were designed to survive the destruction of up to half of their components and still perform their function. Unfortunately, the actual hardware could barely tolerate being installed. One key component, a fiber-optic communication interface, was so sensitive that 29 out of 30 initial boards produced failed before our final demonstration!

The team was led by a former F-14 pilot. He was an outstanding leader who didn't need to understand every detail of how each of us did our jobs. What he excelled at was removing obstacles from our paths.

We were guaranteed to see him every morning at the daily stand-up meeting. Scrum was largely unknown to the world in 1990, but F-14 pilots knew how to have a stand-up meeting. Each of us, in turn, told of our progress, what we were working on next, and what problems we were having.

Our pilot-lead had an interesting habit that I will never forget: He always trimmed his nails during this meeting. He focused on his nail clipper, but we knew he was listening. I didn't realize it at the time, but my inability to make eye contact with him forced me to speak to the group instead. If a discussion got too involved, he cut it short.

One day I reported that the McDonnell Douglas system administrator was not giving us access to a computer that he had promised to a week earlier. It was cutting into our efforts to test the avionics, and the administrator was rude to the contractors. As soon as I said it, our lead's head snapped up. With a steady, steely glare, he repeated what he heard me say. I verified that he had heard me right; the administrator was messing with his team.

Five minutes after the conclusion of the meeting, we heard our lead swearing at the top of his lungs at the administrator. They must have a class for F-14 pilots on the creative application of profanity. It was impressive to hear. It was even more impressive to realize that our pilot-lead had our back. He was our "wingman," and as Tom Cruise's character learned in *Top Gun*, you never leave your wingman.

We received access immediately and never had another problem with the administrator. It was a pivotal moment for the team. We had started the day as a collection of contractors from around the country. By noon, we were the team you didn't mess with. Did it affect our work? You bet. We didn't have any excuses not to solve our own problems with the dedication demonstrated by our lead.

Our lead demonstrated many of the values and practices of Scrum long before any of us had heard of it. Was he prescient? No, he was merely applying good practices known to many good leaders. Scrum does the same thing. Its practices derive from those who have worked in many high-performing organizations or teams for decades.

Scrum is a **framework** for creating complex products. It's not a process or a methodology; its practices aren't specific enough to tell programmers, artists, designers, producers, QA, and so on, how to do their jobs. A studio adopting Scrum merges its own practices into the Scrum framework to form its own methodology.

Scrum compels a studio to create an incremental and iterative development process with self-managing, cross-disciplined teams. The rules of Scrum are simple, but from these simple rules emerge vast improvements in how teams work together. They increase their productivity and enjoy their work more. It's like chess; from the simple rules of chess emerge complex tactics and strategy that take a lifetime to master. Scrum is also a never-ending pursuit for continual improvement, especially in the rapidly changing game development industry.

This chapter introduces Scrum. First, we have a rundown of Scrum and look at some of its components and practices in more detail. Next, we examine the various roles involved with Scrum. We finish up discussing customers and stakeholders and how Scrum scales.

## The Solutions in This Chapter

This chapter introduces the basics of Scrum as defined in the Scrum Guide[1] and how it connects to game development.

1. https://www.scrumguides.org/scrum-guide.html

## The History of Scrum

Product development methods—from the industrial revolution through the information age—have undergone a slow evolution. It's an evolution of how people work together to create products.

The Industrial Revolution arose from the limitations of craftsmanship. The limited supply of craftspeople kept the supply of products low and their cost high. The assembly line transferred product creation to workers on the assembly line who were considered replaceable cogs performing only simple tasks. It removed the value of knowledge at every stage to a centralized few called **managers**.

With the introduction of the assembly line, everyone could afford a product like the Model T car. The cost of doing this was the loss of customization and variety that the craftsperson supplied.[2]

The weakness of Henry Ford's assembly line, which was optimized by Taylor (1911), was that it didn't leverage the knowledge and creativity of the people on the assembly line. Working in a factory became synonymous with the loss of humanity to the large machine of society that seemed to be emerging.[3]

Two world wars created demand for large amounts of material from a limited workforce. This drove innovation at the factory level. Millions of "Rosie the Riveters" had to be trained and made productive. This required more than mindless assembly-line workers. Leadership was required to train and guide this new workforce. Knowledge and skill at every level of the assembly line became recognized as a critical asset as valuable as the capital equipment in the factories themselves.

As the war ended, the soldiers returned to their jobs, and America found itself with the only intact industrial base. This led to a languid attitude toward the wartime lessons, many of which were forgotten in the factories. Additionally, those people who filled the roles in the factories of the departed soldiers left the factories and took much of the new knowledge tools with them.

Overseas the lessons were embraced. For example, as America occupied Japan, many of the industrial consultants, such as William Edwards Deming, who helped American industry ramp up production during the war were brought over to help Japan rebuild its devastated manufacturing industries. Companies such as Toyota merged some of these principles with their own. These companies were able to elevate productivity as American industry had done during the war.

2. Henry Ford's famous quote, "Any customer can have a car painted any color that he wants so long as it is black," highlights this lack of variety of choice. (Source: Ford, H., & Crowther, S., 1922. *My Life and Work*, Garden City Publishing Company.)

3. Read Orwell's novel *1984* to get a sense of this attitude toward the future.

These changes in Japan continued to restore the value of individuals in the workplace and decentralize many of the day-to-day decisions about quality and efficiency. As a result, Toyota, and companies like it, has leveraged the lower cost and higher quality of its products to dominate the world automobile market.

In the mid-eighties, the differences in product development were researched and described in a groundbreaking article titled "The New New Product Development Game" (Takeuchi and Nonaka, 1986).[4] This study described how some companies consistently and rapidly released new, highly successful, and innovative products into the market. What made these companies different was their process for developing products.

These companies didn't develop products using a traditional "relay-race" model of sequential development, such as the waterfall approach in the software industry. Instead, handpicked cross-discipline teams collaboratively iterated on the development of their products to a much higher degree. This approach to development was compared to the scrum formation of rugby teams that move the ball up and down the field together.

Scrum was first identified as a model for software development in the book *Wicked Problems, Righteous Solutions* (DeGrace and Stahl, 1990). This model was first applied at the Easel Corporation in the early nineties by Jeff Sutherland (2004) and Ken Schwaber at Advanced Development Methods. Then, Ken Schwaber and Mike Beedle (2002) teamed up to write a book, which popularized Scrum to a broad audience.

Although Sutherland and Schwaber were the first to use and define Scrum, Scrum integrates ideas from many sources. Teams meeting daily, owning the problem, putting the work to be done on a wall, and graphing the amount of work to be done are not novel ideas. What was novel about the earliest Scrum implementations was putting all of these ideas together.

## The Big Picture

Scrum consists of the Scrum Team, Events, and Artifacts:

- The Scrum Team
- The Product Owner
- The Development Team
- The Scrum Master

---

4. https://hbr.org/1986/01/the-new-new-product-development-game

- Scrum Events
- The Sprint
- Sprint Planning
- Daily Scrum
- Sprint Review
- Sprint Retrospective
- Scrum Artifacts
- Product Backlog
- Sprint Backlog
- Potentially shippable game (Increment)

This chapter and the next define all these terms.

Figure 3.1 shows the Events and Artifacts of Scrum. A game developed with Scrum makes progress in one- to three-week iterations, or **Sprints**, using cross-discipline teams of five to nine people. At the start of a Sprint, during **Sprint Planning**, the team selects a number of features from an ordered list of them called the **Product Backlog**. Each feature on the Product Backlog is called a **Product Backlog Item** (PBI). The team discusses a plan to implement each PBI. If achievable, the plan for each PBI is moved into the **Sprint backlog.**

Once the team feels it has reached the capacity of work it can achieve in the Sprint, based on what it's been able to accomplish in past Sprints, it will finish planning.

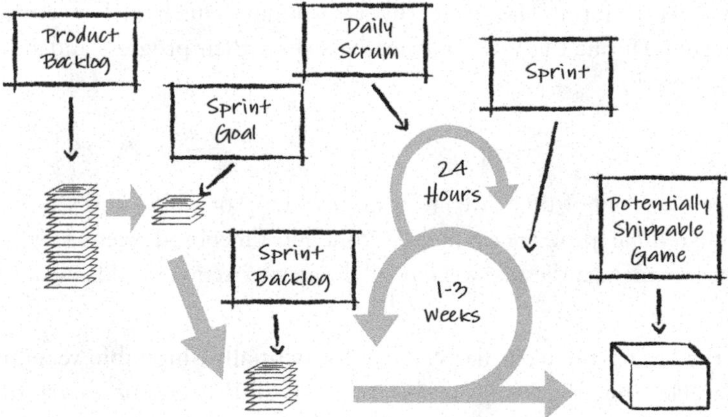


**Figure 3.1** *The big picture*

*Source:* Based on information from Mountain Goat Software

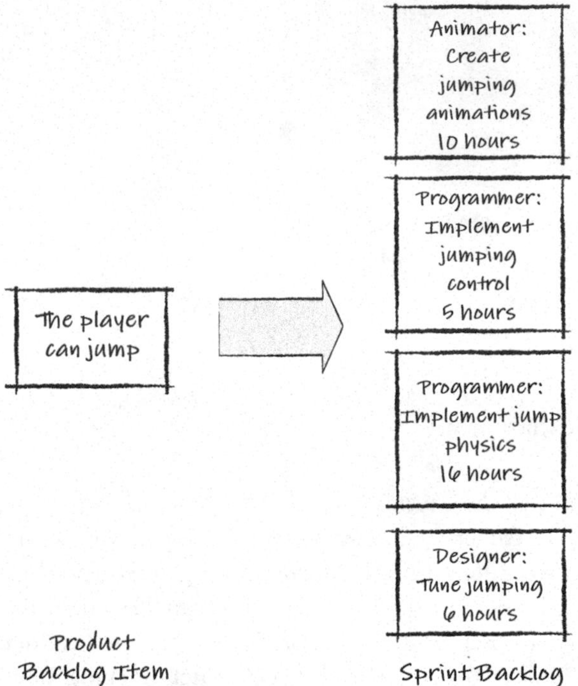


**Figure 3.2** *An example of breaking a PBI into tasks for the Sprint Backlog*

Figure 3.2 shows a simple player jump feature and a Sprint Backlog of tasks to implement it.

The team only commits to features in a Sprint that it judges to be achievable.

The team meets daily during the Sprint in a 15-minute timeboxed meeting called the **Daily Scrum.** During this meeting, members share their progress and any impediments to their work.

## Definition

A **timebox** is a fixed amount of time given to a meeting, task, or work. This sets a limit on the amount of time spent. For example, a 15-minute timeboxed meeting will end at the 15-minute mark regardless of whether all the agenda items are addressed.

By the end of the Sprint, the team has created a **potentially shippable** version of the game: a playable game that won't necessarily pass all the tests necessary to ship. The **stakeholders** (managers, directors, and publisher staff) of the game gather with the team in a **Sprint Review** to evaluate whether the goals of the Sprint were met and to update the Product Backlog for the next Sprint based on what they've learned.

One other practice is the **Sprint Retrospective.** This is a brief meeting held by the team following the Sprint Review to reflect on how effectively the team worked together over the last Sprint and to find ways of improving its practices.

**Note**

Think of a potentially shippable version of the game as something you could run an informal focus test with.

## The Values of Scrum

The core of Scrum is its values. These values guide us in finding ways to execute our work better to achieve success and fulfillment together. The values are:

- **Focus:** We focus on only a few things at a time to deliver value sooner and to guide the next steps of our work.
- **Courage:** Because we are trusted and supported, we have the courage to take chances and create real change.
- **Openness:** We are open and transparent in our work. In this way, concerns can be expressed and addressed.
- **Commitment:** We are committed as a team to the success of our work.
- **Respect:** We share our successes and failures through respect and help each other grow.

If a studio cultivates Scrum with these values, it will discover the benefits.

## The Principles of Scrum

Scrum practices are meant to be adapted and changed over time as teams explore better ways to make games and work together.

The principles of Scrum explain why we execute these practices. As we change practices, we continuously evaluate them against the principles. These principles are:

- **Empiricism:** Scrum uses an "inspect and adapt" cycle that enables the team and stakeholders to respond to emerging knowledge and changing conditions in real time using actual data. An example of this can be seen in the Daily Scrum practice, which enables the team to react to daily issues.

- **Emergence:** As a game is developed, more is learned about what makes it fun, what is possible, and how to create it. Scrum practices don't ban designs from being developed up front. They acknowledge that we can't know everything about a game from the start. The Sprint Review and Planning cycles are designed to maximize the emergence of features as seen in a working game.
- **Collaboration:** Scrum emphasizes collaboration between team members, stakeholders, and the players themselves. Interaction between all three focuses the effort on the best outcomes.
- **Timeboxing:** Scrum delivers value on a regular cadence, which enables stakeholders and developers to synchronize and steer the game as value emerges. Sprints are an example of a timeboxed practice.
- **Prioritization:** Some features are more important to the stakeholders than others. Rather than approaching the development of a game by "implementing everything in the design document," Scrum teams develop features for a game based on their value to the player, who will buy it. The Product Backlog is an expression of this principle.
- **Self-organization:** Small, cross-discipline teams are empowered to organize their membership, manage their process, and create the best possible product within the timeboxes. They use the "inspect and adapt" cycle to continually improve how they work together, often through the Sprint Retrospective meeting.

By preserving these principles, Scrum teams can alter their practices and improve the benefits of Scrum.

## Product Backlog, Sprints, and Releases

In this section, we look at some of the elements of Scrum identified in Figure 3.1 and define releases.

### The Product Backlog

The Product Backlog is an ordered list of the features, called Product Backlog Items (PBIs) for a game, a toolset, or the pipeline for making the game.

The following are examples of such features:

- A filtering function for the animation exporter
- A particle effect for a winning poker hand
- Online multiplayer modes

The Product Backlog is expected to change after each Sprint as we learn more about the game. PBIs that weren't anticipated are added. PBIs that are no longer necessary are removed, and their order is changed as necessary.

The value, cost, and risk of each feature to the player is used to order the backlog. The Product Backlog is not meant to be a detailed list of every feature we may need; that makes it too cumbersome to manipulate. Instead, the PBIs on the top of the list are split, or broken down into small enough features for the team to implement in one Sprint. Figure 3.3 demonstrates some PBIs for an example platform game.

*Jump*, *crawl*, and *fly* are the most important PBIs to implement right now and are at the top of the list. These PBIs are small enough to complete in a single Sprint. PBIs such as *online* or *in-game map editor* have lower value and are not split into smaller PBIs until the team is closer to implementing them.

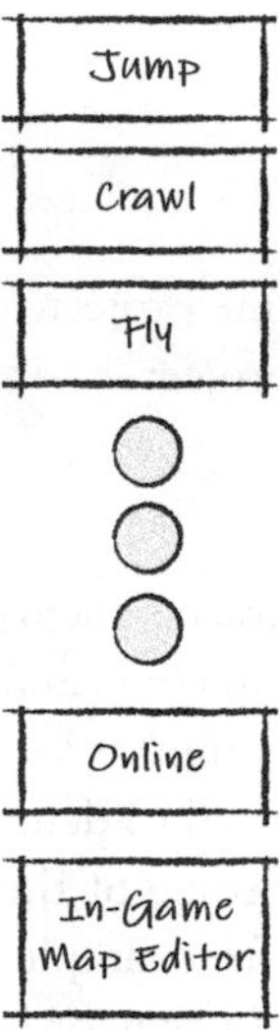


**Figure 3.3** *A backlog of features/PBIs*

## Sprints

A Scrum-developed project makes progress in Sprints. These iterations are the heartbeat of the project.

Sprints have a fixed duration (timebox) of one to three weeks. Teams commit to working on the PBIs that they forecast they can complete within the Sprint. The overall objective of the Sprint is called the **Sprint Goal**. A Sprint Goal is the overall theme of the Sprint to which the team forecasts it can achieve. It is usually expressed as a set of PBIs from the top of the Product Backlog.

### Sprint Goal

Ideally, but not always, a Sprint Goal is an objective unifying what the Scrum Team is aiming to deliver, such as, "The player can navigate a representative level where they navigate obstacles." This would be supported by PBIs that describe running, jumping, and swimming pulled from the Product Backlog in Sprint Planning. Ultimately, the PBIs that the team forecasts in Planning determine how much of that statement they forecast they can deliver on.

The Sprint Goal remains unchanged. At the end of the Sprint, the team shows a new version of the game to the stakeholders, such as the publisher, which demonstrates the Sprint Goal.

### Definition

A **stakeholder** is someone who has a stake in the outcome of the game project. These include people on the publishing side, other members of the project, and studio management.

Sprints produce vertical slices of functionality; they are like mini-projects themselves. A Sprint contains design, coding, asset creation, tuning, debugging, and optimization—everything necessary to produce a potentially shippable game.

Many features require multiple Sprints to develop, but Sprints still need to demonstrate value at every review. Sometimes the stakeholder wants to see some of the uncertainty or risk removed from the project as early as possible. Take, for example, a team delivering AI features: One of the most difficult challenges of AI behavior is navigation in a complex environment. The AI system has to identify obstacles that prevent an AI character from moving and calculate a path around them. With the addition of moving characters and objects, the problem can become intractable. Navigation is one the riskiest problems to solve for the entire game.

We want to solve the navigation problem as early as possible. Other related systems—such as character animation and physics—might not be mature enough to support the Sprint Goal of having a polished AI character walk through a complex environment. In this case, a Sprint Goal for the team could be to demonstrate simple shapes navigating a complex test environment. This goal doesn't demonstrate a complete feature, but it does represent the value of reduced risk.

Does this remove all the risk associated with AI characters navigating complex environments? No. It addresses a core part of the challenge. There still may be other problems that crop up when progress is made with the animation and physics. We want to minimize work built on assumptions. For example, the next Sprint Goal for the AI team could be to demonstrate the test shape "climbing" stairs. Discovering that AI characters can't climb stairs halfway through level production would be a disaster if a number of levels and animations were built assuming this navigation worked, but it doesn't.

## Releases

Releases are a set of Sprints meant to bring a game with major new features to a potentially deployable or shippable state. A typical release cycle lasts between 6 to 12 weeks. The pace of releases is similar to those of milestones on a typical project.

The "potentially shippable" state means "playable by potential buyers of the game but not necessarily ready to package with full content or pass all first-party requirements tests." On a two-year project, releases leading up to the deployed game should have a "magazine on downloadable demo quality." Games deploy following the release that ensures first-party hardware or store (technical certification requirement [TCR] or technical requirements checklist [TRC]) or broad hardware compatibility tests pass.

Releases establish longer-term goals for the team and stakeholders. They require an elevated level of polish and debugging that reduces a great deal of uncertainty about the work left to do to ship the game.

Releases start with a planning session that establishes major goals for the game. A release plan drives the goals for each Sprint. Figure 3.4 shows how the release plan is a subset of features from the Product Backlog and how each Sprint Goal is a subset of the release plan.

**Note**

Chapter 9, "Agile Release Planning," describes the release plan in detail.

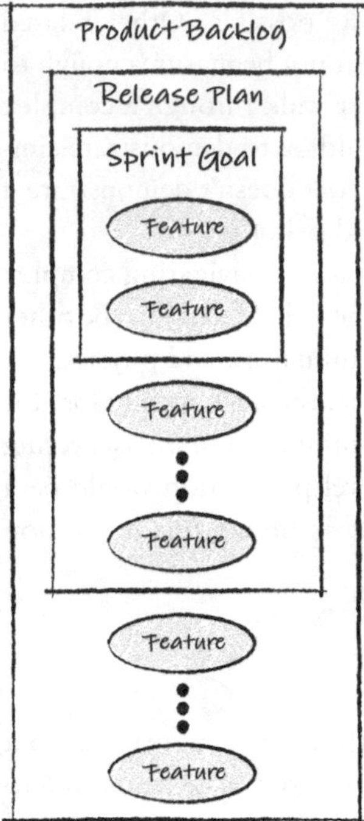


**Figure 3.4** *Subsets of planning*

## Scrum Roles

Scrum gains much of its benefit from Sprints and teams that make commitments to goals and own their work. A distinct separation exists in the roles and responsibilities between Scrum teams and the stakeholders. Scrum teams and stakeholders agree on goals, which satisfy clearly defined needs of the player. Figure 3.5 shows the various roles described in this section.

### The Scrum Team

A Scrum Team consists of a Scrum Master, a Product Owner, and a Development Team.

The **Scrum Master** is responsible for educating the team about Scrum, ensuring the members follow the practices they established for themselves. The Scrum Master facilitates problem-solving and runs interference for the team when necessary. He or she coaches the team on the values and principles of Scrum, helping them to find better ways to work together. The Scrum Master also challenges the studio, helping to improve its overall culture.

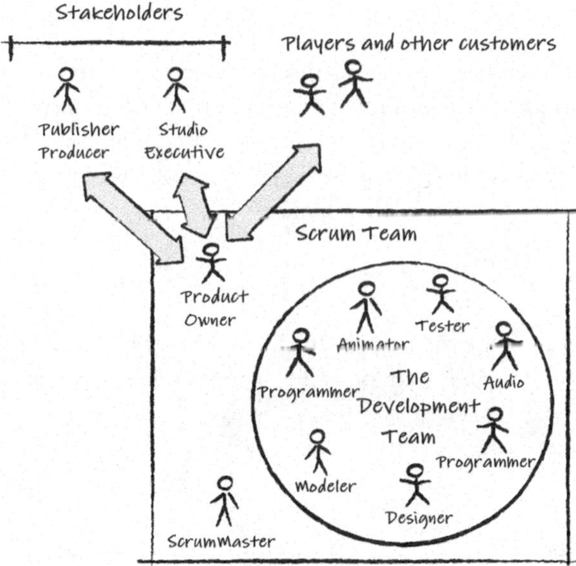


**Figure 3.5** *The Scrum roles*

The **Product Owner** is responsible for communicating the vision of the game and maximizing the return on investment (ROI). The Product Owner maximizes ROI by establishing and ordering the desirable features in the Product Backlog.

The **Development Team** delivers sets of features from the Product Backlog every Sprint that meet an agreed-upon quality. Developers are self-organizing and self-managing; they determine how much work they can commit to at the start of a Sprint and take responsibility to deliver the improved game by the end.

In the coming sections, we'll dive deeper into the roles on a game developed using Scrum.

### Terminology

There has been a lot of debate about these terms in the Scrum community. They have settled on these terms for the benefit of consistency. This book follows the terminology (including capitalization of terms) used in the Scrum Guide. However, for brevity, I'll refer to the Development Team as the "team." When referring to the entire Scrum Team (Scrum Master, Product Owner, and Development Team), I'll use the phrase "Scrum Team."

## Development Team

The Development Team includes everyone from every discipline necessary to complete the goal that the team commits to in a Sprint. For example, a team committing to a goal that requires a walking, talking AI character should have animators, AI programmers, character modelers, and even QA to help the team ensure that the goal is done.

> **Note**
>
> The term *teams* often refers to everyone on a game. In this book, we'll call that group the **game staff**. Therefore, a game staff of eighty people might contain seven to nine Scrum teams.

## Scrum Master

The Scrum Master role is pivotal for the success of Scrum, yet it is the most misunderstood role. It is neither a traditional lead nor a management role. The Scrum Master improves the use of Scrum through coaching, facilitation, and the rapid elimination of anything that distracts the team from delivering value.

### *Responsibilities*

The job of the Scrum Master is to ensure that Scrum is a success. The Scrum Master must apply the principles of Scrum and deftly guide the team through the practices.

When a team starts using Scrum, members should rigorously apply the Scrum practices "by the book." Over time, those practices gradually change as the team finds better ways of working together. The Scrum Master's role is to ensure that the principles behind Scrum remain intact and that the team sticks to the practices it agrees to follow. Chapter 18, "Team Transformations," discusses such adoption strategies in greater detail.

> **Highlight**
>
> Scrum "by-the-book" is a "starting script" for agility. Used correctly, that script will vastly change over time.

The Scrum Master is the conscience of the team; the principles and values of Scrum are inconvenient at times, but the Scrum Master's role is to reinforce their importance. For example, a team may be ignoring bugs or unpolished assets in their rush to deliver on a Sprint. The Scrum Master must remind them that each Sprint delivers a vertical slice of the game and must not defer bug fixing or asset polishing to a future Sprint.

One of the main responsibilities of the Scrum Master is to nurture the sense of ownership within the team. Ownership has great value (see the sidebar "Ownership"). The Scrum Master knows when to let teams occasionally falter and when to lend support. Much like a good parent, the Scrum Master knows that protecting the team too much will not lead to growth and independence of thought and action.

The specific responsibilities of the Scrum Master are as follows:

- Ensures impediments are addressed
- Monitors progress
- Facilitates planning, reviews, and retrospectives
- Encourages continuous improvement
- Helps stakeholders and teams communicate

**Ownership**

A sense of ownership leads teams to solve impediments a bit faster than teams that take little control over their work. Ownership leads to more passion for their efforts. I've seen teams with a sense of ownership work overnight to implement something they felt strongly about. The goal, however, isn't to have teams work overnight but to engage in and enjoy the work. Making games should be a creative and fun process. If it isn't, how can we expect the game itself to be creative and fun?

Teams take ownership of their work during the Sprint. This is an important feature of Scrum because it enables the team to truly commit to the work it estimated it could complete. Teams committed to their work far outperform teams that are not. If Sprint Goal changes are imposed on the team, it loses this sense of ownership and the commitment that comes with it.

*Ensures Impediments Are Addressed*

There is seldom a single event that causes a game to be late; there are usually many hundreds or thousands of problems. Losing just a couple of hours a day can extend the time required to finish a one-year project by several months!

Scrum refers to every problem that interferes with progress as an **impediment**. Impediments take various forms:

- Bugs that crash the game or tools
- Excessive or long meetings that don't produce results
- Constant distractions or interruptions from, for example, a frequently used intercom system
- Waiting for someone to finish something you need to make progress on your task

The list goes on. Scrum focuses the team on solving many of these impediments through the creation of cross-discipline teams and the Daily Scrum. A programmer who needs a test asset can turn to a team artist for help. A designer who shares the same Sprint Goal with a programmer finds that the programmer is easily motivated to help them solve a bug.

A cross-discipline team will rapidly solve most impediments identified throughout the day on their own. The Scrum Master's role is to ensure that the visibility of impediments is raised to the proper level, so they are addressed.

Some impediments cannot be solved by the team. For example, if an animator needs a tool purchased, the team probably does not have the authority to issue a purchase order directly. Much like my former F-14 boss did, the Scrum Master takes ownership of this problem and raises it to the necessary level for the purchase to be authorized. Without this daily support, the tool purchase could take weeks to resolve.

Sometimes impediments take time to be resolved. The Scrum Master tracks these to ensure that they are not forgotten.

*Ensures Progress Is Transparent*

The Scrum Master ensures that the team remains aware of how well it is performing against its goal. A Scrum Team monitors its progress every day and projects progress against the goal. If the team is slipping behind, it must be made aware of it as soon as possible.

**Experience**

Many new Scrum Masters feel it's their job to monitor the team through a tool and to take responsibility for it achieving its Sprint Goal. This actually prevents the team from becoming accountable for the Sprint Goal. It's always a hard habit to break.

*Facilitates Planning, Reviews, and Retrospectives*

The Scrum Master ensures that all team meetings are prepared for and facilitated. Facilitating a meeting includes scheduling the time, preparing the space, and ensuring that the meeting occurs within the time limits to which everyone agreed.

Ensuring that a meeting runs well is a deep skill that Scrum Masters need to continually develop and help teams learn to execute well on their own.

*Encourages Continual Improvement*

The Scrum Master encourages the team to seek ways to improve its performance as a team. This never ceases. Even with the most productive teams, the Scrum Master encourages them to seek even a single percentage point of improvement. This promotes a culture of continuous improvement. Improvements could be as simple as moving desks closer to improve communication or as hard as requesting new technology that improves the efficiency of the production pipeline.

The Scrum Master role is mainly a facilitative and coaching role. The Scrum Master might recognize problems before the team and identify a favored solution but should never lead by implementing the solution. Instead, a Scrum Master will help a team recognize problems and own the solution. This teaches members the invaluable skill of identifying and solving problems on their own. In many ways, the role of the Scrum Master is to coach the team to eliminate the need for a Scrum Master.

*Helps Stakeholders and Teams Communicate*

Stakeholders and development teams speak different languages. Stakeholders speak about return on investment, profit/loss calculations, sales projections, and budgets. Development teams talk about technology, gameplay, and artistic vision. This divide of language prevents real communication from occurring between the two groups. The Scrum Master's job is to facilitate this communication, primarily through teaching the team the necessary amount of business language, coaching the Product Owner, and focusing much of the communication bandwidth through the Product Backlog.

### Attributes

A Scrum Master's role on the team is compared to a sheepdog, guiding the team toward the goal by enforcing boundaries, chasing off predators, and giving the occasional bark. The role of a Scrum Master requires a proper attitude. An overbearing sheepdog stresses out the flock. A passive sheepdog lets the predators in among them.

The Scrum Master trusts the team. The Scrum Master guides the team to do its best work through coaching and facilitation. The Scrum Master role is not easy, but it is rewarding. A Scrum Master has to be stubborn and persistent. Many issues facing a team require intervention at a personal level with people who may not want to change their behaviors. For example, take a manager of considerable authority and many years of experience in a command-and-control environment who does not believe self-organization works. This manager repeatedly interferes with a team in ways that distract the team by assigning new work in the middle of a Sprint. The Scrum Master needs to persistently remind the manager about the purpose of Scrum and the reciprocal commitments between the team and the stakeholders. This needs to be done in a way that does not offend and raise barriers. It's a coaching role. Not everyone can do it.

There are formal courses meant to introduce Scrum or train every role. These courses are an immersion in the practices and principles of Scrum given by an experienced Scrum trainer.[5]

**Should the Scrum Master be Dedicated to Only One Team?**

Scrum Masters can handle two to three teams before their role starts becoming a full-time job.[6] It depends on how many organization impediments exist that the Scrum Master needs to address. This limitation may mean that there are not enough Scrum Masters to go around.

**Note**

Sprint lengths are usually set between one to three weeks and don't change much. The best Sprint length is discussed in Chapter 4, "Sprints."

Teams often ask, "Should the Scrum Master stay as a developer on the team?" I prefer that a Scrum Master not be a developer on the team. The "Scrum Master as a member of the team" role can cause some problems if any of the following occurs:

- They focus on their own tasks more than on the Scrum Master role.
- They prioritize their own impediments over those of other teammates.

5. I also provide a wide variety of courses specifically tailored for game development. Visit www.ClintonKeith.com for more details.
6. However, a novice team new to Scrum might need a full-time Scrum Master for a while.

- The team assumes the role is a leadership one, but they defer ownership to the Scrum Master.

Sometimes there is no choice but to have the Scrum Master be recruited from the developers on the team. When this happens, everyone on the team needs to watch out for these problems.

**Wearing the Scrum Master Hat**

Sometimes when a developer on the team takes on the role of the Scrum Master, they carry a hat around with them. They don the hat when they are in the Scrum Master role and take it off when they are in the developer role. It helps the team know who is speaking to them.

## Product Owner

The Product Owner establishes and communicates the vision of the game and orders its features.

The Product Owner is responsible for:

- Managing the ROI for the game
- Establishing a shared vision for the game among the stakeholders and developers
- Knowing what to build and in what order
- Creating release plans and establishing delivery dates
- Supporting Sprint Planning and Reviews
- Representing the player who buys the game

Most AAA video game projects need the initial shipped version to get things right. AAA games that have launched with a weak feature set cannot overcome reviews and player feedback with patches. This requires great vision; it makes the role of a Product Owner on an Agile video game project critical.

Similarly, live games need Product Owners who not only have a vision for the game, but must understand and react to the metrics and feedback from their existing players.

**Customers**

An Agile team has even more customers than the players and the stakeholders. These are customers of work the team produces beyond features for the game. Examples of other customers are:

- Other developers who need tool and pipeline changes
- Marketers who need demos and screenshots
- First-party hardware owners who have requirements for their platforms

### *Manages the ROI*

The Product Owner is responsible for ensuring that the investment in the game is returned with a profit. This requires the Product Owner to know what the market wants, even years in advance of its initial deployment.

The Product Owner is responsible for other metrics of a project's success. These include the performance of the game on the target platforms, the final cost of the game, and the ship date. Forecasts, such as average game rankings and profit/loss (P&L) calculations, can be applied, but these are marketing projections that can't guide games very well. The Product Owner creates a bridge between marketing, sales, and the Scrum team by demonstrating the emerging game and collaborating on the direction the game is heading.

### *Creates a Shared Vision*

The Product Owner is a single voice for the vision that is shared with the team, igniting creativity and ownership with the team and collaborating with it as the vision evolves with the emerging game.

Having a shared vision is critical for the success of any game. Lacking vision, a large team of developers will go off in separate directions, creating a Frankenstein game of parts that don't mesh. We've all seen these games—the ones that have beautiful art but no great gameplay, the games that have a great mechanic but too many performance problems to be playable, or the games that have dozens of mechanics but not one of them done well.

Sharing a project vision is not easy. It was easier when a game had a few less-specialized developers, but many games being developed today require a small army of specialists. Large development teams allow people to become isolated by discipline. This isolation creates further barriers to a shared vision; programmers sitting together start to see a game project as a computer science project. Artists produce art that satisfies other artists. Designers create baroque control schemes that only other designers can appreciate. Each group focuses on the challenges for its own discipline and loses sight of the business side.

The Product Owner's role in creating the vision for a video game project is comparable to the role played by key visionaries such as Shigeru Miyamoto,[7] Will Wright,[8] Tim Schafer,[9] Cliff Bleszinski,[10] and Sid Meier[11] on their projects. Product Owners represent the ultimate customer during development: the player. The Product Owner has to foresee what the market will embrace up to three years in advance and have to know the mind and emotional responses of the player.

### *Owns the Product Backlog*

The Product Owner owns the Product Backlog and determines the order of features in it. This order reflects their sequence of completion.

The Product Owner cannot manage a Product Backlog alone. The backlog may have features that require a technical, artistic, or design understanding to create or prioritize. Some features support the efforts of sales and marketing to help promote the game, such as in-game advertisements. The Product Owner needs to work with the various customers and stakeholders of the game to understand all of their needs.

### *Manages Releases*

The Product Owner manages the release plans and the delivery date. The Product Owner revises the release plan based on changes to the goals or the progress from the teams during Sprints. The Product Owner guides the various release activities. We cover these activities in more detail in Chapter 9.

### *Supporting Sprint Planning and Reviews*

The Product Owner has the following major duties during a Sprint:

- Establishing and updating the features on the backlog and their priorities
- Participating in Sprint Planning
- Participating in the Sprint Review and accepting or rejecting the results of the Sprints

7. Creator of *Donkey Kong, Mario, Zelda*, and so on
8. Creator of *The Sims* and *Spore*
9. Creator of *Full Throttle* and *Psychonauts*
10. Designer of *Gears of War*
11. Creator of the *Civilization* series

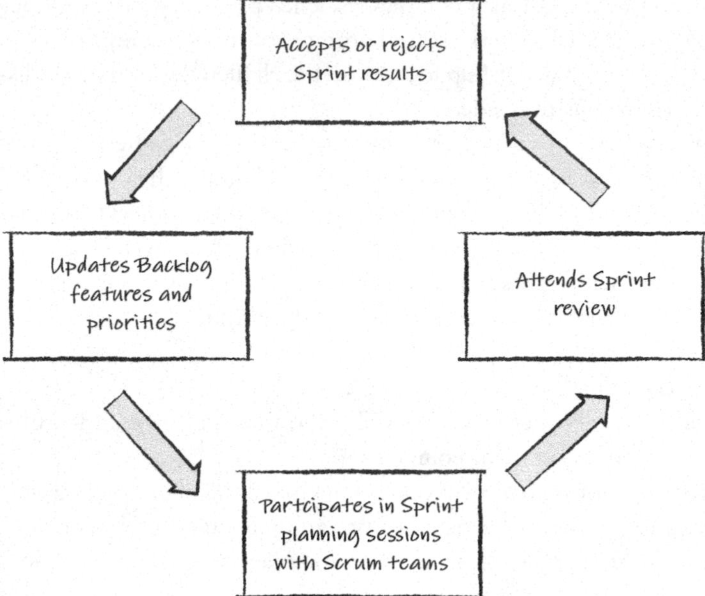


**Figure 3.6** *The Product Owner role*

Figure 3.6 summarizes the role of the Product Owner regarding the Product Backlog and Sprints.

**Should the Product Owner also be a Member of the Development Team?**

Having a Product Owner as a member of the development team can be an advantage or a disadvantage. Being among the developers has the advantage of continuous communication, but the Product Owner/Developer must be careful not to distract the team from the Sprint Goal. I knew of one Product Owner who used to think of new features overnight and ask the team to "just add that to the Sprint"!

## Customers and Stakeholders

The relationship of customers and stakeholders to the Scrum team is important. They define many of the items on the backlog. They work with the Product Owner to help order the backlog. Although the Product Owner is a member of a Scrum team, the Product Owner is considered the "lead customer." This person determines the priority of features on the backlog. The Product Owner provides a service to the team by being the one voice of all the customers and stakeholders.

The ultimate customer is the player who will buy the game. Although the player doesn't directly define the requirements of the game, all stakeholders represent them. The stakeholders are people outside the team who have a stake in the game being made.

The following is a list of typical stakeholders:

- **Publisher-producer:** The publisher-producer communicates the progress and goals between the publisher and the studio. One of the main values of this role is to ensure that both sides have the same vision about the game and that there is transparency about the progress of a game.
- **Marketing:** Marketing provides input on the relative importance of features in the backlog and, by understanding the backlog, more effectively communicates the key features of the game to the market.
- **Studio leadership:** Studio art, design, and technology leadership help the Product Owner order work, especially with respect to cost and risk of feature development. For example, as a former chief technical officer, my role was to work with the Product Owner and the project staff to address areas of technical risk through the Product Backlog.

Each of these stakeholders can introduce feature requests to the Product Backlog. For example, as a CTO, I was mostly concerned with the technical risk in implementing various features in the game and the pipeline. As a result, I introduced PBIs that helped the team gain knowledge about risk or helped everyone understand the cost of implementing a feature.

### The Growing Influence of Players on Development

The growth of mobile and live game development has led to teams being able to interact more with players and measure how they play the game. This is a major advantage for Agile teams that can use this feedback to guide the game's development better.

## Chickens and Pigs

A book describing Scrum can't avoid telling the story about "the pig and the chicken," so here goes:

> Once upon a time, a pig and chicken were talking. "I have an idea," the chicken exclaimed, "let's open a restaurant; we'll call it Ham and Eggs." The pig thought about it for a moment and said, "No, thanks...you'd only be involved, but I'd be committed."

This is how the labels of *pigs* and *chickens* got their start (see the sidebar "Renaming Pigs and Chickens"). **Pigs** are the members of a Scrum team who commit to the work in the Sprint. **Chickens** are the customers and stakeholders outside the team who do not make the personal commitment to the work.

Chickens influence the direction of the project between Sprints. Chickens and pigs discuss the goals of an upcoming Sprint and order the Product Backlog. The pigs (teams) commit to implementing features. The chickens commit to allowing the team to achieve those goals without interference. This reciprocal commitment between the pigs and chickens enables Scrum to work. If the chickens are allowed to change a Sprint Goal, then it is not possible for the pigs to truly commit to it at the start of the Sprint.

### Renaming Pigs and Chickens

The distinction between the pig and chicken roles is important in Scrum. Companies that adopt Scrum are very conscious of the distinction when working out the practices. Some teams come up with new terms to replace the terms *chicken* and *pig* because no one enjoys being called either of those names.

A good example of replacement terms was coined by the developers at Swordfish Studios in the United Kingdom. They decided to refer to themselves as *pirates* and *ninjas*.

These terms are more acceptable, but I was uncertain what they meant, so I asked them about it. "To us, pirates are the chickens; they invade, pillage, cause all sorts of mayhem, and then leave," I was told. "Okay," I said, "that makes sense, but what about ninjas?" The reply was, "Oh, well, we called ourselves ninjas because ninjas are cool."

As it turns out, ninjas and pirates are natural enemies. An Internet meme has grown up around this.[12]

12. http://en.wikipedia.org/wiki/Pirates_versus_Ninjas

## Scaling Scrum

Scrum teams have fewer than ten developers, but most game projects require a larger staff. Scrum supports this through scaling. This is done by having a number of Scrum teams work in parallel and coordinating their work through practices such as the Scrum of Scrums, which the book addresses in great detail in Chapter 21, "Scaling Agile Game Teams."

## What Good Looks Like

The most successful Scrum adoptions I've seen over the past 15 years were with teams that adapted and changed the practices significantly, but maintained the Scrum values and applied the principles to their changing practices.

## Summary

Scrum practices and roles are simple and easy to start using. So, why read an entire book dedicated to using Agile practices for game development? The reason is that the practices previously described are only a starting point.

Scrum creates the opportunity for you to measure and question every practice you use to make games (inspect) and enables you to introduce change to improve them (adapt). Scrum gives you empirical tools to measure the effectiveness of your team. These measurements give you feedback about the benefits and drawbacks of every change and enable you to enter the endless cycle of continually improving your practices. The challenge in adopting Scrum is to learn how and why it works and then modify your practices to leverage the transparency that Scrum creates.

The next chapter rounds out the basics of Scrum by detailing the activities involved in Sprints.

## Additional Reading

Schwaber, K. 2004. *Agile Project Management with Scrum*. Redmond, WA: Microsoft Press.

Schwaber, K., and J. Sutherland. The Scrum Guide, https://www.scrumguides.org/scrum-guide.html

Takeuchi, H., and I. Nonaka. 1986. The New New Product Development Game, *Harvard Business Review*, pp. 137–146, January–February.

# Chapter 4

# Sprints

In the previous chapter, we introduced Scrum practices and roles. In this chapter, we'll go into more detail about Sprints, the iterative cycles of development. We'll see how they are planned, how they are conducted on a day-to-day basis, and how the team and stakeholders review the progress at the end and reflect on how well they worked together. Finally, we'll see how Sprints might fail to achieve their full goals and how the teams and stakeholders deal with that.

## The Solutions in This Chapter

The solutions we are addressing through proper Sprints are ensuring that:

- Developers are part of the planning cycle.
- Developers are focusing on the goals of the game, and the studio leadership is focusing on removing any roadblocks to that.
- Teams and stakeholders are committed to true transparency of the progress of the game's progress and emerging value.

## The Big Picture

Sprints have the following basic rules:

- They are timeboxed, usually between one to three weeks in length.

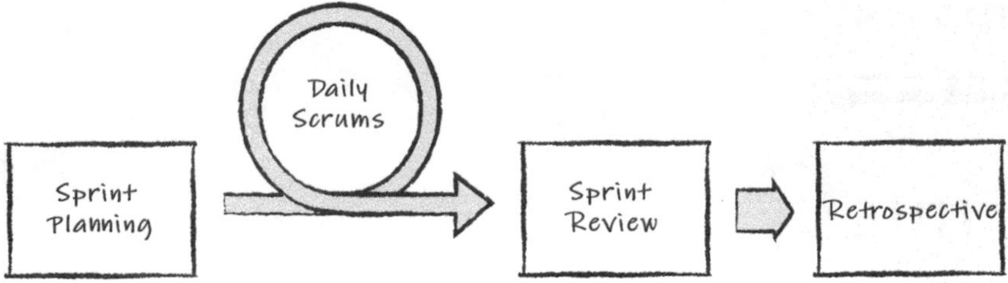


**Figure 4.1** *The flow of Sprint meetings*

- The team forecasts a Sprint goal they will focus on completing.
- The stakeholders commit to do their best not to change the Sprint goal.

Figure 4.1 shows the basic flow of what happens in a Sprint.

At the start of a Sprint, the team and stakeholders establish a Sprint Goal in Sprint Planning. Then the team begins to work on achieving the goal, sharing their progress with one another in the Daily Scrums. At the end of the Sprint, the team demonstrates the improved version of the game to the stakeholders in a Sprint Review. Following the Review, the team conducts a Retrospective, where they discuss how the team worked together during the Sprint and to seek improvements for the coming Sprints.

**Meetings by Any Other Name**

An initial complaint of Scrum is that it identifies four meetings that have to take place every Sprint. People's initial reaction to "more meetings" is usually negative, which often has to do with how poorly many meetings are facilitated. Although the Scrum Master should facilitate effective meetings, the Scrum Guide authors attempted to mitigate this initial reaction by renaming "meetings." Their first attempt was to call them "celebrations," which fooled no one. Currently, the Scrum Guide refers to them as "events." In this book, I still call them "meetings."

## Planning

At the start of a Sprint, the Development Team meets with the Product Owner to plan the next Sprint. Sprint Planning has two parts: identifying the Sprint Goal and planning how to achieve that goal. The participants in this meeting include the entire Scrum Team (the Development Team, Scrum Master, and Product Owner) and any domain expert who may be needed to answer questions or help the team estimate its work better (such as an online programmer, motion capture technician, and so on).

## The Sprint Goal

The Sprint Goal is the coherent objective for the Sprint. It is refined by the Scrum Team during Sprint planning based on an initial forecast or by discussing the highest order of Product Backlog Items (PBIs). As the Sprint progresses, the Development Team will keep its focus on the goal and negotiate the scope of the Sprint Backlog with the Product Owner as needed.

### Note

The practices describing how a team estimates, tracks, and manages the Sprint Backlog here are a typical starting pattern for many teams. However, applying the principle of self-organization, teams will explore and improve how to plan and manage their Sprint. We shouldn't care if a team is using a Ouija-board to plan its Sprint. We should only care about how they improve the game every Sprint.

## Part One: Identifying the Sprint Goal

The meeting begins with the Product Owner describing the highest-ordered features on the Product Backlog that the team is capable of implementing. This is an opportunity for the Development Team to raise any design (game design, technical, art, and so on) questions. For example, if a feature requires the main character to jump, there may be some questions about how the current animation and physics technology is applied. This discussion reveals design and high-level implementation questions such as whether a physics-only, animation-only, or blended solution is best.

Sometimes high-ordered PBIs on the Product Backlog are too large for a team to tackle in a single Sprint. These features are split into smaller PBIs that are expected to fit.

The focus of this part is to identify the Sprint Goal for the coming Sprint. The team selects the top PBIs from the Product Backlog it thinks it might accomplish given the current composition of the team. At this point, the Sprint Goal is merely a forecast that will be adjusted in the second part. For example, if a particular feature requires animation, but no animators are on the team, then the team cannot commit to working on that feature unless it finds one to join them.

Another reason to drop a particular PBI from the initial Sprint Goal is because of a dependency from another team. For example, a feature requiring engine work to be completed first should be postponed if the engine team has not addressed it yet. The organization of the Product Backlog and teams reflect the need to avoid such dependencies, but sometimes they do occur. We want to discuss enough PBIs during this meeting that the team has some leeway in which it chooses to work on during the next meeting, all while generally working within Product Owner priorities.

At this point, the team hasn't committed to any work. It has identified the PBIs it may be able to complete, but until it has broken these PBIs down into a detailed plan to achieve the Sprint Goal—which it does in the planning meeting—it isn't yet ready to commit.

## Part Two: Planning How to Achieve the Sprint Goal

After identifying a potential Sprint Goal, the team creates a plan to implement each PBI, one at a time, creating the Sprint Backlog: the plan to achieve the Sprint Goal.

At the start of the meeting, the Scrum Master helps the Development Team identify constraints that might impact its ability to commit to the Sprint Goal. Here are some examples of these constraints:

- Holidays that reduce the amount of time available
- Time that will be spent outside of the team (interviews, and so on)
- Potential impacts from other areas, such as the integration of a major engine change that has caused problems in the past

The Development Team's ability to commit to work is based primarily on its past performance. This is best determined by examining what the Development Team has been able to accomplish in past Sprints. For example, if the Development Team was able to finish an average of 400 hours of estimated work in the last few Sprints, then it's probably a safe bet for it to sign up for 400 hours of estimated work for the coming Sprint. This becomes the limit in the capacity of planned work it can put into the Sprint Backlog during Sprint Planning.

The Development Team then discusses design and implementation details for every PBI that is potentially part of the Sprint Goal. The attendance of the Product Owner is important for this discussion because there are many subjective aspects to what needs to be implemented. For example, the Development Team might want to discuss potential trade-offs on character motion that looks realistic versus motion that is responsive to player input but more jarring in appearance.

**Note**

The form of the Sprint Backlog is determined by the Development Team. From here out, I'll describe a typical approach of breaking PBIs into time-estimated tasks, but because the Sprint Backlog is owned by the Development Team, it decides how to make the estimate. Some teams don't even use estimates (see Chapter 9, "Agile Release Planning")! If you force teams to plan their Sprint in a particular way, don't expect them to truly commit to owning the work.

The Development Team then starts breaking the PBIs into work items. Figure 4.2 shows one potential way PBIs are taken from the Product Backlog and employed to build the Sprint Backlog.

The Development Team starts filling a Sprint Backlog by taking the highest-priority PBI from the Sprint Goal and breaking it into work items. Everyone on the Development Team is involved at first because design questions are raised. After the requirements of the feature are agreed upon, the Development Team starts writing individual tasks and estimating the amount of effort each one takes to complete.

The work breakdown takes place within discipline groups. For example, if the Development Team has four programmers, they estimate the programming work together. If only one programmer is on the Development Team, the programmer estimates all the programming tasks alone.

Tasks are often estimated in ideal hours or days, which is the amount of time a task should take without interruption or any problems. This means that an eight-hour task is not the same as a one-day task. An eight-hour task usually takes more than one calendar day to accomplish. The reason is that our days are filled with interruptions, problems, and conversations that vary from day to day.

**Note**

Ideal time is better to use than actual time. Teams can forecast just as well with ideal time and, as they find improvements in their practices, they can forecast more ideal time in the same timebox.

Estimates for large tasks are less accurate than estimates for small tasks. I can estimate how long a trip to the local store takes to within a few minutes, but a cross-country drive estimate might be off by a day or two. The limit of task size is arbitrary, but a couple of days is a reasonable limit as a size before it needs to be broken

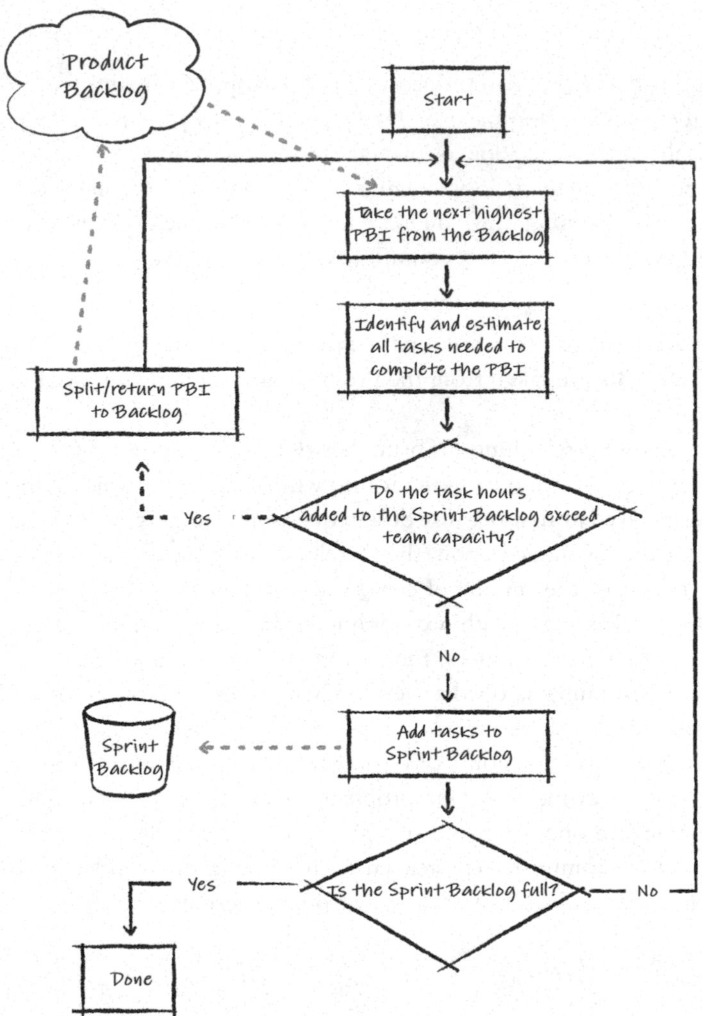


**Figure 4.2** *The flow of creating a Sprint Backlog*

down into smaller tasks. Sometimes a Development Team might not have enough information to break down a task larger than a couple of days into smaller tasks. Instead, it will create a placeholder task with a larger estimate until it is ready to work on the task and know more.

After each PBI is broken down into tasks, the total estimated time is added up. This total is then compared with the remaining time available in the Sprint Backlog. If the Sprint Backlog has room for the time the new PBI adds, then the Development Team commits to completing that PBI. Of course, each specialty on the project needs to be within its capacity.

**Note**

Even though we got 400 hours of combined work done last Sprint, we can't commit to 400 hours of animations this Sprint if half the Development Team are programmers. Apply common sense. Make sure each discipline (specialty or skill group) is within its capacity, and use the amount of work done during the last Sprint as a guide to what can be completed this Sprint. Part III, "Agile Game Development," discusses the disciplines in more detail.

If the work for the new PBI would overflow the Sprint Backlog, then the Development Team won't commit to it. One of three options is available when this happens. First, the PBI is returned to the Product Backlog, and another, smaller PBI takes its place. A second option is to split the original PBI into two or more smaller PBIs. A subset of the original PBI might be identified that fits into the Sprint. As an example, a PBI for creating a level could be broken down into two PBIs, each for one half of the level. A third option is to drop an item already pulled in to enable the new item to fit. The Product Owner can help the Development Team decide which is the best solution.

**How to Estimate Your First Sprint**

While planning a Sprint, the Development Team considers the amount of work accomplished over previous Sprints to judge the approximate amount of time it uses to estimate its capacity for work in the coming Sprint. A natural question that comes up is, "How do we estimate our capacity for our first Sprint?" I recommend that the Development Team aim for one-third fewer hours/days than it initially estimates. The reason for this is that Development Teams new to Scrum underestimate the effort to create potentially shippable features at first. This includes time for bug fixing and polishing, activities not traditionally included in waterfall task estimates.

If the Development Team runs out of work during the Sprint, it conducts a mini-planning meeting and picks another PBI or two to fit into the remainder of the Sprint. It'll have a better feel for and be able to more accurately measure the work it can commit to with every successive Sprint.

**Note**

If the team runs out of work a day or less before the end of the Sprint, it can usually find some tuning, polishing, or refactoring work that needs to be done!

## Length

What is the ideal length of a Sprint? Sprints typically last two to three weeks, but many factors influence this:

- The frequency of stakeholder feedback and change
- The experience level of the Development Team
- The overhead time for planning and reviews
- The ability to accurately plan the entire Sprint
- The intensity of the Development Team over the Sprint

Over the course of a project, these factors will change, and the length of a Sprint may change as well.

### *Stakeholder Feedback*

The duration of a Sprint depends on the amount of time the stakeholders can go without seeing progress and providing direction on the game. Some core mechanics require frequent feedback in the early stages of development, so a shorter Sprint is required to be sure the game is headed in the right direction. For example, the motion of the character, behavior of the camera, and layout of the controls may require frequent feedback. Some Development Teams don't need such a rapid cycle of feedback (such as content production teams), so a longer Sprint is more appropriate for them.

The Development Team must not have the goal changed within the Sprint. If three weeks is unbearably long for stakeholders to wait for a review, then it needs a shorter Sprint.

#### One-Month Sprints?

When we first started practicing Scrum, the published wisdom was that one-month Sprints were ideal. After trying and failing at one-month sprints, I asked one of the authors of that advice what we were doing wrong. He told me that we weren't wrong, but that the original advice was. Apparently he'd chosen that Sprint duration because he didn't want to fly out to the clients; he was coaching every Sprint more than once a month!

### *Development Team Experience*

Teams new to game development, Agile, or even just working together should start with shorter Sprints. This enables them to iterate on the practices and learn how to

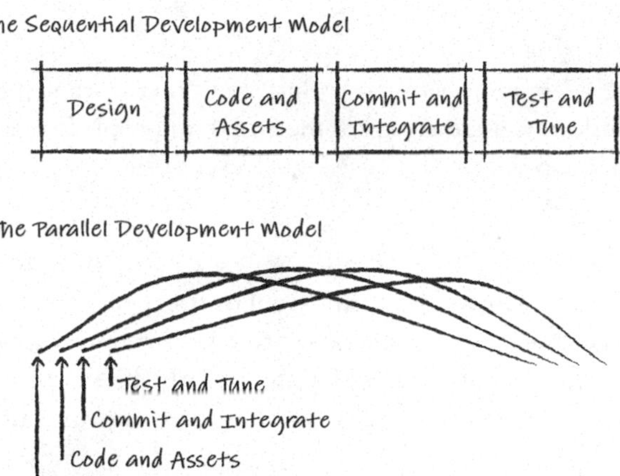


**Figure 4.3** *Sequential versus parallel development models*

develop more iteratively and incrementally. Teams new to Scrum should be discouraged from practicing longer Sprints because they tend to approach a Sprint like a mini-waterfall project (see the top part of Figure 4.3). They'll spend a couple of days exclusively in design, spend a few weeks creating code and assets, and finally integrate, test, and tune during the last few days of the Sprint and end up crunching to reach the finish line. This doesn't give them the opportunity to achieve the best possible result because there is little time left to iterate and polish their work.

Experienced Development Teams will perform these activities more in parallel, designing, coding, creating assets, testing, and debugging every day. Working this way creates better results and enables the team to iterate more during the Sprint and increase the quality of their work.

### *Planning and Review Overhead*

Shorter Sprints often require a larger portion of a team's time for planning and review. Review and planning usually require a good portion of a day regardless of the length of the Sprint. Even though planning for a shorter Sprint may take less time, the remainder of the day following the meeting is never 100 percent effective. Imagine that you had a Sprint that lasted one week. You'd probably spend one day that week in review and planning. That's 20 percent of the team's time spent in planning!

### Plan to Party

Allow the team to have a little celebration between Sprints, but don't disrupt the cycle of the Sprint for it. Set a little time aside as part of the Sprint for people to play the game and relax. Besides, game developers don't need much excuse for a party!

### *Ability to Plan the Sprint*

If the team is uncertain about how to achieve the Sprint Goal or if experimentation or prototypes need to be done, then the Sprint should be shorter. Uncertainty implies that the work eventually required for the Sprint might be significantly different from what was anticipated at the start. If this is the case, it's better to change direction after two weeks than four.

### Short Sprints

Some prototype teams have chosen an extremely short Sprint duration of days! I've seen web-based games deploy versions of a game twice a week.

### *Balanced Intensity*

Sometimes three weeks is too long for a Sprint because it leads to a low-intensity mini-design phase up front and a high-intensity debug mini-crunch phase at the end. Although the mini-crunch phase isn't going to kill anyone, it's not the most efficient way to work.

### Choosing a Sprint Duration

On my last team, a one-week Sprint felt too short. It was as though the review was too soon to "do anything too challenging." A three-week Sprint was too long to create a sense of urgency. We compromised and chose a two-week Sprint because "it felt right."

### *When Is the Sprint Too Long?*

Stakeholders usually limit a Sprint's duration to three weeks as the longest amount of time they let pass to direct the goals of the game. Some may argue that some technical areas (such as engine or pipeline development) cannot achieve any significant progress in as little as three weeks. The need for longer Sprints to show value usually indicates that the technical practices need to be more iterative. Any development practice that can't demonstrate progress at least once every two to three weeks should be addressed. Interim goals should demonstrate a reduction in risk and have value. For example, if a team is implementing the infrastructure for online gameplay, it might demonstrate simple object messaging across a local area network after the first Sprint. The longer a team goes without proving or disproving architectural assumptions, the greater the potential waste.

**Note**

We'll discuss this in more detail in Chapter 12, "Agile Technology."

### *Who Selects the Sprint Duration and When?*

The stakeholders and the Scrum team need to determine the duration of a Sprint. If there is a disagreement, the Product Owner has the final say. The length of the Sprint must be changed only between Sprints, and it shouldn't be changed too frequently. Frequent changes to the length of Sprints are disruptive. It takes some time for the team to adjust to the rhythm and pace of a particular Sprint length and refine its ability to estimate the appropriate Sprint Backlog.

**Sprint Commitment**

One of the reasons that the phrase *Sprint Commitment* is no longer in the Scrum Guide is because it has often been weaponized to force teams to complete everything they had estimated in Sprint Planning regardless of what problems emerge during the Sprint. This has resulted in teams compromising quality to get every feature in the game "done" by the end of the Sprint.

The Sprint Guide now uses the word *forecast* instead of commitment for Sprints, even though *commitment* is still a core value. I agree that *forecast* is an accurate way to express what the plan is, but I think we've lost something by dumping the word *commitment*.

It comes down to what we mean by commitment. Often forecast means "We'll get done what we get done," or better yet, "We'll do our best to get everything done, but we might have to drop some less important features." To me, commitment goes a step beyond that, but not so far as to mean "We must do everything."

Commitment means doing our best to achieve a goal, but also being accountable as a team when things don't go according to plan.

A good example is when you commit to picking up your child at daycare. You'll obviously do your best to be there on time, but sometimes things go wrong. Let's say your car breaks down a few miles away from daycare. Do you just say, "Oh well; I tried my best"? No! You call your spouse, friend, and/or the daycare to let them know. You do this because you hold yourself accountable to pick your child up.

Similarly, if teams run into problems with a feature in their Sprint goal, they need to hold themselves accountable. They need to raise the issue. They grab the Product Owner and discuss ways to address it. If they can't solve the problem themselves, they recruit the Scrum Master to help out. It still might mean the feature gets dropped, but the accountability results in better risk management.

Commitment is a core value for Scrum Masters to grow with a team. Sometimes the first step is to stop solving problems for the team and start asking it, "What should you do about it?"

## Tracking Progress

During a Sprint, the team needs to share information about its progress and identify any threats to its Sprint Goal. The team needs to have the proper information to make the best decisions. It needs easy access to the Sprint Backlog of tasks. It needs to understand where it stands in terms of achieving its goals. It needs to recognize as early as possible when it won't achieve its goal.

Scrum teams use a number of low-tech practices and artifacts to provide this information to teams. Task cards, burndown charts, task boards, and war rooms have proven their value for tracking progress throughout the Sprint. This section describes these in detail.

**Note**

The Development Team doesn't track actual time spent; it tracks the estimated time remaining to accomplish tasks. When first starting Scrum, actual time spent may be double that of the estimated time because the Development Team isn't used to including debugging and tuning time. This is consistent across all tasks, and so is predictable, but it will improve over time.

### Task Cards

Tasks can be recorded and tracked in many ways. The most useful form to store tasks are on 3-by-5 index cards, called **task cards**. These cards have many advantages that no tool can match. The major benefit is that they enable everyone on the team to participate in task creation and management. The task card enables easy customization using various color cards and markings. For example, a cinematics team decided to categorize the order of asset creation tasks by using stamps with pictures of fruit to help them better prioritize their tasks. The "low-hanging" fruit were picked off the board first. Try doing that as easily with a tool!

### Sticky Notes

Many teams use sticky notes. These work well unless you use cheap off-brand notes or post them in a windy location.

## Burndown Chart

During Sprint Planning, the team commits to accomplishing the Sprint Goal based on the sum of the estimated work expected to complete it. The team updates the estimate of work remaining daily to help track progress toward its goal. The team plots this day-to-day measurement on a graph, called a **burndown chart** (see Figure 4.4), a tool for the team to use to gauge how well its efforts are leading to achieving its goal by the end of the Sprint.

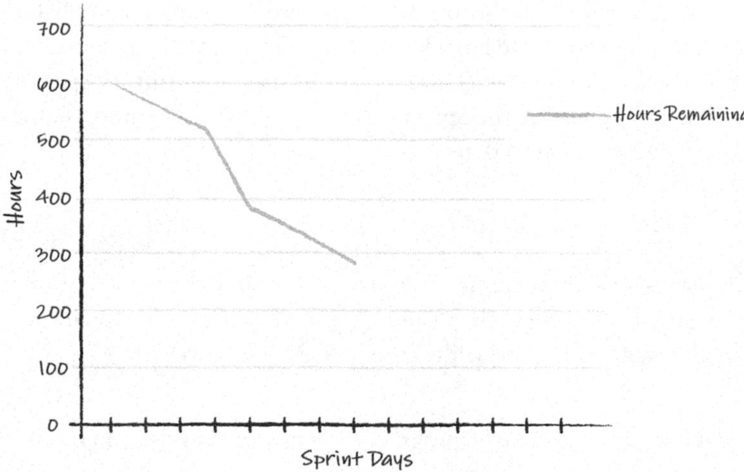


**Figure 4.4** *An example burndown chart*

**Burndowns Deprecated**

The Scrum Guide, the definition of Scrum that is maintained by Jeff Sutherland and Ken Schwaber, eliminated Burndown Charts as a standard practice in Scrum a few years back. This was a good decision because the use of any tool or practice used within a Sprint should be decided by the team. It was also good because many managers were "weaponizing" Burndown Charts. I've seen managers monitor burndowns and even reward or punish teams based on "how straight" their burndowns were. Management tracking of a sprint burndown is like measuring how hard a canoeist is paddling. It doesn't tell you if he or she is headed in the right direction or if the current is pushing the canoeist backwards. That said, I feel that burndowns, when used properly, can be a great benefit to Development Teams.

## The Burndown Trend

As described in the planning section, tasks are typically estimated in "ideal" time. An ideal hour/day is an hour/day of work accomplished without interruptions, bugs, tool problems, questions, coffee breaks, friends on the phone, and so on. We're lucky if we accomplish four ideal hours of work per eight-hour workday with all this competition for our time and attention.

The burndown chart tracks the ideal time remaining to accomplish the Sprint Goal. The rate that ideal time decreases per actual day is called the **burndown trend**. Measuring this trend is a useful tool for Scrum teams.

The burndown trend is for the team to track its progress toward accomplishing the Sprint Goal. Figure 4.5 shows the burndown chart of a team a little more than halfway through its Sprint. Using this chart, the team, in mid-Sprint, projects its trend (the dotted line) to the end of the Sprint. The trend line is a warning that the team is falling behind and won't achieve its goal.

**Note**

The burndown trend is a valuable empirical tool for examining the impact of any change that the team makes to how they work. Teams should see the downward slope of that trend increase over time as they improve how they work.

Some teams will draw an ideal line of progress from estimated time remaining at the start of the Sprint to zero hours on the last day. Figure 4.6 shows this trend line. This shows the team how far it is above the ideal projection of remaining time.

The team needs to understand that the goal isn't to have its burndown line match the ideal line. The goal is to use the burndown to show progress daily.

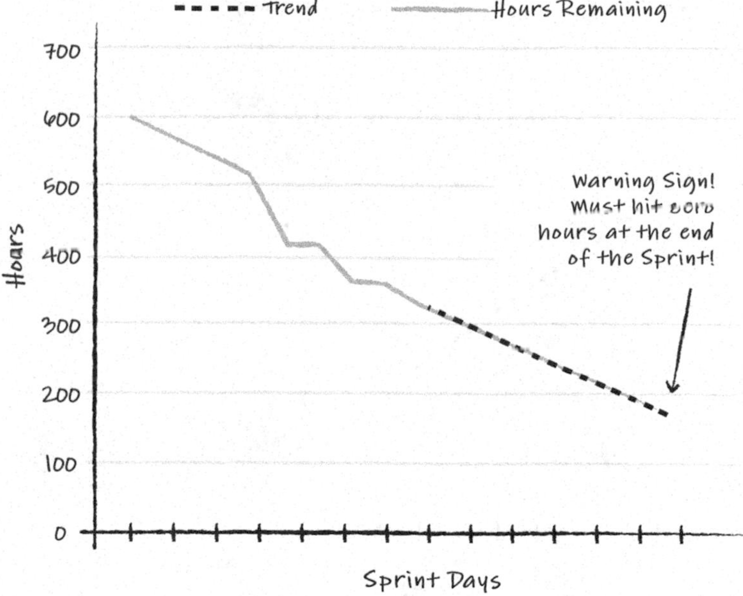


**Figure 4.5** *Projecting the Sprint Backlog rate by adding a trend line*

**Note**

We'll discuss the options available when the team is running out of time later in this chapter.

### Burndown Charts are Not New

Long before I learned about Scrum, I encountered the power of burndown charts. When our team entered alpha, the publisher threw a couple dozen testers on the project, and all of us fixed bugs.

Once a week, we triaged the bug database to prioritize the bug "backlog." We tracked the total bug count and used a "burndown chart" to measure bug resolution velocity, bug discovery velocity, and the projected "zero bugs" date that we were trying to reach. All I had to do was fix bugs and achieve the best possible resolution velocity.

Does this sound familiar? It's no coincidence that many of the Scrum practices reflect these practices.

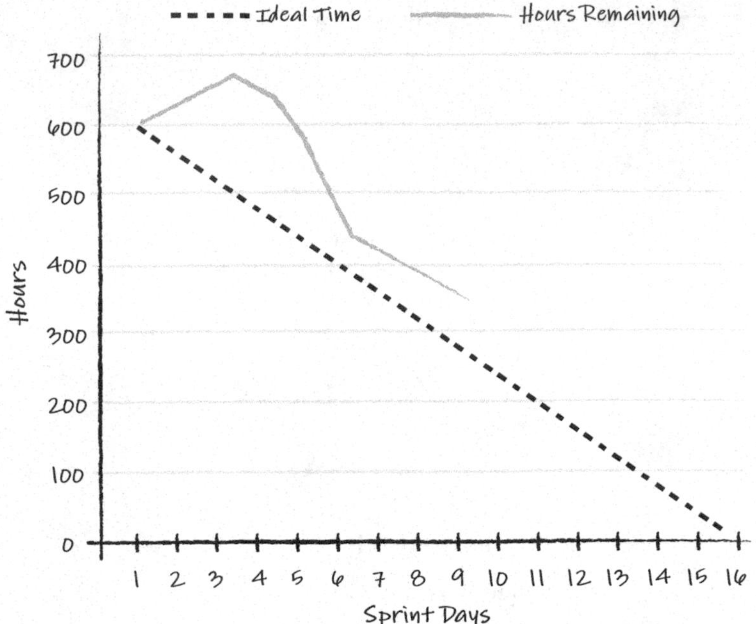


**Figure 4.6** *An ideal trend line*

> **Note**
>
> Given clear goals, discrete tasks, and an empirical measurement of progress toward a goal, teams achieve a high level of focus and effectiveness.

## Task Board

A **task board** displays the goal, burndown chart, and tasks for a Sprint. The team gathers around it daily and pulls the work that it needs to accomplish from it. The task board often occupies a section of a wall. Figure 4.7 shows an example task board.

Task cards move from the "not started" column to the "done" column as the work for each card is started and completed. A benefit of this movement, with the addition of the burndown chart on the board, is that the task board provides an immediate view of the progress of the Sprint.

Task boards have at least four columns. The first column contains the ordered list of PBIs that the team has committed to completing (the Sprint Goal). The second column contains all the tasks that have yet to be started. Following Sprint Planning, all the PBIs and tasks are placed in these two columns. The third column contains all the tasks in progress. As team members decide what they will "work on next," they

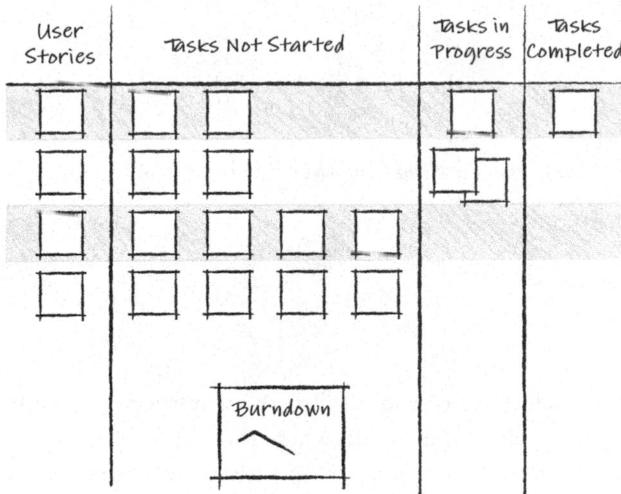


**Figure 4.7** *An example task board*

move the associated task card from the second column to the third column. The last column contains all the tasks that have been completed. Cards are moved into this column when team members finish tasks.

Tasks are usually lined up in rows with their associated PBIs. This enables the team to see the overall progress of work for each feature quickly.

Teams might add columns to task boards to represent additional task states. For example, they could add a "pending" column, between the in-progress and completed columns, for tasks that need external approval before being moved to the "tasks completed" column. For example, tasks to complete models or animations that require aesthetic approval from an art director are placed in a pending column.

### Scrum Master Tip: Have the Team Talk to the Board

If the team is quiet when asked the three questions during the daily stand-up, encourage members to talk to the board instead.

#### The Practice

The Scrum Master will go to the board and, starting at the highest ordered PBI with unfinished work associated with it (tasks in the "not started" or "in progress" columns) ask the team about what needs to be done to complete that PBI. Remind the team that higher priority PBIs should ideally take precedence over lower priority PBIs.

**Benefits**

- Some people will speak up more when facing a board than other team members.
- The practice focuses the team on finishing PBIs over finishing tasks.
- It highlights impediments quickly.

### War Room

Many Agile teams set aside a small space or room called the **war room**. The war room is where the team has their Daily Scrums and where the tasks board is displayed. A war room is an austere place. Chairs or other furniture for people to sit on during the Daily Scrum are not allowed. Depending on the wall space, a half dozen teams can share a war room.

Some teams prefer to have the task board in their local team area and have their Daily Scrums there.

## The Daily Scrum Meeting

Each day, teams gather for the Daily Scrum. Many teams new to Scrum underestimate the purpose and value of the Daily Scrum. A number of reasons exist for the Daily Scrum:

- To synchronize effort among all team members.
- To commit to the work to be accomplished in the next day and reaffirm the team's commitment to the Sprint Goal.
- To identify any impediments to be addressed by the team.
- To ensure the team members are "on the same page." The full team needs to hear about the problems facing each member so that solutions can be addressed after the meeting. The Daily Scrum enables them to micro-steer their progress toward their goal together.

### The Practice

A Daily Scrum is a 15-minute timeboxed meeting that every member of the team attends. No one is allowed to sit down in the meeting, which reinforces the idea that this is a quick huddle and not an open-ended laboriously long meeting. Daily Scrums get to the point.

As the team gathers in a circle, each member of the team answers these three questions:

- **"What have I done since the previous Daily Scrum?"** This should relate to anything done for the Sprint Goal or what may have impeded progress (for example, "I spent the entire day trying to get the game to run on my PC!").
- **"What am I going to accomplish between now and the next Daily Scrum?"** Each team member describes what he or she plans to accomplish by the next Daily Scrum. If there is any work not related to the goal, the team member should mention it (for example, "I need to interview a candidate this afternoon").
- **"What are the problems or impediments slowing me down?"** Impediments are anything that gets in the way of delivering what was promised during the previous Daily Scrum (for example, "It takes two hours to bake assets for the PlayStation build").

**Scrum Master Tip: Ask a Fourth Question**

The three Daily Scrum questions are not fixed and are often modified and supplemented by the team to make the meeting more effective. One example of this is to ask an additional question about the team's view of the Sprint's progress.

Sometimes the team can feel a little pessimistic about the Sprint, and this question helps to address any issues as early as possible. One way to do this is to use a Roman vote. Ask the entire team "*Are we going to achieve our Sprint Goal?*" On the count of three, members either vote thumbs up (if they believe they will achieve it) or thumbs down (if they believe they won't).

The Daily Scrum is not for solving problems. Keeping all side conversations to a minimum is important so that the meeting doesn't become protracted and ineffective. Solving problems is part of what occurs throughout the entire day.

The Daily Scrum is probably the most frequently modified Scrum practice, so this definition of the practice is just a starting point. As a team takes more ownership of how it works, it is free to modify the practice as long as the purpose of the meeting (status, commitment, and improvement) remains intact. For example, some teams will answer the questions one member at a time, whereas others will address the progress of each PBI.

### Try This

If you, as Scrum Master, don't know whether the team is holding the Daily Scrum for you or its members, disappear a few minutes before it is scheduled. If they hold it without you, it's serving them. If they ignore it, it might mean they don't see the value in it.

## Improving the Daily Scrum

When visiting a studio, I'll often ask to observe the Daily Scrums. It's the best way to sense where a team is and how to focus coaching time for the visit. An effective Daily Scrum is an energetic swarm of engaged Development Team members who need to quickly synchronize their efforts and identify anything that is threatening their shared goal.

Some Daily Scrums aren't like this. They are monotonous, manager-led, and useless to the Development Team. Teams here lack any sense of commitment or ownership, and they eventually question the merit of the practice and perhaps even abandon it. Unfortunately, abandoning the stand-up doesn't improve their chances of building commitment or ownership, which are principles of Scrum. I've compiled a list of pointers on ways to improve the Daily Scrum and improve commitment and ownership.

- **The stand-up is for the team.** This meeting is for the team to synchronize its efforts towards achieving its goal, not just as a status report. If there are any "management artifacts" that need to be created (such as an update to a tracking tool), it should be done outside the meeting.
- **The rules aren't fixed.** The "answer the three questions" rule you read about in books is only the starting place. Teams add questions, change the format, and do anything necessary to address their needs.
- **It's about the commitment to the goal, not just the tasks.** Task tracking is critical, but work will arise on a daily basis that wasn't considered during Sprint Planning. Teams need to react to this new work and balance it daily against their goal. They need to inform each other about new developments and threats to their goal. They should care about accomplishing the tasks, but they should care about the goal more.
- **Scrum Masters must know their role.** Scrum Masters do not run the Daily Scrum. They facilitate them. The difference is that the rules for the stand-up come from the team and the Scrum Master ensures that those rules are followed. If the team has decided that being late to the stand-up is not acceptable,

they'll likely have a rule in place to humorously chastise those who are late. Paying $1 or singing a song is common. Scrum Masters must not let them off the hook.

- **It's a "stand-up" meeting.** If you took the same meeting and had everyone sit down, its duration would increase by 50 percent. Standing creates a sense of urgency. Try making another meeting "standing only" and see what happens!
- **Respect the timebox.** Some of the most effective stand-ups I've seen were five-minute "hurricanes of energy and activity." The team members shared what they needed to share and went back to work. Stand-ups that take longer than 15 minutes are just wrong and need to be fixed.
- **Prefer a physical task board.** This is not always possible to have, but there is no electronic replacement that is equivalent. A physical task board with cards allows everyone on the team to handle the tasks simultaneously at the same location. It encourages team ownership.
- **Avoid projectors.** This might seem a bit redundant given the last point, but projectors used in a stand-up meeting should be renamed "engagement killers." Projectors usually involve a software tool that provides information in a linear, one-at-a-time way with someone, unfortunately often the Scrum Master, at the keyboard/mouse controls. It defeats the non-linear, swarming-on-the-goal, value of the stand-up. Software tools are often a critical part of project planning and tracking, but they have no place in a co-located Daily Scrum.
- **It's owned by the team.** The team picks the format and time of day of the Daily Scrum. Because the team owns it, it should run the same way, regardless of whether the Scrum Master is there or not. One simple test I recommend to Scrum Masters is to occasionally hide around the time of the Daily Scrum and see what happens. If the team meets and runs the stand-up the same way as when you are there, you are doing a good job. If the team doesn't meet or stands around wondering what to do, it has some things to fix.

**Experience**

When teams adopt Agile, the Daily Scrum is usually a good practice to start even though they may resist it. However, I've noticed that some teams that function well eventually abandon the practice because their communication throughout the day is so effective, they don't need a separate "ceremony" to communicate.

## Sprint Reviews

The Sprint Review occurs on the last day of the Sprint. The Review brings the team and stakeholders together to play the game and discuss the work accomplished. During the Review, the Product Owner officially accepts or rejects the results of the Sprint. If the results for a particular feature are declined, then the Product Owner decides whether it returns to the Product Backlog or is deleted.

> **Note**
>
> The Product Owner is a member of the Scrum Team and should be engaged with the team throughout the Sprint. Although the Product Owner officially accepts or rejects Sprint results at the review, he or she should always know what the team has accomplished before the review. Being surprised there means the Product Owner is not doing his or her job!

Sprint Reviews should be structured to enable the best level of communication between the stakeholders and the teams. This is the opportunity for the stakeholders to inspect the game and communicate with the Scrum Team. If this communication doesn't occur, the project can go off in directions that won't return the best results for the stakeholders or players.

Reviews enable a more informal conversation between the team and the stakeholders. They help communicate the progress of the game more directly.

> **Note**
>
> Chapter 21, "Scaling Agile Game Teams," describes Sprint Reviews for larger games with more than a few teams.

### Review Format for Smaller Games

For games with fewer than four to six Scrum teams, Reviews take place with individual teams. The stakeholders visit each team area and review the Sprint results. This creates a casual and comfortable environment for the review.

The meeting starts with a member of the team explaining the Sprint Goal and the overall results. If any of the PBIs were dropped, the reasons are discussed here. Then one or more team members play the game and demonstrate where each goal has been achieved. The controller is often passed to a stakeholder to play.

Team Reviews offer numerous benefits:

- It fosters high-bandwidth communication between the stakeholders and the team. Individual team members and stakeholders directly communicate in-depth, which creates an improved vision for the game.
- It enables more hands-on time for the stakeholders.

However, small Reviews have some drawbacks:

- If other people on the project want to observe the Reviews, it creates a roaming crowd that moves around a studio. This might interfere with some of the benefits previously listed.
- It can inhibit cross-team collaboration. Teams might see their work as isolated products, which creates integration issues (among other problems).

Even with smaller games, occasionally having a single review format is useful, as described in Chapter 21.

**Note**

We always modified Sprint Reviews not only as we learned what worked better, but also as we modified team formations and as teams grew.

## Remote Stakeholders

One of the biggest challenges for game projects using Scrum is having the publisher's voice represented in the Sprint Reviews. Many of us have worked on games where the publisher ignores the progress for the first 80 percent of the project and then overwhelms the project with feedback during the last 20 percent, when the opportunities for change are at a minimum. Always include the publisher (if the project has one) to avoid late course corrections.

However, having a representative from a publisher that is thousands of miles distant visit for every Sprint Review is usually impossible. This doesn't mean publishers cannot provide useful feedback, however. Every effort should be made to have publishers play builds and have their feedback incorporated into the next Sprint. We always demand that the publisher visit at least for Release Planning and Reviews. These are just too critical to ignore. Chapter 17, "Working with Stakeholders," explores working with remote stakeholders in more detail.

**Note**

Having publishers present during a Review has a big impact on the project. Have them speak to all Scrum Teams about the progress made. There is nothing like hearing feedback directly from the publisher!

### Studio Stakeholders

Studio executives and managers need to attend reviews as well. Reviews provide a very concise and transparent view into the progress and challenges of a project.

### Players

Agile values and principles emphasize customer collaboration. The ultimate customers for our games are our players. Because our players can number in the millions, we usually can't invite them to Reviews. With live games, we can use metrics and player forums to measure and hear feedback. Chapter 22, "Live Game Development," addresses how to incorporate these into the Product Backlog.

### Honest Feedback

It's critical that stakeholders provide honest feedback to the team. Too often, they see the progress but don't always insist that Sprints need to deliver vertical slices of functionality. If the team has committed to delivering a character that walks and runs but has a few transition bugs, the stakeholders need to call the team on it. Many stakeholders don't want to discourage teams by criticizing anything, especially when the team has worked hard and delivered value. However, allowing debt (such as bugs) to accumulate does the team a disservice later by creating further debt. Honesty is the best policy in Reviews.

## Retrospectives

The Sprint Retrospective is possibly the most important, yet often most neglected practice. The goal of the meeting is to continually improve how the team creates value for the game. This is accomplished in the Retrospective by identifying beneficial practices, stopping detrimental practices, and identifying new practices to be tried in the next Sprint.

The Retrospective is where much of the improvement of development practices occurs. Changes don't necessarily have to be large ones; a 1- to 2-percent improvement in the effectiveness of the team every Sprint compounds into huge improvements over the long term. Usually an improvement is something small like "Don't commit anything untested at the end of the day." That one saved many morning hours!

## The Meeting

The Retrospective occurs after the Review. The entire Scrum team attends. It's facilitated by the Scrum Master and is a timeboxed meeting. The team selects a time limit for the meeting before it starts. Teams will select times from 30 minutes to 3 hours, depending on how much needs to be addressed.

The following three questions are raised at the meeting:

- **"What things should we stop doing?"** The team identifies detrimental practices identified during the last Sprint that it wants to stop.
- **"What should we start doing?"** The team identifies practices that help it improve how members work together.
- **"What is working well that we should continue to do?"** The team identifies the beneficial practices that should be continued. Usually these are changes introduced at recent Retrospectives.

It's up to the team whether it wants to invite people from outside the team. If a team interacts with people outside the team during the Sprint, then including these people in the Retrospective is valuable.

A lot of discussion should occur during the Retrospective. The Scrum Master should facilitate these discussions to help keep the pace of the meeting within its timebox.

The purpose of the Retrospective is to identify changes in the ways the Scrum team works together, usually in the form of action items. The answers to the questions asked result in action items. These action items aren't always assigned to individuals during the meeting; it depends on the action item itself. The following are examples of answers to the question "What should we start doing?" and some potential actions that could result:

- **"Start having QA approve all tasks marked 'done,' if possible."** This doesn't require an action item; it is a working agreement for all of QA to adopt.

- **"Make sure Joe tests his animations before committing them."** Clearly, Joe has to follow up on his animation testing, but because this has to happen daily, a specific action item isn't needed.
- **"Have the build server send an e-mail when the build is broken."** If the team has programmers who can implement this change, then they could implement it themselves. If not, this generates an action item to pass along this request to the team that maintains the build server.

### Keeping Retrospectives Fresh

The format of Retrospectives should always be mixed up from time to time. Using the same format leads to them becoming boring and unproductive. The book *Agile Retrospectives: Making Good Teams Great* (Derby and Larsen, 2006) describes many formats and techniques to use to keep them interesting and productive.

### Posting and Tracking Results

Scrum Masters record all the answers given for each question. Following the Retrospective, they post the results of the meeting in the team area and check off all the items on the list that have been fulfilled during the next Sprint. Any items left unchecked from the last Retrospective are discussed at the next Retrospective. These items are either carried forward to the next Sprint or removed from the list based on what the team decides.

Retrospectives help the team become more effective over time. Ignoring this critical practice prevents the benefits of Agile adoption from being realized.

### Should the Product Owner Attend the Retrospective?

Some argue that Product Owners shouldn't attend the Retrospective, that it's only for the Development Team. I feel that they should be invited. Issues such as improving communication between the Development Team and the stakeholders is something that impacts Team productivity. After all, what's the use of having a team efficiently create something the stakeholders and players don't want? It's important that the discussions in the Retrospective remain focused on improving "how" the team works, not "what" it is working on.

## Sprint Challenges

The goal of a Sprint is to advance the value of a game within a fixed amount of time. The team meets with the stakeholders and negotiates to find a goal that it commits to achieve. The team then implements the code, assets, and behaviors. What could be simpler?

Sometimes things don't work out quite so simply—unforeseen roadblocks slow progress. Stakeholders change their mind. The process has to accommodate the vagaries of life and development.

Scrum handles these problems in a number of ways. Small and large impacts to the Sprint are quickly exposed. The Scrum team addresses these and works with the stakeholders to react to the problems. Sometimes these problems can't be handled through daily fixes and result in the team's failing to achieve all or part of the Sprint Goal. This section looks at what the team is able to do when this occurs.

## Sprint Interrupted

In the fall of 2007, following an unusually warm weekend, we woke up to a different world in San Diego. The southern sky was different; a horizontal column of dark orange sky fell across it like a wall. Blown from the east by a Santa Ana (desert) wind, it could only mean that there was a wildfire out of control again.

A quick check of the news assured me that the fire was distant and no immediate threat to our town, so I decided to head into work. The studio was like a ghost town; many employees had distant commutes, and they decided not to press their luck that day.

Shortly after lunch, our fortunes changed. The main fire had spawned a number of other fires, some of which were a direct threat to the studio and surrounding homes. This happened so suddenly that we found ourselves in an evacuation zone. I faced the imminent threat of being cut off from my family by closed roads, so I raced for the door.

On the way out, I was met by one of our Scrum Masters. Although he was just as determined to escape, he paused to ask, "What do you think this means to Friday's Sprint review?" I initially thought he was joking, but his expression was one of concern. I had to admire the tenacity of his Scrum Master training. I told him that all bets were off and wished him and his family the best of luck.

Fortunately, none of the studio employees lost their homes (or worse) this time around, and the studio was spared. People trickled back in over the next week, and the Sprints resumed. The studio probably lost close to two weeks of work.

We discussed restarting a new Sprint or finishing the remainder of the Sprint in progress, but we decided to finish. Work picked up smoothly where we had left off, and we had a successful Sprint.

## Sprint Resets

One of the most drastic practices in Scrum is called the **Sprint Reset**. A Sprint Reset allows the team or the stakeholders to declare that the Sprint Goal needs to change or that the team is unable to complete much of that goal by the end of the Sprint. When a Sprint is reset, all the incomplete PBIs are returned to the Product Backlog, and the team returns to Sprint Planning.

Sprint Resets are costly. Much of the work in progress is potentially lost. Resets should be rare. They must always lead to ways the stakeholders and team improve communication and its ability to plan.

## Problems with the Sprint Goal

Although you may not have wildfires and earthquakes, there are a few more common reasons for Sprints to run into trouble. The two main reasons are when the Sprint Goal changes. or the team realizes it will not achieve its Sprint Goal because it has run out of time.

### *Goals Change*

Imagine a team is working on its jump feature when the CEO runs in with an emergency; he's agreed to demonstrate an online feature in two weeks! This new feature is suddenly more important to him than any other feature. What does the team do?

First, the team does nothing. The Scrum Master must intervene at this point. The first thing that the Scrum Master does is separate the CEO from the team and firmly remind him or her that interrupting a Sprint has great costs. The CEO needs to understand the cost of changing Sprint Goals. Next, the Product Owner is brought into the discussion. The two of them discuss the feature in more detail. The Product Owner then brings in domain experts to discuss the feature, if necessary. For example, if the CEO wants an online feature, an online programmer may be consulted.

If the group decides the online feature should be pursued (or if the CEO is adamant), then a proper PBI encompassing the feature is written. The team best suited to accomplish this feature is gathered to perform a preliminary Sprint Planning session to evaluate the scope of this new feature and whether it could possibly be finished in a two-week Sprint.

If the team determines that the goal cannot be accomplished, then the CEO must be told "no." Perhaps a smaller portion of the original feature is discussed, but the team must not commit to the work. If the team determines that completing the feature within a new Sprint is possible, then the Sprint is reset, and a new Sprint is fully planned to deliver the online feature within two weeks.

### Objection: My CEO Doesn't Take "No" as an Answer

There is a saying that "A dead Scrum Master is a useless Scrum Master" (Schwaber, 2004). If you are fired for standing up to the CEO because he is not following the "Scrum rules," you aren't helping your team. Live to fight the battle another day and to influence stakeholders to do these things less often.

### *Running Out of Time*

Estimating work for even a two-week Sprint isn't 100 percent certain. Problems can blindside the team; tasks that seemed minimal can balloon into large challenges. Sprint teams sometimes find themselves approaching the end of the Sprint with too much work and not enough time left to accomplish it.

A useful tool in evaluating the progress of a Sprint is the burndown chart. As previously described, the burndown chart is a tool to monitor the work remaining. In some cases (refer to Figure 4.5), the burndown chart shows that the team will not hit zero time by the end of the Sprint. Projecting the burndown trend clearly shows this. The end date of the Sprint is always set and never changes, but sometimes the scope of work isn't so predictable and expands significantly.

In this situation, the team then has one of three choices:

1. If the extra work isn't too great, put in some overtime to make up the difference.
2. Negotiate with the Product Owner to remove one or more of the lower-priority PBIs in the Goal or remove part of a PBI.
3. Request a Sprint Reset. Set a new Sprint with more achievable goals.

The team explores the solution to the problem in this order; it committed to the work and should do its reasonable best to accomplish it. If the debt of work remaining exceeds what can be accomplished with a reasonable amount of effort, the team should approach the Product Owner and request that some PBIs be dropped from its list of goals for the Sprint. If the Product Owner agrees to drop some PBIs, they are usually among the lower-priority ones. Dropping individual PBIs may not be possible if they are highly interrelated. In this case, the team and Product Owner should call for a Sprint Reset.

> **Note**
>
> For teams I have been on, we commit to work evenings during the week if we need to catch up, but we avoid any weekend work. After the Sprint we will discuss the reasons for why this extra work was necessary and try to find ways to avoid it in the future. Chapter 16, "The Myths and Challenges of Scrum," explores overtime and crunch more.

The question is often raised about how much overtime the team should put in before they request that some of the work be dropped. There is no specific answer to this. Teams typically abhor dropping PBIs. They prefer to work some reasonable amount of overtime. Overtime should not be invoked very often. If teams experience overtime every Sprint, they need to reduce the amount of work to which they are committing.

**Note**

This is a balancing act; as a stakeholder and coach, I expect a team to not deliver all committed PBIs in perhaps one out of every four of their Sprints. If the team never needs to drop something from its Goal, I suspect that the team fears "overcommitment." If the failure rate is significantly higher, I suspect that the team is not taking its Sprint Goals seriously enough. It's a fine line, and one of the biggest challenges that Scrum Masters and coaches encounter with teams.

Whatever the cause, when teams need to drop PBIs during a Sprint, the reasons should be discussed in the Retrospective.

### Running Out of Work

Occasionally a team accomplishes its goal well before the end of the Sprint. If it's a day or two away from the end of the Sprint, the team can come up with useful work to fill the time and can usually identify enough housekeeping and polishing tasks. If it runs out of work sooner than that, it can meet with the Product Owner to find a small PBI on the Product Backlog to estimate and complete.

**Note**

If teams encounter this problem a few times, I encourage them to commit to more work during Sprint Planning.

## What Good Looks Like

The challenge of adopting these practices isn't their complexity. Scrum has been defined as being easy to start but hard to get good at. The hard part is cultural. Culture pushes back on these practices largely because transparency often reveals things we don't want revealed. But when teams and studios overcome these cultural issues, we see

- Teams being trusted to determine their own pace and process within the Sprint and becoming engaged in the work.

- Stakeholders increasingly trusting teams to do so and demanding less documentation up front.
- Issues being raised as early as possible and risk being communicated and accounted for early, when the cost for resolution is lowest.
- True progress is measured, and a game's plan responds quickly to what the game is telling us, Sprint to Sprint.

Chapter 18, "Team Transformations," and Chapter 19, "Coaching Teams for Greatness," explore overcoming the cultural challenges.

## Summary

Sprints provide the heartbeat of iteration on an Agile game project. They are a contract between the stakeholder and the team to provide value demonstrated within the game rather than promised in a document. However, a game project isn't made of a series of Sprints that all look the same. We start many projects by iteratively exploring the possibility and end them by creating many assets to provide hours of entertainment. The next part of the book examines practices that help with longer development cycles, called **Releases**, and how we plan in an Agile way over the entire duration of the project.

## Additional Reading

Derby, E., and D. Larsen. 2006. *Agile Retrospectives: Making Good Teams Great.* Raleigh, NC: Pragmatic Bookshelf.

# Chapter 5

# Great Teams

I've worked on creating various products, from the F-22 fighters to games, for more than 20 years. The highlights of my career are clearly marked in my mind by the teams I was a part of. These teams were more consequential to enjoyment and productivity than the company or project we were working for at the time.

Working with the project team on the first Midtown Madness game was a highlight. The team was largely composed of developers who had never worked on a game before. Microsoft, our publisher, and the studio we worked at, Angel Studios, left us largely alone to develop the game. As a result, many of the smaller details of the game were left to us to discover. We were never far away from being canceled either…in some cases hours away. We had to prove ourselves.

What emerged was a team with a shared vision, a sense of ownership, and pride. We worked hard on the game. For example, we started a LAN party with the game every day at 6 p.m., and at 8 p.m. we met in a conference room to talk about improving the experience. I would often have an idea pop into my head during the night, and I would rush back in during the early hours of the day to try it, often finding teammates who had arrived earlier or had even spent the night working on their own idea. Although we spent long hours on the game, it seemed more like a hobby we were passionate about than a job, but it never felt like a "crunch."

The game we shipped was a success, but the real reward was the experience of working with that team. Much of the chemistry of that team is a mystery to me. There doesn't seem to be a formula for how such teams can be created, but I've found that it's quite easy to prevent such teams from forming. Scrum's focus is on allowing such teams to form, if possible, and nurturing them to grow.

## What Are Great Teams?

Great teams are one of the most influential factors for creating a successful game. Great teams are also the most difficult teams to foster. They cannot be created through the application of rules or practices alone. Studio and project leadership are required to facilitate them.

Great teams share the following characteristics:

- **Follow a shared vision and purpose:** Everyone on the team understands the goal of what they are working on.
- **Complement other team members' skills:** Team members depend on each other to achieve their goals by applying their unique skills to a shared goal.
- **Exhibit open and safe communication:** Team members feel safe to communicate anything to one another.
- **Share decision making, responsibility, and accountability:** The team succeeds or fails together, not as individuals. Everyone earns their spot on the team daily. There is no room for titles or egos.
- **Have fun together:** They spend time together and enjoy each other's company. They care for one another.
- **Deliver value:** Great teams take pride in their work and deliver high value consistently.
- **Demonstrate shared commitment:** Great teams have a unified cause. When one member has a problem, the entire team will pitch in to help them out. As a result, great teams deliver value because they focus on the whole rather on their own parts. Great teams are committed to their goals. They'll go the "extra mile" to achieve a goal that they believe in.

Scrum creates a framework through its practices and roles to support these teams, which require facilitation and support of leadership and management to evolve. Great teams are uncommon. They create experiences—like the one I mentioned in the chapter introduction—that people strive to be a part of over their entire career.

When baking a cake, a few ingredients are needed before you start. If you are missing any of these, such as eggs, flour, and so on, you can't make a cake. However, just how these ingredients are prepared together and baked into the cake is the main difference between a memorable wedding cake and something that might taste like it that came from an Easy-Bake oven.

Leadership and talent are the required ingredients for a great game, but like the cake, how these ingredients are brought together, such as in a team, is the main determinant of the quality of the game. An Agile framework, like Scrum, doesn't provide the ingredients for great teams but helps them "mix and bake" what's there to achieve that goal.

## The Solutions in This Chapter

Great teams can emerge anywhere. The Midtown Madness team described earlier was a waterfall-driven project that was faced with many challenges, yet still formed a highly effective team.

This chapter explores some of the basic Scrum principles and practices that support such teams.

## An Agile Approach to Teams

Scrum creates conditions that enable such teams to achieve greatness through its practices and principles:

- **Cross-discipline teams:** Enables teams to deliver features and mechanics that have clear value to customers and stakeholders
- **Self-management:** Enables teams to select the set of features they establish as a Sprint Goal, organize the plan to achieve that goal, and execute on that plan through whatever means they find appropriate
- **Self-organization:** Enables teams to have a degree of authority and responsibility to select their membership and the processes and practices they use.
- **True leadership:** Provides leadership focused on mentoring and facilitation to free the best performance possible from the team

The rest of this section examines the principles and practices in greater detail.

**Experience**

"At the heart of Scrum is the interaction of the team. A daily meeting around the task board is interactive, vibrant, collaborative, visual, and tactile. It is a visual way of showing the goal the team is striving toward and the progress they are making. They, each and every member of the team, are peers.

"They own the goal. It's a team effort. They gather around the board to align themselves with each other, to honor others' contribution to the effort, and to course-correct when they are missing the mark. They argue, discuss, share, learn, continually improve, celebrate, boost each other up, and create solutions.

"There is another thing that Scrum does for the team: It creates transparency. Since Scrum depends on collaboration and continual forward progress, problems are addressed by the team as they crop up instead of dealing with them later or covering the problem under a layer of 'spin.'

"A structured, militant environment will never create a team. A team works together toward a shared goal. A group works together toward a goal given to them. Scrum is messy and noisy. It lives, it breathes, it stretches, it morphs, and it expands. Interaction is the heart of the team. The heart of Scrum is the team."

—Shelly Warmuth, freelance writer and game designer

## Cross-Discipline Teams

When the various documents are written, and schedules are created, the priorities of each discipline's schedules don't often mesh. Programmers often read the design document and architect a number of systems based on the goals established in the document. Complexity and risk prioritize this work, not feature value.

For example, if the design identifies characters that walk on walls, then they architect that requirement into the character system. This requires a great deal of work to alter the physics system and the camera system. The programmers consider these changes as high priority, because they affect core systems at a fundamental level. As a result, they begin working on these changes from the start. The problem is that the "walking on walls" feature may not be very important to the designers. The feature may even be dropped when it is seen.

This lack of synchronized prioritization between disciplines leads to delays in building knowledge about the game: knowledge that comes only from using each mechanic in a working game.

Scrum requires a synchronization of the disciplines every Sprint. This forces change in how each developer works daily regardless of their discipline. A cross-discipline team uses value to explore a solution, which addresses the needs for technology, design, and animation. This drives changes in the way each discipline works to avoid one discipline getting too far ahead of the others, such as creating speculative architectures. Programmers on a Scrum team may eventually adopt test-driven development practices, discussed in Chapter 12, "Agile Technology," to enable value-prioritized development without the cost of late changes that up-front architectures attempt to avoid.

Cross-discipline Scrum teams minimize the delays and costs that are incurred by large discipline-focused hierarchies. Team members share the same goal and, therefore, the same priorities, which encourage collaboration. Practices such as the Daily Scrum reinforce a team's commitment to the Sprint Goal and to solving the problems that ordinarily would "fall between the cracks" between the disciplines on a daily basis.

**"We're Not Sitting Next to Them!"**

When we first adopted Scrum, we asked the developers to form cross-discipline teams. Their reaction was swift and negative. I recall someone on a team of animators saying, "We're not sitting next to any propeller heads!" As a CTO, I could only imagine they were referring to the modelers.[1]

As a result, the initial Sprints were chaotic. Single-discipline teams generate a lot of dependencies and delays.

Eventually, I was approached by someone from the animation team who asked if they could have a programmer, we'll call Sean, join their team. I was astonished to hear they wanted Sean. I considered Sean to be the weakest of all our programmers. None of the other programmers wanted him on their team.

When I asked why they wanted Sean, I was told "He will drop anything he's doing to help us out. He fixes exporters, animation state machines, and any other technical issue we have."

This was a revelation. I suddenly realized that Sean was probably one of our most productive programmers; he was keeping a team of animators happy!

1. They weren't.

## Generalizing Specialists

One of the most insidious problems I see is the lack of accountability that can occur when excessive separation exists between specialists and their work. This separation reveals itself with handoffs between specialists. Designers hand off a document to programmers, who will hand off a tool or feature to art and so on. Eventually, a build of the game is handed off to QA to test. After testing, a list of bugs is handed back to the team through a database.

Although we can't expect everyone to be effective at every discipline, having specialists understand the workflow and constraints of other specialists can be beneficial. It allows a dialogue around the constraints and the ultimate goal for a feature or game, which handoffs are not best at.

### Experience

Several times in my career, I worked with the SEAL teams training in San Diego. In a SEAL team, everybody can shoot and use all sorts of weapons. However, a sniper is still the best in long-range shooting. An explosive expert is still the best in handling explosives. No matter how hard you get trained, some are just naturally specialized in some fields and keep specialized through their dedicated training full time.

When this occurs, you see unanticipated benefits. I can't count the number of times I've seen a programmer look over the shoulder of an artist struggling to put an asset into the game using a clunky tool and comment that they could modify the tool to "make it easy."

Ultimately, everyone on the team should be a "game developer" first and a designer/programmer/artists/tester second. A problem with the game is the team's problem, not just the problem of a single specialist.

### Experience

Sometimes a coaching day with a studio will be spent facilitating pair conversations between specialists. Usually one explains a problem he has been dealing with for years, and the other offers a quick solution. Such problems shouldn't hang around for years.

To me, this highlights the need for better internal coaching (See Chapter 19, "Coaching Teams for Greatness").

## Self-Management

Scrum addresses the problems of communication on large teams not by adding management layers but by dividing the project staff into small teams. Development Teams are usually composed of five to nine cross-disciplined developers who take on major game features and create vertical slices of those features every Sprint. Teams take on an increasing level of self-management by doing the following:

- Choosing the set of features from the top of the Product Backlog that they are able to accomplish in their Sprint.
- Deciding the best way to work together
- Planning their own work and monitoring progress toward their goal daily
- Demonstrating an improved game to the stakeholders every Sprint

Team self-management doesn't happen overnight. It requires mentoring and practice to achieve. It requires trust to be built between management and the teams and the clear definition of the dividing line of responsibilities.

## Team Size

Scrum literature recommends teams have sizes of seven to nine members (Schwaber, 2004). This is based on studies (Steiner, 1972) and first-hand experience that shows that team productivity peaks at these sizes.

A challenge for Agile game development is to build cross-discipline teams that don't exceed this size. For some teams, the number of disciplines desired to achieve a goal can be large. For example, a level production team may need the following:

- Two level artists
- One prop artist
- One texture artist
- One animator
- One sound designer
- One concept artist
- One level designer
- One gameplay designer
- One graphics programmer

- One gameplay programmer
- One AI programmer

This is a 12-member team that begins to exhibit some of the problems seen on larger teams. For example, some members are more likely than others to speak up and be heard. This can prevent key information from being shared.

Another problem with larger teams is that subteams or cliques tend to form. I was on such a team. The designers and artists formed separate cabals that raised communication barriers. Whenever I visited one of these cliques, they would criticize the other. These criticisms weren't shared between the two factions, so problems lingered. This had a major impact on the quality of the levels and the speed at which they were created. Scrum Master intervention eventually resolved this, but a smaller team would have self-corrected this problem sooner.

A team like this might consider separating into two teams with smaller goals that "stage" the development of prototype levels, but that introduces dependency and accountability issues. I encourage teams to try different arrangements for a few Sprints, and if that doesn't address the problems, they can reform into a larger team again.

**Note**

Some studios have used teams of three to five people in size and report that it worked very well.

### Collaboration, Interrupted

There is no shortage of ways in which companies try to build morale with large cross-discipline teams. I've been involved in a few of these potentially dangerous exercises myself in the past.

I still recall the day that a team-building exercise nearly maimed me. It was on a paintball field located in high chaparral land east of San Diego. I was lying flat on my back, nearly out of ammunition, while nearly 30 electrical engineers were trying to shoot me.

I was a young software engineer working for a military avionics company. During my career in the defense industry, I witnessed the animosity between electrical engineers and software engineers. To the electrical engineers, we lacked true engineering discipline and were overpaid. They often considered our code as a "necessary evil." We saw the electrical engineers as elitist in attitude and outdated in their technical philosophy.

I believed the electrical engineers hated us because we were often the heroes of a project. The software we wrote often worked around the flaws in their hardware that threatened a project in its final hours.

It started with a division into two teams. Naturally, one consisted of electrical engineers, and the other consisted of us software engineers.

I won't lie and say we were better fighters that day. We weren't. I won't make excuses and accuse them of cheating, although they brought some suspicious-looking tools with them. The plain fact was that the software team lost the most games, and we lost them badly.

I faced the greatest challenge during the last game of the day. We were playing an elimination match in a small plywood "village." The goal of the game was for one team to eliminate every player on the opposing team to win.

It was another bloodbath for the software team. We were quickly decimated. I survived by hiding, with several other programmers, on the roof of a plywood hut. The partial cover of three walls protected us, and the only way to enter the roof was through a hole in the floor from the room below.

One by one, my roof mates were killed off in heroic displays of gallantry and ignorance of the value of cover. I was content to hunch low and survive.

Suddenly the referees blew their whistles signaling the end of the game. They believed that all the software engineers were dead! I jumped up, roaring in defiance at what I hoped was one or two remaining enemies. My roar quickly choked when I saw that nearly the entire enemy team of 30 electrical engineers was still alive. Endless seconds seemed to pass as we considered each other. Then one of the referees announced, "Game on!" and blew his whistle. I will never forget the sight of all those electrical engineers, shouting with gleeful nerd rage, running toward me as I ducked back into cover.

I held out for a while. I even managed to kill a few of the enemy engineers. I would love to say that I was a hero that day, but it was not to be. Someone eventually shot me. The electrical engineers completed their victory over us, and we went back to work with renewed feelings of antagonism.

## What Good Looks Like

### A Team to The Rescue

One of my all-time favorite games was *Mech Warrior 2*. The core mechanics, interface, levels, and even the music were outstanding. The game was a financial success for a struggling Activision as well.

I've come to find out that it was a bit of a miracle that the game ever saw the light of day, which was due to the team coming to its rescue:

"MW2 went through two rebirths: one on the engineering side, and one on the design side. The original team had implemented something with promise, but it barely ran (not enough memory to hold more than two mechs) and it lacked narrative (just mechs on a flat surface shooting lamely at each other).

"After a couple of years of effort, with a major deadline looming, management had no option but to retrench and down-scope the project. The existing team leadership departed at that point (lead engineers, lead producer, etc.).

"In an effort to salvage the massive effort invested, a couple of remaining engineers went rogue while VP Howard Marks was away at a tradeshow for a week: Without permission, they attempted to convert the game to protected mode. This would theoretically provide access to enough memory to render a full set of mechs, but it had been deemed impossible in anything less than nine months, which was way more time than was available.

"As of 9 p.m. the night before Howard returned, they were ready to concede defeat: Protected mode conversion requires extensive Intel assembly language programming, something they had no experience with—and there was no Internet to use as a reference; they just had a single Intel tech manual. They thought they had done the right things, but there was no telling how many bugs remained before the game loop would run. Howard's arrival would spell the end of their effort, since his priority was to ship something, even if massive compromise in scope was required.

"Against all odds, that midnight the game successfully looped in protected mode for the first time, and they were rewarded with a full set of mechs rendering, albeit in wireframe and without sound. They were elated to have cracked the hardest problem, opening up the possibility to build a better game.

"Howard returned, recognized the potential that had been unlocked, and helped set the team up for success by bringing in proven problem solvers from *Pitfall: The Mayan Adventure*. John Spinale and Sean Vesce stepped in to build a new team on the skeleton that remained and to establish a vision for a product that to that point was nothing more than a bare bones tech demo.

> "The design rebirth of MW2 is something that Sean can speak better to, but it's fair to say that the technology rebirth was just an enabler—the design team innovated on so many levels under tight time pressure to produce something that was revolutionary for the time. Without that innovation, I have no doubt that MW2 would languish in obscurity today. Likewise, without the successful leadership of John rebuilding the team and protecting the team from outside interference, we would not have achieved the success that we ultimately did."
>
> —Tim Morton, Production Director at Blizzard Entertainment

In my training classes, I often ask the group, "If you decided to start a new game and hired 50 random people off the street who had never made a game before, but had them use Scrum, would Scrum be effective?"

Most answer "no." I tell them that the answer is "yes." Scrum would show you very quickly that this group will not be successful. This is a reminder about the benefit of Scrum. It doesn't solve problems. It creates transparency.

While Scrum doesn't ensure any team will be great, it provides the tools to recognize team chemistry and performance quickly and lets you do something about it. If a team is dysfunctional, it is immediately evident. That team can be coached, which can help it grow to greatness or, if coaching fails, can simply be disbanded. Very often, members from a dysfunctional team will find better chemistry on another team that will become great.

Chapter 19 explores ways of coaching teams to become great.

## Summary

There is no single formula for what a great team is. Exploring roles and team structures is an ongoing process. Teams must use Retrospectives to find ways to improve how they work together and with the stakeholders (Chapter 17, "Working with Stakeholders,") of the game. By allowing teams to take ownership and authority over some of the daily aspects of their life, they are more likely to take responsibility for their work. This doesn't happen overnight. It takes years in many cases and will create head-on collisions with studio leadership culture. The results are worth the effort.

Scrum also drives changes across specialties, focusing the team on changing how it works day to day to improve communication and the pace of iteration. It also drives changes in how each discipline works. Part IV of this book explores those discipline changes in more detail.

The goal is to foster teams that love their work and make games players will love.

## Additional Reading

DeMarco, T., and T. Lister. 1999. *Peopleware: Productive Projects and Teams, Second Edition*. New York: Dorset House Publishing.

Katzenbach, J. R., and D. K. Smith. 2003. *The Wisdom of Teams: Creating the High-Performance Organization*. Cambridge, MA: Harvard Business School Press.

Steiner, I. D. 1972. *Group Process and Productivity*. New York, NY: Academic Press.

# Chapter 6

# Kanban

Early in our adoption, Scrum exposed many problems for us to solve. Later we encountered other challenges that presented problems using Scrum for all aspects of video game development:

- The team supporting engines and tools for multiple games kept receiving urgent requests that interrupted their Sprints.
- The teams that were producing assets such as levels and characters couldn't cleanly fit their work into timeboxed Sprints.

After some experimentation, these teams decided not to Sprint anymore. Instead, they decided to plan work as needed and release it as completed. This worked well.

This problem had been seen elsewhere before. Jeff Sutherland, one of the founders of Scrum, had encountered this at his company and had called his similar variation "Scrum Type C."[1] Later on, we came across writings by David Anderson and Corey Ladas, who had adapted Lean practices from Japan into a method called Kanban.

## The Solutions in This Chapter

This chapter introduces the basics of Kanban for game development. Later chapters employ those basics for content creation (Chapter 10, "Video Game Project Management") and to support teams (Chapter 22, "Live Game Development"). It covers

1. https://xebia.com/blog/type-c-scrum-explained/

- Why Sprints aren't a perfect match for some types of work
- How Kanban visualizes and measures work differently
- How Kanban tools help manage work to address bottlenecks and improve flow
- The difference between Scrum and Kanban roles and practices

## What Is Kanban?

Kanban is a method for visualizing, measuring, and managing the flow of work. It employs many practices for improving that workflow by making problems immediately visible and their impact on the workflow measurable.

### Why Scrum and Kanban?

One of the most surprising reactions to talking about both Scrum and Kanban with some people is anger. Scrum and Kanban overlap in principle, and the practices unique to each are complementary. Just as carpenters have different tools for different needs, teams can employ practices that best serve them regardless of the label they fall under.

### Visualizing the Workflow

Applying the Kanban method starts with visualizing the workflow of an item. Figure 6.1 shows an example workflow of a character asset.

A single-discipline executes each step of the work, and the arrows between represent a handoff of that work to another discipline.

After we capture the workflow of an item, we represent that flow on a Kanban board (shown in Figure 6.2). A Kanban board is a bit similar to a Scrum task board, and is also sometimes called a *Heijunka board*.

A Kanban board visualizes the current state of the workflow and identifies where it is being disrupted.

A Kanban board has columns that represent each state of work for an asset or feature, which are identified on **Kanban cards**. In Japanese, the word *kan* means "card,"

**Figure 6.1** *The flow of creating a character*

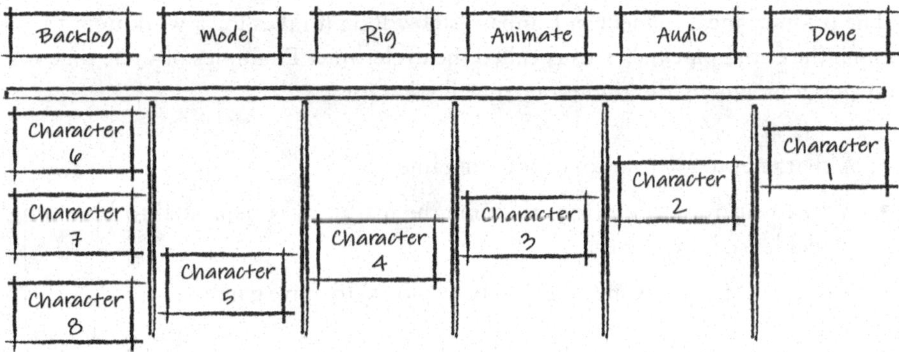


**Figure 6.2** *A Kanban board*

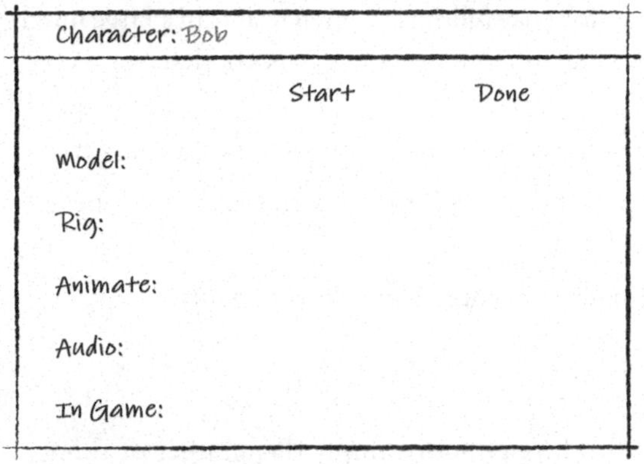

Character: Bob

Start Done

Model:

Rig:

Animate:

Audio:

In Game:

**Figure 6.3** *A Kanban card*

and *ban* means "signal," so **Kanban** refers to "signal card." A Kanban card is a signal meant to signal action, such as "work on this next" or "I need an animation."

A Kanban card (see Figure 6.3) contains information we want to capture for each stage of work on a character.

In this example, the Kanban card captures the date of completion for each stage of work. This is useful for measuring and smoothing out the flow of work. Kanban cards contribute to the visualization of workflow by showing, at a glance, where work might be falling behind or where someone has nothing to work on.

## Measuring the Workflow

Kanban incorporates the same inspect-and-adapt approach to continuous improvement as Scrum. As with any empirical approach, improving something is easier to do if you can measure it.

The primary measurement in Kanban is how long it takes for a work item to go through the entire pipeline. This is called the **cycle time**. Examples of cycle time for game development are the amount of time it takes for

- A character to go from concept to in-game
- A tool feature starting from the time the feature was requested to becoming available to the tool user
- A proposal for a new mechanic to be deployed to a live game

What's common with these examples is that Kanban is focused on measuring the entire pipeline. This principle is based on the discoveries in Lean manufacturing that optimizing parts of a workflow often works against the whole of the workflow. For example, if we focus on keeping a character animator busy fulltime, it often results in a large inventory of unfinished characters. This backlog of unfinished work is a debt that can

- Lead to long lead times between the concept and deployment of a character
- Lead to throwing out those animations when the first character to appear in the game reveals animation problems
- Slow iteration time, resulting in fewer iterations and lower quality

**Note**

Some teams use **throughput** instead. Throughput is simply the number of things completed in a certain amount of time; so instead of saying a character model took a day of cycle time, the throughput might be five characters per week.

## Managing the Workflow

One of the easiest aspects of Kanban initially is that you don't change how you work when you start it. You just capture your workflow on a board, add some measurements, and continue working as you always have. It doesn't stay that way, though. Over time you start applying some different ways of managing the work to better highlight the issues that are slowing that work down.

This section describes ways Kanban manages workflow differently, and the next section shows how workflow is improved using these techniques.

### *Pulling Work*

Kanban employs a pull system, where people working "downstream" (work that will be done later) pull work from "upstream" (work that is done earlier). In the example from Figure 6.2, when the animator needs more work, he pulls the next character to be animated from the column containing the previously rigged characters.

This is different from "pushing" work to an animator, usually in the form of a predetermined schedule. The reasons why pulling work is better are

- **Schedules are more realistic:** Work is "pulled" when it hits a quality bar. "Pushing" is usually driven by a fixed schedule and often results in unfinished work that requires late rework, which creates schedule delays. When this initial work items make it through a pull system, we can better forecast the schedule for the remainder of the work.
- **Quality drives pace:** As mentioned, with a push system, work is rushed, and quality suffers. The built-in definitions of done in Kanban (covered later in this chapter) allow a balance to be established between speed and quality that can be continually refined.
- **Pull systems allow more task ownership:** This results in the entire team being more engaged with finding improvements.

### *Defining Done and Buffering*

As each stage of a work item is completed, it moves into a done state for that stage. For that to happen, it has to meet a Definition of Done (see Chapter 7, "The Product Backlog"). For example, with the flow shown in Figure 6.1, for a character model to be considered complete, it has to

- Pass an art Review
- Meet budget constraints (polygon count, texture limits)
- Meet asset naming conventions

If it meets these definitions, it moves into a buffer between it and the rigging stage. This buffer signals to artists doing the rigging that they can pull that model in when they are ready.

### *Limiting Work in Progress*

One of the more powerful techniques of managing work in Kanban is to limit the *work in progress* (WiP) in every stage and buffer in the workflow. These limits, when reached, trigger a rule (called a **policy**) that says no more work can enter that stage or buffer. This prevents a pile-up of unfinished work. It signals to the team that it has reached a limit and that something needs to be done, usually resulting in improvements to the workflow (discussed later in this chapter).

**Lean Thinking and Boats**

A useful metaphor for how Lean thinking encourages continual improvement is that of a boat traveling down a river. The river is filled with boulders of various sizes that impede the flow of water. When the water level of the river is high, the crew sailing the boat doesn't encounter the boulders and isn't concerned about how they are slowing them down.

However, when the water level in the river drops, the boulders begin to appear. They are then recognized not only as impediments to the flow of the river, but also as real danger! Now the crew reacts to the boulders and steers around them.

In this metaphor, the boat is the project, and the flow of water represents the flow of money or time being spent on it. The boulders stand for the things that slow development down, such as unreliable build systems or asset pipelines that take hours to create a build.

Lean thinking not only causes the water level to be lowered, through WiP limits and reduced batch sizes, but also arms teams with the equivalent of a cannon, through transparency and self-organization, to start blowing the boulders away. This makes it possible for the boat to go faster and straighter.

### *Ordered Work*

As with Scrum, the team's work comes from an ordered Product Backlog that a Product Owner manages. For a support team, this allows the Product Owner to balance the urgency of requests coming in.

### *Planning on Demand*

Kanban teams don't have timeboxed iterations, like Scrum Sprints. Instead of planning a Sprint every one to three weeks, Kanban teams pull a set of work from the Product Backlog when they need to.

**Ready Columns**

If planning is needed for Product Backlog Items (PBIs) brought in from the Product Backlog, a Kanban team will add a "ready" column. A ready column will have a set of tasks associated with each PBI. An empty ready column is a signal to the team to hold a planning session to refill the column.

Ready columns will usually have a WiP limit that determines how many PBIs to pull in from the Product Backlog.

### *A Cadence of Review and Retrospectives*

As with Scrum, having regular Reviews of the work with the stakeholders is useful to evaluate progress and to have team Retrospectives discuss improvements in how they work. Unlike Scrum, these are not tied to a Sprint timebox. Instead, Kanban teams establish a cadence (rhythm) of Reviews and Retrospectives. The cadence of Reviews is negotiated with the stakeholders based on how long they want to go without seeing what the team has accomplished since the last Review.

The cadence of the Retrospective, in my experience, shouldn't be longer than once every three weeks. When it's longer than that, then the urgency of fixing things that impacted the team more than three weeks ago starts to fade.

**Optional Cadence**

Reviews and Retrospectives can also be held on demand instead of a cadence but be careful not to let too much time pass between them.

## Improving the Workflow

After the workflow is visualized and is being measured, everything is in place to inspect and adapt and continually improve it. This section describes the major tools of improvement that teams use. Future chapters on live support and content production explore these tools and others more fully.

### Reducing Batch Sizes and Waste

One of the biggest wastes in game development is throwing out assets that were created too soon. This often results from the assets being created before the technology or design assumptions, used to drive asset requirements, are proven to be too optimistic.

Lean development, like Agile, promotes more frequent and low-cost iterations, which gives us more opportunities to find improvements in what we're making and to ensure we're making it the right way. By sending small batches of assets through the entire workflow and into a working game, we can avoid this waste.

The same applies to technical work. By sending smaller batches of code through the workflow and proving their functionality, we build up a better architecture rather than just coding to a lengthy technical design document and integrating the work in the distant future.

## Reducing Handoffs

Studios often organize developers by disciplines that even sit in separate rooms. These are called *silos*. Silos work with each other by passing documents. Designers write documents that are "handed off" to programmers who develop architectures and tools that are handed off to content creators who put assets in the game, which is then handed off to testers who then hand off bug reports back to the developers.

Each of these handoffs represents not only a handoff of work, but a handoff of responsibility. When a programmer hands off an architecture, he can feel his responsibility for the game has been handed off as well. If an asset doesn't work within that architecture, the responsibility for that can be confusing. At best this results in a delay in a solution (assigning tasks to fix bugs can result in many handoffs) or at worst a culture of blame as the artist and the programmer blame the work of the other for the problem.

The Lean principle of **reducing handoffs** addresses this. As described in earlier chapters, documents are an imperfect means of communication. When teams find ways to be more closely involved with the entire workflow, and not just their own part, the result improves. Chapter 10 explores examples of the benefits of reducing handoffs in content pipelines.

## Responding to Bottlenecks

WiP limits create hard stops in the workflow when those limits are hit. For example, if testing has hit its limit of new features currently being tested, it can't pull in any more. That might create a bottleneck for development upstream. As a result, its own WiP limit is hit, and no more development tasks can be pulled in.

As with Scrum, we first ask the team what to do. Using Lean methodology, it can apply the "Theory of Constraints,"[2] which says that you solve the bottlenecks one at a time and wait for the next bottleneck to show up and repeat the process.

For the testing bottleneck example, a number of things might be done:

- **Hire more testers:** This solves the problem of testing, but then your testers might run out of things to test, and the programmers then become the bottleneck.
- **Have the developers stop developing for a few hours and help test:** Some developers might look down on doing this, but in my opinion, developers often need to test their own work more to experience the impact of cutting corners.

2. https://www.Leanproduction.com/theory-of-constraints.html

- **Create fewer bugs:** This may sound flippant, but the easiest way to reduce debugging time is not to introduce bugs to begin with. More automated tests, such as with unit testing (see Chapter 12, "Agile Technology") are often the best solution.

### *Buffering Between Stages*

The time it takes to model a character can vary considerably. A simple character variation can take a day, whereas a boss character can take weeks. We don't want this variation to cause times when the person who will rig the character has to wait around. Inserting a buffer between the two stages of character work allows a small backlog of models to exist so that a character is always waiting to be rigged. Care must be taken to limit the buffer's WiP so we don't impact the character cycle time too much.

Too much buffering can also slow down cycle time, so putting WiP limits on buffers is useful as well.

**Buffers**

A mailbox is an example of a useful time buffer. Mail delivery can vary by hours, and nobody wants to stand around waiting for the carrier to show up. That's why we have mailboxes: They are a buffer between the carrier and recipient!

### *Kanban at My Local Coffee Shop*

A few years ago, I pulled into one of the many local coffee shops, as I did every day. If, like me, you are a straight-coffee drinker who frequents coffee shops, you probably appreciate that you don't have to wait for all the lattes, cappuccinos, and so on, ordered ahead of you.

The barista works on those exclusively, and the cashier can directly pour your coffee for you.

That day at my local shop, a light bulb turned on; I suddenly realized they were applying Kanban!

At a coffee shop, the empty coffee cups, marked with your (often misspelled) name and order details, are the Kanban cards. Based on how many there are between the cashier and barista, this informs them of what they should do next.

Looking at a hypothetical coffee shop Kanban board in Figure 6.4, my coffee goes from the "order" column to the "leave" column directly.

Based on the size of the line, the barista and cashier might help one another out. If the line is long and the barista has nothing to do, he will ask people in line what drink they want and start making that before the cashier takes their order.

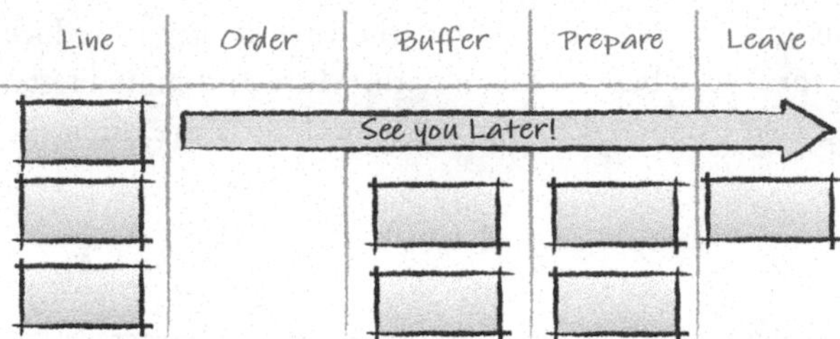


**Figure 6.4** *Coffee shop Kanban*

Conversely, if the line empties, but there is a backlog of unfinished drinks, the cashier will join the barista in making drinks.

This benefits everyone. A key metric for Starbucks is the customer cycle time: the amount of time it takes between walking in the door and when you walk out with your drink.

The critical path for coffee drinkers and latte drinkers isn't the same, but it isn't entirely separate; much as I personally would enjoy it, there is no separate cashier line for coffee drinkers. Starbucks has chosen not to optimize specifically for us straight-coffee drinkers for a good reason.

This is similar to the approach you might use for asset types. Although every asset will have a large variation of effort needed (like that between coffee and a latte) and partially separate paths, measuring every asset's cycle time will still give us valuable information.

The goal isn't to achieve a uniform cycle time for all assets, just as people who order lattes should expect to wait longer at Starbucks than us super-efficient coffee drinkers.

## The Difference with Scrum

Besides the shift away from timeboxed Sprints and planning on-demand, very little needs to be different between Scrum and Kanban. The Scrum Master and Product Owner are still useful roles, and the meetings, such as Reviews, Retrospectives, and Daily Scrums, are still held.

### Definition

Sometimes Kanban teams will refer to the "Daily Scrum" as the "Daily Standup."

Often, teams exploring game behaviors in pre-production—exploring character behaviors and budgets—will start shifting into mass-producing more characters and will sense the need to abandon Sprint timeboxes and start measuring cycle times instead. This should be a smooth transition with very little change in roles and practices, except those introduced in this chapter.

When teams using Kanban return to using Sprints, they'll often bring useful habits back, including applying WiP limits on their Sprint task boards and focusing on getting PBIs finished one at a time rather than near the end of the Sprint.

## What Good Looks Like

When our level production teams introduced Kanban in 2007, they were able to reduce the cycle time of levels production by 56 percent over the course of several months by

- Reducing handoffs with concept artists, as described earlier
- Raising the priority of reducing export times with the tools support team
- Reducing the batch sizes of levels by finishing portions of levels divided across streaming boundaries, reducing iteration times to increase the pace of improvements
- Developing a better way of building levels (in Unreal rather than in Maya)

These improvements were driven by members of the team who were focused on reducing the cycle time of level production. It almost became a game with them to find ways to shave a few hours off every week.

## Summary

This chapter covered the basics of Kanban as applied to areas of game development, such as content production and support (live and services). Later chapters dive into more detail for each application.

## Additional Reading

Brechner E., and J. Waletzky. *Agile Project Management with Kanban*. Redmond, WA: Microsoft Press, 2015.

DeMarco, T., and T. Lister. 1999. *Peopleware: Productive Projects and Teams, Second Edition*. New York: Dorset House Publishing.

Katzenbach, J. R., and D. K. Smith. 2003. *The Wisdom of Teams: Creating the High-Performance Organization*. Cambridge, MA: Harvard Business School Press.

Keith C, Shonkwiler G. 2018. *Gear Up!: 100+ ways to grow your studio culture, Second Edition*.

Larman C., and B. Vodde. 2017. *Large-Scale Scrum: More with LeSS*. Boston, MA: Addison-Wesley.

# Chapter 7

# The Product Backlog

When we start working on a game, it's natural to want to know what we are going to make. That perhaps sounds pretty obvious, but it takes effort to achieve. Without a shared vision of the goal, everyone would start developing a game with separate points of view.

But we often go too far. We create design documents that have hundreds of pages that describe the mechanics of the game and the levels and characters in great detail. If you've ever worked on a game that had a large design document written up front, ask yourself:

- How closely did the finished game resemble the original design?
- If the document evolved with the emerging game, was it a good artifact to communicate those changes (that is, a "living document")?
- Was the design document ignored after the game was signed by the publisher or stakeholders?

## The Solutions in This Chapter

What we need is a planning method that does the following:

- **Communicates the order and value of the features:** The team needs to focus on delivering the highest-value features ahead of the lower-value ones.

- **Enables change and communication of change:** Change is going to occur, and discussions about those changes need to happen regularly and frequently.
- **Is a placeholder for future communication:** Documentation can't replace conversation. There must be a balance between the two.
- **Enables details to emerge as more information is learned:** It shouldn't require all design details up front or impose a great deal of effort to spread knowledge or change.
- **Delivers potentially deployable features in value-first order:** Features are built in the order of the value they add for the players who buy the game. Delivering the highest-value playable features ahead of lower-value ones drives the development of the game rather than a preset ordered list of work. This enables the true value of the game to emerge earlier, when we can make better decisions about its direction.
- **Plan by feature, which creates cross-discipline behavior:** Delivering features every Sprint encourages separate disciplines to collaborate to produce results that matter to the stakeholders. Problems that impact one discipline impact the rest and are likely to be solved more quickly rather than ignored for the sake of a schedule.
- **Avoid debt to allow better measurement of progress:** Sprints combine the full cycle of feature development. This reduces the debt of debugging, tuning, polishing, and optimization and makes the pace of development easier to forecast. Establishing a Definition of Done with the Product Owner enables the team to understand each Sprint Goal and the quality required.

A Product Backlog addresses all these needs. This chapter describes Product Backlogs, a different form of planning, that addresses the problems with traditional forms of planning, such as detailed design documents.

## A Fateful Meeting

I'll begin this chapter with an example from my own experience. I recall a certain meeting years ago on a game project called *Smuggler's Run*. Although I've attended hundreds of meetings like it, none other would change the focus and course of my career as this one did.

The purpose of the meeting was to review the work remaining to achieve the alpha milestone, which was two weeks away. Alpha was the cut-off date for incomplete features; features planned for but not fully implemented were to be cut from the game. You could sense how close alpha was. *Smuggler's Run* needed to be out for Christmas. It was also a launch title for the PlayStation 2. Everything rested on this game being on time. No one really wanted to be at this meeting; there was much to do, but the meeting was critical and, as the director of product development for the studio, I had to know whether we would achieve alpha.

All the leads attended. I had to keep an eye on the lead programmer and lead designer; they often clashed over the ideals of design and the feasibility of what our technology could accomplish. They approached their roles perfectly, and the natural tension between them benefitted the game. I just had to make sure it didn't go too far.

That day tested that tension. The lead designer had brought a big concern to the meeting. "When are the animals going to be added to the game?" he asked. The lead programmer didn't have a clue about this feature. So, the lead designer pulled out the game design document and pointed to a paragraph on page 97, which described the feature. The game was to have animals wandering about the levels in herds that avoided the player vehicles. The feature had been added to the game design document partway through the project, and the lead programmer had not read it.

The lead programmer didn't know whether to laugh or explode in anger. "How am I expected to know when a new paragraph was added to the design document?" he demanded. "I barely read it the first time!"

We spent some time calming everyone down and were finally able to discuss options for the feature. In the end, a simplified version of the feature was added. Rather than herds of animals avoiding the vehicles, lone animals wandered about ignoring the vehicles and, when hit, turned into tumbling rag dolls. As it turned out, this was a popular feature in the game. Players spent hours hunting down the entire populations of animals. Had this feature been more exploited, the game would have met with even more commercial success.[1]

## Why Design Documents Fail

As the project director, that meeting was a wake-up call about the issues of documentation and communication. I saw the futility of trying to know everything about a game up front and using monolithic documents to capture change and knowledge. This started my path to Agile.

The *Smuggler's Run* game design document was well maintained by the designers, but it still failed in a few basic ways:

- **It failed to communicate the value of features:** Each team member evaluated the value of each feature on their own.

1. And the ire of animal rights groups everywhere.

- **It failed to communicate changes to the rest of the team:** Few team members reread the document on a regular basis to keep up with the frequent changes.

The conversation that occurred two weeks before alpha was very fortuitous, but which features make it into the game shouldn't be left to chance. What we had was a failure to communicate. The information in the document was valuable, but the document itself was a poor medium for communicating change and order.

This underscores some problems with the traditional requirements of gathering and tracking. One way to avoid these communication pitfalls is by using a Product Backlog, which is a Scrum artifact designed to provide planning centered around change and communication.

## The Product Backlog

The Product Backlog is an ordered list of everything believed to be needed for the game. A Product Backlog:

- Is written in "business language." It's focused on what is important and valuable to the player of the game or the user of a tool or pipeline
- Is ordered, so that the team is always working on what is most important
- Supports continual planning as the game emerges, so the plan matches reality
- Accommodates frequent change and emergence in a low-cost way to allow better transparency and communication between the team and stakeholders
- Encourages team engagement and alignment with the vision of the game by having it participate in defining and discussing the emergent detail
- Is organized to reflect team structures, which reduces dependencies and the debt of unfinished work

### Product Backlog Items

The features and other work identified in the Product Backlog are called Product Backlog Items (PBIs). Unlike detailed sections of a design document, PBIs briefly express the desired behavior for something in the game, tool, or asset pipeline from the point of view of the user of that functionality (for example, a player or artist). PBIs can describe any type of work:

- Features
- Content

- Tools/pipeline work
- Technical/architectural work
- Bug fixes
- Prototypes and experiments

Chapter 8, "User Stories," and Chapter 9, "Agile Release Planning," explore how to write PBIs that express the reason for their implementation and the value the implementation provides.

## Ordering the Product Backlog

The Product Owner manages the order of PBIs in the Product Backlog. It's done with the input of stakeholders, team members, and domain experts. The following guides help determine the order of each PBI in the Product Backlog:

- **Value:** The value that a PBI adds for the player who buys the game is the main criteria in determining the order of that PBI on the Product Backlog. By focusing the team's effort on adding the highest value every Sprint, Product Owners generate the best possible ROI. They measure value using their own judgment, feedback from focus testing, and feedback from stakeholders. Value applies to the "nonfunctional requirements" as well. Tool and pipeline PBIs that improve productivity have a place in the Product Backlog because improving productivity also improves ROI.
- **Cost:** Cost is a key factor in the Product Owner's ROI calculation. Some highly desirable features might cost too much to implement. An example of this is implementing fully destructible geometry for a shooter. Although this feature may add a great deal of value to the game, the Product Owner must weigh its value against the cost of developing the technology and producing level assets that leverage it. Two equally valuable features are often ordered by cost; the lowest-cost feature is given a higher order.
- **Risk:** Risk implies uncertainty about value and cost. As a team refines its knowledge in these areas, the Product Backlog becomes a better tool for the Product Owner. PBIs with higher risk are often ordered higher to refine a Product Owner's understanding of value and cost. If they are not, then potentially valuable PBIs might be left at the bottom of the Product Backlog and potentially dropped because of schedule or budgetary limitations.

- **Knowledge:** Sometimes Product Owners don't know the value, risk, or cost of a feature. They simply need more information. Early prototypes, experiments, and investigations will allow you to learn more about the value, cost, and risk of features being considered.

> **Note**
>
> This book uses the term *ordered* rather than *prioritized* when talking about the Product Backlog to reflect the idea that sometimes the order of work doesn't match the priority. For example, a roof might be more valuable than the foundation of a house in a rainy environment, but the foundation still has to come first.

## Continual Planning

The work done by a Scrum team is determined by the order of PBIs on the Product Backlog and what the team is capable of accomplishing. Every Sprint, a team pulls PBIs off the top of the Product Backlog and considers the development tasks to implement them. For this to happen, each PBI the team considers must be small enough to be accomplished in a single Sprint. Therefore, ensuring the PBIs on top of the Product Backlog are broken down enough is where most of the continual planning (usually about an hour a week) takes place.

Note though that not every PBI on the Product Backlog should be small enough to fit into a Sprint. If they were, then the Product Backlog might contain thousands of PBIs, which is too cumbersome to maintain. Instead, the lower-order PBIs are not broken down until the higher-order PBIs are completed. This is an advantage because the lower-order PBIs, which are more distant from implementation, are expected to change as the team and stakeholders learn more about what is possible and what is fun.

A useful metaphor for the Product Backlog is an iceberg (Cohn, 2008), as shown in Figure 7.1. The highest-order PBIs are represented by snowballs at the top of the iceberg, which are small enough to be completed in a single Sprint. Below them are the lower-order PBIs, or larger chunks of ice, called **epics**.

Everything above the waterline represents the work we want to complete in the current release. Each Sprint sweeps off the snowballs (PBIs) from the top of the iceberg. The stakeholders and team break down the larger chunks of ice (epics) into snowballs for the next Sprint.

## Allowing for Change and Emergence

As we're breaking out the detail of a game as we're developing it, the Product Backlog never grows too large. Even the largest games rarely have more than 200–300 PBIs

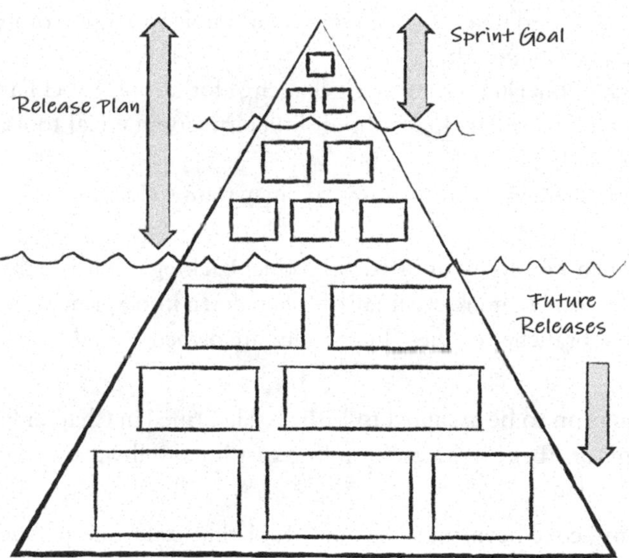


**Figure 7.1** *The product-planning iceberg*

on them. Because of this, revisiting the Backlog every Sprint to make any changes based on what the emerging game is telling us doesn't take much time. This is something we can't do with 300-page design documents.

### Encouraging Team Engagement and Alignment

Every Sprint, as teams complete PBIs at the top of the Product Backlog, they participate in breaking down larger PBIs further down the list into smaller PBIs that could fit in coming Sprints. This activity engages the team in conversation with the Product Owner and helps them participate in the decision making and understand the vision of the game.

## Creating the Product Backlog

Unlike a traditional game where a large design document has to be created up front, an initial Product Backlog only has to have enough detail to get teams started. Typical PBIs on an initial Backlog could be:

- Some prototypes to experiment with
- Initial architecture dependencies
- Basic camera, control, and character features

A small set of PBIs can be created in less than an hour in a simple workshop or in a Release Planning meeting (see Chapter 9).

Managing several hundred PBIs isn't a significant challenge for a tool. Excel has been used by teams to manage their Backlog without difficulty. Commercial tools, such as Jira, are common as well.

When searching for a tool, there are a few features you may want to look for:

- **The ability to manage a hierarchy of PBIs:** A Product Backlog is a hierarchy or set of hierarchies of epics that are eventually broken down into Sprint-sized PBIs. Often, individual branches of these hierarchies are owned by individual Scrum teams.
- **Allows sizing information to be assigned to PBIs:** As described in Chapter 9, tracking size estimates of PBIs can be useful to forecast how well we are progressing towards target dates.
- **Ease of use with low-cost licensing:** Having a tool that only one person can use at a time or is so difficult or costly for others to use can limit team collaboration.
- **Has good visualization options:** Teams will often examine the Product Backlog through different "lenses." Sometimes, they'll want to examine one branch, and other times individual PBIs, and often the entire tree.

### Different Forms of Backlog

I've seen and experienced many different forms of Product Backlog. Some worked, some didn't.

Initially, we tried using index cards to store our Backlog. A physical Product Backlog had its benefits, but after a while, we felt nervous about having the Backlog for a $40 million game on a deck of cards that someone could easily leave in their pocket and send through the wash.

Our favorite form of Backlog was in a mind map. It represented the hierarchy very well, and using a 42-inch plotter, we were able to create large posters of epic branches for individual teams to hang in their area. Chapter 21, "Scaling Agile Game Teams," explores mind mapping a Product Backlog in more detail.

**What if our Stakeholders Demand the Big Design Document?**

Few stakeholders (publishers, managers) still believe that a big design document ensures a good game will be delivered on schedule. Often the reason they still ask for it is due to a lack of trust; fatter documents make some managers feel better.

The way to build trust is to create transparency (see Chapter 17, "Working with Stakeholders"). Invite them to help build the Product Backlog and maintain it. Invite them to Sprint Reviews.

Building trust takes time, and they might not drop the demand for the detailed design right away.

## Managing the Product Backlog

Even for the largest games, to stay manageable, a Product Backlog should never grow beyond several hundred PBIs in size. Live game Backlogs should be even smaller (see Chapter 22, "Live Game Development").

### Backlog Refinement

After a Sprint, teams will refine the Product Backlog based on the progress of the game. This is done in a meeting called the **Backlog Refinement**. In this meeting a team (including the Product Owner) will

- Add any new PBIs identified in the last Sprint Review
- Break any large PBIs on the top of the Backlog into smaller PBIs that will fit in the coming Sprints
- Estimate the size of any new or split PBIs and update the forecasted Sprint Goals (see Chapter 9)
- Eliminate older PBIs that are no longer desired or valuable

Teams often include some of the work done in the first part of Sprint Planning in the refinement meeting, such as discussing the potential goal for the upcoming Sprint. This can reduce the amount of time needed in Sprint Planning.

## Who Attends the Refinement and When?

The Scrum Team decides when and where to hold a Backlog Refinement. It can invite anyone else, but keep in mind that a limit exists as to how many people can participate before conversation starts to slow down.

Teams hold Refinement sessions just before or after the Sprint Review. Although refining the Backlog before the Review might lack full stakeholder feedback, teams are often aware of what they've accomplished and find refining the Backlog before the Review a time saver.

Having the Development Team participate is useful. The conversations that lead to how the Product Backlog is ordered and how the Backlog items are created helps share the vision of the game with the team and leads to its making better decisions about achieving Sprint Goals.

The Product Owner can add or remove PBIs from the Backlog at any time. The Scrum Master has to ensure that the Product Backlog is being maintained and shared and that the Product Owner is not ignoring the Product Backlog.

## Techniques for Ordering the Product Backlog

The order of PBIs in the backlog determines the order in which they are developed. It is a balance of cost, risk, knowledge, and value.

For example, while we might think that value to the player may be the sole factor that determines a PBI's order, cost is often the limiting factor. Just as I might want to drive a Ferrari, my bank account and spouse might have something to say to discourage that choice.

The following are techniques commonly used to evaluate these factors.

### *Evaluating Cost*

Ordering by the cost of a feature is often the most attractive to stakeholders because they can attempt to use numbers (such as time, people-days, and so on) to do so.

However, evaluating cost isn't as easy as it might sound. Cost depends on the risk associated with a feature and the experience and skill of who is implementing it.

Chapter 9 explores the challenges and techniques of evaluating cost in greater detail.

### *Evaluating Risk*

Risk is harder to quantify. In this case, like other hard-to-quantify elements, a variation of relative ordering (often referred to as a **rank ordering**) is useful. A risk matrix is a valuable tool for this.

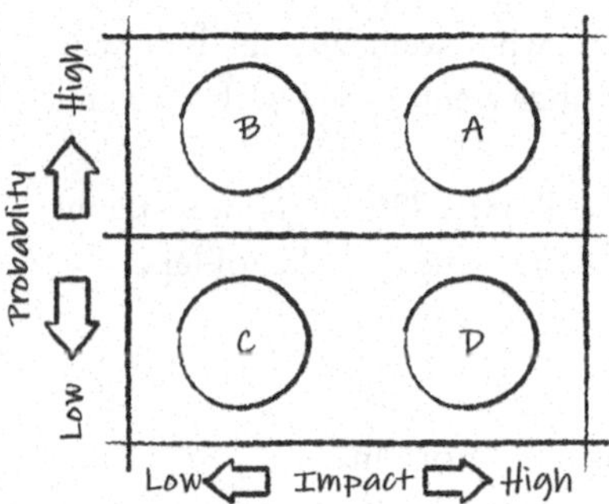


**Figure 7.2** *The risk matrix*

A risk matrix is a simple tool. Each area of risk that has been identified is placed on a 2 x 2 map sorted, relative to other risks, by the probability of the risk occurring as well as its impact (cost or schedule) on the game (see Figure 7.2). The risks are then ordered by which quadrant they occupy on the map.

Looking at the matrix in Figure 7.2, the risks in the "A" square are the ones we would be most concerned about. These could be risks like "we can't find enough good programmers to hire and train in time." Risks in the "B" squares are next. Those risks remaining in square "C" can usually be ignored. They are unlikely to manifest, and if they do, their impact will be minimal.

With a set of risks ordered by impact and probability, you can establish a plan to manage them. Chapter 10, "Video Game Project Management," explores an approach for doing that.

### Try Running a Premortem

A premortem (Brown S., Macanufo J., 2010) is an imaginary postmortem held at the start of a game. Participants put on their "future hats" and imagine themselves gathering a month after the game has been shipped. They then describe all the problems with the game and with the effort to develop it. These scenarios are used to populate a risk matrix and identify solutions long before these potential problems occur.

#### The Practice

Small groups of people (five to nine in size) gather to create a poster for the game. On this poster, they write the game's goals (genre, market positioning, major features, and so on) and create the plan (critical dates, cost, team structures, and so on) on one half. The other half of the poster is set aside to capture "what went wrong." Teams fill the "what went wrong" half with sticky notes, each containing one area where things went wrong with the game in the market or in the effort to develop it.

After a team completes the aforementioned steps (30–40 minutes), one member of the team presents their poster to other teams or stakeholders.

### Tips

Here are some tips that can help when running a premortem.

- If there are a lot of "what went wrong" sticky notes on a poster, ask the team to pick the three items that are most impactful to present.
- Identify areas where differences exist in the goals and plan section. This is a great opportunity for a Product Owner to create and discuss a shared vision of the goals and plan for the game.

## *Evaluating Knowledge*

One of the best ways to gain knowledge about something unknown is to perform an experiment. A useful tool for prototypes is using a timeboxed PBI called a **spike**, which limits how much time the team spends working on it before it can be evaluated. An example of this is a two-week prototype to determine whether the physics engine supports destructible geometry. If this spike demonstrates that the value, cost, and risk of implementing the system and toolset is not too great, the Product Owner is more likely to raise the order of a PBI to develop the full feature.

## *Evaluating Value*

Knowing what your players want can be a challenge, especially the further out in time you try to forecast. Although live games can use Key Performance Indicators (KPIs) and frequent releases to guide value over the short term, identifying feature value over the mid- and long term can be nebulous. The following tools can help categorize value.

### *Kano Analysis*

The Kano analysis model prioritizes features into the following market categories:

- **Delighters:** These are features that are rare in other games or have never been seen before. They would be heavily promoted in a marketing campaign and would delight players; for example, massively persistent/destructible MMO environments.

- **Satisfiers:** These are features that players are not surprised by, but enjoy. Competitors may or may not have all of these; for example, collaborative online zombie maps in a first-person shooter.
- **Basic expectations:** These features are not advertised but are expected by the player, and their absence will upset them; for example, save game checkpoints.

**Batman Quality!**

"Product Backlogs are great for prioritization, but that doesn't necessarily correlate to quality. But we've found a way to measure quality through the Backlog by adding a few more dimensions: customer impact and quality goal. Customer impact would be used to specify how much impact the implementation of the user story would have to the end customer, and quality goal would be used to set several expectations and alignment per quality level.

"You can measure customer impact at three levels:

- **Minimum** is the minimum passable version of the story.
- **Awesome** is making the story good or better than competition or user expectation.
- **Batman** is something noteworthy and amazing, because, well, it's Batman.

"Each has their Definition of Done, which establishes the quality goal. These metrics allow us to look at completed stories and measure the number of stories at certain quality levels, completed by customer impact. If everything is minimal, that gives us a good view of how it may be perceived.

"Having user stories with additional clarity of quality goals allows the ability to do a competitive marketing analysis and make more informed scoping decisions. It is extremely unlikely that any project can implement every user story at the highest level. But it's also not necessary. By having the customer impact measure for items that are low impact, it is most likely safe to implement the minimum version.

"Before adding these measures, all user stories can be seen to be equal in impact and quality. Throughout the project, you can run a Backlog report; using the measures of customer impact and quality on completed features will give you the ability to view the current quality state. We can then put a higher weight on the high customer impact items and calculate a quality score for the product. Using this helps make better scoping decisions, to at least give us better odds at delivering the right quality, in the right places."

—Brian Graham, Production, Playful Corp.

### *MuSCoW Analysis*

MuSCoW Analysis prioritizes features into the following categories:

- **Must have:** Features we cannot ship without. If we cut them, we'll fail; for example, online gameplay on a first-person console shooter.
- **Should have:** Features that can be cut, but would impact us if we do; for example, particle effects for a mobile slots game.
- **Could have:** Features we would like to keep, but can cut without much impact to the game; for example, posting game progress on Facebook.
- **Won't have:** Features we will not keep; for example, a small character that follows the player around in the game incessantly giving them advice.

MuSCoW is especially useful for identifying an initial feature set for a live game with a minimum set of features. Its benefit over Kano is to explicitly identify features that won't be included with the stakeholders.

### *Value/Cost Ordering*

The matrix in Figure 7.2 can also be used to order PBIs using cost on the horizontal axis and the value on the vertical axis, as shown in Figure 7.3. PBIs are then ordered through the four quadrants:

1. High Value, Low Cost
2. High Value, High Cost
3. Low Value, Low Cost
4. Low Value, High Cost (don't bother with these!)

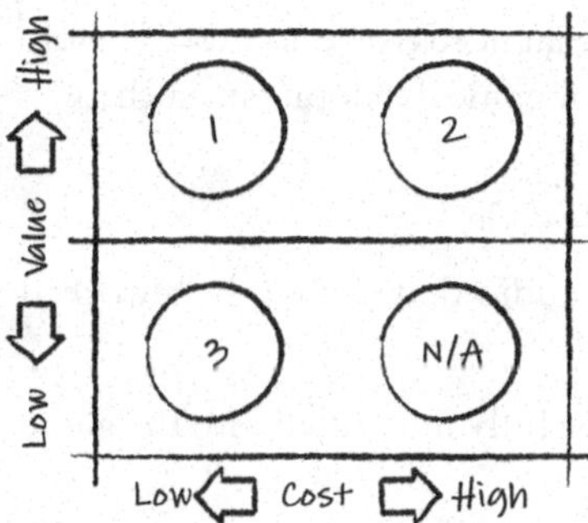


**Figure 7.3** *The value-cost matrix*

## Defining "Done"

Each Sprint, teams commit to completing a number of PBIs from the Product Backlog and demonstrating that these are done in the Sprint Review. However, defining what *done* means can be challenging. There are many bad examples of what "done" means in the game industry, such as

- "It runs on my PC."
- "It looks good in Maya."
- "It compiles."
- "I checked in the asset."

These loose definitions result in debt piling up in the game. Let's look at the types of debt that exist in video games, how debt is managed, and how Definitions of Done can help.

### Types of Debt

Ward Cunningham, one of the authors of the Agile Manifesto, once likened the problems with technology, such as bugs and unmaintainable code, with financial debt—it grows the cost of payback over time.[2]

2. http://wiki.c2.com/?WardExplainsDebtMetaphor

Debt results in an ever-expanding amount of work that needs to be addressed before the game is deployed. Numerous forms of debt exist for game development, such as

- **Technical debt:** Bugs; slow and unmaintainable code
- **Art debt:** Assets such as models, textures, and audio that need to be reworked or improved
- **Design debt:** Unproven mechanics waiting to be fully integrated into the game to prove their value
- **Production debt:** The amount of content that the game needs to be commercially viable (for example, 12 to 20 hours of gameplay)
- **Optimization debt:** Work waiting to be done to prove the game can run at acceptable frame rates on the target platforms

If unmanaged, the amount of work to address debt is unpredictably impactful and results in crunch and a compromise in quality as key features or assets are dropped in favor of maintaining a schedule.

**Game Development Debt Example**

One typical example of game development debt is in the creation of characters. Characters are often designed, modeled, rigged, and animated wholesale before we really know what we want them to do or before we know their budget. This is done because of schedule pressure or a plan that optimizes discipline allocation over the delivery of working assets.

As a result, by the time we figure out what we want the characters to do, we realize that the requirements for rigging and animation have changed, and instead of having to re-rig and reanimate one character, we have to do it for 20.

Demonstrating one character behaving the way we want in the game before mass-producing the remaining characters would have avoided this debt. If the character production schedule is a critical path for the project, then prioritize it as a risk and order the work that removes the uncertainty of character budgets and requirements early.

## Managing Debt

The benefit of managing debt is to reduce the cost of development, avoid crunch, and avoid compromising quality. This is easier said than done due to the pressure of delivering quantity over quality. When we estimate the time to deliver scope, we don't estimate fixing bugs, refactoring code, or even the overhead of iteration. That work has to be factored in to create the space to manage debt.

**Note**

I've never seen anyone write a task that said, "The bug we'll find next Wednesday will take 5 hours to fix."

That work is emergent and results from the quality bar that is established and refined between the Development Team and the Product Owner. That bar is called a **Definition of Done** (DoD).

After every Sprint, the Product Owner and the Development Team can refine the DoD. This refinement often takes place in the Retrospective.

When first establishing a DoD, start with the basics. An example is

*"When added, this feature will not crash the game."*

**Tip**

Don't change the DoDs too much every Sprint. Each change will impact development practices and take a while for the team to adjust to, and some DoDs may need to be reversed after exploring those impacts.

DoDs are added based on growing or newly identified areas of debt. For example, if the addition of new features drops the frame rate too low on a regular basis, the team might introduce a DoD that says:

*"The game's frame rate stays above 20 frames per second."*

Some areas of debt, such as slow frame rate, can be hard to track down, but it's far easier to find a cause soon after the work that caused it is introduced.

**Note**

The goal isn't to eliminate all debt. A certain amount of debt is reasonable to carry. For example, prototypes don't have to have production code or deployable assets up front because we may be throwing most of them out. You just don't want 50 percent of the code to be "prototype quality"!

## Development DoDs and Stakeholder DoDs

DoDs result from a negotiation between the Product Owner and Development Team as they balance effort and quality. They define two categories of DoDs, which are described in the following sections.

#### *Development DoDs*

Development DoDs are white-box (internal) standards for the Development Team. They guide how code is written and assets are created; for example:

- All functions have sufficient unit test coverage.
- All assets conform to standard naming and budget conventions.

These are managed by the Development Team and guide work within the Sprint. For games with more than one team, make an effort to unify the development DoDs so there is a consistency of quality across the entire game.

> **Note**
>
> Development DoDs introduce additional work during a Sprint, which can measurably slow the pace of introducing features to the game, compared to the pace that was measured before they existed. This additional work saves time over the long term by reducing debt (see Chapter 12, "Agile Technology").

#### *Stakeholder DoDs*

Stakeholder DoDs are external requirements, often called *non-functional requirements*, which are needed to satisfy market and publishing needs. Examples of these are

- TRC/TCR and App Store requirements
- Platform requirements
- Performance requirements

## QA and DoDs

The Development Team is responsible for ensuring that each PBI completed in a Sprint meets the DoD. Teams often recruit testers to help validate them as well by running the game on various platforms and verifying each DoD during the Sprint.

This was one approach we used to slowly transform members of a "QA pool" to members of Scrum teams, where they become more effective at helping teams improve quality (see Chapter 15, "Agile QA and Production").

## Sets of Done

Ideally, an Agile game should be "potentially deployable" every Sprint; live games can truly be deployable. For games that have not reached their first deployment, we should have a playable game that would demonstrate value to players every Sprint but would have some epic features that still require work.

As a result, teams establish sets of DoDs as shown in Figure 7.4. Each set encompasses a group of DoDs appropriate to the development maturity of an epic. For example, we might have a set of DoDs that a prototyped epic would need to satisfy, such as running only on a PC, not crashing, and exhibiting reasonable frame rates. Another set would incorporate the DoDs necessary to deploy an epic to players.

Here is a simple example set of DoDs:

- **Prototype:** Demonstrates potential value. Assets are for demonstration purposes, and the game only runs on development PCs.
- **Internal Demo:** Demonstrates feature value and identifies areas that need to be polished before the feature can be shown internally. The game runs on target debug platforms with lower than shippable frame rates.
- **External Demo:** Demonstrates demo quality (90 percent assets, not all TRC/TCR requirements). The target frame rate and hardware resource budgets are met.
- **Deployable (Ship!):** Ready to be deployed. It passes all TRC/TCR tests and has no memory leaks. All assets are polished.

During Sprint planning, each PBI can have a different set of DoDs assigned to it. For example, they might be prototyping one feature while preparing another for deployment.

| | Prototype | Internal Demo | External Demo | Ship! |
|---|---|---|---|---|
| Design | Story board, blocked out level | First pass | Core mechanics Shippable | Full story playable |
| Assets/UI | Concept | Stand-in assets, Wireframes | Shippable animations & textures UI flow final | Final assets |
| Code | Throw Away | Production, Unit tested | production, Unit tested | Production, Unit tested |

**Figure 7.4** *Sets of Done*

**Note**

Having the DoDs posted for the team to see is useful to remind the team during planning what the target is for each story.

## Challenges

Here are some typical challenges that teams encounter with Product Backlogs:

- **They contain tasks:** Sometimes Product Backlogs look like large Sprint Backlogs, which contain discipline tasks. The Product Backlog is meant to express business value, not development work. Otherwise, the Product Owner is unable to order it properly.
- **Too many PBIs:** When a Backlog contains thousands of PBIs, it becomes impossible to refine it frequently enough to keep pace with the emerging game. This is often the result of making many design decisions too early.
- **PBIs are too detailed:** PBIs are meant to be placeholders for conversation. When each PBI has a large document's worth of detail attached to it, conversations don't occur.

## Dysfunctional Product Ownership

The "visionary" aspect is central to the role of the Product Owner. Regardless of the methodology used, if there is a bad vision or a vision that isn't shared, the chances of making a great game are diminished. This is an area of vulnerability with any project and no less so with Agile projects.

The advantage that Scrum teams have is that the visionary role of the Product Owner is more transparent and defined. A dysfunctional Product Owner should be quickly identified. Teams demand communication and Scrum Masters hold visionaries accountable for serving that demand.

**Where is Matt Damon?**

One of our first Agile-run projects was *Bourne Conspiracy*, which was based on the *Jason Bourne* franchise, written by Robert Ludlum and the basis for the successful Bourne movies starring Matt Damon.

We were given the job to create a game that followed the first movie's plot. This was a challenge for us, because the game needed to ship when the next movie was released, on the next generation of consoles using an engine that hadn't ever been used on a console. Added to that, we had never made a third-person action-adventure game. There was a lot of risk!

Our stakeholder wasn't familiar with Scrum and so to build trust with them, we asked one of their executive producers to be the Lead Product Owner for the game (see Chapter 21). This was a big mistake.

Our Lead Product Owner didn't visit the teams very often, and when he paid attention to the Product Backlog, he described a game that felt more like *Splinter Cell* than what you would expect from a *Bourne* game; Jason Bourne should use objects around him, such as rolled-up magazines, to defeat enemies rather than the high-tech gadgets in *Splinter Cell*.

We just collectively shrugged and focused on the technical and schedule risks of the game.

Unfortunately, the Ludlum estate, which had final say over the game's release, wasn't going to ignore this. It also turned out that Matt Damon wasn't interested in participating either.

Unfortunately, our Lead Product Owner wasn't communicating with these important stakeholders. As a result, we had to rebuild the game when the Ludlum estate rejected it, and we had to scramble to find a new lead actor.

Missing the movie's release, not having Matt Damon, and the impact on quality from last-minute changes killed any chance of success. We learned a number of lessons about dysfunctional Product Ownership (described later in this chapter).

I've seen many examples of dysfunctional Product Ownership over the past decade. This section lists the most common dysfunctions and ways to address them.

## The Proxy Product Owner

A proxy Product Owner is an underpowered Product Owner who stands in for the actual Product Owner. This can be due to many reasons, including:

- The actual Product Owner is too distant or too busy to interact with the teams on a daily basis.
- There is no one with the authority or accountability of a Product Owner, so one is created in name only.
- There is a group of people to instantiate the Product Owner role, rather than one, and they need a single voice to speak with development.

Anytime an additional layer of communication exists between developers and decision-makers, it impacts effectiveness. Product Owners must have the authority to make calls with the accountability that they are the right ones. A proxy Product Owner can lead to disengaged teams due to a lack of a shared vision or decisiveness.

On the business side, the project can suffer from a lack of transparency. The different areas of focus can lead to delayed integration and delayed knowledge of what makes a game good or not.

Proxy Product Ownership can be hard to address because the roots are cultural and the shift to a single voice that speaks to the vision and project management aspects of the game will

- Threaten those who currently occupy those aspects of the role
- Be hard to fill because very few people are good at being both a visionary and project manager

## Product Owner Committees

Product Owner Committees form when there are many equal stakeholders who hope to prioritize the Backlog through collaboration or when there is fear of elevating one of their own into the role of the "single voice of the game."

The main potential dysfunction seen with this arrangement is from the team's point of view. The feature POs or teams often don't know who to speak with, and the committee members usually have a different perspective. Often, a release plan from a committee is the combined set of all desired features from the committee, which leads to long release cycles.

***Example:*** A Product Owner Committee prioritized hand-to-hand combat as the highest priority epic for the next release of a game. The team invited one of the committee POs to its first Backlog Refinement meeting in which it discussed the design options in breaking the epic down. The only member of the committee that showed up was Amy. In the discussion, Amy emphasized that the hand-to-hand combat had to "look cinematic" at all times. This led to the team focusing on ways to avoid animation popping and adding more transitions. At the first Sprint Review, one of the committee POs, Dan, complained that the fighting was responsive enough and that the team should focus on the movement mechanics, such as jumping and running. A third committee PO, Steve, thought that multiplayer online needed more work and that the team should work on that.

**The Dirty Dozen**

I once worked with an MMO that had a committee of 12 Product Owners. Because they couldn't narrow down the goals for the next expansion pack, it had to have all of their required features. As a result, it took well over a year to release each expansion pack, which frustrated their players.

The solution was to run an exercise called "Buy a Feature" (Keith and Shonkwiler, 2018), which helped reduce the set of desired expansion features to approximately six months of effort.

The main issue with transitioning from a Product Owner committee to a single-voice lead Product Owner is to address the concern that prevents it. The other committee members might fear a loss of influence or prestige if it's seen that one of them is being elevated over the others. To overcome these fears, the lead Product Owner's responsibilities must be communicated and demonstrated (see above) to the others in the committee. Coaching is often necessary to reinforce that the lead Product Owner acts in an inclusive way, and the other members of the former committee do not lose their voice.

## Silo Product Owners

Silo POs are similar to a committee POs in that there is no single voice, but silo POs are a bit worse: These POs don't even talk the same language. They focus on the underlying means to build features and not the outcomes. Silo POs usually result from adopting the Product Owner role in a siloed or matrix-driven organization where design, art, and technology department leads run the studio. As with a committee Product Owner, it was easier to assign the Product Owner title to the existing leadership and ignore the need for a single voice.

Silo Product Ownership can create confusion among teams and leave a lot of "loose ends" with the game. This can demoralize a team that doesn't understand the vision because, regardless of whether a vision has been shared, if the prioritization doesn't match the vision, the work will not align to it.

As with the Product Owner committee, one of the silo POs has to step up to be the single voice for the team. This can also raise concerns about roles.

***Example:*** Project *Zeppelin*, a mobile game, has two Product Owners who are the founders of the small studio creating it. One is a designer, and the other is a programmer. Several teams are developing a World War I flight simulator game, which is the sole game being worked on at the small studio. When planning and executing sprints, teams will get a different set of priorities from their Product Owners. The design Product Owner will want to try out different mechanics and prioritize prototypes to the top of the Backlog during Sprint Planning. The technical Product Owner will prioritize technical risk reduction work to the top of the Backlog for teams that invite him to their planning sessions.

In the preceding example, with two founders providing guidance to the one project the entire studio is focused on, the founder who doesn't take on the Product Owner role might be feeling diminished or threatened. As a coach, I would remind him that a Product Owner must rely on close collaboration with his peers to make the best decision about the prioritization of the backlog. Let's say the designer became the Product Owner and began ignoring all the technical input for reducing risk. This points to a dysfunctional relationship between the two founders. This was the real dysfunction that instantiating the Product Owner role has exposed. It's probably always been there and has been a threat to the studio from the start. A coach can work with these two to establish better trust and communication and help them fix the true root cause of the problem.

## Attention Deficit Product Owner

I have heard some POs claim, "We need to focus on everything!" It's great when a Product Owner has a strong vision. It's not so great when that vision changes daily. Some famous game designers have been known for this. They have a dream one night, or their cat does something interesting that sparks an insight, and so on. Next thing you know, they are running through the studio excited about their new insight and impatient to see it being implemented.

Enthusiasm is great, especially when it can be shared, but it needs to be combined with a focus on demonstrating fun in the game. Focusing on too many things that will somehow come together months later is a debt we don't want to owe.

***Example:*** Nearly everyone has heard of the *Duke Nukem Forever* development story.[3] The sequel to the hit game *Duke Nukem 3D* took 15 years to develop due to a continually changing series of goals, in addition to changing publishers and so on. Although it wasn't a Scrum-based project and probably didn't have a Product Owner, per se, it's an extreme example of how a lack of focus can impact a game's development. Teams with a wandering focus waste a lot of money and cause stakeholders to cancel projects.

A continually changing focus can have a bad effect on the team. It can lead to disengagement among the team members: No matter how engaged they get in a vision, it's going to change, so why bother? Also, the sense of urgency that comes with these changes is not sustainable, which leads to poor quality decisions (reduced testing, refactoring, tuning, and polishing).

Additionally, this constant change of focus will have an impact on the velocity of the team over the course of a release and beyond.

The Scrum Master needs to intervene with Product Owners to help them understand the impact the constantly changing focus is having on the team. The main barrier is that this is the Product Owners need to "be heard by the team." They can see the Scrum Master's intervention as a threat to their authority. Therefore, the Scrum Master must take care to ensure the ideas of the Product Owner are being collected, ideally as user stories, to be addressed. The best place to do this is in a Backlog Refinement meeting. This is where the Product Owner can discuss insights along with development impacts and costs with a smaller group of experienced developers. It will also create a buffer between the developers who are focused on the current Sprint's goal, because any decisions made during the Refinement meeting will only impact future Sprints.

If these changing goals impact release targets, the stakeholders must be informed. The Scrum Master has to ensure that they are aware of this and have discussed it with the Product Owner. Stakeholders who are engaged with the decision-making process are much less likely to make drastic decisions about the project.[4]

## Tunnel Vision Product Owner

Bill Gates supposedly claimed in 1981 that 640K ought to be enough for anybody. No vision is perfect, but sometimes the hardest person to convince of that is the visionary. Given that a shipped game rarely resembles the original detailed design document, an equally detailed and prophetic vision buried inside someone's head can be

3. http://en.wikipedia.org/wiki/Development_of_Duke_Nukem_Forever

4. Ask any *Duke Nukem Forever* developer.

just as capricious. A common result is that the emergent gameplay quality is not taken into account and teams become disengaged.

I call this dysfunction "tunnel vision" Product Ownership. It's common in studios transitioning from a design-document approach to an Agile one. Although the visionaries admit that detailed design documents fail to create a shared vision, they haven't yet adopted an Agile mindset, which requires

- Frequent face-to-face engagement with developers
- The ability of teams to produce iterations of an emergent game that validates the vision (or not)
- The ability of Product Owners to evaluate their vision against the emergent game

This leads to many patterns of dysfunction, as the example illustrates.

***Example:*** The Product Backlog becomes a component list of features and functions necessary to fulfill the vision…someday. This reminds me of someone building all the parts for a prototype car. They build a carburetor, then the tires, and so on. Eventually, when all the parts are built, an assembly phase is entered. Even if all the parts fit together, it rarely results in a very functional car.

The same dysfunction happens in games. The following dysfunctional practices are seen with a tunnel vision Product Owner:

- There are too many component (or functional) teams; for example:
    - AI team
    - Animation team
    - Design team
    - Graphics team

  This is not to say that component teams are all bad. They are often necessary, but having the majority of a project composed of component teams usually results in delayed integration and knowledge (that is, debt).
- Crunch Sprints (usually called something less obvious) occur with lots of overtime, little velocity, or just to tackle user stories created to address debt (refactors, bug fixes, polishing, and so on). If most user stories don't read like features users would pay for, it's generally a strong indication that a good Definition of Done is not in place, teams are doing a lot of component work, or debt is piling up.

- Teams that don't have a tangible vision or one that is months away from being realized have a hard time engaging in their work. This is especially true on larger projects. Nothing will drag velocity down more.

As with any cultural issue, tunnel vision is hard to fix. Transforming a detailed design document–focused culture to one of frequent communication and inspection doesn't happen overnight. There needs to be some bridgework between the two. Before the documents are shrunk, a Product Owner needs to gain skill in communicating vision and in learning to respond to the emergent game. To start with, find ways to improve communication in Sprint Planning, Reviews, and Retrospectives. Establishing a better Definition of Done, and phrasing the Sprint Goal in terms of true value (for example, "What are we going to be able to play at the end of the Sprint?") sets the context for what is expected (in the playable game). Focusing the Sprint Review on the state of the gameplay sends that message as well. For the team, it's easier: Having a Product Owner responding to gameplay communicates priorities.

Having a vision is better than having none at all, but a vision must be tempered against reality.

## Distant Product Owner

Distant Product Owners are physically distant from the people making the game. They could have the best vision for the game and be the creative soul, but because they are not near the team, they don't get the same traction with the game. This is a very common dysfunction with large, distributed teams. The Product Owner can only be at one place at one time, and so all but one of the development locations will suffer from a distant Product Owner dysfunction.

***Example:*** This was one of the problems with the *Bourne* Product Owner. When a Product Owner is distant, teams drift and stakeholders lose their voice. Each fall back on their assumptions about the game or lose sight of any vision.

If development is occurring in one studio, the solution to this dysfunction is to get another Product Owner. This can be a challenge due to a perceived loss of influence from the existing distant Product Owner (especially with a licensed game), but it has to be made clear to the distant Product Owner that his influence is already diminished from his distance. One solution is to create a developer-side Product Owner who has a good working relationship with the distant Product Owner, whom I'll call the business-side Product Owner. This relationship works with a publisher/developer relationship where many of the marketing and funding decisions are made at the distant publisher site.

The developer-side Product Owner will own the Product Backlog and be able to make decisions about it but will also be able to develop a shared vision with the business-side Product Owner. The business-side Product Owner will have the responsibility of maintaining a shared vision with the marketing, franchise, sales, accounting, and executive stakeholders local to him.

Care must be taken that the developer-side Product Owner does not become a proxy Product Owner.

For large, distributed teams, please refer to the distributed development section (Chapter 21) for advice on avoiding the distant Product Owner dysfunction.

### Ditching Product Owners

CCP Games, the developer and publisher of EVE Online, was founded in 1997. After the transition to Agile and Scrum in 2009, the EVE Online team at CCP had a fairly mature organization. One of the significant adaptations it made was the elimination of the Product Owner role and the shifting of that responsibility to the teams themselves. Andie Nordgren, former Executive Producer of EVE Online, describes the transition.

"Agile practices were seen as a given, and work on process was mostly about optimizations rather than any challenges to the form itself—a "mostly Scrum" setup with cross-functional teams with designers, developers, and quality analysts collaborating and taking responsibility for their work all the way into production. There were monthly release trains and smaller patches in between.

"The investment in cross-functional teams was a clear direction we wanted to stay with, and the problems at the time that disrupted these teams were all about how teams were directed and managed. At the time, teams had been cross-functional for a long time, but people management was still done matrix-style by work role: Managers for Engineers, Producers, Designers, Artists, and QA, respectively. For each discipline, there was also a director, and each team had a Product Owner, normally a Producer filling that role for one to three teams. It was a mix of team-based, discipline-based and individual-based practices that created a number of disruptions that hindered teams from performing well—mostly because individuals on these teams just had too many people telling them what to do. Also, Product Owners were hard to find. They ended up being Producers who could easily handle the production-style tasks of Backlog and stakeholder management, but lacked the knowledge of the users and the game to really make product decisions themselves, or they would be designers who could make good calls on game features, but didn't have time to do so, because they were (often badly) managing the Backlog and the stakeholders. Either way, teams often felt victimized by both managers, directors, and their Product Owner, who—by the rules of Scrum—had the power to prioritize and make decisions about what the team should work on, and in practice represented the team in many key product discussions, when the actual product knowledge sat in the team. Frustrations were everywhere.

"With the compass pointed towards a structure that would support whole teams rather than individuals, we made two changes: First, we created a Development Manager role that was responsible for staffing a team and for its processes and work practices and the team's deliverables once they were committed. From a user value perspective, these managers led from below—supporting the team that knew what user value to build, with the right resources and process to do so.

"For Product Ownership, we decided to move the role to the team as a whole, and ask every member to step up to take responsibility for what they were building and why: engineers, QA, designers, artists collaborating to define and build features with process support from their development manager. The responsibility would no longer sit with an individual outside the team, but with the team as a whole, driving home the point that everyone on the team was needed and a crucial part of how to deliver value to the players of the game. In practice on gameplay feature teams, designers often led the work on what to build but they now didn't need to drown in Backlog management to do so, as they had that support from their Development Manager.

"This created a new type of commitment from teams and also a more empowered autonomy. New types of team collaborations emerged as teams realized they truly owned their own time and could make commitments to other teams. But it also became harder to coordinate and collaborate between teams as teams became reluctant to ask other teams for work or sign themselves up for work with a lot of dependencies on other teams. Eventually, some more explicit process for cross-team planning and commitments was brought in to counter these tendencies. Another gap was that a number of tasks and skills normally performed by Product Owners didn't get the appropriate amount of staffing on teams. To ditch the Product Owner role, teams should have had embedded people or access to better data analysis resources and user research resources.

"Overall the change recognized that with entertainment products the uncertainty of what will work for users, and the fact that you can often not just ask them what they want, creates a product development environment less suitable for having a single person represent the customer needs. And in that case, having product ownership move from an individual to being a responsibility for the whole team working to deliver value to users might be a better fit."

## What Good Looks Like

A good Product Backlog:

- Is easily accessible by any member of the team
- Contains PBIs that express the reason and value of the work
- Contains no more than 200–300 PBIs
- Is refined regularly
- Is ordered by a single voice: the Product Owner

A good Product Backlog reflects an alignment with the vision of the game between stakeholders and developers alike. It's one single list of ordered work rather than separate lists of discipline work that is derived from a design document written at the start of the project.

## Summary

The biggest cultural challenge in adopting a Product Backlog is the shift from writing detailed specifications up front to leaving questions unanswered until more is known. While there is great comfort for stakeholders in reading exacting specifications about all proposed features in a game and the details and cost of how they will be implemented, those are usually guesses, and first guesses on uncertain features are usually wrong.

It's fine to document things we are certain about, but we can't document away uncertainty. Uncertainty has to be executed away. We have to focus the team on the goal and work with it closely to find the best path to the best outcome.

## Additional Reading

Cohn, Mike. 2006. *Agile Estimating and Planning*. Upper Saddle River, NJ: Prentice Hall.

Gray, D., S. Brown, and J. Mancuso. 2010. *Gamestorming: a playbook for innovators, rulebreakers, and changemakers*. Beijing: OReilly.

Keith, C., and G. Shonkwiler. 2018. *Gear Up!: 100+ ways to grow your studio culture, Second edition.*

# Part III

# Agile Game Development

## Chapter 8

# User Stories

Communication is one of the biggest challenges for developing games, and one of the largest communication problems is language. Stakeholders often speak the language of business. To them, cost and consumer value influence how they see the world and communicate.

Developers speak a different language. Their language pivots around their specialty. Programmers speak the language of math, code, and algorithms. Designers speak the language of pacing and reward. Artists speak the language of polygon color, texture, and lighting. These languages are not exclusive of one another, but they present communication challenges when everyone on the team needs to understand the same vision of the game.

The solution is for developers to speak the language of the stakeholders. We can't expect stakeholders to learn the language of development (although many stakeholders are often familiar with the jargon). As a business, the language of the player must be the universal language of game development. To this end, we need to be sure that the critical lines of communication between the stakeholders and developers—and even between developers of separate disciplines—are made and kept open using this universal language.

This is where user stories come in. A **user story** is a short description of a game, tool, or pipeline feature that has a clear value to a user. If the feature is a tool or pipeline change, the user can be a developer who uses the tool or pipeline to make the game.

Up to this point, we've used the terms *feature* and *PBI* to define what is developed. This chapter introduces user stories as a replacement for those terms and describes how good user stories are created.

## Speaking Different Languages

Many years ago, our studio was working on a *Resident Evil* port for the Nintendo 64. It was a very challenging project to port a CD game filled with video cinematics onto a much smaller cartridge, but the biggest challenge was communicating with the Japanese stakeholders from Capcom.

First, it was very important to them that player control be responsive. When someone moved the controller, they wanted the character on the screen to reach the next frame. Somehow that wasn't clear to us, and we kept adding embellishments, such as animation blending, which slowed the responsiveness down slightly. After months of wasted effort, we found ourselves being screamed at in Japanese by a Capcom producer while his poor translator tried to keep up.

The second, and worst, blunder in communication was with the alpha version of the game. As a Christmas title, it was important for us to hit that date and we thought we had. Unfortunately, our definition of alpha, where all the features were in the game, but not fully debugged and optimized, was not the same as theirs, which they defined as fully debugged and optimized. Apparently, both definitions were in different documents, and they were never reconciled beforehand. As a result, we missed the Christmas launch and were yelled at in Japanese again.

## The Solutions in This Chapter

This chapter addresses the traditional issues of communication in video game development and introduces user stories as a solution. While not a complete replacement for all documentation, user stories provide the following solutions:

- They communicate business value that allows better communication between stakeholders and developers.
- They promote continual conversation among all groups, which is better than a pure documentation approach.
- They are hierarchical, allowing a breakdown of detail for the work that is immediate and needs refinement of understanding.
- They allow for testability through specific criteria.

## What Are User Stories?

User stories were created to express the value of features to a customer, set quality expectations, and elicit conversation (Beck, 2000). Identifying the value of individual features coupled with the benefit of Agile development, demonstrating value throughout a project, is a powerful combination. User stories represent the requirements of the game from the point of view of the user, not the developer. They don't fully describe design details. Stories are placeholders for conversation about the details. User stories follow a template determined together by the team and stakeholders. Mike Cohn (2004) recommends the following:

As a <user role>, I want <goal> [so that <reason>].

This template includes the following:

- **User role:** A customer of the game or a user of the pipeline who benefits from this story.
- **Goal:** The goal of the story. This is a feature or function in the game, tool, or pipeline.
- **Reason:** The benefit to the customer or user when this feature or function is used.

The last portion of the story template, "so that <reason>," is optional. It's often left out when the reason is apparent.

Examples of user stories follow:

As a player, I want a mute player button so that I stop being distracted by some of the other players online.

As an animator, I want to change animations directly in the game without restarting it so that I can iterate faster on animations.

As a prop modeler, I want the exporter to check the naming conventions of the props to ensure that they are correct, so a poorly named prop does not crash the game.

As a player, I want to see my health level.[1]

1. It's apparent why I want to see my health level, so we don't need to state the reason.

## Levels of Detail

Teams complete one or more user stories per Sprint. These user stories have to be small enough to fit into a Sprint. Had we used stories on *Smuggler's Run (Chapter 7)*, we may have had an initial story something like the following:

> As a player, I want to see herds of animals running around the environment so that it seems more realistic and alive.

As it increased in priority and approached implementation, it could have been split into smaller stories such as the following:

> As an animal in the game, I want to run away from vehicles.

We don't want to break down every large feature into Sprint-sized stories at the start of the project. That creates too many stories to be practically managed by the Product Owner. Instead, priority determines when features are broken down. Higher-priority stories are worked on sooner, so they are broken down into smaller stories in a planning meeting. User stories that are too large to be accomplished in a single Sprint are called **epics**, such as the animal herd story. Sometimes a number of related user stories are gathered together in a **theme**. Themes are beneficial for aggregating user stories together for estimating.

> **Note**
>
> Some projects have required an even higher level of scope than an epic and have introduced what they call the **saga**!

User stories, epics, and themes can be decomposed into smaller user stories. Figure 8.1 shows an example of an online epic broken down into smaller stories.

In this example, the stakeholders identify the lobby and online game as two online epics. They split the gameplay story further into death-match stories. This decomposition of stories occurs throughout the project. A Product Backlog can be considered as a hierarchy of user stories that change. Branches grow in detail or are pruned as we learn more about what is fun. This chapter defines how to split stories in more detail later.

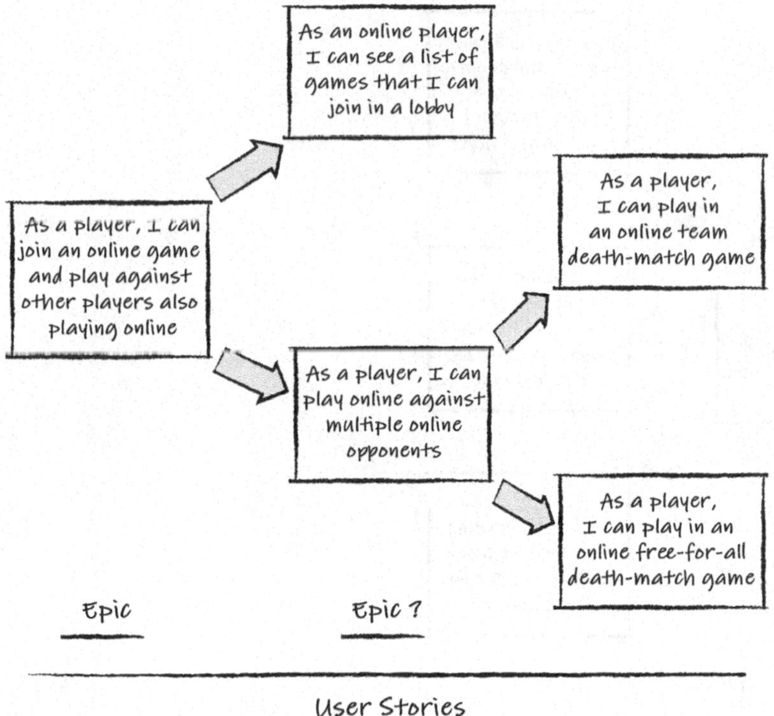


**Figure 8.1** *Splitting an epic into smaller stories*

## Acceptance Criteria

Sometimes we want to add some specific details to a small story.

Take the following example story:

> As a player, I want to shoot an enemy character and see it react so that I know when it is hit.

If this leaves a bit of uncertainty in the details, the stakeholders and team decompose the story into smaller stories, as shown in Figure 8.2, to add those details.

However, if the initial story is small enough to fit in a Sprint, then this decomposition is not necessary. Another approach is to list these substories as **acceptance criteria** (AC), as shown in Figure 8.3.

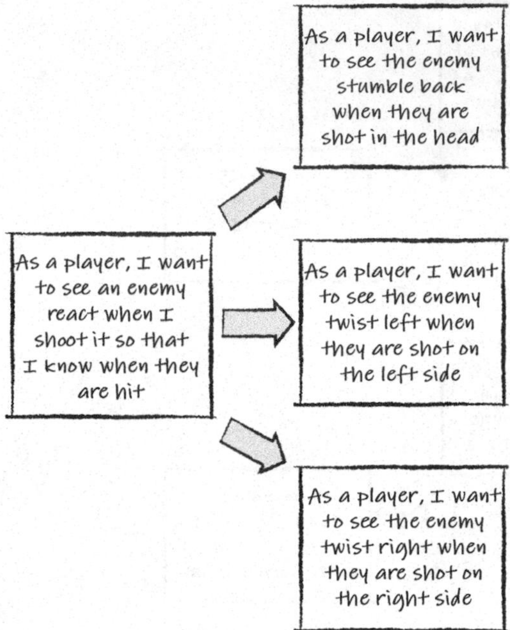


**Figure 8.2** *Splitting a story to add details*

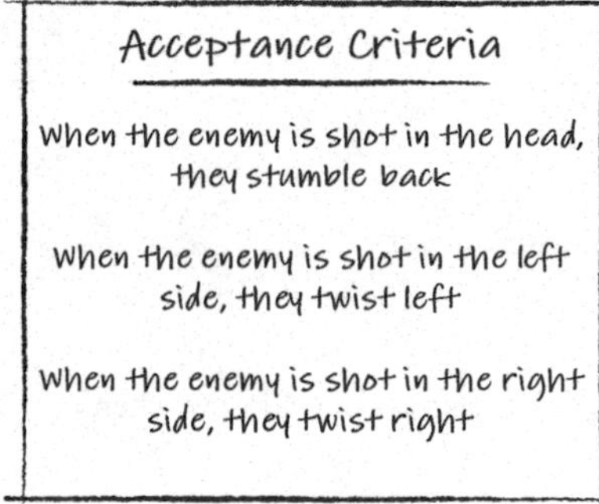


**Figure 8.3** *Adding details as acceptance criteria*

This is a very powerful tool. AC help the team understand the ultimate goal for every user story and avoid delivering the wrong feature at the Sprint review.

AC have to be testable. The team should verify whether the AC are met by running the game and ensuring that the behaviors described exist.

**Experience**

"I really thought user stories worked well in the development of our game. It forced the designers to really think out what they wanted. On my last project, programmers worked closely with the designers on the acceptance criteria so that everyone knew what was expected. It was critical that the programmers found out as much detail as possible. It kept any creeping seat-of-the-pants design to the planning session where all the interested parties were present. Programmers debated the merits of some of the design decisions, and designers came to understand the technical effort involved. Programmers with design skills had an opportunity to get their input heard."

—Mike Riccio, Lead Programmer, High Moon Studios

## Using Index Cards for User Stories

As with tasks, user stories are often represented in the form of a 3-by-5 index card. These cards are a great medium for handling user stories for a number of reasons:

- The size of the card constrains the amount of detail in a story. We don't want stories to be large documents that include every necessary design detail. A small card prevents this from happening.
- Cards can be physically manipulated (sorted, edited, replaced, and passed) by many hands in collaborative settings (Daily Scrums and planning meetings).
- The backside of the card is an ideal location and size for listing AC. Once again, the constraint imposed by the size of the card prevents pages of AC from being listed, which interferes with the story being negotiable.

**Experience**

Constraint is really hard, even when limited to an index card. At first, we stuffed lots of written detail on our cards by printing them with tiny fonts or stapling ten-page documents to them. Our coach eventually limited us to using only permanent markers.

## INVEST in User Stories

What makes a good story? Mike Cohn and Bill Wake (2003) suggested the acronym *INVEST*, which stands for the following attributes of a good story:

- Independent
- Negotiable
- Valuable
- Estimable
- Sized appropriately
- Testable

### Independent

Stories should be independent from other stories in the order they are implemented. Dependencies create problems that make them hard to prioritize and estimate. For example, suppose we have the following two stories:

> As a player, when I shoot a door, it splinters into hundreds of pieces of wood.
> As a player, when I shoot a window, it shatters into hundreds of shards of glass.

If the technology for creating this effect does not exist, then the first of these stories to be implemented requires underlying technology to be developed as well. Because these stories appear almost identical, they should not have such a discrepancy of work to implement. The dependency inherent in the first story implemented does not make this possible. There are two solutions to this. The first is to combine these into one larger story:

> As a player, I want to shoot certain objects and have them break into many pieces.

The door and windows could be handled as two acceptance criteria. This works when the larger story fits within a Sprint. If the aggregated story takes longer, we break the story into the one that creates the base technology:

> As a designer, I want to shoot certain objects and have them break into many pieces.

and into two others, which allow the window and door instances of this effect:

> As a player, when I shoot a door, it splinters into hundreds of pieces of wood.
>
> As a player, when I shoot a window, it shatters into hundreds of shards of glass.

These stories aren't truly independent because the first story must be completed before the others, but dependency is now clear, where it wasn't in the first place.

**Note**

One key difference to note is that the customer for the first story is the designer who uses the system to finish the second story. This enables the team implementing the first story to focus on the needs of the designer, including an interface to tune the system, which the player does not need. Beware of the "parts on the garage floor" problem described in Chapter 14, "Agile Design."

## Negotiable

Stories are not contracts or detailed requirements. They are placeholders for conversation between the stakeholders and the team. A story that is too detailed and specific shortcuts those conversations by creating the illusion that all details are known and don't require any dialogue. For example, consider the story in Figure 8.4.

The detail in the story may not be as comprehensive as it implies. Did the customer forget about sound effects of the tires on these surfaces? Do they want more effects in the future? Would they like wheel friction to change depending on the surface? Figure 8.5 shows a better version of this story.

This story is a better placeholder for the conversation. It drives conversation. The requirements of the water spray and grass particles could be added as acceptance criteria on the backside of the card if the stakeholders want to ensure that these things are demonstrated.

As a driver, I want to see water being sprayed when driving through a puddle and grass flying when driving through a park

**Figure 8.4** *A story that doesn't allow much negotiation*

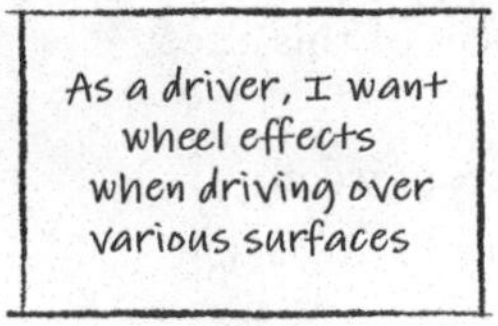

As a driver, I want wheel effects when driving over various surfaces

**Figure 8.5** *A more negotiable story*

### Note

A missing requirement in an overly detailed story is more likely to lead to that requirement being overlooked by a team focused on fulfilling the "letter of the law." Negotiable stories serve the "spirit of the law" better.

### Harness the Creativity of Teams!

Negotiable stories raise questions on purpose. They enable anyone on the team to suggest ideas. Talk about being motivated when millions of people love a feature that you thought up!

## Valuable

Stories need to communicate value not only to the player but also to the team developing and marketing the game. The Product Owner adjusts the priority of user stories on the Product Backlog by judging their value. Stories not expressed in terms of value are difficult to prioritize. Consider the following story:

> Sort rigid bodies in the environment into islands of objects local to one another.

This story does not communicate value to the player or pipeline users, but it may be a story that has a great deal of value. In this example, a physics programmer may request that these changes be made so that the game runs at 30 frames per second (fps). If this is the case, the story can be written to express this value to the player:

> Sort rigid bodies in the environment into islands of objects local to one another so that we maintain 30 fps.

Note that the expression of the user role is missing in this story. The player and the developers all benefit from the game running at 30 fps, which is far more enjoyable than a game running at half that rate.

## Estimable

Stories need to be estimated. This requires knowledge about what we are building and how we are going to build it. If not enough is known or the scope of the story is too large, then we cannot estimate it well enough.

Sometimes stories push the boundaries of knowledge about what our technology can do or the level of effort required. For example, suppose the following story was introduced:

> As a player, I want to knock over stacks of boxes to block the AI players from approaching me and to allow me to escape tight situations.

This story could present a number of problems to the programmers:

- The physics engine might not support a stable stacking of objects.
- The AI navigation system may not "see" dynamic objects such as boxes in the environment.

Implementing this story may be simple or require months of effort. To mitigate this risk, a story is introduced to explore these risks. This story is timeboxed, or limited, in the amount of effort spent on investigating these risks; we don't want to sign a blank check. This type of story is called a **spike**, and its purpose is to add knowledge about the cost of implementing the main story. After the spike, the Product Owner and the team should better understand the cost of implementing the full feature.

**Spikes and Tracer Bullets**

Spikes are important for video game development. Spikes are timeboxed stories. The reason for this importance is that spikes address areas of great uncertainty, and their only goal is to create knowledge that helps the Product Owner evaluate the cost of other stories. For example, the Product Owner may have a spike defined that says the following:

*As a Product Owner, I want to see a mock-up video of how our fighting mechanic might look on an iPhone.*

The Product Owner may only be willing to spend a Sprint or less of the team's time investigating something. In this case, he wants to know what a mechanic might look like on the iPhone before developing the iPhone technology. At the end of the Sprint, the team shares what it has learned so far. If the Product Owner decides to investigate further, he can create another spike.

A variation of a spike are **tracer bullets**. In warfare, tracer bullets are special bullets that glow when they are fired from a machine gun. There is usually one tracer bullet for every 10 or 20 normal bullets. These tracer bullets allow the gunner to see where the other bullets are headed. For game development, a tracer bullet is a spike that is used to measure the cost or quality of a small piece of work that will help us estimate the larger set. An example of a tracer bullet would be to create a shippable section of a level that will help the team understand the cost of all the levels anticipated for the game.

## Sized Appropriately

Stories need to eventually be made small enough to fit into a Sprint when implemented. If they are too large, they are split up.

A group of small stories can be combined into a larger story more easily managed as a theme. Examples of this are minor bug fixes and polishing tasks placed on the Product Backlog. We don't need to track and estimate small one-hour fixes within separate stories.

**Tip**

One trick teams do is to collect all their small polishing tasks into a single spike each Sprint and dedicate a fixed and predictable amount of time polishing the game. Over time these tasks are included at the start of the Sprint, and the spike becomes unnecessary.

## Testable

The story should be written so that it is verified before the end of the Sprint. Without this, the team cannot determine whether it satisfied the stakeholders. Using the acceptance criteria on the back of the card to define those tests is best. Some stories require approval to check off.

Consider the following stories:

The prototype shooting level is fun.
The boss character model is complete.

Both of these stories are subject to interpretation. In this case, the team had a lead designer or lead artist to sign off on the level or model, respectively. The AC should identify when these approvals are needed. Sometimes a team adds a column on the task board between the "in progress" and "done" columns called "needs verification." This is a holding stage for all the stories that are considered complete only when a lead signs off on them. If a team has many subjective stories or tasks, this is a good solution.

**The Impossible Story**

One time I was handed a user story that read "As a player, I want the camera view to shift to the side a half-second before I hit the jump button, so I can see a cinematic view of my jump." To this day, I have no idea how anyone could implement that feature!

## User Roles

Many games provide difficulty levels for the players who buy the game. They usually implement several levels of difficulty as a means of adding replayability and accommodating a range of player skills. The levels are differentiated by scaling challenges in the game, such as the number of opponents and damage from weapons hits.

Games benefit from considering a broader range of players and placing more emphasis on their roles. As an example, consider the popular *Battlefield* games, which enable players to adopt specific roles. If you are not familiar with the games or the specialties, they are divided across these roles:

- **Assault specialist:** Is equipped with an assault weapon and grenades for close quarter combat
- **Sniper:** Carries a high-power sniper rifle and a targeting device used to call in precision strikes
- **Engineer:** Has a bazooka and mines and can repair vehicles

- **Special forces:** Carries a light automatic weapon and C4 explosives for sneaking around behind enemy lines disrupting opponents
- **Support:** Totes a heavy automatic weapon and a radio to call in mortar strikes

These specialties require different behavior from the player. Inserting these roles at the end of a project is difficult. They need to be developed in parallel during preproduction because they have an impact on level design and should be added before production starts.

User stories allow roles and their associated features to be clearly defined. A good method for differentiating roles is to use them in the story template. Instead of saying this:

> As a player, I want a bazooka so I can blow up tanks.

The story becomes this:

> As an engineer, I want a bazooka so I can blow up tanks.

What's the difference? It's mainly one of value and priority. For a generic player, the bazooka is one of a host of weapons. However, for the engineer, the bazooka is probably the most valuable weapon because the engineer role exists to counteract tanks. There's nothing more gratifying than taking out a tank with a well-placed shot. The bazooka is useless for a sniper to carry because snipers maintain a distance from the fight that is greater than the bazooka's range and firing it leaves a trail of smoke that reveals the sniper's position.

Even if your game isn't going to use such specialties, there is a lot of value in brainstorming the various types of players early in development. Who is buying your game? Do you hope to attract casual and hardcore players to your game? If you do, it benefits you to identify the "casual player" role in some of your stories. It may lead to many small decisions such as offering an option to simplify the controls or adding more checkpoints, so the casual gamer doesn't become frustrated.

User roles also apply to developers who use the pipeline and tools to make the game. Pipeline and tool stories have to express value as well as gameplay stories. This enables the Product Owner to better order the stories to be implemented. For example, if animation creation is a bottleneck for a project, the Product Owner raises the order of stories that address the animation pipeline. This is best accomplished by having those stories start with the phrase "As an animator...." Here's an example:

> As an animator, I want the animation exporter optimized so I can create and test more animations.

**When to Avoid User Stories**

User stories are fine to a certain point, but they don't have to be used everywhere. Stories used to address bug fixes or asset changes are pointless. Do we really need to define which user doesn't want the game to crash?

## Collecting Stories

Collecting stories in the Product Backlog is an ongoing process that occurs throughout development. At the start of an Agile project, the team and stakeholders collect enough stories to encompass all the major requirements (epics) known and enough detailed stories to enable the team to start iterating.

The collection of stories for an Agile project isn't the sole responsibility of a few leads. Instead, there are many ways to gather stories, including marketing studies and focus group questionnaires, but the most beneficial method for game developers is the story-gathering workshop.

The story-gathering workshop brings stakeholders and teams together to brainstorm user stories for the game. The Product Owner facilitates the workshop and invites everyone who can contribute ideas.

Attendees discuss the goals and constraints for the game. This is especially important if it's the first workshop. For example, if the title is to be tied to a license, then the customer who represents the licensor describes what is allowed in the game, such as not allowing a licensed car to catch fire. The publisher shares the major goals of the game, including the product's position in their portfolio, release date options, and targeted demographics. User roles are explored. Domain experts discuss risks and opportunities. For example, the design leadership may identify areas of strength and weaknesses in the level design feature set related to delivering on requested mechanics.

> **Note**
>
> Many of these points do not directly lead to the creation of stories right away but are placed in a "parking lot" of topics to be discussed in detail as time permits.

At the first workshop, the major epics are identified. An example of an initial summary of epics for a first-person shooter might resemble Figure 8.6.

The story-gathering workshop identifies enough detailed stories to fill the next release. This requires the Product Owner to identify story priorities and discuss the capacity and capabilities with the teams. For our first-person shooter project, the Product Owner identifies that the player control and artificial intelligence epics are the most valuable areas to focus on for the next three or so months. If the teams confirm that they have the necessary specialists to accomplish work in these areas, then the workshop focuses on breaking out stories sized appropriately. As the workshop drills down on smaller epics, then the subtrees become populated with stories that fit into Sprints. Figure 8.7 shows some of the smaller epics identified for player control.

The team and domain experts are critical in contributing their ideas here. If, for example, the physics engine causes problems with player controller development, they should discuss it in this meeting. This may lead to work that investigates the potential issues with physics.

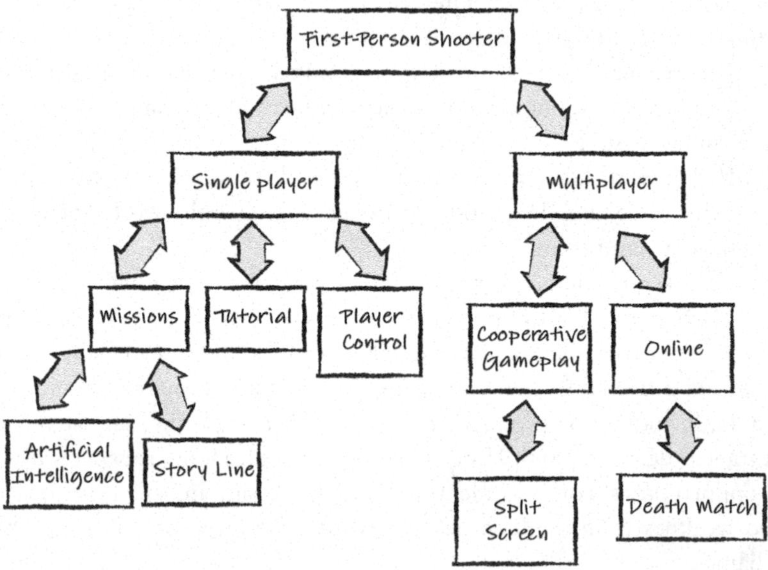


**Figure 8.6** *Identifying a hierarchy of epics is valuable in communicating the big picture.*

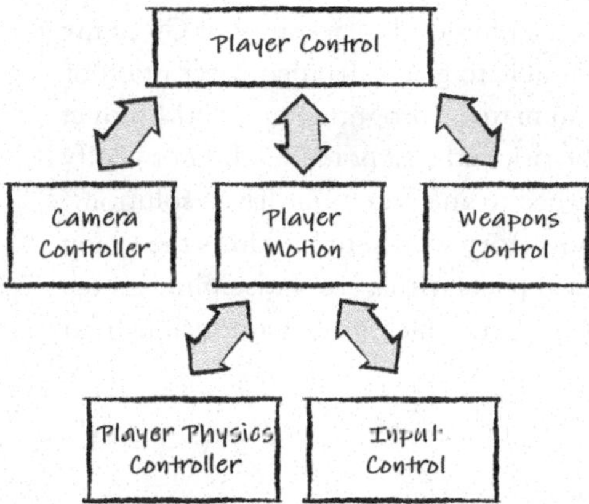


**Figure 8.7** *Smaller epics*

### Planning a Hand-to-Hand Combat System

I've worked on two projects that have included hand-to-hand combat. The first game was a sequel to a popular fighting game developed by another studio. The hardship the original project suffered—it took more than four grueling years to develop—was due to the complexity of its hand-to-hand combat system.

The challenge of hand-to-hand combat systems is to create a proper blend of responsive player control and smooth, seamless animation. The approach chosen for the original game was entirely physics-based. Animations drove the motion until a collision occurred. The force of a collision then controlled the motion of the character. It was an ambitious system that promised flexibility and a great degree of player control. Unfortunately, it didn't allow for a very good-looking character movement. Much of the contact between characters was resolved incorrectly. After wasting enormous amounts of effort trying to make this system work, the team reworked the system, eventually settling with an entirely animation-driven solution. The publisher wanted the sequel to implement the physical solution, but after several months of experiments, we could offer no good solution, and the project was abandoned.

Based on this previous experience, I had some opinions about the technical approach when I attended the story workshop for another game with a hand-to-hand combat system. The Product Owner introduced the feature and told us that the most important value of this feature was that it be fun and look good.

The discussion eventually touched on a physics-driven solution. Given my experiences from the past project, I was able to give a detailed description of the problems this created. When the animators, programmers, and Product Owner heard this, they decided that the risk and cost potential did not justify the physics approach, and attention turned to an animation-driven solution.

This small example demonstrates how story workshops address the vision of each feature and the potential design impacts with a cross-discipline group. Too often, projects don't discuss this impact, which leads to decisions that take the project down a bad path.

## Splitting Stories

Splitting epics into smaller stories is a bit of an art form. Teams new to Agile tend to split stories into requirements or development tasks, or simply split stories too soon.

Every time you split a larger story into smaller ones, you are making design decisions. We want such design decisions to be made "just in time," or "as late as we can responsibly make them" simply because the longer we wait, the more we will learn and our decisions will be better.

### Splitting Too Far

The most frightening Product Backlog I've seen was at a client working on a large MMO. I was asked to see their "Product Backlog Room," which I had never heard of before. They brought me to a large windowless room whose walls were completely covered with more than 1,000 highly detailed index cards. I immediately felt like Shelly Duvall's character in *The Shining*, when she encountered her husband's draft novel only to experience the horror of the detail of what he was writing. I quickly exited the room, and we had a conversation about the dangers of splitting stories too soon. One thousand story cards on a wall are just as bad, if not worse than, a huge design document!

This section lists some useful strategies and tips for splitting stories.

## Split Along Research or Prototype Dependencies

Doing some exploration before you can decide how to split an epic further is often necessary. Start with splitting out a research or prototype story first.

***Example epic:*** As a player, I want to react to impacts.

***Example split:***

- As a designer, I want to know where an impact occurs.
- As a player, I want to react based on the impact location.

***Reasoning:*** The first story allows some research on collision physics and helps the team and designer experiment with different strategies. (For example, would a simple strategy of having high, middle, and low collision volumes be good enough, or do we need something more complex?)

***Example epic:*** As a player, I want to buy weapons using my PayPal or my credit card accounts.

***Example split:***

- As the Monetization Product Manager, I need a system for processing and recording payments in a secure way.
  - *Acceptance criteria:* A player can buy a weapon with PayPal.
- As a player I can buy weapons with a credit card.

***Reasoning:*** An infrastructure or architecture often needs to be in place, which requires a dependent story to be implemented first.

## Split Along Conjunctions

If your epic has a conjunction (for example, and, if, but), you can often split out stories from either side.

***Example:*** As a player, I want to smash wooden crates and doors open.

***Example split:***

- As a player, I want to smash wooden crates open.
- As a player, I want to smash wooden doors open.

***Reasoning:*** Do the simplest or most important first. Also, note that the first of *anything* is usually more expensive, so this makes it easier to see costs by sizing these stories individually.

### Split by Progression or Value

Sometimes we split an epic into stages of progression, ordered by their value to the player.

***Example:*** As a player, I want to be coached on the rules of poker and ways I can improve my home game.

***Example split:***

- As a player, I want the game to have some first-time user experience (FTUE) tips for playing poker.
- As a player, I want the game to give me tips for improving my home game.
- As a player, I want the game to evaluate my hand strength and suggest the next move.

***Reasoning:*** This split details some of the ways players can improve with a progression of stories that are a bit more specific, from players first encountering the game to later in the game as they become better.

### Other Splitting Tips

The following are some other splitting methods to try:

- Split by acceptance criteria. Acceptance criteria often make perfect stories themselves.
- Split by discipline capacity. For example, if you don't have enough animation support, then you might have to split off an "Add polished animations to....." story for the next Sprint (after you've done everything else to avoid this).
- Make sure your split stories still meet the INVEST criteria and are not at the task level.

## Advantages of User Stories

User stories have many advantages over the traditional practice of written requirements. This section emphasizes the face-to-face communication advantages and ease of comprehension.

## Face-to-Face Communication

At the beginning of Chapter 7, "The Product Backlog," I told the story about a misunderstood feature in *Smuggler's Run*. This misunderstanding was driven mainly by a lack of ongoing communication between the designers and the rest of the team. User stories encourage an ongoing face-to-face conversation between separate disciplines that must happen for game development teams to be effective.

Consider the following requirement:

> As a player driving a vehicle, I want a rearview mirror to see behind my vehicle.

On the surface, this requirement seems clear. However, there may be a number of issues with delivering this function to the player:

- Do we show a mirror in the third-person camera view? Wouldn't a mirror floating above the vehicle look a little odd?
- If the AI opponents cheat by using "rubber banding" or other tricks to catch up with the player, wouldn't the mirror reveal these tricks?
- Does the second view of the environment reduce the overall rendering budget?

Many of us have seen issues like these crop up during implementation that impact the schedule by adding work not foreseen at the start of the project. By having these conversations at the start of every Sprint, we create opportunities to address such issues when we know far more about the immediate value they provide.

## Everyone Can Understand User Stories

Mike Cohn writes, "Because stories are terse and are always written to show customer or user value, they are always readily comprehensible by businesspeople and developers."[2] Consider an actual story I've seen:

> As a programmer, I want a checkbox in the audio objects menu to control the Looping boolean flag.

Although this story follows the template, it fails to communicate value. It's a task, not a story. Does the programmer benefit from this change? Perhaps they don't have to write separate looping audio object code, but that is not communicated here.

---

2. Cohn, M. 2004. *User Stories Applied: For Agile Software Development*. Boston: Addison-Wesley. Reproduced by permission of Pearson Education, Inc.

More than likely, the audio designers wanted looping sounds in the game. If this is the case, the story should be written as follows:

> As an audio designer, I want to set a looping flag on a sound object so that I control looping environmental sounds in the game.

This story represents real value that the Product Owner understands. Alternatively, we could have expressed the story in terms of the player. The average player does not understand looping sounds but certainly would miss the depth of the sound environment if the designers didn't include the capability to loop sounds in the background such as a babbling brook or the sounds of combat off in the distance.

**What Happens to the Design Documents?**

User stories collected on a Product Backlog are meant to replace much of the design documentation. However, external stakeholders, such as publishers, may demand to see design document in a traditional format, and many tools that manage Product Backlogs will output the Backlog in a single document.

Personally, I would still maintain a technical design document that listed technical risks and strategies for handling those risks, but I would use that document to help order the Product Backlog, which is where all work done by the team originates.

## What Good Looks Like

User stories aren't the only form of written documentation on teams. As mentioned earlier, they are placeholders, primarily for conversation, but also for other forms of communication:

- Licensed games, which will have extensive documentation that describes specific requirements for a property
- Storyboards and other art
- Reference art

Teams will explore the dividing line between what needs to be written down and what needs to be explored and communicated frequently. The bottom line is that you can't document away uncertainty.

## Summary

This chapter has covered the creation of stories and explained how they clearly communicate intent between the stakeholders and developers. Stories encompass what have been called features, PBIs, and requirements. Now that we have this powerful tool, we'll examine how to use it for planning over the longer term.

## Additional Reading

Cohn, Mike. 2004. *User Stories Applied*. Boston, MA: Addison-Wesley.

# Chapter 9

# Agile Release Planning

*In preparing for battle I have always found that plans are useless, but planning is indispensable.*

—Dwight D. Eisenhower

Agile planning is a commonly misunderstood part of Agile project management. Many consider "*Agile planning*" to be an oxymoron—that Agile teams plan very little and iterate with no end in sight.

Agile planning does not call for a complete plan up front but spreads the work of planning throughout the entire project. In fact, Agile teams spend more time planning than traditional teams; it's just not concentrated at the start of a project.

## The Solutions in This Chapter

This chapter explores the practices used to avoid the typical planning pitfalls based on the following principles:

- **Apply a higher tier of planning than Sprints:** Release planning allows for a longer planning horizon.
- **Create a shared vision of the game:** This ensures that everyone working on the game understands what is being made and why.
- **Enable continuing refinement of the work estimated for each feature as the team learns more:** Uncertain features can't have precise estimates. Accuracy can grow as the feature requirements are refined.

- **Plan continually:** Plans created at the start of a project are very good at hiding when a project is "going off the rails." Agile planning continually fine-tunes the course of the project to avoid or immediately respond to pitfalls and to double down on valuable practices and features. Plans help teams find success.
- **Work with clear objectives:** The ongoing communication between the team and the stakeholders enables clear objectives to be created.
- **Prioritize scope to control the budget and delivery date:** Many projects that run into trouble first choose to add people or delay delivery dates. This is usually done because many key features are developed in parallel and need continuing development to produce any value. Sprints and releases implement features in order of value. This gives the project the option of meeting a ship date by allowing the stakeholders to draw the line and ship with a set of the highest-valued features.

**Experience: Can Agile be Used for Fixed Deadlines?**

A common concern with Agile is that "it cannot be used for games with a fixed ship date." A decade-and-a-half of experience has proven otherwise. Many studios I've worked with publish AAA sports titles. These games can lose a large portion of sales if they miss shipping their game at the start of a season.

The Agile approach to implementing features in a value-ordered way while managing debt and risk is the best way to hit a deadline. For sports titles, ensuring that the proper team assets (uniforms, logos, rosters, stadiums) for each year are up to date is most critical and that any new features be managed in a risk-averse fashion. For example, challenging features are often undertaken more than a season in advance so as not to risk the coming season's build.

Additionally, these teams usually have excellent test automation and defect control to manage debt.

## What Is Release Planning?

Chapter 3, "Scrum," describes releases as major goals that occur every several months, comparable to milestones or E3 or marketing demos in the level they are polished.

Planning a release is different from Sprint Planning. A release plan has more flexibility as features emerge from the Sprints.

Releases begin with a planning meeting that establishes major goals, a set of forecasted Sprint Goals, and a completion date. A release makes progress through a series of Sprints. As each Sprint implements Product Backlog Items (PBIs) and the game emerges, the release plan is updated. The release date can change as well.

### Forecasting Versus Estimating

We often use the word *forecast* instead of *estimate* with release planning, because the word implies that it's a prediction of something uncertain. A weatherperson forecasts the weather for this reason. You never hear them "estimate tomorrow's weather."

## Release Planning Meetings

A release planning meeting uses the steps shown in Figure 9.1.

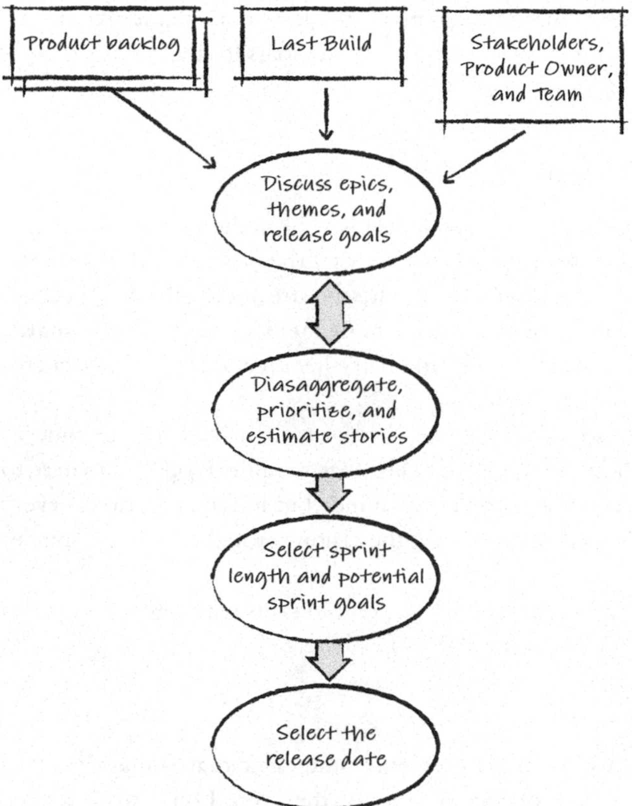


**Figure 9.1** *The flow of a release planning meeting*

The Product Owner, stakeholders, team members, and domain experts attend the meeting. It begins with a review of the progress made in the last release and the Product Backlog. The group then deliberates on the major goals for the release. These goals, often referred to as **big hairy audacious goals** (BHAGs), represent a challenge for the entire team and establish a vision to aid prioritization. For example, a BHAG to "fight other players online" might raise the priority of spikes to demonstrate that the animation system works in an online setting.

**Tip**

A release planning meeting can take most of a day. Finding a location with minimum disruptions is useful. A conference room at a local hotel is a good option.

After BHAGs for the release are agreed upon, stories needed to implement them are identified, ordered, and estimated using techniques described in the upcoming sections. The group uses the estimations and priorities, based on the progress teams have demonstrated in past Sprints, to lay out the Sprint Goals for the release. This is called the **release plan**.

## Chartering a Shared Vision

Having a shared vision among all game developers is vital to the success of a game. Too many times developers on big games complain that they "don't know how their part will fit into the whole" or that they don't honestly care about the game because they've only seen some high-level marketing plan. Game developers need a shared vision that will engage them meaningfully and help them make better daily micro-decisions, which determine a game's quality.

Because Agile games "respond to change," this vision will drift over time as features change based on how they emerge. This drift requires Product Owners to continually refresh this vision, not only in their minds but in the thoughts of every developer. A release cycle is ideal for revisiting the vision through the establishment of BHAGs.

Many useful practices have been established for doing this with a team regularly, often referred to as *chartering a vision*. I'll list a few here.[1]

### *Elevator Statement*

The elevator statement is a one- or two-sentence statement that summarizes the game for a high-level stakeholder or any member of the team. I once worked on a

1. I've found a useful source of these practices in the book *Innovation Games* by Luke Hohmann.

game that had the elevator statement, "Halo meets GTA3, where street gangs are the heroes battling an alien invasion." It created an image in the minds of every developer and sparked conversation and excitement around that vision.

### *Game Box*

Every three releases we would mock up a Blu-ray box with some concept art of what the release version of the game would look like.[2] The epic goals for the release, written in user story form, sound like the marketing bullet points on the back of the box:

- Execute amazing tricks jumping your skateboard over large objects.
- Skateboard on places you're not allowed to go, like the Hoover Dam.
- Meet your friends online and invent contests.

Combined with concept art, a game box communicates a vision and promotes an ongoing conversation about how to get there.

### *Game Positioning Map*

A game positioning map is a one- or two-dimensional map that positions games similar to yours on a chart whose dimensions are significant market segments. This is a standard marketing tool that game developers should use more. Figure 9.2 shows a simple example of a positioning map for a racing game based on the dimensions of the physics realism (sim versus arcade) and the realism of the environments (real versus fantasy).

We would create this map in a release planning meeting from scratch and populate the map with suggestions from the team about existing games, past and present. As we would fill the map, we would get more debate about the meaning of the dimensions. For example, while *Mario Kart* is more "arcadey" than other games, its wheel friction might be quite realistic. Discussing this subject with the physics programmer is beneficial.

However, the real debate begins when we ask, "Where does our game belong?" It also raises questions about our assumptions. For example, if we are making an arcade game with fantasy worlds, we might see the market flooded with such titles, but there are fewer games in the "sim in a fantasy world" area, which might identify a market opportunity.

2. Online games can mock up a website.

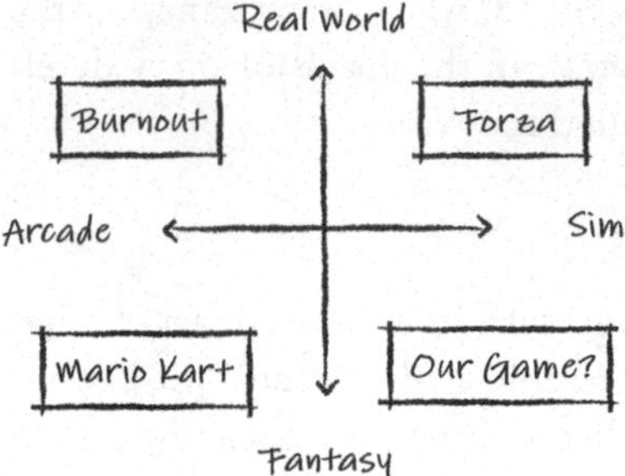


**Figure 9.2** *Game positioning map*

### *Other Approaches*

Various approaches to chartering a vision to explore include the following:

- Mock magazine reviews
- MVP canvases
- Product presentations (Steve Jobs style)

The benefit of creating a shared vision results mostly from the discussion among developers and stakeholders. These aren't "design by committee" meetings, and not everyone will agree with the decisions made, but it's an opportunity to create a shared understanding of why these decisions are made.

## Estimating Feature Size

As discussed in Chapter 7, "The Product Backlog," ordering features on the Product Backlog depends on their individual value and cost. Predicting the cost of a feature is a bit tricky because it can have a feature that has never been worked on before, and it depends on who is doing the work. This section explores techniques for such estimations.

### Velocity

Most estimation techniques used by Agile teams use an approach different from traditional project management. Instead of estimating the time it takes to implement work that leads to features, Agile teams estimate the size of features relative to one another and forecast the time they will take by using the average size of features implemented in past Sprints. This average is often referred to as a team's **velocity**.

We're all used to using velocity outside of work. To measure the velocity of anything (a car driving or a ship sailing), we measure the size of something changing over the passage of time (such as miles driven per hour or nautical miles per day). Similarly, for measuring velocity on an Agile project, we use the size of stories completed per Sprint.

Measuring the size of features has been a product management challenge for decades. Project managers have tried measures such as "lines of code," which turned out to have very little to do with the actual progress made on the project.[3] The Agile approach, instead, is to measure completed features, which have value to a user.

This section describes proven methods for estimating user story sizes to be used for measuring velocity.

**Note**

Because most of the published material uses the phrase *story points* instead of *PBI points*, this chapter will refer to PBIs as *user stories* or simply *stories* as described in the previous chapter.

## How Much Effort Should We Spend Estimating?

How much time should we spend estimating stories? We could spend anywhere from a few minutes to a few hours. In a few minutes, we could discuss a broad outline and come up with a guess. In a few hours, we could break a story down into the detailed tasks required to implement it.

We want to spend our planning time wisely. One assumption of planning is that the more time we spend planning, the more accurate our plan becomes. This is, in fact, not true. Figure 9.3 shows that beyond a certain amount of effort, our accuracy decreases (Cohn, 2006).

Planning provides an initial spike of accuracy with little effort spent. As more effort is spent, the accuracy of estimates actually starts to decline! This is surprising at first glance, but it makes sense. Say we spend an entire day estimating a single story. Given this time, we would eventually create very detailed tasks. These define work creating classes and functions, creating art assets, and tuning variables. As it turns out, this level of detail is too speculative. By the time we start defining functions and variables, chances are we are defining things that won't be needed or will be changed during implementation.

3. In fact, it only led to more lines of code.

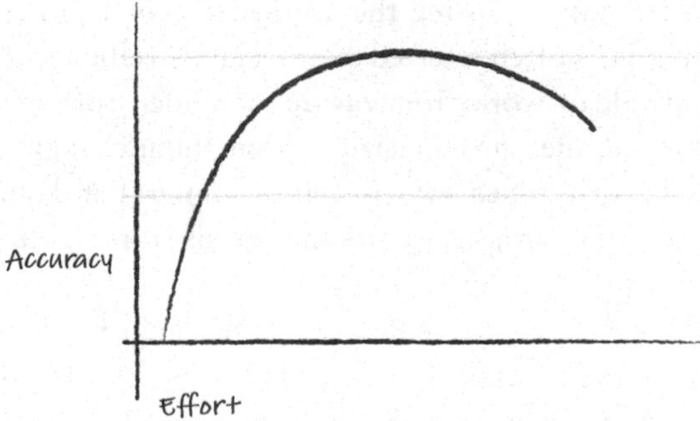


**Figure 9.3** *Accuracy versus effort for estimating*

*Source:* Cohn, M. 2006. *Agile Estimating and Planning*. Upper Saddle River, NJ: Prentice Hall.

> **Rule**
>
> It's better to be "roughly right" than "precisely wrong." Your range of accuracy cannot exceed your range of certainty.

The purpose of story estimation is meant to be efficient and to occupy the left side of the curve in Figure 9.3. It's a quick, low-effort estimating practice that provides accuracy valuable enough for forecasting but not enough for a team to commit to the work.

## Where Are Story Sizes Estimated?

Chapter 8, "User Stories," described a story workshop where a hand-to-hand combat system was debated. The debate included not only my technical perspective and experience but also those of the animators and the lead designer. As a result, we had good cross-discipline agreement about the story before we estimated the work.

This is a benefit of story workshops. When teams estimate the size of stories, it drives the discussion of vision, design assumptions, and challenges of implementation. As a colleague once remarked, "It helps remove the fuzziness and hand-waving when you have to come up with a number."

These cross-discipline discussions refine a team's understanding of what they are trying to achieve. An estimate for a story needs to reflect this cross-discipline understanding and produce a value that everyone agrees with, regardless of the skills required to implement it. Creating a universal scale for all stories is challenging. For example, a story about a procedural physics effect and a story about animating a character are difficult to directly compare. However, over time, as a team builds a repository of estimated stories and the experience of implementing them, finding comparable stories becomes easier.

Estimating stories should be a quick process that involves the following:

- **Expert opinion:** Inviting domain experts to story workshops helps inform the group about the issues and effort of implementing something the expert is familiar with. For example, if a story includes an online component, a network programmer would provide value to the discussion about it.
- **Analogy:** Analogy is used to estimate story size. When stories are compared to each other, a far more accurate estimate can be achieved than estimating stories on their own. Using triangulation, a story is compared to one larger in complexity or size and one smaller to produce the best results. A story that requires significant specialization, such as a weapon creation story, is best compared to other weapon creation stories to provide the best results.
- **Splitting:** Large stories are more difficult to accurately estimate than smaller ones, so often these stories are split into smaller ones, which are more accurately estimated. However, stories shouldn't be broken down into a pile of tiny ones because a false sense of detail emerges, as described previously.

## Story Points

Stories are often estimated using **story points**, which are a relative measure of a feature's size or complexity. For example, modeling two vehicles is estimated at twice the points of modeling one vehicle and possibly the same as modeling a character. This relative measure of story points allows for a more accurate measure of size, as explained later in this chapter.

### Note

Although points are not durations, keeping durations out of your mind when estimating points can be impossible. For example, I mountain bike a lot, but I take downhill sections slowly. I occasionally ride with Shonny Vanlandingham, a former U.S. mountain biking champion and neighbor. She "bombs down" the rockiest sections at twice my speed. While I might estimate two different downhill sections to myself in time and say the first will take 20 minutes and the second 40 minutes, my friend would argue that the first should be 10 minutes and the second 20. We would never agree on the times between us, but we would agree that one was half the "size" of the other. As long as we keep our personal time estimates to ourselves, we can work toward an agreement.

A story point estimate is not a commitment to when a story will be completed. There are two reasons for this. First, a story point estimate takes only a few minutes. A team's commitment to completing a story requires a more precise and time-consuming estimation process. This happens when the team breaks a story down into individual tasks in Sprint Planning. Second, different teams have different velocities. For example, one team might implement a 10-point story twice as fast as another team based on their membership and experience.

**Note**

Story point estimation is a bit like estimating the price of a car to within $5,000 to $10,000. I don't need to know the exact price of a *Porsche* to know that I can't afford one, but if I know that the small truck that can carry my surfboard is around $20,000, I'll go to the lot to learn more.

### *Planning Poker*

A favorite technique for estimating stories is the Planning Poker game (Grenning, 2002). Planning Poker combines expert opinion, disaggregation, and analogy in a fun and efficient practice. Planning Poker should be part of release planning meetings and story workshops. It should be used whenever new stories are introduced that need an estimate.

In Planning Poker, attendees discuss stories that have not yet been estimated. After a story is discussed, each person estimates the points they think should be assigned to the story by simultaneously raising a card with their estimate on it for all to see. The first vote often reveals a wide disparity of estimates. The group discusses the range, first by asking the outlying voters to describe the reasoning behind their estimate. This exposes the uncertainties and assumptions of the story. As a result, the vision, design, and implementation details are discussed and refined. These discussions often lead to adding acceptance criteria for a story or defining new stories that were not previously considered.

This practice is repeated until everyone produces the same estimate. If a couple of people have different but close estimates, they may concede to the group's estimated points and allow the meeting to move to the next story.

**Note**

Don't average the votes. The different point estimates often hide what needs to be discussed! Assigning an average doesn't solve potential problems with the story.

Estimating an entire release plan can take four to eight hours. Often teams won't tackle all stories for a release in one sitting. They split and estimate the highest-priority stories and then meet once a Sprint to estimate lower-priority or new stories for upcoming Sprints.

### *Story Point Sizes and the Fibonacci Series*

Story points provide a quick and relative estimate of size and complexity for a story. Alone they are not perfectly precise, but with a mass of stories, they average out well enough for planning.

Projects need to define a set of numbers that they use for story point estimates. The two rules of thumb for selecting a set of story points are that the entire scale be within two orders of magnitude. For example, a range of 1 to 100 or a range of 1,000 to 100,000 works. Second, the numbers used should be closely spaced out at the small end and widely spaced out at the high end of the scale. The reason is that our ability to judge the difference between stories with sizes of 20 and 21 points, for example, is not the same as our ability to tell the difference between two stories with sizes of 1 and 2 points.

A useful set of story points that follows these two rules is derived from the Fibonacci numbers. In a sequence of Fibonacci numbers, each number is the sum of the two preceding numbers. An example set of Fibonacci numbers useful for story point estimation follows:

0, 1, 2, 3, 5, 8, 13, 20, 40, 100

The numbers at the high and low ends of the set depart from the Fibonacci sequence. We use zero-point estimates for trivial stories that require very little effort, such as changing a user interface (UI) font color.[4] The upper range of these numbers departs from the Fibonacci series rule, but they exist to allow a couple of rounded-out values in the high range.

**Tip**

If Planning Poker encounters a story whose estimate exceeds the highest point value, splitting that story into smaller stories before estimating each is best.

The team members should constrain themselves to use only numbers within the set and not use values between them to create averages or compromises. This creates a false sense of precision with story point estimation and slows down a Planning Poker session!

4. Be careful not to accumulate too many zero-point stories...zeros add up with this math!

**Story Point Limits**

Story point velocity is like the odometer in a car. For a long trip, an odometer is not very accurate on an hour-to-hour basis. One hour you might stop for lunch and cover very little distance. Another hour, you might be on a rural highway and cover a great deal of distance. However, an odometer can be very useful looking at a daily average and it lets you refine your plan for arriving at your destination. The same goes for story points. They're never too accurate when looked at closely, but when used for release planning, they average out pretty well as a forecasting tool.

### *Ideal Days*

The concept of story points is difficult to introduce. Teams accustomed to time estimates often find story points too abstract and instead use ideal days as a benchmark to begin estimating. An ideal day is the measure of work accomplished in a single day with no interruptions (phone calls, questions, broken builds, and so on). Because of this association with something real, the team more readily embraces ideal days.

Ideal days are still a measure of size alone. A story estimated to be one ideal day in size doesn't mean it takes one day of actual work to complete. We want to avoid any translation of ideal days to actual days of effort. Ideal days, like story points, are valuable measures for quick relative forecasts of effort but not precise enough to use for making commitments.

### *Abusing Story Points*

Used in the way they were originally intended, story points work well. During the British rule of India, officials were concerned about the number of cobras in Delhi so they offered a bounty for each dead cobra brought to them. Instead of reducing the number of cobras, the bounty incentivized people to breed them for the income.

I often see the cobra effect with story points. When they are used to drive team commitments, instead of being used to measure and forecast, they incentivize teams to inflate story point estimates to look good.

Unfortunately, because of management pressures or inertia to demand more predictability and certainty where none exist, many studios end up abusing story points, as discussed next.

#### *Converting Points to Time Estimates*

Story point estimation is a quick way to get a forecast of a release plan and of future print goals. However, a five-minute Planning Poker discussion will not give a precise estimation of the effort. Unfortunately, some studios see story points as a cheap and precise way to estimate. Teams end up being told "how many points of scope" they need to accomplish every Sprint because someone applied an hours-per-point formula. It's always wrong.

*Teams Using Large Point-Sized Stories to Commit to a Sprint*

Similarly, teams commit to a Sprint Goal using the sum total of stories with large point sizes. As mentioned earlier, large point-sized stories are simply not precise enough for accurate forecasting.

I've seen teams successfully commit to a set of very small-sized (one- or two-point) stories, due to the detailed conversations that occur while splitting large stories into smaller ones.

### Advantages and Disadvantages of Velocity

An advantage of measuring velocity is to measure the effectiveness of change. Positive changes to practices improve velocity. For example, teams that collocate often see up to a 20 percent improvement in velocity. This is mainly because of the enhancement of communication within the team. Most changes create smaller increases in velocity, but their impact accumulates and compounds over time. Without measuring velocity, many small changes might be overlooked. Quoting Peter Drucker, "You can't manage what you can't measure."

Unfortunately, experience has shown velocity being "weaponized" and used against teams in ways they weren't intended:

- **Used to compare teams:** Teams are composed of different individuals with different skills and experience, usually working on different things. Comparing their velocity makes no sense.
- **Used to commit teams to future work:** An example is when teams are assigned the number of story points to complete every Sprint. Velocity is an output that can be useful to forecast the future, but story point estimation is never precise enough (see the earlier odometer analogy) to predict the future.

When velocity is used as an input, then the team often adjusts for the uncertainty that emerges by varying the quality they deliver. Some have suggested using a different word, such as "capacity" to avoid these disadvantages, but it's a cultural issue, not one of vocabulary.

## Alternatives to Story Points

Teams have explored a number of alternatives to story points that have worked for them.

### *T-Shirt Sizing*

T-shirt sizing requires a team to size items on the Backlog by using the "small," "medium," or "large" tag. Teams will start by rank ordering (discussed next) stories from the top of the Backlog and then divide the list into three size buckets. Once sized, teams will be able to forecast initial Sprint Goals by pulling in a certain number of t-shirt sized items. Although t-shirt sizing doesn't rely on point sizes, teams will often create a point conversion (for example, small equals one point, medium equals two points, and large equals four points).

Variations include the following:

- Teams also use outlier sizes XL, XXL, XS to expand the range of sizes.
- Teams will split any story bigger than a "medium" into "small" or "medium" stories before pulling them into Sprint Planning.

### *Rank Ordering/Sizing*

Rank ordering is a visual mapping practice that focuses on the relative amount of effort features or assets will take to get into the game, compared with other, similar assets or features. Identifying their point size comes at the end. Here is how to do it:

1. Features are written on cards (one per card) and are spread out in random order in front of the group so that they can be easily read as others are being written.
2. The cards are then collected into a deck.
3. A card is drawn from the top and placed in the middle of a space (table or wall).
4. One at a time, each member takes a feature card from the stack and places it, based on the effort needed to implement that feature relative to the other cards. **Example:** If feature A is easier to implement than feature B, it is placed to the left. If harder, it is place to the right, and if the same, it is placed above or below B.

   Instead of placing a card, a member can swap two existing cards if they disagree with how they were previously placed.

With every action, a team member will explain their reasoning to the rest of the team.

5. The team then returns to step 4 until the deck is emptied.
6. The ranked list can then be divided into story point buckets or t-shirt sizes.

**#NoEstimates**

In 2012, Woody Zuill started a conversation on Twitter about the alternatives to conventional estimation techniques using the provocative hashtag #NoEstimates. This led to a useful and heated debate about the usefulness and abuse of estimating things that have an element of uncertainty. There was even a book published on the topic.[5]

While I don't believe that all estimation is bad, I've certainly seen many cases where the desire for certainty, where little or none exists, has led to very speculative and detailed estimates that somehow get transformed into solid do-or-die deadlines. When this occurs, we often see quality of the game and the life of the developer negatively impacted due to the pressures of hitting an arbitrary deadline.

Although the discussion continues to this day, the bottom line is that a continual conversation about the usefulness and the time teams spend creating estimates is a valuable part of continually improving how we spend our time.

5. *NoEstimates: How to Measure Project Progress Without Estimating* by Vasco Duarte

## Release Planning with Story Points

The release plan identifies potential Sprint Goals for the release. With a history of what has accomplished in the past, teams can forecast those goals using a Product Backlog that has been sized with story points.

Figure 9.4 shows a release plan based on a historical velocity of 15 story points per Sprint. The goals for Sprints 1 through 3 each contain stories that add up to 15 points. The stories for the more distant Sprints in the release are lumped together. In this example, the Product Owner has called for six Sprints in the release because the release plan and projected velocity tells him that this is how many Sprints are needed (for example, 89 points at 15 points of velocity every Sprint tells him the need for six Sprints).[6]

6. We always round up.

| Story | Points | Sprint |
|---|---|---|
| As a player... | 5 | Sprint 1 |
| As a player... | 5 | |
| As a player... | 5 | |
| As a player... | 10 | Sprint 2 |
| As a designer... | 5 | |
| As a player... | 6 | Sprint 3 |
| As a player... | 3 | |
| As a player... | 6 | |
| As an animator... | 7 | Sprints 4-6 |
| As a player... | 5 | |
| As a player... | 8 | |
| As a player... | 4 | |
| As a player... | 9 | |
| As a player... | 5 | |
| As a player... | 6 | |

**Figure 9.4** *Splitting the release plan across future Sprints*

As Sprints are finished, the goals and stories for the subsequent Sprints are refined. For example, after Sprint 1 is completed, the goal for Sprint 4 is identified.

It's important to understand that the Sprint Goals identified in the meeting are a forecast of work that can potentially be accomplished by the team; they're not a commitment. They are useful benchmarks for measuring progress.

## Why Not Create a Release Backlog?

People often refer to a release backlog instead of a release plan. It's best not to create a different backlog for the release. The release plan is a subset of the Product Backlog that changes during the release. Having separate backlogs creates a lot of extra work and confusion over what backlog we are talking about.

## Updating the Release Plan

Following each Sprint review, the release plan is reexamined. Sometimes the Sprint has identified new stories to be added. These are stories that were either overlooked or not anticipated in release planning. Other times, stories are removed. These stories are considered unnecessary, or their priority was reduced enough to push them into a future release. As with the Product Backlog, the Product Owner makes the final decision on the addition, deletion, or reprioritization of any story in the release plan.

The release plan may also need refinement based on the team's actual velocity. Figure 9.5 shows an example of an original release plan on the left, which forecasted 16 user story points of velocity per Sprint. However, the first Sprint accomplished only 13. As a result, the Product Owner updated the new release plan—shown on the right—which dropped the last two (lowest-priority) stories.

The Product Owner also had the option of adding another Sprint to the release if he didn't want to drop those stories.

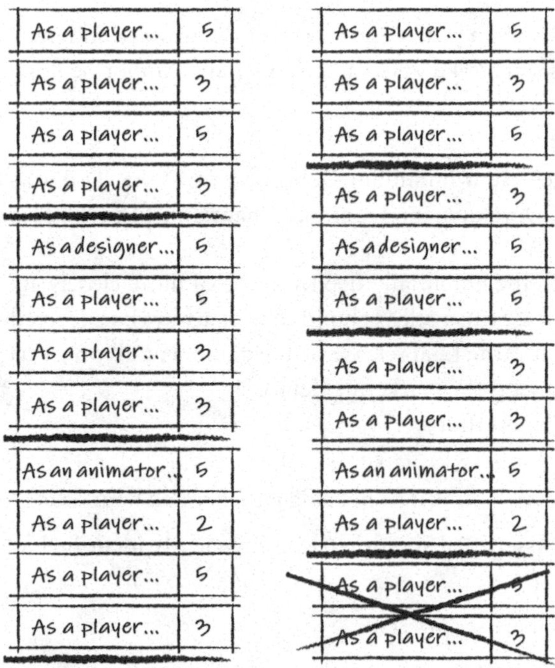


**Figure 9.5** *Updating the release plan based on velocity*

**Note**

In practice, the release plan isn't dependent on the results of a single Sprint. The velocity used to forecast the Sprint Goals for the release is usually based on the average velocity of the past several Sprints.

## Marketing Demos and Hardening Sprints

Scrum describes Sprints as delivering a potentially deployable version of a product at the end of every Sprint. This allows the Product Owner to decide to ship the product on short notice. This is a challenging goal for many games that are deploying for three reasons:

- Slacking off on addressing debt is easy to do when you are months or years away from deploying the game.
- Many features and assets require a number of Sprints to implement (for example, production levels).
- To be deployable, games must often pass rigorous tests for hardware and first-party compliance. These tests can take weeks to conduct and cannot be done every Sprint.

Nevertheless, Sprints should achieve a minimum Definition of Done (DoD) as defined by the Product Owner and Development Team (see Chapter 7, "The Product Backlog").

A release build should approach the potentially deployable goal more closely. Its DoD should be higher than a Sprint's. Still, a release build cannot always be expected to pass all shipping criteria unless it is the final release of the game. For all previous releases, a good example of a DoD set is the marketing demo.

A marketing demo has certain expectations:

- It has no major memory leaks preventing it from being played for an hour or two.
- There are no major missing assets. All stand-in assets are clearly identified as such.
- The game has a clean and usable user interface.
- The player has a clear objective and experiences the fun of the game.

These are typical requirements for a demo version of a game in any publication, so they are easy to communicate.

As a result of the different completion bars for releases and Sprints, release builds require additional testing beyond what is tested for every Sprint. If this testing identifies issues with the game that aren't found in Sprint testing, the additional work created to address them creates the need for a special Sprint at the end of the release called a **Hardening Sprint**.

Work for the Hardening Sprint is derived from the difference between the Definition of Done for Sprint builds and release builds. If the Definition of Done is the same for both, there should be no reason for a Hardening Sprint.

**Note**

The need for a Hardening Sprint is often driven by testing practices considered too time-consuming to be done every Sprint. For example, testing a marketing demo requires many hours of "burn-in" testing to ensure that there are no significant memory leaks.

Hardening Sprints are often run using a list of bugs and polishing tasks that need to be worked on. They are not used to complete stories from the Product Backlog (see the sidebar "Hardening Sprint Example").

**Hardening Sprint Example**

At High Moon Studios, we created simple practices for planning and managing the work for a Hardening Sprint.

A Hardening Sprint was shorter than our typical three-week Sprint; it was usually one week long. The Sprint Planning session started with a simple triage. The Sprint Backlog emerged from a play-through of the game during the meeting with the team, stakeholders, and Product Owner in attendance. During the play-through, anyone in the room could identify a potential fix for the Sprint. If the Product Owner agreed with the value of the fix, it was written down on a whiteboard.

Following the review, the Product Owner roughly prioritized the bugs. This consisted of labeling each bug with an *A*, *B*, or *C*. The A bugs were the most important to fix, the B bugs were medium priority, and the C bugs were not considered very important to fix. This prioritization raised much discussion; some A bugs were considered too challenging to fix in a single week and were demoted, while some C bugs were judged trivial to fix and were promoted.

The team then identified and estimated the tasks to fix all the A bugs and as many of the B bugs as they could within the coming week.

Unlike normal Sprints, changes to the Hardening Sprint priorities were allowed. It was important for the Product Owner to be involved in evaluating the daily build during the Hardening Sprint. Sometimes new bugs caused the Product Owner to change the items or priorities of the bug list. As a result, teams weren't able to commit to a fixed set of tasks.

Not all fixes on the list were completed in the Hardening Sprint, but the prioritization helped the team accomplish work in the best order. For us, the Hardening Sprint was more like a series of one-day Sprints to improve the game.

## What Good Looks Like

How teams plan and execute releases varies considerably, but consistent patterns are common to them all:

- The entire team participates in the breakdown of epic stories into a release plan's forecast continually throughout the release.
- The release plan is fine-tuned as the game emerges with the stakeholders participating in the refinement of the release plan.
- Story points and other story sizing practices are used only as a rough forecasting tool, not for forcing progress. Successful teams and stakeholders know the limit of estimating uncertain work and respond to the emerging reality by adjusting the plan and not blaming the team.

## Summary

Agile teams plan in ways that allow iteration, transparency, and change. They adjust planning to match reality rather than trying to make reality match a plan.

Stories, measured in relative size, allow the measurement of work accomplished per Sprint, which is the velocity. Velocity is used to examine the rate of development and forecast future progress. Measuring velocity early and frequently allows the project to be steered when many options are available to it.

Release cycles allow major goals to be achieved over a longer time frame. Because of the longer time frame, releases have flexibility in planning that does not exist with Sprints. Release plans can be altered in duration or in scope. Releases also demand a more refined Definition of Done to bring an almost deployable level of polish, stability, and tuning to the game, rather than postponing it to near the end of the project.

For many projects, this is enough. The release cycle is sufficient to release versions of the product to players on a regular basis. Many video game projects don't have this luxury. They have pre-production and production phases that have a different focus and challenges. The next chapter describes these phases and how Scrum, Agile planning, and Lean practices can be combined for planning over the entire development life cycle.

## Additional Reading

Bockman, Steve. 2015. *Practical Estimation: A Pocket Guide to Making Dependable Project Schedules*.

Cohn, Mike. 2006. *Agile Estimating and Planning*. Upper Saddle River, NJ: Prentice Hall.

Duarte, Vasco, 2016. *NoEstimates: How to Measure Project Progress Without Estimating*. OikosofySeries.

Hohmann L. *Innovation games: creating breakthrough products through collaborative play*. 2007. Boston, MA: Addison-Wesley.

# Chapter 10

# Video Game Project Management

In Chapter 2, "Agile and Lean Development," a major challenge identified with adopting Agile for game development was matching phase-less Agile practices with the needs of game development stages, such as pre-production and production.

A typical Scrum project is always kept in a near-deployable state. The reason for this is that the work traditionally separated across multiple phases (design, coding, testing, optimization) is part of every Sprint. By doing this, Agile projects keep the debt of typically late project work, such as fixing bugs, to a minimum.

Agile game development follows the same model of combining all phases into each Sprint. However, game project stages create a different form of debt, or necessary work that must be accomplished, such as content production, which requires some new practices to be introduced over the course of the project.

This chapter addresses the needs for stages and the challenges they create. It focuses on production—the most expensive stage that derails many Scrum teams. By introducing Lean practices, Scrum teams manage complex asset production pipelines while maintaining the benefits over traditional preplanned methods.

## Midnight Club Story

Of the score of games that I have worked on, only a few have shipped on time and within budget. Of these, *Midnight Club* was the most successful. *Midnight Club* was a PlayStation 2 (PS2) launch title where players illegally race in the large, open cities of London and New York. The project was a grueling 18-month struggle with a new platform and new publisher.

Our launch title was originally designed to include six cities. We considered two major risks to delivering a good game in time for the launch of the console. First was the uncertainty of developing for the PS2. The PS2 was powered by a custom CPU referred to as "the Emotion Engine," marketed as a supercomputer on a chip. The hype of the machine's power was so great that when it was revealed that Saddam Hussein had ordered 4,000 units, it was theorized he was going to use them to design nuclear weapons.[1]

Working with the early development kits, we knew this wasn't true. The only emotion we experienced was continual frustration with the weaknesses of the kits and the poor state of the support libraries and their documentation.

Second, we were uncertain about the effort to produce six large cities in the time we had before launch.

We focused pre-production on creating one city that would run well on the PS2. This effort took four times longer than we anticipated. Armed with this knowledge, we were forced to scale our plans down to three cities. Our publisher, Rockstar Games, took these cuts in stride. It knew how hard we were working.

During production, we slowly realized that we had a crucial decision to make. The time to create the necessary polish for deployable cities was taking even longer than we had planned. We had to choose between shipping three low-quality cities or two polished ones. After much teeth gnashing, Rockstar Games decided to ship with two cities.

In the end, it was the best decision and contributed to the game's shipping as a PS2 launch title that sold millions of copies. A major reason for maintaining the schedule was the constant attention to the production costs of creating and polishing the cities. For many game projects—especially those with fixed ship dates—the production costs and schedule pressures create the greatest risks.

## The Solutions in This Chapter

This chapter explores the challenges of managing a game project using Agile and Lean principles to

- Manage fixed ship dates
- Manage risk
- Manage project constraints such as cost, schedule, and scope
- Refine content production debt

1. https://www.eurogamer.net/articles/article_29913

- Choose when and how to employ Kanban practices for content production
- Optimize and improve the flow of content production work using Lean principles

**Definition: Project**

The Project Management Institute's PMBOK (PMI, 2013) defines a project as "a temporary endeavor undertaken to create a unique product or service."

Because they are temporary, projects have a beginning and ending, which leads to constraints such as cost, schedule, and scope. A decade ago, most game development efforts were just projects. After they shipped, apart from some ongoing support, teams transitioned to the next game project.

Now, due to mobile and digital marketplaces, many games continue to grow beyond their first deployment. The practices used for the fixed constraints of projects change.

This chapter focuses on the practices of project management. Chapter 22, "Live Game Development," focuses on the methods of continued development of live games after their initial launch.

## Minimum Viable Game

Many projects outside the game industry are challenged with an obligation of delivering on certain expectations from the start. For example, a word processor would have to have undo, printing, font management, and so on. The feature and content set might require a year or more of effort before a minimum viable game (MVG) or the smallest possible set of features, content, and constraints required for a successful launch, are met.

Example MVG requirements are

- Gameplay content (levels, characters, and so on)
- Fixed ship dates such as holidays or movie co-release dates
- Minimum required feature sets—such as online multiplayer for a first-person shooter—that must be shipped with the game

These requirements demand budget and staff planning. For example, content production costs are refined over the course of pre-production releases to identify the number of content creators and the time needed to produce a minimum amount of gameplay time.

Minimum required feature sets necessitate similar long-term plans. For the first-person shooter example, the following is a minimum required feature set:

- Single-player gameplay
- AI
- Weapons
- Online multiplayer gameplay

These features create a debt of work, much like the content production debt, that takes multiple releases to deliver. Often, stakeholders demand that resource management plans be developed to support a predicted ship date for these features.

**"Resources"**

I always cringe a bit when I hear individuals called "resources." It sounds like we're talking about oil or bauxite. It reflects the old approach of **scientific management**, established more than 100 years ago with the emergence of the assembly line, which introduced the idea that product development could be made more efficient if factory workers were considered low-cost interchangeable parts of a machine. Despite the fact that the philosophy has been disproven, we still say *resources*. I use the word here to refer to the cost of development and the range of disciplines needed, and not individuals.

How does resource management planning work with Agile planning? A proven approach is to identify a range of resource needs to implement epic-level stories and continually refine both through Sprints and releases.

This is a balancing act of cost and value. Imagine you are buying yourself a new PC, but you have only $2,000 to spend, and not a cent more. You would start with a breakdown of the parts of the PC and the cost of each:

| Component | Cost |
|---|---|
| CPU, motherboard, and memory | $800 |
| Graphics card | $500 |
| Monitor | $400 |
| Case, mouse, and keyboard | $200 |
| Hard drive | $100 |

You might decide later to buy the latest graphics card that costs $100 more. This money has to come from another part of the computer. This is how long-term planning works with epics. Large epics are defined and thought about to produce a cost of time and resources. If any budget item is wrong, the time has to come from another bucket. That needs to be a deliberate and visible decision and needs to be publicly proclaimed.

For each item, the first estimate might be largely based on experience with previous games, which is not very accurate. For the first-person shooter example, a Product Owner identifies the large online multiplayer epics that a team of eight might complete in six to eight months. Some of these epics are not split until more is known. For example, cooperative online gameplay with AI may or may not be valuable or even possible within this resource plan until more is known, so the epic that might contain that feature is not split until more is known and a team is available to work on it.

This provides the flexibility necessary as more is discovered about the challenges, velocity, and opportunities for online as the game emerges. It does not ensure that every minimum required feature will be completed within budget and schedule—no planning process does that—but it enables decisions to be made earlier that help steer the project in the right direction.

## Contracts

The typical game development contract has a series of defined milestones. Each milestone is associated with a specific date and features that need to be delivered on that date. If developers deliver those features on schedule, they are paid for the milestone. Milestone payments are the lifeblood for most independent developers; they will do almost anything to avoid missing a milestone. This includes avoiding change that would improve the game if it threatens the milestone with additional work. Who can blame them? Many developers who miss a milestone payment miss payroll; that is a very bad thing for them to do. The contract is an impediment to change.

On the other side, a publisher doesn't have the full freedom to add features or change the milestone definition when it thinks the game would benefit from the change. The contract impedes working with the developer to fix the game.

Fixed-milestone deliverables have led to an adversarial relationship between developers and publishers. Both recognize the need for change to improve the game but lack the necessary level of trust to allow the change to occur.

Collaboration between developer and publisher should be valued more than a fixed contract. However, very few publishers allow a developer to work without a detailed contract. Outside our industry, many contracts in an Agile environment follow the **time and materials** form, which is where the client pays for the cost of the last iteration. This style of contract requires greater trust between both parties. The client has to trust that the developer is spending money wisely. The developer has to trust that the client won't cancel the ongoing contract without good reason.

Although most Western publishers don't support this model, many have adopted flexible milestone definitions that allow some level of collaboration with developers every few months. As the use of Agile spreads, we will see more collaborative business arrangements as trust is built through greater collaboration.

## Hitting Fixed Ship Dates

There is an old project management saying: "Time, budget, scope—pick two," which is fundamentally flawed. Projects always balance variables such as these and they are not independent of one another.

For example, it's often assumed that we can throw more money at a game that's late or in trouble and solve its problems. In practice this means adding developers, which usually puts the game in even greater peril because the new developers need to be brought up to speed by the developers currently working on the game, delaying it further.

Most plans for a new video game have a ship date in mind. However, very few actually fail if they miss that date. They're mostly one of the main constraints that stakeholders put on teams to ensure they have a target to aim for. But some of the game teams I've worked with over the past decade do have critical ship dates. These are often sports titles that must be out for the start of a new season.

For these games, a disciplined Agile adoption has given them the best set of tools for hitting the fixed ship dates by

- Managing debt with a robust definition of done, automated testing, and solid technical practices
- Refining content production forecasts using tracer bullets while still in pre-production
- Managing scope in an ordered fashion to ensure delivering an MVG, while not risking the dates on non-essential scope
- Closely collaborating with the stakeholders on trade-offs

**Early Failure Can Be Good**

One of my first independent consulting engagements was with a AAA team that was starting a new console game project. I was shown a large room with a dozen developers and told of the plan to grow to more than 200 within the next few months. The goal of the project was to ship a game within 18 months based on an engine that hadn't been used for a shipped game yet.

It was clear that this project had no chance of hitting that ship date, but the project's director was convinced that applying Scrum would solve that problem. When asked, my advice was that Scrum, properly applied, would quickly provide the data that the schedule would be impossible to meet.

Within a single release they had shown this to be the case, and the stakeholders agreed to slow down the growth of the team and extend the targeted ship dates.

I've always found that revealing bad news early is far more welcome to stakeholders and far more humane to developers than revealing bad news late.

## Managing Risk

Game development probably has to handle more risk than any other product outside of the defense industry. We have rapidly evolving, cutting-edge technology and fixed ship dates for sports seasons, movie releases, or seasonal markets. The market's whims also change suddenly. As a result, many games don't meet expectations or developers are asked to work miracles. Many of these problems could be avoided if projects embrace risk instead of avoiding it and accept that, inevitably, things go wrong from time to time.

**My Worst Job**

My first job after I graduated college was with a small software consultancy firm. Many of the contracts we took on were fun to work on, such as installing new displays for the New York Stock Exchange trading floor or installing new gadgets in factories.

One contract we signed was a nightmare. It was to conduct Independent Validation and Verification of software that allowed the F-15 fighter to drop a nuclear bomb. The purpose was to help eliminate the risk that a bug would allow an armed nuclear weapon to be dropped where and when it shouldn't.

This wasn't easy software to test. It was written in assembly, which is very low-level code, and took up hundreds of pages when printed.

My job was to trace the flow of code using five colored pencils on the printout. The five colors were for places where the code might branch out. It was extremely boring work and eventually led to my quitting the job. Somehow, I didn't feel good about falling asleep and missing a critical bug in the code that controlled a nuclear weapon.

I found out years later when the testing was complete and the software was validated as safe that an F-15 pilot had pointed out that this "safe" software could not prevent a rogue pilot from "jettisoning" an armed nuclear weapon where he shouldn't via a mechanical lever. As a result, the weapon was immediately canceled.

This was one of many stories I heard and witnessed about our inability to eliminate risk in complex weapon systems. Although games are often more complex than nuclear weapon fire control systems, the failures in our products are far less "impactful."

## Incorporating Risk in the Product Backlog

It's quite easy for anyone who has shipped a game before to identify many potential risks. That's the easy part. The hard part is to incorporate risk management into your plan. Stakeholders often don't want to see unanswered questions in a Product Backlog, but we can't plan away uncertainty.

A better way to manage risk is to stand watch for it and have a plan in place to mitigate it if it rises up. An approach I've found successful is an adaptation from the book *Waltzing with bears: managing risk on software projects* (DeMarco, Lister, 2003).

The approach is to

1. Create a list of possible risks.
2. Prioritize the risks according to impact and probability (see the prioritization matrix practice in Chapter 7, "The Product Backlog").

3. Take the most impactful and likely risks and identify the following:
   The trigger date or condition (also called risk transition).
   Example: *If this critical middleware isn't ported to our game's hardware platform by October*
4. Create a mitigation strategy for each risk (including a plan and cost for eliminating the risk)
   Example: *Six engineers working for two months to port the middleware ourselves, starting in November*
5. Communicate this risk strategy plan widely with all the stakeholders
6. Revisit the plan on a regular basis (once every Sprint)

Approximately 20 percent of the risks we identified were realized. Although we weren't able to identify every problem we encountered, we did avoid many. Our stakeholders appreciated the proactive approach of not only identifying potential problems but also having plans in place to solve them ahead of time.

**Tip**

Applying the Diamond of Participatory Decision-Making from Chapter 19, "Coaching Teams for Greatness" is a good approach for building a list of risks. Identify a complete set first (refer to step 1) before prioritizing them (steps 2 and 3). After they are prioritized, then create a mitigation strategy (steps 4 and 5).

## The Need for Stages

For many games developed using Agile, a need still exists to separate some of the development activities. The three major reasons for this are

- **Publishers require concepts:** To gain publisher approval (which includes marketing and often franchise or license owner approval), developers need to create a detailed concept treatment at the start of a project. They are unable to stray too far from this vision throughout the project.
- **Games need to deliver eight-plus hours of gameplay:** Games typically deliver 8 to 12 hours of single-player gameplay. Games tell stories that need a great deal of production content to be created using mechanics discovered during pre-production.

- **There is one launch:** For many PC and console games, there is only one deployment date at the end of a 24+ month development cycle. Intensive hardware compliance testing by the first party platform owner is often delayed until the end.

**Live Games**

Massively multiplayer online games (MMOs), such as *World of Warcraft* or *Eve Online*, which regularly deliver expansion packs to existing customers, balance the pressures of schedule and scope to determine deployment dates on a release-by-release basis. Other games, such as iPhone or casual online games, have similar deployment cycles. After these games are live, their stages of development can be more easily streamlined (see Chapter 22).

## The Development Stages

Agile game projects spread activities such as concept, design, coding, asset creation, optimizing, and debugging more evenly throughout their life. This doesn't mean that the project is a homogenous string of Sprints.

Most game development projects have stages regardless of whether they are Agile or not. These stages change how teams develop the game:

- **Concept:** This stage occurs before pre-production. Concept development is almost purely iterative. Ideas are generated, possibly prototyped, and thrown away on a regular basis. This stage is usually timeboxed to deliver one or more concept development plans to a green-light approval process required by the publisher or a license holder.
- **Pre-production:** Teams explore what is fun and how they are going to build assets to support it during production. They also create levels and other assets that represent production quality. This stage is fully iterative and incremental. Teams iteratively discover what is fun and incrementally adapt development planning with this knowledge.
- **Production:** The team focuses on creating an 8- to 12-hour experience using the core mechanics and content production flow discovered during pre-production. This stage focuses on efficiency and incremental improvements. Teams iterate less on core mechanics discovered during pre-production because they are

building a great deal of assets based on them. Changing those mechanics during production is usually very wasteful and expensive. For example, consider a team in production on a platformer genre game. Platformer games challenge the player to develop skills to navigate treacherous environments (such as Nintendo's *Mario* series). The production team creates hundreds of assets that depend on character movement metrics such as "how high the character can jump" or "the minimum height that the player can crawl under." If these metrics are changed in the midst of production, it wreaks havoc. For example, if a designer changes the jump height of the character, hundreds of ledges or barriers would have to be retrofitted. This creates a great deal of wasted effort during the most expensive phase of development. Discovering and locking down such metrics during pre-production is critical.

- **Post-production:** With the content brought to deployable quality, the team focuses on polishing the whole 8- to 12-hour game experience. This stage improves the game incrementally. Following this, the game is submitted to hardware testing. Although much of this testing is spread throughout the entire project, some of it cannot be. For example, Microsoft and Sony hardware testing is expensive and only occurs in the months prior to shipping the game.

## Mixing the Stages

Stages aren't isolated to distinct periods of time. For example, although a great deal of concept work is done up front, concept development needs to be refined as the game emerges over the entire project.

Figure 10.1 shows a typical distribution of efforts on an Agile game project. Note that although more design and concept is done up front and more tuning, debugging, and optimization are done at the end, many overlap with one another. For example, rather than an official "production start date," teams see a gradual buildup of production activities and a drop-off of pre-production work in the middle of the project.

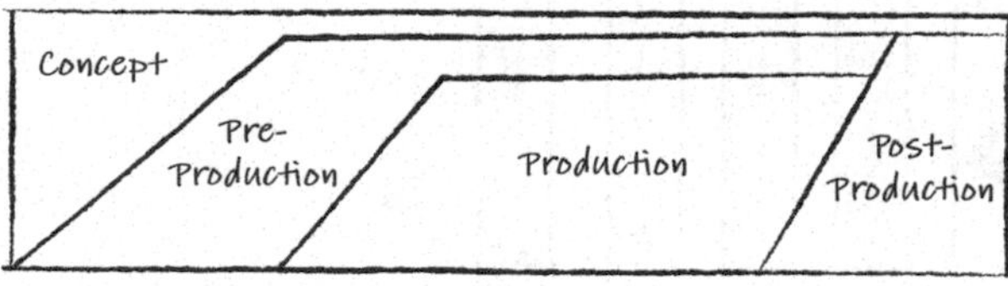


**Figure 10.1** *Overlapping stages*

## Managing Stages with Releases

Releases are a series of Sprints linked together to deliver major features and assets. Similarly, a game project is a series of releases that deliver a finished game to the consumer. Figure 10.2 shows a typical series of two- to three-month releases that make up a two-year project.

> **Stages With Live Games**
>
> Instead of stages split across releases, live games will have stages split across weeks or even days. Chapter 22 explores this topic in detail.

Each of these stages requires a different emphasis on the practices used. The transition between stages such as pre-production and production can be gradual with various asset types transitioning at different times.

The reasons for the change in practices are illustrated by an enhanced version of the Stacey diagram shown in Figure 10.3. As the game progresses from concept to post-production, the level of technical and requirements uncertainty drops. As the Stacey diagram indicates, the practices should reflect these levels of uncertainty.

The framework used is still Scrum, but teams adjust the practices for the current stage:

- **Concept:** Sprints are shorter, and most of the stories in the very small backlog are spikes. The main goal of the conceptual stage is to create knowledge for the team and stakeholders, not shippable value for the players. Release goals are concept treatments and perhaps a prototype to demonstrate to stakeholders.
- **Pre-production:** Scrum is used to discover the fun of the game and incrementally and iteratively build value and knowledge about production costs. Development is paced by Sprints and releases. Release goals are major features.

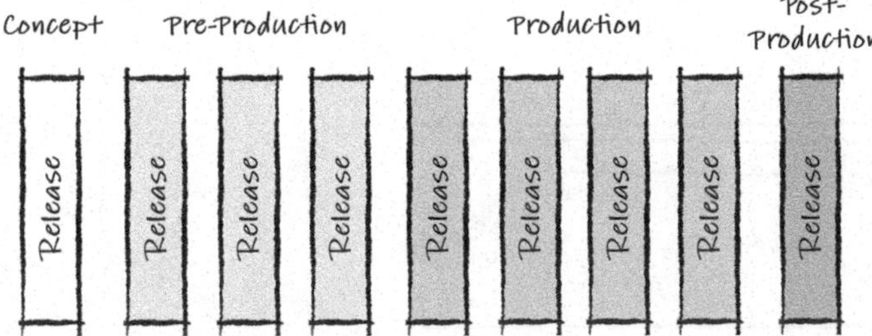


**Figure 10.2** *Releases in a multiyear project*

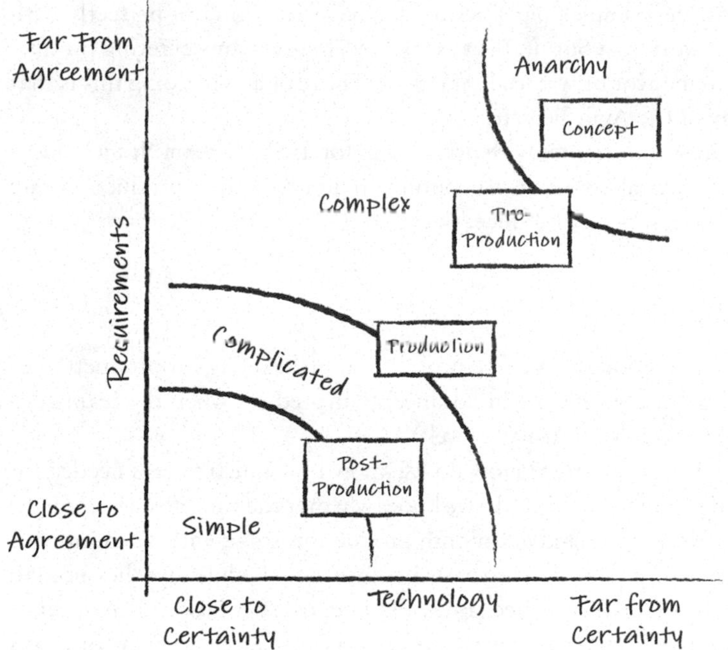


**Figure 10.3** *Stages of decreasing uncertainty*

*Adapted from:* Schwaber, K., and M. Beedle. 2002. *Agile Software Development with Scrum*. Upper Saddle River, NJ: Prentice Hall.

- **Production:** Teams produce assets that were identified in pre-production and incrementally improve the asset pipelines. Although Sprints and releases are still used, the pace of asset production becomes the metric for measuring velocity.
- **Post-production:** Teams focus on tuning, polishing, and bug fixing tasks they identify daily. Although Sprint and release reviews are held, the goals are driven more by the daily triage backlog (which includes bug fixes and polishing tasks) and upcoming key dates such as submission. Post-production starts on the alpha date and includes the beta and shipping dates.

## Lean Production

Production is the most challenging and expensive stage. It represents a large debt of work that is dependent on pre-production decisions and timing.

For Scrum teams, the complex pipelines of asset creation don't fit perfectly with the iterative flow of work in a Sprint. Because of this, many teams entering production abandon Scrum in favor of waterfall practices. The problem in doing this is that they abandon many of the Agile benefits.

This section addresses the issues with production for an Agile team. It introduces some Lean concepts that allow teams to continually improve their production rate and the quality of the assets they produce.

## Production Debt

Have you ever seen a schedule for a game project that picks a day for production to begin? A date is chosen, a year or so in advance, that predicts when the team is to begin creating production assets (usually levels).

Where does this date come from? How do we know how much time is needed for pre-production and production? How do we know whether the time given is enough? How many times have you entered a 9-month production stage with 12 months of work? Many games enter production too early because the schedule says they need to do so. The problem is that the core mechanics and budgets that production depends on are still being iterated. This creates wasted work, because large numbers of assets must be reworked as this information emerges.

The work that needs to be done in production to create the 8 to 12 hours of content many games need is called **production debt**.

### *Measuring Production Debt in Pre-Production*

One of the goals of pre-production releases should be to measure and refine knowledge about the size of the production debt. During the first few releases, that debt is uncertain. For example, a project early in development might estimate its production debt to be 1,000 people-months of work, plus or minus 20 percent. Changes to the feature set may impact those ranges as well. Toward the end of pre-production, it should be more accurate, such as 1,050 people-months, plus or minus 5 percent. Figure 10.4 shows how this range of estimates will change over time. Although this estimate will never be perfect, it is always better than the first guess made at the start of the project.

These estimates are refined with Sprint and release goals that call for assets with increasingly higher quality. By developing these assets, the team learns more about the actual cost required to create them. These estimates aren't frozen in production either. During production, the team should be finding ways to improve how assets are created to further reduce costs.

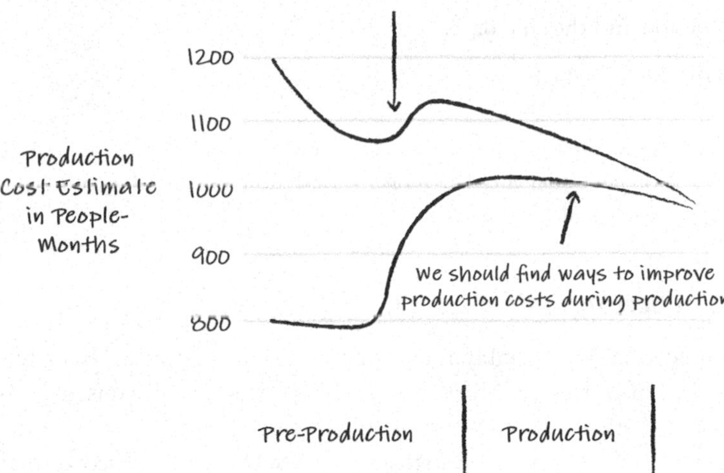


**Figure 10.4** *Production cost estimates over time*

### Making Games is Like Making a Car

A lot of problems and solutions for game development have their parallels in automobile design and production. During the design of a car like the Prius, Toyota not only had to design a car that the green market would buy, but one they could mass-produce at a price point that the green market could afford. In other words, they had to design the factory at the same time they designed the car (Liker, 2004).

## *Why Measure Production Debt?*

Measuring the cost of production during pre-production is important to help make decisions about the features that impact that cost. If Product Owners do not know the cost impact of such features, they are inclined to accept them at face value.

Imagine you are working on a first-person shooter game that has 12 months of production scheduled to build 10 levels. During development, the team implements technology that enables every part of the world to be destroyed or have holes blown in it. This is a great new addition, but it doubles the amount of work required to build a level.

If Product Owners know this, they can make an early decision. The following are some choices:

- Drop the feature because the project can't afford it.
- Drop half the levels.

- Start production earlier.
- Extend production and the ship date.
- Scale up the production staff.

Some of these choices are better than others, but they are all better than the one taken if production debt isn't measured: trying to stuff 24 months of production effort into 12 months of schedule.

## The Challenge of Scrum in Production

Production is dominated by an assembly-line approach to asset creation characterized by sequential steps of specialized work. These asset production streams are easily stalled or starved of work at various points within by impediments.

When Scrum teams fit asset production streams into Sprints, they discover that some of the benefits they've enjoyed in pre-production, such as ad hoc iteration and transparency, are somewhat reduced.

### *Scrum Task Boards and Production Streams*

At the start of a Sprint, a team forecasts the tasks it estimated it could complete by the end of the Sprint. Those tasks are placed on a task board that is reviewed every day. Many of the tasks are worked on out of sequence or in parallel. If someone is held up waiting for another task to complete, then he works on something else. This organic flow of task execution fosters communication among the team and prevents impediments from stopping it cold. Scrum task boards are great for supporting this.

However, for a long series of asset production steps that must be completed in order, the team loses much of this benefit. Tasks must flow in an ordered and steady pace to ensure that the specialists on a production team are not waiting for work. Scrum task boards don't clearly show this flow.

For example, consider the asset production stream for a single character to be produced in a Sprint (see Figure 10.5). The team estimates it will complete this work before the end of the Sprint. As this stream shows, each task has to occur in order before it is handed off to the next one.

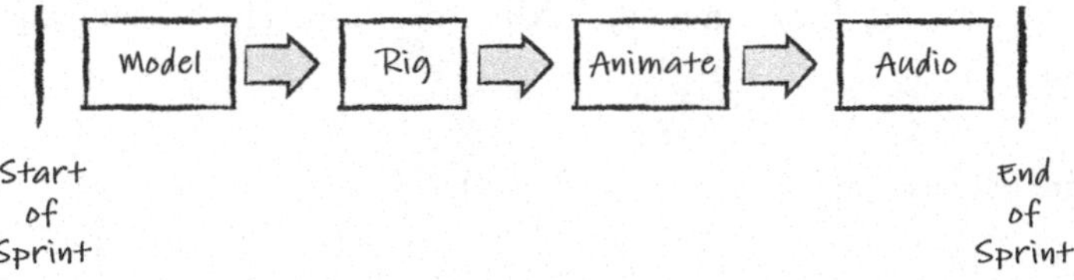


**Figure 10.5** *A production stream in a Sprint*

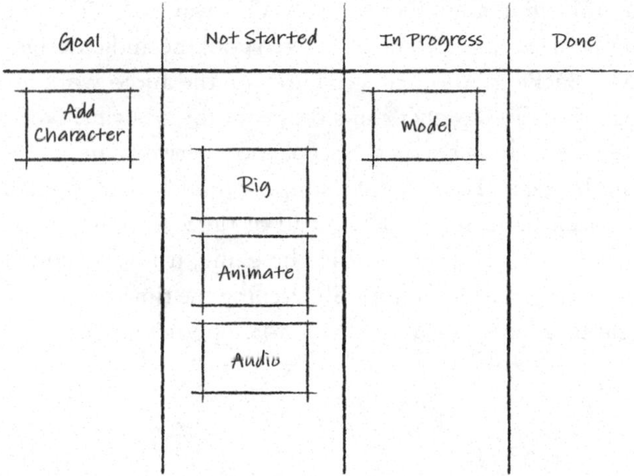


**Figure 10.6** *A character production stream visualized on a task board*

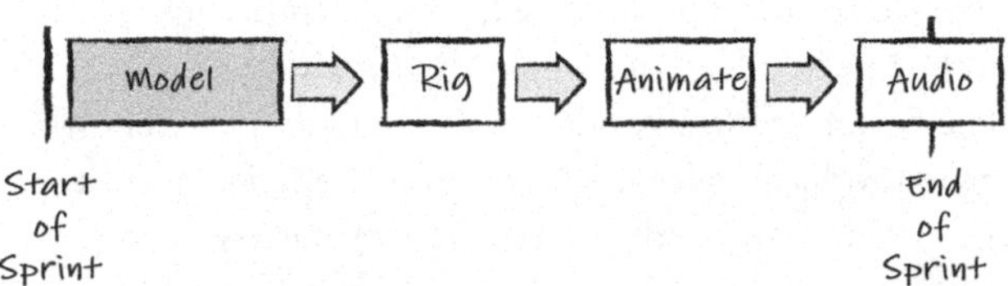


**Figure 10.7** *What happens if modeling is delayed*

When this stream of work is placed on a task board, it looks like Figure 10.6.

This task board shows that the character model is being created first. One problem with displaying streams on a task board is that the flow rate of the stream is not sufficiently visualized. This lack of visualization fails to alert a team to problems.

For example, what happens if modeling takes longer than estimated? Figure 10.7 shows the likely result. The modeler, rigger, and animator are able to finish their work, but the last person in the chain, the audio designer, does not have enough time to do his work before the end of the Sprint.

The team needs to see the impact of delays within the stream while they are occurring at any time.

### *Keeping Everyone Busy*

Another problem with fitting asset production streams into Sprints is keeping all the specialists busy. In the previous character production stream example, what is the audio designer doing before the animation is completed?

Scrum teams address this problem in a number of ways. One way is to share the composer with another team that needs audio. The other is to pool the audio designers into a team that has its own Backlog. Another is to batch up the audio work for a number of characters until the audio designer joins the team for a Sprint. None of these solutions is ideal because each increases the separation between an asset's creation and its appearance in the game. For example, suppose modelers are pooled together where they create a dozen character models ahead of time. If a problem is revealed the first time one of the characters appears in the game, it might require major rework of all 12, which is a big waste of effort. Shortening the time between a model's creation and its appearance on the screen creates more opportunities to "do it right" the first time.

### *Less Use of Iteration*

Asset production pipelines are similar to assembly lines. In this sense, a Scrum team completely empties the assembly line by the end of every Sprint, which doesn't make sense for assembly lines. They have to be continuously filled because each step in the line only works on what was passed from the previous step. An assembly-line run like a Sprint creates many gaps in the line that leave team members waiting.

This is the reason that some Scrum teams abandon Agile practices entirely when they enter production. However, production is never 100 percent efficient. The team cannot foresee every potential problem. It needs to seek improvements in pipelines right up until the game is shipped. For this reason, the Agile and Lean values and principles should be maintained in production. If production is driven by fixed schedules and deadlines, the best the team can hope for is to meet those deadlines, but unplanned problems will continue to appear and threaten them. Practices that are still Agile are needed—practices that anticipate change, that encourage continuous efficient flow, and that focus attention on continually improving how assets are produced.

This is where "Lean" thinking can help. As described in Chapter 2, Lean is a set of principles applied to production environments that have more certainty about what is being created but still want to introduce improvements continually. The remainder of this chapter describes how Lean practices such as Kanban can help a team remain Agile during production.

## Lean Production with Kanban

As teams transition from the complex exploration of pre-production to the complicated flow of production, a Lean production method such as Kanban can be a better fit for their work.

### *Visualizing Flow with Kanban*

A team employs a Kanban board to visualize an asset production stream and provide the transparency that a Scrum task board cannot.

We'll use an example level production stream to demonstrate how Kanban and Lean thinking are applied to production. Figure 10.8 shows a simplified level production stream, from concept to tuning.

The first step is to represent the stream on a Kanban board, which uses columns to represent individual workflow steps and capacity. Figure 10.9 shows a simplified Kanban for the level production stream.

There are six columns, which represent the steps of this production stream, including the Product Backlog. The cards within the columns represent individual levels in production. As the work for each step of a level is completed, a card for the next level to work on is pulled from the column immediately to its left, if that level is ready.

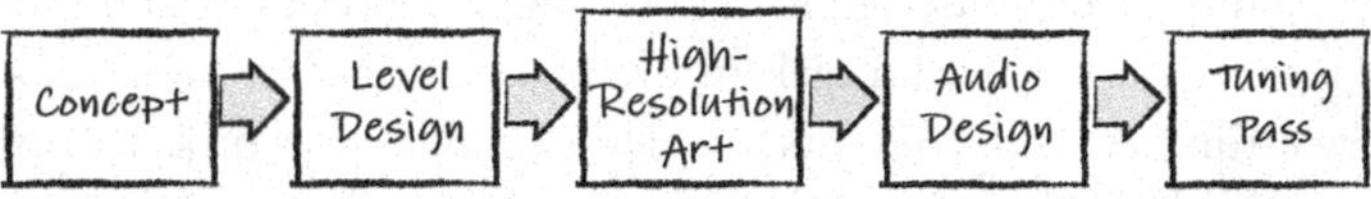


**Figure 10.8** *A simplified production stream for levels*

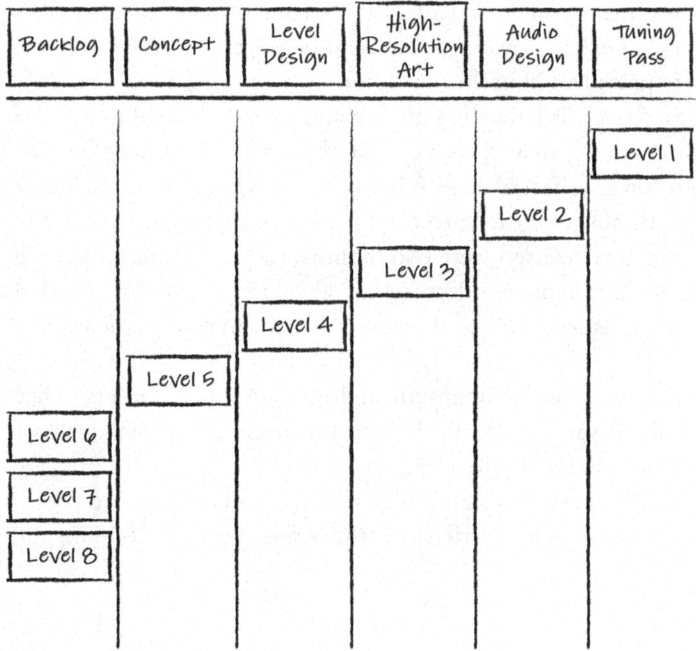


**Figure 10.9** *A simple Kanban board*

## *Leveling Production Flow*

Now that the team has a Kanban board representing the level production stream, the team members can start applying Lean tools to smooth out the fluctuations of production. This allows them to create production assets at a more constant and predictable rate.

There are two basic tools for leveling production flow. The first is establishing timeboxes for each step of the production stream. Following this, the flow is leveled by balancing the resources supporting every step.

### *Timeboxing*

Every developer who uses Scrum recognizes that a Sprint is a two- to three-week timebox. The benefit is to create a measurable cadence of value being added to the game.

In Lean production, this is taken a step further. Each step of a production stream is often timeboxed. For example, audio design for a level might be timeboxed to 10 days. This is different from a similar Scrum task in pre-production that the audio designer independently estimates and commits to. This changes for production because the team has established, during pre-production, the ideal timebox for a level's audio design. This timebox is based on the trade-off of time (cost) of creation and quality desired by the Product Owner.

Timeboxing does not mean content creators are forced to meet a set quality within a fixed amount of time. It's an average. The quality is determined by what the content creator is able to provide within the time limit.

The key to timeboxing assets is balancing quality and cost, measured in time. If the timebox chosen is too short, then the quality of the asset will be too low. For example, if the timebox for a section of high-resolution level geometry is set to one day, an artist might only be able to create a section filled with untextured cubes! On the other hand, if the timebox selected were two months, the artist might deliver a section with too much detailed geometry. It would be absolutely beautiful, but that beauty would come at too great of a cost to the stakeholder compared to the value it provides to the player.

Balancing asset quality and cost is the responsibility of Product Owners. They have to judge what the player values. Figure 10.10 demonstrates a notional curve of the trade-off between cost and value to the player.

It's not a straight line, because of diminishing returns; a player driving past a 10,000-polygon fire hydrant does not experience 50 times the value of a 200-polygon fire hydrant.

> **Note**
>
> As the Product Owner of a driving game, I asked the artists to create "95-mile-per-hour art." This quality bar depends on what the player cares about when they play the game; the player doesn't care about a high-resolution fire hydrant they pass at 95 miles per hour!

Figure 10.11 shows the area of the trade-off curve where the timebox selection is made. Pre-production refines the shape of this curve and the best range for a production timebox.

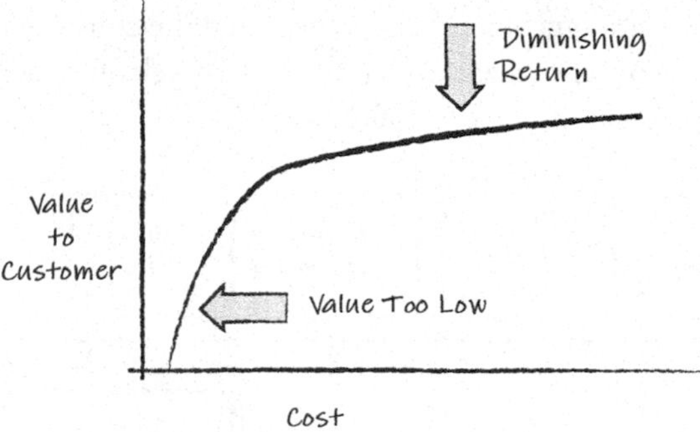


**Figure 10.10** *The cost/trade-off curve of assets*

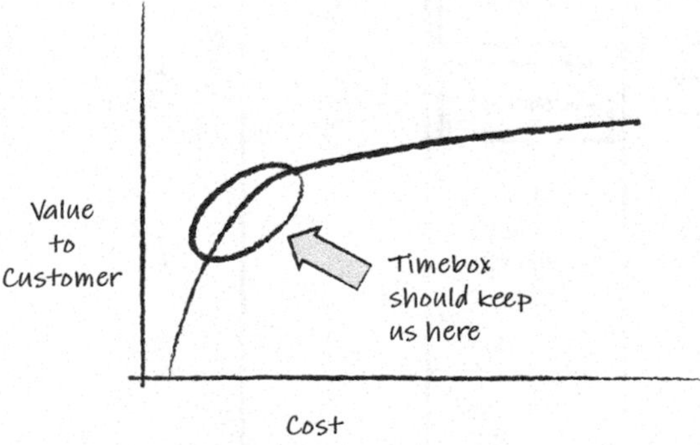


**Figure 10.11** *Selecting a timebox for an asset*

Timeboxes are not absolutely precise. Some levels take more time than others. The timebox chosen is an average of best- and worst-case times. The team uses small buffers, described next, to avoid underflow or overflow of work that this might cause.

**Note**

The timebox curve changes during production; it shrinks as it is refined and moves to the left as the team improves how it performs.

*Leveling Work*

Each step in the stream usually requires a different-length timebox. This causes gaps and pileups of work, which is to be avoided. For example, in Figure 10.12, if level design takes a week but the high-resolution geometry takes two, then the completed design work piles up. Conversely, if conceptualization requires two weeks for each level, the level designer eventually runs out of work and has to wait.

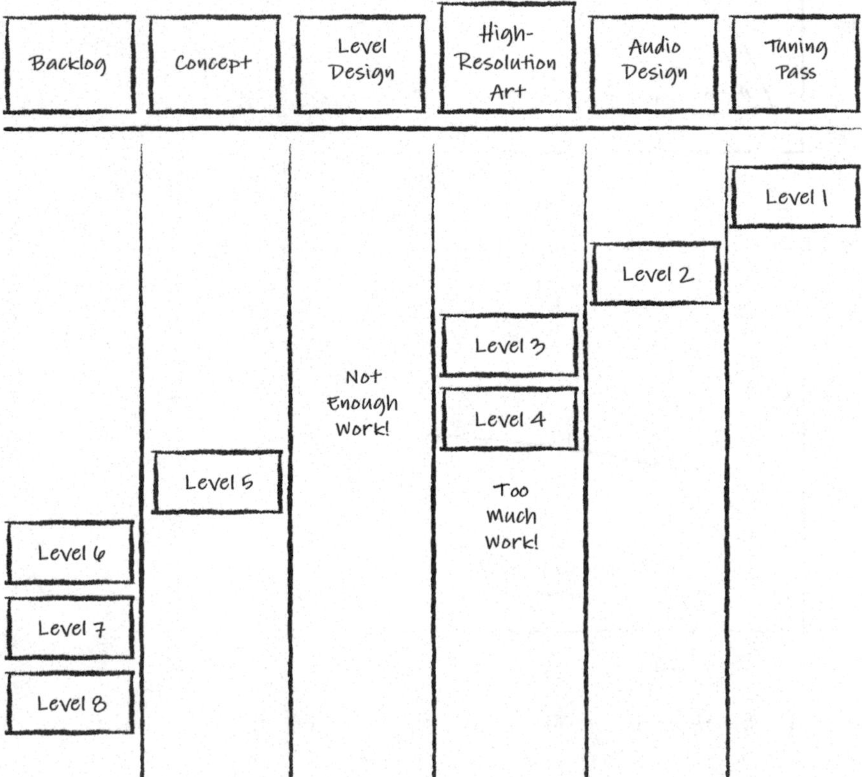


**Figure 10.12** *A Kanban board showing starvation and overflow*

Workflow needs to be balanced so that everyone always has work to do and that large amounts of work in progress don't pile up too much between any step. One way of doing this is to balance the amount of time each step takes, called its **cycle time**.

For example, if the team wants a 10-day cycle time for each step, it starts by examining the timeboxes for each person working on the stream (see Table 10.1).

Concept art and audio design already have a cycle time of 10 days. However, the other steps have different cycle times. For example, tuning takes less than 10 days per level. This means the designer who tunes levels runs out of work from time to time and has to find other things to do. This could mean helping out another team, level design, or QA.

For steps that require more than 10 days per level, the team needs to add people or find improvements to the process. For example, because the high-resolution artists require 30 days per level, the team could dedicate three high-resolution artists to balance the flow. Artists can work together in a number of ways, but each has challenges:

- **Have all high-resolution artists work on the same level:** This may not be an option if the editing tools do not support simultaneous editing on the same level.
- **Break up the high-resolution step into a specialized flow** (for example, texture artist, prop artist, static geometry artist)**:** It may be hard to balance these specialties.
- **Have the high-resolution artists working on multiple levels in parallel:** This solution might pose challenges with creating consistent quality and pace.

Each member of the team adds capacity, represented by a work in progress (WiP) limit for each column, as shown in Figure 10.13. This number defines the maximum number of cards (levels) that can reside in each column. When the number of cards in a column hits its WiP limit, no more cards can be pulled in.

**Table 10.1** *The Starting Cycle Times for an Unbalanced Stream*

| Step | Timebox per Step |
|---|---|
| Concept | 10 days |
| Level design | 20 days |
| High-resolution art* | 30 days |
| Audio design | 10 days |
| Tuning pass | 7 days |

* **High-resolution art** is the creation of detailed geometry, textures, and lighting.

### Limiting Work in Progress

Limiting WiP is an essential part of improving flow and quality. Simply improving the productivity of each step is not enough.

A useful analogy is that of a pizza restaurant. Say you're hungry, and you want to get a pizza. Your local shop makes great pizzas, and it takes them 20 minutes to bake one.

You enter the shop, but notice there is a long line. You're not going to get your pizza in 20 minutes because of all those people waiting ahead of you.

That line of people is the WiP for the pizza shop. WiP adds delay. In game development, that delay results in

- Fewer iterations, therefore less quality and fewer opportunities to experiment with improving the flow of production
- More waste because if we find a problem when an asset finally gets into the game, there might be another dozen in the pipeline, due to a high WiP count, that need to be reworked

Teams will continually explore ways to reduce WiP limits at every stage of a pipeline.

Our Kanban board now looks like Figure 10.13.

The team has now balanced the level production stream and established the rate at which levels are completed, called the **takt time** (see the sidebar "Takt Time and Cycle Time"), which is also 10 days. They apply Lean tools to maintain and even reduce takt time so as to continually improve the cost and quality of the levels.

### Takt Time and Cycle Time

Lean uses two measures of time for asset production streams. One is takt time, which is the rate of external demand for completed assets to be delivered. For video game production, this is determined by a schedule established in pre-production. One goal of Lean practices is to continually put pressure on reducing takt time—increasing the rate at which finished assets are delivered—by finding improvements in the pipeline.

Cycle time is used to measure the interval of time between the start and finish of a step or an entire stream.

Ideally, the cycle time of each step is less than or equal to the takt time. This is the goal of leveling flow. In the level creation example stream, the high-resolution art step required a 15-day cycle time. This could not be reduced to the takt time goal of five days by simply improving the pipeline. The solution was to create three high-resolution art stations working in parallel to meet the demand for one level of high-resolution art to be completed every five days.

### *Continual Improvement*

One of the main advantages of applying Lean production is that teams maintain the drive to continually improve what they are making and how they are making it. This is a benefit over fixed production schedules, where teams concentrate on keeping pace with deadlines, and unanticipated problems add delay.

In production, teams apply the same planning paradigm of using velocity measurements to forecast the pace toward achieving a goal. This allows fixes and improvements to be quickly appraised.

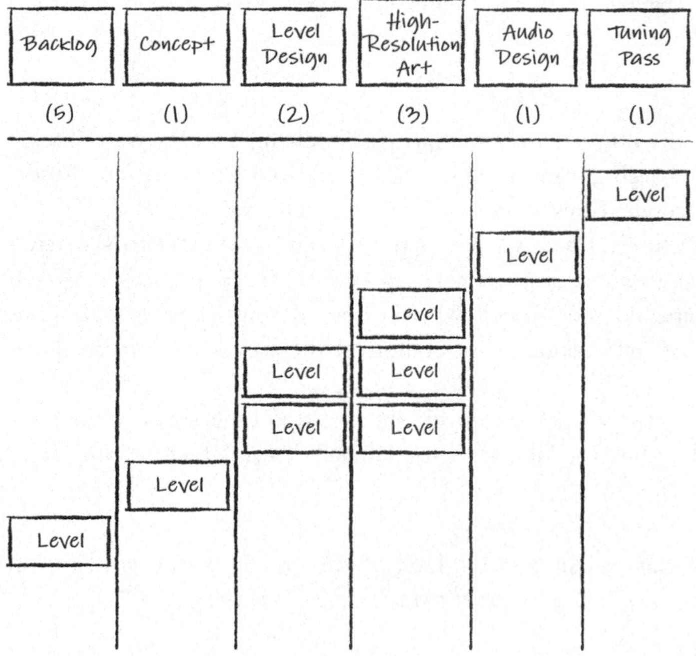


**Figure 10.13** *A Kanban board showing balanced flow*

This section uses the level production example to describe some of the ways Lean thinking enables teams to continually improve how they work together to increase the quality and production pace of assets.

**Example Benefits of Kanban for Production**

- "A lot more visibility and clarity on where things are and what needs to be worked on."
- "Easy to quickly see the overall project schedule and what can and can't get done. This helped many times for re-aligning resources to meet our goals."
- "Planning is actually much easier and straightforward for a Kanban team working within the Scrum structure."
- "Kanban got us to realize improvements to our process and pipeline. Specifically, making 'blockout' animations and 'proxy' models to get things in game as quickly as possible and keep everything moving."

—Dante Falcone, Game Industry Producer and Engineer

*Improving Cycle Time*

The pace of iteration has a direct impact on quality. For example, if the wait time on changing a texture and seeing it in the game is reduced from 10 minutes to 10 seconds, an artist iterates on textures more, and the game looks better.

The same principle applies to asset production streams. We want to shorten a stream's iteration time to allow improvements to be introduced as quickly as possible. These include pipeline, tool, workflow, and teamwork improvements. Shortening the iteration time of such changes enables more of them to be implemented and seen.

In Lean production, we focus on improving the iteration time, or cycle time, for the entire stream rather than the individual steps. The following factors influence a stream's cycle time:

- **Asset size:** Large assets, such as full levels, have large cycle times. If a team completes portions of a large asset, it reduces asset cycle time.

- **Batch size:** This is the number of assets processed at one time at any individual step. The larger the batch size, the longer the cycle time. An example of this is completing a dozen character models before handing them all off to the rigger. This is one of the benefits of establishing smaller WiP limits.
- **Waste:** This is the effort spent on things that don't add value to the final asset. For example, the time spent waiting for an approval is non-value-added time, or waste.
- **Knowledge, skill, and empowerment:** The greatest factor in determining cycle time is the knowledge and skill of everyone who adds value along the stream and their ability to influence change. For example, knowing when and where to reuse an asset rather than building one from scratch has a large impact on cycle time.

*Smaller Assets*

By breaking large assets into smaller ones, teams receive faster feedback. There are three types of feedback:

- **Gameplay feedback:** Very large assets, such as levels, can have month-long cycle times and, despite how detailed their design is, deliver uncertain gameplay. This long cycle time provides little opportunity for feedback to influence the asset. As a result, levels are shipped based on their initial design assumptions. By breaking levels into smaller areas, teams are given valuable feedback about the gameplay emerging and use this knowledge to influence subsequent portions of the level.
- **Production feedback:** Improvements to the production flow are applied more quickly and cheaply. For example, if the team discovers that a particular piece of static geometry interferes with character motion in the first section of the level, it fixes that section and changes its standards of work to apply the improvement on every subsequent section. This is a big time-saver.
- **Velocity feedback:** Gauging the effectiveness of individual practice changes or tool improvements when the cycle time is measured in months is very difficult. If the cycle time is reduced to weeks, then changes to the pace of work from improvements are more apparent.

One level production team I was working with did this by breaking up their levels into seven smaller "zones." Zones were the sections of levels that were streamed in and out of memory as the player moved.

After they began building zones, their cycle times became one-seventh of what they were before. Zones were completed every few weeks, and each one added improvements in quality and production that fed into subsequent zones. This team eventually reduced its cycle time by more than 50 percent.

*Smaller Batches*

Traditional production pipelines focus on the efficient utilization of content creators, rather than the flow of asset production streams. The imbalance of disciplines often causes project managers to level the work being done so that nobody runs out of work to do. Because "discipline leveling" predictions are never too precise, large inventories of works in progress are built in between the steps.

For example, if a project has dozens of levels to ship, the team may start producing batches of concept art or level props well before the end of pre-production. To a certain degree, this is necessary, but it often goes too far. For example, a half-dozen levels of concept art created before gameplay is fully understood leads to waste if the concepts have to be redone or, worse, levels are produced using these obsolete concepts.

With Lean thinking, teams try to reduce or eliminate batches of work. Because of the uncertainties within the timeboxes for each step, teams often need to create small buffers of works in progress between the steps of an asset production stream. They choose the smallest possible buffer size, because buffers increase the cycle time. The buffers should prevent waiting but not excessive pileups of work between each stage of work.

Figure 10.14 shows how buffers are represented on a Kanban board. Buffers have WiP limits, like every other step, that signal when the buffer is overflowing or underflowing.

*Reducing Waste*

A good portion of the time spent in production is wasted on work or activities that don't add value to the final product. Examples of this are the time waiting for exports, waiting for asset approvals, or syncing with the latest assets. Reducing these wastes greatly benefits productivity and cycle times.

Many of these wastes are identified and corrected by the team itself. The subtle pressures of takt time and timeboxing largely drive this. Timeboxes exert a pressure on the content creators to use their time wisely. As a result, it encourages them to seek ways to be more effective in how they work and point out the problems that were not so impactful when they had more time.

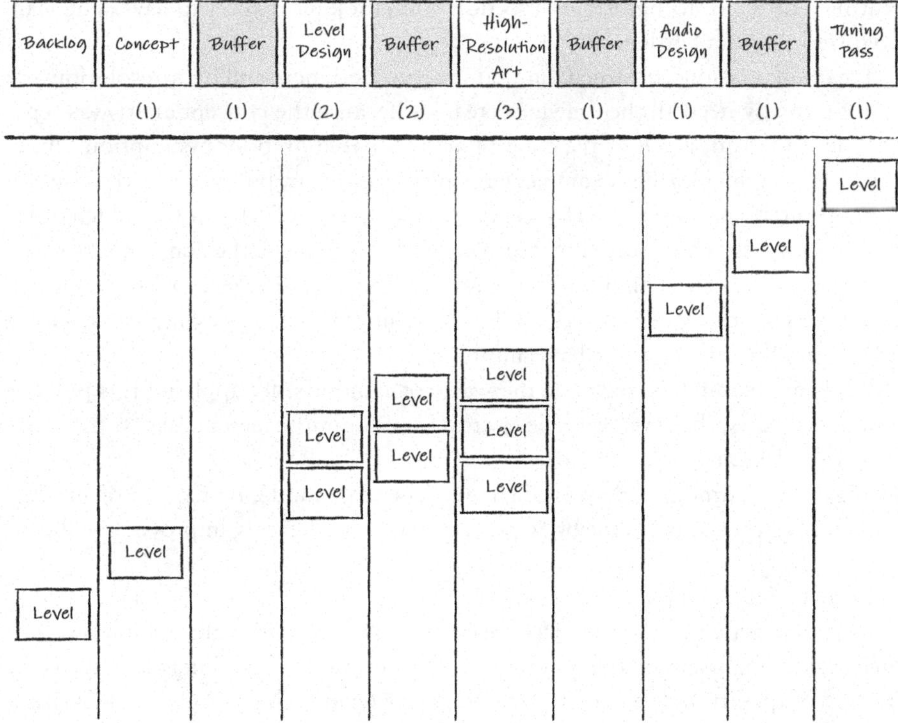


**Figure 10.14** *A Kanban board with buffers*

## Limiting Creativity?

One concern about Lean is that it limits the creativity of artists in production. I have found that the opposite is the case. A quote from T.S. Eliot seems to apply: "When forced to work within a strict framework, the imagination is taxed to its utmost and will produce its richest ideas. Given total freedom the work is likely to sprawl."

One production team I was working with had a 10-day takt time for level sections. This pace was challenging and exposed many problems with the flow of work. The biggest problem was with the concept art step. The team had only one concept artist available who was sitting with the other concept artists in another part of the studio.

Creating a dozen drawings for each section often took more than 10 days. The team recognized this as a bottleneck.

In team discussions, it turned out that the level designers and high-resolution artists didn't really need all the drawings created. Because the concept artist was separate from the team, much of the concept art was based on poor assumptions about the level and gameplay. For example, gameplay was linear, but much of the concept art represented open areas. The concept artist was surprised to hear that much of his work was useless. The solution the team created was to move the concept artist next to the level designer and high-resolution artists. This enabled them to discuss the layout of levels as concept art was created. As a result, far fewer drawings needed to be created, and the quality of the levels improved.

This is an example of reducing the waste of handoffs. By applying this practice to other handoffs, the team was able to create similar improvements across the entire production stream.

This is one example of dozens of changes the team made. By the end of production, it had improved takt time by 56 percent while significantly improving quality.

#### *Knowledge, Skill, and Empowerment*

Like Scrum practices, Lean practices create transparency in the production pipeline, which makes quality, velocity, and waste visible. One of the first things revealed is the variation of quality and velocity between separate teams. This visibility enables leads to know where to focus mentoring. In many cases, all that is required is to help a struggling content creator use a tool correctly or understand how to reuse assets to improve his effectiveness.

Lean thinking focuses skills on the final product, rather than on individual steps. Part IV, "Agile Disciplines," discusses this topic in greater detail.

Many of the Lean tools described require teams to be empowered to make decisions and take ownership of their practices. In the previous example, the team decided to move the concept artist with the rest of the team. In many studios, teams are not allowed to make such decisions. It comes back to the lack of transparency. With transparency, teams are entrusted to make greater and greater decisions because of the performance metrics that ensure their decisions demonstrate higher productivity and quality. The difference in the number, quality, and frequency of beneficial changes increases as ownership of them is spread. Leaders might be skilled and insightful, but they can't be everywhere. They need to rely on empowered teams to recognize and solve issues daily.

### *Outsourcing*

Outsourcing has established its benefits for asset production. However, many studios have found that outsourcing limits the amount of iteration that takes place in the

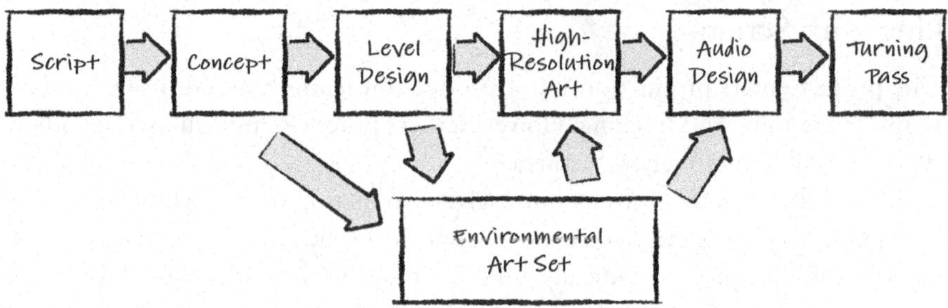


**Figure 10.15** *Outsourcing a portion of the stream*

creation of large assets such as key characters or levels. This limited iteration impacts quality or introduces expensive rework that limits outsourcing's cost benefits.

Lean production outside the game industry evolved to work with external suppliers. Suppliers to Lean companies need to become Lean themselves. Lean suppliers deliver smaller batches of parts to the main production line. This is done to allow quality improvements to be introduced more frequently and at lower cost.

How does this translate to game asset production? With our example, we don't want to outsource the entire level production stream. The key is to outsource parts of the production stream that don't require larger iterative cycles that should remain in the studio. For level production, studio teams retain large layout tasks and outsource the component assets used in these layouts. An example of this is environment sets, or collections of assets, common throughout a level. If a project needs a large city level, the team outsources all the props, such as light posts, mailboxes, vehicles, building components, ambient sounds, and so on. These environmental sets are brought into the layout steps (high-resolution art and audio layout). This enables continued iteration of the layouts at the studio.

Figure 10.15 shows a production stream with the environmental art outsourced.

The outsourced assets are identified in level concept and design to give sufficient lead time. These assets are delivered as they are developed rather than in a single batch.

### Note

Many layout tools support late introduction of outsourced components. An example is the Unreal Engine 3 editor. The packaging system allows for levels to be laid out with proxy assets that are automatically replaced as the high-quality outsourced assets are delivered. For example, the studio artists could use blue rectangles in place of doors, and when the outsourced doors are delivered, a single instance change replaces them all.

## Working with Scrum

When the project enters production, asset production teams may not use practices such as Sprint planning and tracking. However, these practices are still used by other teams to continue innovating new features.

Sprints are still valuable in production. Asset production teams demonstrate the assets that have been completed since the last Sprint review. Production teams don't plan Sprints. Instead, they periodically fill a Backlog buffer with a set of ordered assets to work on next. The team selects a Backlog buffer size limit and fills it to that limit every time it is emptied.

Teams might also mix production and feature development work. For example, consider a level production team that has a few programmers adding effects, enhancing AI, and improving tools. The programmers plan typical Sprints with user stories and a Sprint Backlog, while the level creators use a Kanban workflow. Figure 10.16 shows how the two task boards are combined using a Scrum "swim lane" added to a Kanban board.

Retrospectives and Daily Scrums are still essential practices for production teams to address impediments and to improve how the team performs together.

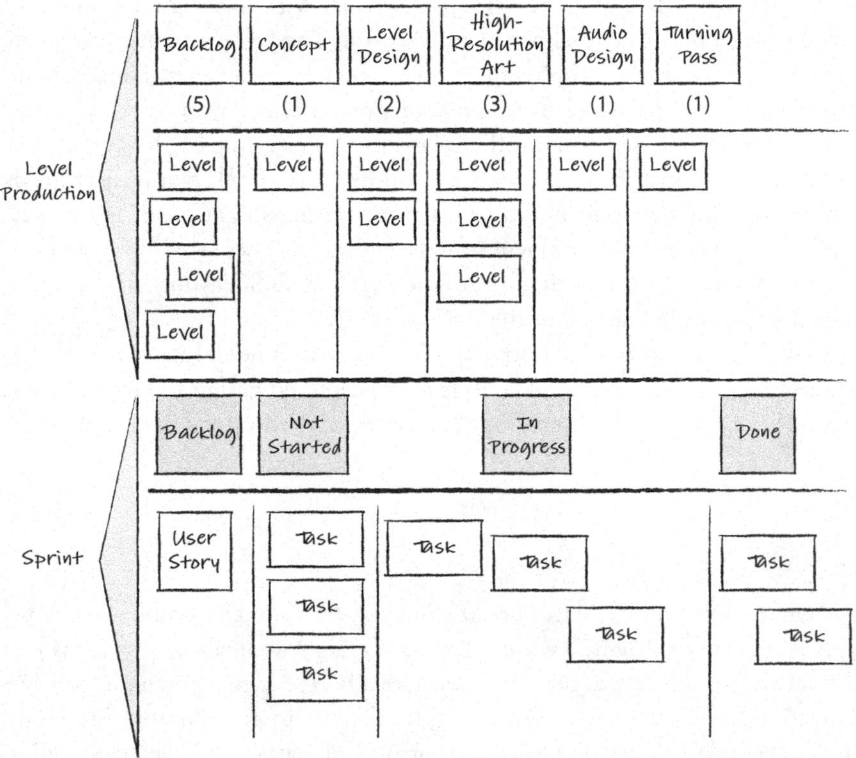


**Figure 10.16** *A Kanban board with a Sprint swim lane*

### Transitioning Scrum Teams

Scrum teams exploring gameplay in pre-production don't instantly reorganize their workflow into asset streams overnight. They gradually build up to them by iterating on assets that approach production quality and refining each stage or workflow. Each team approaches this transition differently, but the common set of steps is as follows:

1. Explore what is correct (fun and cost).
2. Refine the timeboxes.
3. Understand how much content is needed and who is needed to create it, and refine the production budget.
4. Establish the asset streams.
5. Start adding columns to task boards with Kanban limits.
6. Level the flow. Adjust the teams.

As the teams level the flow of an asset stream, their size might far exceed 10 members. Some teams might break the team into two, but more often they maintain themselves as a single team. This allows them to "see the whole" asset stream as one continuous flow. The downside is that it makes team meetings, such as Daily Scrums and Retrospectives, less productive because of the communication overhead.

## What Good Looks Like

There is no project management approach that can turn a studio into a factory that mass-produces hit games that ship on schedule and budget. Some goals are impossible, at least with the constraints we're given. The best a project management approach can do under those circumstances is to discover that fact as early and cheaply as possible.

I learned the "find the fun" and "fail fast" lessons for pre-production from Nintendo in the '90s, but found that managing risk and content production needed far more planning than an iterative approach. This is what sets game project management apart from software project management.

Good is managing risk, protecting developers and the quality of the game from the pressures of hitting very specific targets on a very uncertain and speculative plan.

## Summary

The additional challenge of stages with game projects doesn't diminish the value of Agile or require complex plans or project management structures. It requires Product Owners to be aware of impacts that features have on production costs and for teams to adapt their practices as they enter production.

## Additional Reading

DeMarco T., and T. Lister. 2003. *Waltzing with bears: managing risk on software projects*. Dorset House Pub.

Ladas, C. 2009. *Scrumban: Essays on Kanban Systems for Lean Software Development*. Seattle: Modus Cooperandi Press.

Liker, J.K. 2004. *The Toyota way: 14 management principles from the world's greatest manufacturer*. New York: McGraw-Hill,

PMI. 2013. *A Guide to the Project Management Body of Knowledge*. Pennsylvania: Project Management Institute.

Poppendieck, M., and T. Poppendieck. 2007. *Implementing Lean Software Development: From Concept to Cash*. Boston, MA: Addison-Wesley.

# Chapter 11

# Faster Iterations

According to Voltaire, "The best is the enemy of the good." In Agile circles, iteration means one thing: It's the timebox in which product increments are made. For Scrum, the iteration is a Sprint. For game developers, the term *iteration* means something more. It refers to the practice of creating an initial version of something (artwork, code, or a design), examining it, and then revising it until it's sufficiently improved.

Unfortunately, iterating isn't free. It takes time to revisit a bit of art, code, design, audio, or other game element. The challenge facing all teams is to find ways to reduce the cost of iteration. A team that reduces the cost of iteration benefits in two ways: They iterate over gameplay elements more often, and they do so more frequently. These benefits result in an increase in their velocity.

Scrum focuses game developers on improving iteration time everywhere. The benefits of doing this are reinforced daily among cross-discipline teams and over the course of Sprints through the measurement of velocity. As described in Chapter 9, "Agile Release Planning," velocity is measured as the average amount of scope, which means a Definition of Done is accomplished every Sprint. Product Backlog Items (PBIs) not only require coding and asset creation but also debugging, tuning, and a degree of polishing to be considered done. These additional requirements drive the need for more iterations, and the longer the iteration time, the slower the velocity. Faster iteration improves velocity.

This chapter examines where the overhead of iterating code, assets, and tuning comes from and ways that a team can reduce this overhead and greatly increase its velocity on a project.

**A Sea Story**

One of the best things about developing games is that mistakes don't kill people or cost tens of thousands of dollars. The pace of development can be slowed under these conditions.

My last job before I joined the game development industry was developing autonomous underwater vehicles. These vehicles were meant to perform dangerous operations such as searching for underwater mines. When launched, these multimillion-dollar vehicles were counted on to conduct their mission and return to us.

No matter how much we tested the software and hardware before a mission, some problems always surfaced at sea (no pun intended). Often these problems resulted in the vehicle's failing to return at the appointed time or location. When this happens, you realize how big the ocean really is.

As a result, changes to the vehicle were very carefully tested over the course of weeks. Even the smallest mishap would "scrub" a day at sea. This long iteration cycle slowed development progress to a crawl.

## The Solutions in This Chapter

This chapter explores ways of balancing the drive for quality with its cost by

- Measuring and reducing the cost of iterations
- Reducing the cost of defects by finding them quickly, or simply not creating them in the first place
- Increasing the speed and effectiveness of testing through automation and more strategic quality assurance (QA)

## Where Does Iteration Overhead Come From?

Iteration overhead comes from many places:

- **Compile and link times:** How long does it take to make a code change and see the change in the game?

- **Tuning changes:** How long does it take to change a tuning parameter, such as bullet damage?
- **Asset changes:** How many steps does it take to change an animation and see it in the game?
- **Approvals:** What are the delays in receiving art direction approval for a texture change?
- **Integrating change from other teams:** How long do changes (new features and bug fixes) from other teams take to reach your team?
- **Defects:** How much time is lost to crashes or just trying to create a stable build?

These time delays between iterations last seconds to weeks in duration. Generally, the longer the time between the iterations, the more time is wasted either waiting or having to find lower-priority work to do before another iteration is attempted.

## Measuring and Displaying Iteration Time

The complexity of a game, asset database, build environment, and pipeline grows over time. While this happens, iteration times tend to grow—there is more code to execute, and more assets in the database to sort through. Iterations are rapid at the start of a project but grow unacceptable over time. Before you know it, half your day is spent waiting for compiles, exports, baking,[1] or game loads.

The key to reducing iteration overhead is to measure, display, and address ways of reducing iterations continually.

### Measuring Iteration Times

Iteration times should be measured frequently. To ensure that such measurements are performed frequently, the measurement process should be automated. A simple automated tool[2] should do this on a build server with a test asset, for example. A nice feature to add to this tool is to have it alert someone when this time spikes.

> **Note**
>
> One time a bug nearly doubled the bake time for a game, yet no one reported it during any of the Daily Scrums for a week. It seemed that people became immune to long iterations, which was more worrying than the bug itself.

1. **Baking** refers to the process of translating exported assets into a particular platform's native format.
2. If not automated, it is easily skipped or forgotten.

## Displaying Iteration Times

An iteration time trend chart displays the amount of time that an individual iteration time, such as build time, is taking and shows its trend over time. Like the Sprint burndown, this chart displays a metric and its recent trend. Figure 11.1 shows an example iteration trend chart.

Showing a longer-term trend of iteration time is important because it is often hidden in daily noise. How frequently the chart is updated depends on how often a particular iteration time is measured and the need for updating it. Significant iteration metrics (based on how many people execute the iteration and how often) should be calculated daily, and the charts should be updated weekly.

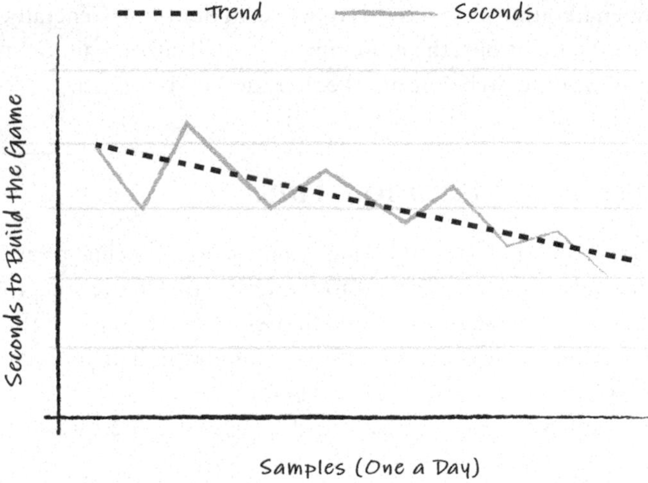


**Figure 11.1** *Recent iteration times and trend line*

> **Note**
>
> A tool that automatically measures iteration time should also alert someone immediately when that time spikes.

### Experience: Playstation Asset Baking

When iterating on art assets, the largest amount of the time it takes to iterate on changes typically comes from baking or exporting an asset to a target platform's native format. On a PlayStation project I worked on, every asset change required a 30-minute bake. Because the actual game executable was used to perform the baking, this time continued to creep up as features were added. It reached the point where everyone working with the PlayStation spent half the day waiting for this process!

The team began by plotting asset iteration time on a daily basis. Over time, it dedicated a portion of its Sprint Backlog toward optimizing the baking tools and process. During a release, the team saw the trend of bake times slowly declining (33 percent in three months).

Without this regular measurement and display, it would have been easy for the team to lose track of the overall trend. Without keeping an eye on the metric, the bake times would have crept up gradually. Equally important was the value of introducing a large number of very small optimizations and seeing the effect over time. Often the "one big fix" simply doesn't exist, and nothing else is done because a significant benefit isn't immediately visible. The burndown demonstrates the value of "a lot of small fixes."

## Personal and Build Iteration

It's useful to consider three types of iteration: personal iterations for each developer iterating at his own development station, the build iterations when code and asset changes are shared across the entire project, and deployment iteration time for live games. All require constant monitoring and improvement. We'll look at deployment iteration time in Chapter 22, "Live Game Development."

Improving personal iteration is mainly a matter of improving tools and skills. Build iteration requires not only tool improvements but also attention to the practices shared across teams to reduce the overhead inherent in sharing changes with many developers.

### Personal Iteration

Personal iteration time includes the time it takes to do the following:

- Exporting and baking assets for a target platform a developer is iterating on

- Changing a design parameter (for example, bullet damage level) and trying it in the game
- Changing a line of code and testing it in the game

These are the smallest iteration times, but because they happen most frequently, they represent the greatest iteration overhead. Removing even five minutes from an export process used a dozen times a day improves velocity by more than 20 percent![3]

Some common improvements can speed up personal iteration times:

- **Upgrade development machines:** More memory, faster CPUs, and more cores increase the speed of tools. This is usually a short-term solution because it hides the real causes of delay.
- **Distributed build tools:** Distributed code-building packages reduce code iteration time by recompiling large amounts of code across many PCs. Tools also exist for distributed asset baking.
- **Parameter editing built into the game:** Many developers build a simple developer user interface into the game for altering parameters that need to be iterated.
- **Asset hot loading:** Changed assets are loaded directly into a running game without requiring a restart or level reload.

**Note**

The ideal iteration is instantaneous! Achieving this ideal after a game engine has been created is far more difficult. For a new engine in development, I consider zero iteration time and hot loading to be necessary parts of the engine that must be maintained from the start of development.

## Build Iteration

Build iteration is the process that spreads changes from one developer to all the other developers on the team. Sometimes this cycle is weeks long, but because members of the team do other things while waiting for a new build, it is not given as much attention as personal iteration times. However, the larger the team, the more impact the build iteration has on the team's effectiveness. It often results in a near disaster when there is a rush to get a working build out for a Sprint or release. Bottlenecks and

3. This is based on four to five hours of useful work done per day.

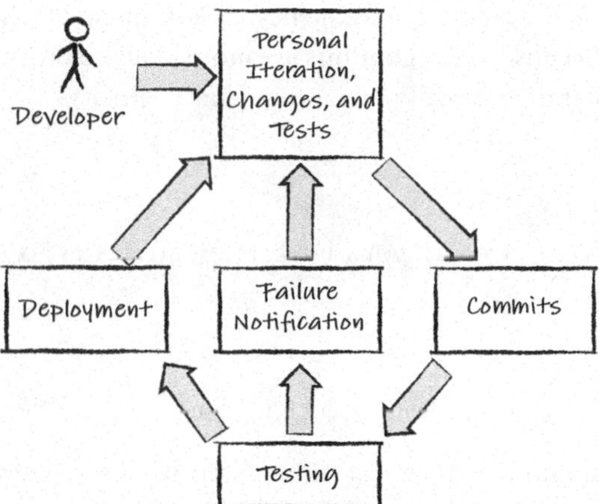


**Figure 11.2** *A build iteration cycle*

conflicts inevitably occur when everyone is trying to commit changes at the same time. The solution is to reduce this overhead so builds are safely iterated more frequently.

Figure 11.2 shows the build iteration cycle discussed.

Following personal iteration, a developer commits changes to a repository or revision control system. This is followed by a battery of tests. If these tests find a problem, the developer is notified and asked to fix the problem. Otherwise, if the tests pass, the build is shared with the team.[4]

## *Commits*

Commits are changes made to a project repository for the rest of the team to access. For example, an animator commits a new set of animations for a character to the repository, and subsequent builds show characters using those new animations.

There are two main concerns regarding commits:

- The commits should be safe and not break the build.
- The build is in a working condition so that any failure is more likely to be tied to the last commit and quickly fixed.

The developer must first synchronize with the latest build and test his changes with it. This is done to avoid any conflicts that arise with other recent commits. If the latest build is broken, it must be fixed before any commit is made.

4. If your project is not doing this, stop reading and implement it now!

When builds are chronically broken, they slow the frequency of commits, which means that larger commits are made. Because larger commits are more likely to break the build, they create a vicious cycle that dramatically impacts a team's velocity.

> **Note**
>
> Chapter 12, "Agile Technology," discusses continuous integration strategies to minimize the size of code changes commits.

## *Testing*

After changes are committed, there should be a flurry of more extensive tests made to ensure that those commits haven't broken anything in the build. There are two competing factors to consider. First, we want to ensure that the build is solidly tested before it is released to the team. Second, a full suite of tests often takes the better portion of a day to run, which is too long. We need to balance testing needs with the need to iterate quickly on build changes.

### *Test Strategies*

A multifaceted approach to testing is best. A combination of automated and QA-run testing catches a broad range of defects.

Figure 11.3 shows a pyramid of tests run in order from bottom to top. The tests at the bottom of the pyramid run quickly and catch the more common defects. As each test passes, the next higher test is run until we get to the top where QA approves the build by playing it.

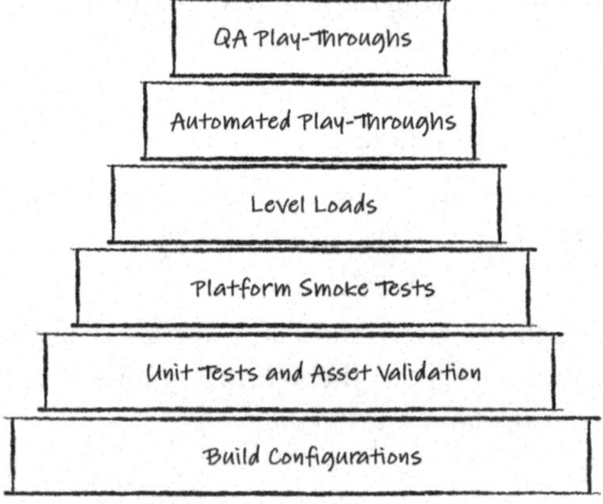


**Figure 11.3** *A testing pyramid*

The tests are as follows:

- **Build configurations:** This testing simply creates a build (executable and assets) for each platform. This discovers whether the code compiles on all your target platforms with multiple build configurations (for example, debug, beta, and final). This could cover dozens of platforms for a mobile game.
- **Unit tests and asset validation:** This includes some of the unit tests (if they exist) and any asset validation tests. Asset validation tests individual assets before they are baked and/or loaded in the game. These are examples of asset validation tools:
  - Naming convention checks
  - Construction checks, such as testing for degenerate triangles
  - Platform resource budget checks (for example, polygon count or memory size)

**Note**

Unit testing is described in more detail in Chapter 12.

The list of validation tests should be built up as problems are discovered.

- **Platform smoke tests:** These tests ensure that the build loads and starts running on all the platforms without any crashes.
- **Level loads:** One or more of the levels are loaded to ensure that they run on all the platforms and stay within their resource budgets. Usually only the levels affected by change are loaded, but all of them are tested overnight.
- **Automated play-throughs:** A game that "plays itself" through scripting or a replay mechanism benefits testing. In fact, implementing this type of feature into the game from the start is worth the investment. If conditions at the end of the play-through do not meet expectations (such as all the AI cars in a racing game crossing the finish line in a preset range of time), an error is flagged.
- **QA play-throughs:** If the build passes all previous tests, then QA plays through portions of the game. QA is not only looking for problems that were missed in the previous tests but also looking for problems that tests could not catch such as unlit portions of the geometry or AI characters that are behaving strangely.

### Robotic Phone Interface Testing

One of the most challenging aspects of mobile game QA is the overhead of testing the interface on all the various phones. It's a slow manual process, but we're starting to see companies introduce "robotic hands" to automate even this.[5]

*Test Frequency*

As development progresses, the time required for running all of these tests grows to the point where keeping up with every commit is impossible. At this point, the scope of build approval needs to be tiered. The following list shows four tiers of build tests that apply increasing levels of testing:

- **Continuous build tests:** These builds have passed the unit and asset tests for the committed modules or assets. These tests take minutes.
- **Hourly build tests:** These builds have passed every test up to the level load test.
- **Semi-daily build tests:** Two or three times a day, QA selects the latest hourly build and plays through it for 30 minutes.
- **Daily build tests:** These are builds that have been completely rebuilt (code and asset cooking) and for which every possible automated test has been run. These take hours to run and are usually done overnight.

As each build is approved, it is flagged (or renamed, and so on) to reflect the testing tier it passed. This lets the team know how extensively the build was tested and to what degree they should trust it.

### Note

Sprint Review builds should pass all the daily build tests!

## *Failure Notification*

When a commit is made that breaks the build, two things must happen:

- The person(s) who made the last commit must be notified immediately in a way they can't ignore. This can take the form of a dialog box that pops up on top of all other windows.

5. https://www.youtube.com/watch?v=mv69ZxKOFSw

- The rest of the team should be notified that the build is broken and that they shouldn't "get the latest" code and assets until the problem is fixed. This notification requires less intrusive means to communicate. An example of a notification is an icon in the system tray that turns red.

**Note**

At High Moon, whenever the build was broken, every development machine warned its user by playing a sound bite. One time I broke the build and 100 PCs started playing the Swedish Chef's theme song from the *Muppet Show*.

### The Loaf of Questionable Freshness

Most of the time when a commit is broken, it is because of someone ignoring the established testing practices. Teams often devise "motivational tools" to help ensure that teammates remember to perform these practices. An example of this took place on the Midtown Madness team in the late nineties at Angel Studios. We didn't have extensive build testing automation then. We had a dedicated PC, the "build monkey," where any change committed had to be tested separately following every commit. Verifying the build on the build monkey could be a tedious task. Some people occasionally found excuses to skip it, sometimes to the detriment of the team.

After a while, I thought of a cure. I purchased a loaf of Wonder bread, and we instituted a new practice: If you broke the build monkey, you had to host the loaf of bread on top of your monitor (everyone had CRT monitors back then, with plenty of warm space on top) until someone else broke the monkey and took ownership of the loaf.

At first things didn't change. At first, no one seemed to mind a loaf of bread on their monitor. However, as time passed, this changed; the bread became stale and then moldy. Someone on the team started calling it "the loaf of questionable freshness." Eventually, we all desperately wanted to avoid being the owner of the loaf. As a result, build discipline improved, the monkey stayed unbroken, and eventually the loaf of questionable freshness was given a proper burial.

Technology has changed these practices a bit (in other words, we can't fit a loaf of bread on top of an LCD monitor). These days automated test tools play embarrassing music, or the team holds impromptu ceremonies for team members who break the build (have you ever come back to your workspace to find it completely wrapped in Saran wrap?). It's all done with a sense of fun, but it works.

### *Stable Builds*

The last step in build iteration is to share a stable build with the developers. There are two main considerations here: communicating stability and reducing transfer time.

#### *Communicate Stability*

Communicate the level of testing performed on working builds to reflect the testing tier each one passed.

In the past, we've used a simple homegrown tool that shows all the builds available on the server, their build date, and the test status. The developer selects a build to download based on their needs. Usually, the developer downloads the latest build that was fully tested (usually the daily build). When developers want very recent changes, they select the hourly build.

**Note**

Keeping a few weeks' history of builds around is useful in case a subtle bug needs to be regressed to discover which commit introduced it.

#### *Reduce Transfer Time*

Reduce the amount of time to transfer the build from the servers to personal development machines.

Games require many gigabytes of space, and when 100 developers transfer builds daily, it challenges the company network. It's common for a new build to take 30+ minutes to transfer from a server to a personal machine. Reducing this time is crucial. A number of ways exist to attack this problem:

- **Server/client compression/decompression:** A number of tools are available to improve the transfer speed of large amounts of data over a network.
- **Partial transfer:** Does everyone need to transfer every asset? Do some developers need just a new executable? Make it possible to do selective transfers.
- **Overnight transfer:** Set up a tool for pushing daily builds (if working!) to all the developer stations overnight.

- **Upgrade your network:** Move to higher-bandwidth switches and mirrored servers. This is costly, but a simple return-on-investment calculation usually shows that the reduced time to share a build and assets pays for itself in productivity gains.

### *Focusing a Team on Build Iteration*

When I was a child, I desperately avoided cleaning my room. As I became older, my mother told me that "She was not put on Earth to clean up after me." Imagine my surprise! However, when I had to clean up after myself, I quickly learned that it was better to avoid making the mess in the first place. At the very least, I learned to clean up a mess before it dried on the carpet!

Improving build iteration and debugging is the responsibility of every team. Making it the responsibility of one group of people removes some of that sense of responsibility. However, creating a better build system to catch problems and share stable builds requires specialists and expertise beyond the capabilities of any one team. Having every team create its own system isn't efficient. They are better off adopting a studio-maintained system and focusing on their game.

The role of creating and maintaining the build system is often the responsibility of an engine or tools team. Members of this team see patterns of failure and work to plug any holes that enable problems to slip through. Additional build server tests are the easiest remedy, but teams often need to improve their practices to avoid commit failures. An example of this is to show individuals how to write better unit tests or improve their unit test coverage or to work with an artist to avoid using nonstandard texture sizes or formats.

The team that supports the build servers and tools also needs a metric that shows its progress. A useful metric used for measuring build stability and availability is to record the percentage of time a working build is available to everyone on the team. The ideal is 100 percent. A perfect level of stability will not be maintained forever, but it is a powerful goal.

> **Note**
>
> On one team, the "working build availability percentage" started at 25 percent. The team recorded this metric daily and plotted it on a burn-up chart. After a year, it averaged 95 percent. Some weeks after a major middleware integration, the availability rate dropped back to near zero, but the burn-up chart enabled the teams to see the long-term picture and slowly improve the trend.

**A Word about Revision Control**

A detailed discussion of revision control is outside the scope of this book. A good article to read further can be found at https://www.gamasutra.com/blogs/AshDavis/20161011/283058/Version_control_Effective_use_issues_and_thoughts_from_a_gamedev_perspective.php

## What Good Looks Like

When visiting teams, I often explore where the responsibility for quality lies. For effective teams, responsibility lies with them, not with a group of testers in another building. Helping teams accept this responsibility is a major purpose of the Definition of Done and the reason for continually and slowly raising the bar on what *done* means; it drives cultural and practice changes that often result in the practices you see in this chapter. It influences developers to care more about quality and not just task completion.

## Summary

The source of iteration overhead comes from many factors. These sources must be relentlessly tracked down and reduced. Left unattended, they will grow to consume more time and bring velocity to a crawl.

Faster iteration time is a big win. It improves velocity and quality by enabling more iterations of features and assets. Faster iterations improve the life of a developer and the quality of the game. When a designer has to wait 10 minutes to test the effects of a wheel friction tweak on a vehicle, they'll likely find a value that is "good enough" and move on. When the iteration time is instantaneous, they'll tweak the value until it's "just right."

## Additional Reading

Crispin, L., and J. Gregory. 2009. *Agile Testing: A Practical Guide for Testers and Agile Teams*. Boston, MA: Addison-Wesley.

Lakos, J. 1997. *Large-Scale C++ Software Design*. Reading, MA: Addison-Wesley.

## PART IV

# Agile Disciplines

# Chapter 12

# Agile Technology

Software developers have been battling the challenge of creating complex software projects since the first program was written. Even in the infancy of computers, the challenge of programming with primitive tools pushed the limits of what people could accomplish. Seminal books on project management such as *Mythical Man Month*, written in the sixties, address challenges that are seen to this day.

### Complexity is Not New

The complex Apollo program was almost undone by unanticipated glitches in the Lunar Module's navigation and guidance computer in the final seconds before the historic landing. That computer had only 4,000 words of memory[1] (one-millionth of the memory in a typical desktop computer).

This chapter begins with a description of some of the major problems encountered when creating technology for games. The remainder of the part discusses some of the Agile practices—including the Extreme Programming methodology—used to address these problems.

I've avoided low-level technical discussion and code examples in this chapter on purpose. The goal is to communicate the issues and solutions that people in every discipline can understand.

1. https://history.nasa.gov/computers/Ch2-5.html

## The Solutions in This Chapter

Technology creation is the greatest area of risk for many video games. Video games compete on the basis of technical prowess as much as gameplay and visual quality. Consumers want to experience the latest graphics, physics, audio effects, artificial intelligence, and so on. Even if a game isn't using the next-generation hardware, it's usually pushing the current generation to new limits.

This chapter addresses the typical technical problems that often impact development and their solutions. These problems impact all disciplines and lead projects down dead-end paths.

## The Problems

Common development problems include uncertain goals, high costs for addressing change, and "over-architecture."

### Uncertainty

I originally joined Sammy Studios as the lead tools programmer. What intrigued me about Sammy was the vision for the studio's technology. It was to give the artists and designers the best possible control over the game through customized tools, while engine technology was to be largely middleware-based. This was in stark contrast to my previous job where engine technology was the main focus and tools meant to help artists and designers were considered far less important.

The first tool I was tasked with developing was meant to tune character movement and animation. This tool was meant to integrate animation and physics behavior and allow animators to directly construct and tune character motion. The tool effort was launched with an extensive 80-page requirements document authored by the animators. This document had mock-ups of the user interface and detailed descriptions of every control necessary for them to fully manipulate the system. I had never seen this level of detail in a tool design before, least of all one created by an artist. At my last company, the programmers developed what they thought the artists and designers needed. This resulted in tools that didn't produce the best results.

Another programmer and I worked on this tool for several months and delivered what was defined in the design document the animators wrote. I looked forward to seeing the amazing character motion that resulted from this tool.

Unfortunately, the effort was a failure. The tool did what it was supposed to, but apparently the animators really couldn't foresee what they needed, and none of us truly understood what the underlying technology would eventually do. This was shocking.

We reflected on what else could have been done to create a better tool. What we decided was that we should have evolved the tool. We should have started by releasing a version with a single control—perhaps a slider that blended two animations (such as walking and running). Had this tool evolved with the animators' understanding of their needs and the capabilities of the emerging animation and physics technology, we would have created a far better tool.

We had developed the wrong tool on schedule. This suggested to us that a more incremental and iterative approach was necessary to develop even technology that had minimum technical and schedule risk.

**Experience: A Moving Target**

Years ago, we signed a game project with a Japanese publisher that didn't want any design documentation at all. It wanted us to explore gameplay for an idea it had. The idea was to create a SWAT game with squad-based AI. The team developed technology and gameplay for six months. Then the publisher changed its mind and wanted the game to be a first-person sci-fi shooter that didn't have squad behavior. The team pursued this direction for several more months. Other changes came and went including an acquisition of the studio and a change of publisher. The team eventually shipped as a third-person cowboy-based shooter series called *Red Dead*.

During development, progress slowed to a crawl. One of the main reasons for the lack of progress was that the codebase had become so convoluted from all the changes in direction. It was only through the heroics of a few programmers refactoring major portions of the code that any progress was made.

## Change Causes Problems

At the core of any game's requirements is the need to "find the fun." Fun cannot be found solely on the basis of what we predict in a game design document. Likewise, technical design and architecture driven by a game design document are unlikely to reflect what we may ultimately need in the game. If we want flexibility in the design of the game, then the technology we create needs to exhibit equal flexibility, but often it does not.

## Cost of Late Change

The curve in Figure 12.1 shows how the cost of changing something in a project grows over time (Boehm, 1981). Changes made late in a project can result in costs that are a magnitude or more greater than if those changes had been made early. Many reasons for this exist:

- Design details are forgotten by the programmer who wrote the code. It takes time to recall the details and be as effective as when the code was written.
- The original author of the code may not be around to make the change. Someone else has to learn the design and architecture.
- Changing assets that were created based on the original code's behavior can take a lot of time and effort.
- A lot of code may have been built on top of the original design and code. Not only does the original code have to be changed, but all the other code built upon the expected behavior of the original code has to be changed as well.

Identifying and making changes as early as possible are important.

Both uncertainty and the cost of change point to the benefits of short iterations of development. Short iterations test features quickly, which reduces uncertainty for those features. Uncertainty implies the potential for change. Because the cost of change increases as time passes, carrying uncertainty forward also carries the potential for increased cost. For example, some teams implement online functionality late in development and discover that much of their project's core technology (such as animation and physics) does not work across a network. Had they discovered this earlier in the project, the cost of fixing the problem could have been far less.

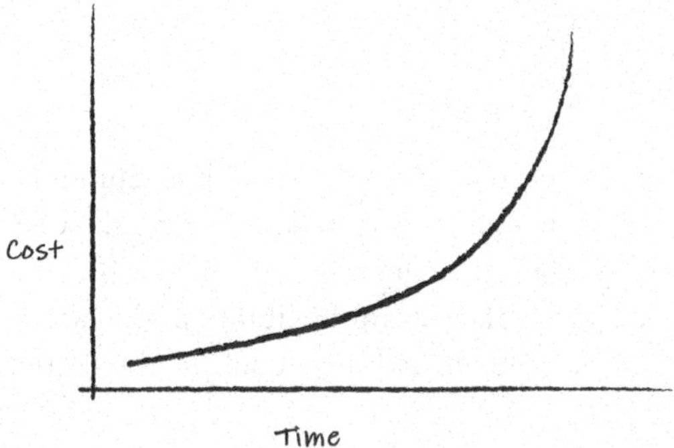


**Figure 12.1** *The cost of change*

**Note**

This potential cost of change being carried forward is a form of **technical debt**. The concept of debt is used for many elements of game development in this book.

## Too Much Architecture Up Front

One approach to the problem of creating technology for changing requirements is to "over-architect" a solution. This means implementing a solution that encompasses all the potential needs. An example is a camera system for a game initially designed to be a first-person shooter. A programmer might architect a camera system that includes general-purpose tools and camera management that handles a variety of other potential cameras, including third-person cameras and others. The goal is that if and when the designers change their minds about the game (such as going from a first-person view to a third-person view), then the changes to the camera can be accommodated through the architected system.

There are three problems with this approach:

- **It slows the introduction of new features up front:** At the start of the game, the designer wants a simple first-person camera to begin prototyping gameplay. He has to wait for the baseline architecture to be created (or brought in from an existing codebase) before the camera is introduced.
- **Architectures designed up front often need to be changed:** The assumptions built into the architecture are often proven wrong during development and need to be changed anyway. Changing larger systems takes more time than smaller systems.
- **The "sunk costs" of up-front architecture often prevent beneficial changes to the game:** After spending months architecting and implementing a solution, there's often a lot of resistance to changing or rewriting it for a better one due to the cost already sunk into the first solution.

**Experience: Build what you Need, Not what you Think you Might Need**

"Too many developers spend months working on the technology for their next game before starting the game itself. Sometimes, they never make it to developing the game! The most pragmatic solution to this is using preexisting technology. However, if custom technology is required, then only create what is needed as you go.

"A trap many developers fall into is thinking 'We'll be using this feature in the next five games, so it's worth putting a lot of time into it now.' If this is done for all features, the first game will never be finished, let alone the next five. My rule of thumb is that until I've solved a problem at least a couple of times, I don't have enough information to make a generalized solution.

"A great way of achieving these goals is adopting an Agile development practice. We are using Scrum for our current game, keeping us focused on creating just enough infrastructure to reach our current sprint/milestone."

—Alistair Doulin, CTO at Bane Games

## An Agile Approach

This section describes Agile solutions to the problems discussed thus far in this chapter. These solutions focus on an iterative and incremental approach to delivering value and knowledge early.

**Flaccid Scrum**

The technical practices described in this chapter not only improve engineering performance, they can also help overcome a typical problem that teams transitioning to Agile commonly experience.

The problem, coined "Flaccid Scrum" by Bob Martin,[2] refers to the problem teams encounter when they move from a mostly architecture-first to an iterative approach to creating technology.

An iterative approach requires continual refactoring as the best architecture emerges and changes to meet the needs of the player. Because refactoring isn't a part of the technical practices of a team new to iterative development, the architecture becomes less stable and more unwieldy, which can slow a team's velocity to a crawl.

On our first Scrum-based game, we encountered Flaccid Scrum, which led us to the practices described in this chapter.

2. https://martinfowler.com/bliki/FlaccidScrum.html

## Extreme Programming (XP)

Scrum, by design, has no engineering practices. Many teams using Scrum soon find that their original engineering practices can't keep up with the changing requirements. These teams often turn to the practices of Extreme Programming for help.

XP was a methodology developed after Scrum that adopted many of the Scrum practices. XP iterations and customer reviews, though slightly different, aren't hard to integrate into Scrum teams used to these concepts. XP introduced new practices for programmers. Among them are the practices of test-driven development (TDD) and pair programming.

Covering the concepts and practices of XP in great detail is outside the scope of this book. There are great books that already do that (see the "Additional Reading" section at the end of this chapter). Numerous studies have shown that XP increases the velocity of code creation and its quality (Jeffries and Melnik, 2007).

Programmers pair up to work on tasks. They apply the TDD practices, described next, to implement technology in small, functional increments. This enables functionality to emerge incrementally that remains stable in the face of change. The goal is to create higher-quality code that can be changed with minimum cost.

### *Test-Driven Development*

TDD practices include writing a number of unit tests for every function introduced. Each unit test will exercise the function to be written a single way by passing in data and testing what the function returns or changes. An example of this is a function that sets the health of the player in a game. If your game design defines 100 as full health and 0 as being dead, your unit tests would each set and test valid and min/max parameters and check to make sure those values were assigned by the function. Other unit tests would try to assign invalid numbers (greater than 100 or less than 0) and test to make sure the function handled those bad values correctly.

If you follow the strict TDD practices, the tests are written before you write the logic of the function that will allow those tests to pass, so the tests actually fail at first.

Unit tests and their associated code are built in parallel. When all the tests pass, the code is checked in. This happens quite frequently when the team is using TDD, sometimes every hour or two. This requires a server that acquires all changes as they are checked in and runs all the unit tests to ensure that none of them has broken the code. This server is called a **continuous integration server** (CIS). By running all the unit tests, it catches a majority of the problems usually caused by commits. When a build passes all the unit tests, then the CIS informs all the developers that it is safe to synchronize with the changes. When a submission breaks a unit test, the CIS lets everyone know that it is broken. It then becomes the team's job to fix that problem. Because the culprit who checked in the error is easily identified, he is usually the one who gets to fix the problem.

This provides big benefits to the team and project. As a project grows, the number of unit tests expands, often into the thousands. These tests continue to catch a great deal of errors automatically that would otherwise have to be caught by QA much later. These tests also create a safety net for refactoring and for other large changes that an emerging design will require.

One of the philosophical foundations of XP is that the programmers create the absolute minimal amount of functionality to satisfy customer requests every iteration. For example, suppose a customer wants to see one AI character walking around the environment. Many programmers want to architect an AI management system that handles dozens of AI characters because they "know that the game will need it sometime in the future." With XP, you don't do this. You write the code as if the user story needs only one AI character. When a story asks for more than one AI character in a future Sprint, you then introduce a simple AI manager and refactor the original code. This leads to an AI manager that is a better fit for the emerging requirements.

A major benefit of TDD is that it requires "constant refactoring" of the codebase to support this behavior. There are a number of reasons for this, but here are two of them:

- Systems created from refactoring, coupled with implementing the absolute minimum needed, often match final requirements more closely and quickly.
- Refactored code has much higher quality. Each refactoring pass creates the opportunity to improve it.

The barriers to TDD are as follows:

- There is an immediate slowing of new features introduced into the game. Writing tests take time, and it can be hard to argue that the time gained back in reduced debugging time is greater.
- Programmers take their practices very personally. Rolling out a practice like TDD has to be done slowly and in a way that clearly demonstrates its value (see Chapter 16, "The Myths and Challenges of Scrum").

**Note**

Personally, I don't fully agree with the purist approach that XP programmers should always do the absolute minimum. I believe that knowledge and experience factor into how much architecture should be preplanned. It's very easy to plan too much ahead and "over architect," but I believe there is a sweet spot found between the two extremes.

TDD is very useful and is not a difficult practice for programmers to adopt. In my experience, if a programmer tries TDD for a while, the practice of writing unit tests becomes second nature. The practice of refactoring takes longer to adjust to. Programmers resist refactoring unless it is necessary. This practice reinforces the mindset of writing code "the right way, the first time," which leads to a more brittle codebase that cannot support iteration as easily. Lead programmers should ensure that refactoring is a constant part of their work.

**Experience: Refactoring**

"Refactoring code is a strong part of our engineering culture at IMVU. Initially, product owners would question the introduction of work into a sprint by the engineers, asking, 'Do we really need to fix this technical debt? Isn't there a faster way to implement this feature?'

"It didn't take long for several concrete examples to appear highlighting the value of engineering things correctly from the outset, and of paying back technical debt that causes ongoing drag on engineering efficiency. At present, Product Owners trust engineers who say, 'I'm delayed on my task because I needed to make time to refactor code.' Engineers also trust Product Owners to help ensure that the team has time to build and maintain solid engineering infrastructure and repay technical debt.

"We've had plenty of conflict, though. To help manage that, we put a simple process in place: if the team technical lead and Product Owner couldn't agree on a how to handle an issue, then the matter was simply resolved by escalating the issue to the management team. Overall, our Product Owners consistently report that our development teams are the most productive that they've ever worked with."

—James Birchler, Engineering Director, IMVU

### *Pair Programming*

Pair programming is a simple practice in principle. Two programmers sit at a workstation. One types in code while the other watches and provides input on the problem they are both tasked with solving.

This practice often creates a great deal of concern:

- "Our programmers will get half the work done."
- "I do my best work when I am focused and not interrupted."
- "Code ownership will be destroyed, which is bad."

Changing personal workspaces and habits can generate a lot of fear, uncertainty, and doubt. This section examines how the benefits of pair programming outweigh or invalidate these concerns.

*Benefits of Pair Programming*

Let's look at the benefits of pair programming:

- **Spreads knowledge:** Pair programming isn't about one person typing and the other watching. It's an ongoing conversation about the problem the pair is trying to solve and the best way to solve it.

  Two separate programmers solve problems differently. If you were to compare these results, you would find that each solution had strengths and weaknesses. This is because the knowledge of each programmer does not entirely overlap with that of the other. The dialogue that occurs with pair programming helps to share knowledge and experience widely and quickly. It results in solutions that contain the "best of both worlds."

  Although this is good for experienced programmers, it is an outstanding benefit for bringing new programmers up to speed and mentoring entry-level programmers. Pairing brings new programmers up to speed much more quickly and therefore rapidly improves their coding practices.
- **Assures that you'll get the best out of TDD:** TDD requires that comprehensive tests be written for every function. The discipline required for this is made easier by pairing. First, it's in our nature to occasionally slack off on writing the tests. From time to time, the partner reminds you to write the proper test or takes over the keyboard if you are not fully motivated. Second, it's common to have one programmer write the tests and the other write the function that causes the tests to pass. Although this doesn't need to become a competition between the two, it

usually ensures better test coverage. A programmer who writes both the test and function may overlook the same problem in the function and tests. The saying "Two heads are better than one" definitely applies to pair programming!

- **Eliminates many bottlenecks caused by code ownership:** How many times have you been concerned about a key programmer leaving the company in mid-project or getting hit by the proverbial bus that drives around hunting down good programmers? Pairing solves some of this by having two programmers on every problem. Even if you are lucky enough not to lose key programmers, they are often too busy on other tasks to quickly solve a critical problem that arrives. Shared knowledge that comes from pair programming solves these problems.
- **Creates good standards and practices automatically:** Have you ever been faced with the problem late in a project that one of your programmers has written thousands of lines of poor-quality code that you depend on, and it is causing major problems? Management often tries to solve this problem by defining "coding standards" and conducting peer reviews.

  The problem with coding standards is that they are often hard to enforce and are usually ignored over time. Peer reviews of code are a great practice, but they usually suffer from not being applied consistently and often occur too late to head off the problem.

  Pair programming can be thought of as a *continuous peer review*. It catches many bad coding practices early. As pairs mix, a company coding standard emerges and is improved daily. It doesn't need to be written down because it is documented in the code and embedded in the heads of every programmer.
- **Focuses programmers on programming:** When programmers start pairing, adjusting to the unrelenting pace takes several days. The reason is that they do nothing but focus on the problem the entire day. Mail isn't read at the pair station. The Web isn't surfed. Shared e-mail stations can be set up for when a programmer wants to take a break and catch up on mail. E-mail clients and web browsers are a major distraction from the focus that needs to occur for programming.

### Experience

At High Moon Studios, we didn't enforce pair programming 100 percent of the time. For example, programmers didn't always pair up to solve simple bugs. However, it was done long enough to become second nature. Had we abandoned pair programming, I would have wanted to make sure that we retained the same benefits with whatever practices replaced it.

*Problems with Pairing*

There are some problems to watch out for with pair programming:

- **Poor pair chemistry:** Some pair combinations should be avoided; namely, when the chemistry does not work and cannot be forced. If pairings are self-selected, it works out better. In rare cases, some programmers cannot be paired with anyone. Any large team switching to pair programming will have some programmers who refuse to pair. It's okay to make exceptions for these people to program outside of pairs, but they still need a peer review of their work before they commit. As time passes, they will often do some pairing and may even switch to it. You just need to give them time and not force it.
- **Pairing very junior people with very senior people:** Pairing between the most experienced programmers and junior programmers is not ideal. The senior programmer ends up doing all the work at a pace the junior programmer cannot learn from. Matching junior-level programmers with mid-level programmers is better.
- **Hiring issues:** Make sure that every programming candidate for hire knows they are interviewing for a job that includes XP practices and what that entails. Consider a one-hour pair programming exercise with each candidate in the later stages of a hiring process. This does two things: First, it's a great tool for evaluating how well the candidate does in a pair situation where communication is critical. Second, it gives the candidate exposure to what they are in for if they accept an offer. A small percentage of candidates admit that pairing is not for them and opt out of consideration for the job. This is best for them and for you.

## *Are XP Practices Better Than Non-XP Practices?*

Measuring the benefit of XP practices when the team first starts using them is difficult because the pace of new features immediately slows down. This corresponds to studies (Jeffries and Melnik, 2007) that show that a pair of programmers using TDD is about 1.5 times as fast as one separate programmer introducing new features. The additional benefits we've seen with XP/TDD more than offset the initial loss of productivity:

- **Very high stability in builds at all times:** It adds to the productivity of designers and artists as well as programmers when the build is not constantly crashing or behaving incorrectly.

- **Post-production debugging demands vastly reduced:** More time is spent tuning and improving gameplay rather than fixing bugs that have been postponed.
- **Better practices required in Scrum:** Iterative practices in Scrum have a higher level of change. TDD helps retain stability through this change.
- **Less wasted effort:** A project wastes less time reworking large systems by avoiding large architectures written before the requirements are fully known.

**Branching versus Continuous Integration**

Branch and merge commit strategies often result in weekly commits that bundle hundreds of lines of changes together in a big lump that causes problems that can require days to fix.

This is the reasoning behind continuous integration; it enables frequent commits that—coupled with unit testing—work well to ensure that the changes are testable, small, and safe. They also make the commit process quick and usually painless.

## Debugging

One of the biggest differences between an Agile game development project and a traditional game development project has to do with how bugs are addressed. In many projects, finding and fixing bugs does not happen until the end when quality assurance (QA) focuses on the game. The resulting rush to fix defects usually leads to crunch.

One of the ideals of Agile game development is to eliminate the "post-alpha bug-fixing crunch." Adding QA early in the project and addressing bugs as we find them significantly reduces the amount of time and risk during the alpha and beta portions of a project.

### *Debugging in Agile*

An Agile project approaches bugs differently. Fixing bugs is part of the work that needs to happen before a feature is completed each Sprint. In an Agile project, we are trying to minimize debt, especially the debt of defects, because the cost of fixing those bugs increases over time. Although QA is part of an Agile team, this doesn't relieve the other developers from the responsibility of testing their own work.

When a bug is identified, we either add a task to fix it in the Sprint Backlog or a story to fix it in the Product Backlog.

*Adding a Task to Fix a Bug to the Sprint Backlog*
When a bug is found that relates to a Sprint Goal and it's small enough to fix, a task to do so is added to the Sprint Backlog. Fixing bugs is part of development velocity. Adopting better practices to avoid defects increases velocity.

In some cases, if enough bugs arise during a Sprint, then the team may miss achieving all the user stories.

*Adding a Bug to the Product Backlog*
Sometimes a problem is uncovered that does not impact a Sprint Goal, cannot be solved by the team, or is too large to fix in the remaining time of the Sprint. For example, if a level production team that contains no programmers uncovers a flaw with AI pathfinding on a new level, a user story to fix this is created, added to the Product Backlog, and ordered by the Product Owner. Often such bugs are addressed in a hardening Sprint if the Product Owner decides to call for one (see Chapter 9, "Agile Release Planning").

If the team is uncertain about which Backlog the bug belongs on, they should discuss it with the Product Owner.

### *A Word About Bug Databases*

One rule I strongly encourage on every Agile team is to avoid bug-tracking tools and databases before the "feature complete" goals (often called **alpha**). It's not that the tools are bad, but tools encourage the attitude that identifying a bug and entering it in a database is "good enough for now." It's not. In many cases it's a root of the evil that creates crunch at the end of a project.

When a team enters alpha and the publisher ramps up its off-site QA staff, then a bug database may become necessary.

## Optimization

Like debugging, optimization is often left for the end of a project. Agile game development projects spread optimization across the project as much as possible. Unfortunately for projects that have large production phases and single true releases, much of the optimization must be left to the end of the project when the entire game is playable.

Knowledge is the key element that helps decide between what is optimized early in the project and what is optimized in post-production. Projects optimize early to gain knowledge about the following:

- **Is the game (feature, mechanic, and so on) fun?** It's difficult to know what is fun when the game is playing at 10 fps. There must be an ongoing effort to avoid a debt of badly written code or bloated test assets that need to be redone in post-production.
- **What are the technical and asset budgets for production?** Projects shouldn't enter production unless the team is certain about the limitations of the engine and tool sets. Knowing these limitations will vastly decrease rework waste. The following are examples:
  - **How many AI characters can be in the scene at any one time?** Often this variable depends on other parameters. For example, a game may afford more AI characters in a simpler scene that frees up some of the rendering budget for AI.
  - **What is the static geometry budget?** This should be established early, and it should be very conservative. As the game experience is polished with special effects and improved textures, the budget often shrinks. In post-production, adding static geometry detail is easier than removing it from scenes.
  - **What work will be necessary to get the game working on the weakest platform?** Sometimes the weakest platform is the most difficult to iterate on. It's better to know as early as possible if separate assets need to be created for another platform!
  - **Does the graphics-partitioning technology work?** Don't count on some "future technical miracle" to occur that enables levels to fit in memory or render at an acceptable frame rate. How much work needs to be done to make a culling system work? Make sure the level artists and designers know how a culling system works before they lay out the levels.

### *Postponed Optimizations*

So, what optimizations are left until post-production? These include lower-risk optimizations such as those made to the assets created in production to reduce their resource footprint. Such optimizations are best made after the entire game is fully playable. Here are some examples of post-production optimization:

- **Disc-streaming optimization:** Organize the data on the hard drive and disc to stream in effectively. This is always prototyped to some degree in pre-production.
- **AI spawn optimization:** Spread out the loading and density of AI characters to balance their use of resources.

- **Mobile app load and server optimization:** Optimize how long your mobile app takes to load and reduce the bottlenecks between it and your app server.
- **Audio mixing:** Simplify the audio streams, and premix multiple streams when possible.

A project can't discount the benefits from engine improvements made during production. At the same time, they can't be counted on. It's a judgment call about where to draw the line. As a technical customer, I set the goal of a project to achieve a measurable bar of performance throughout development as a Definition of Done for releases. An example of a release Definition of Done is as follows:

- 30 frames per second (or better) for 50 percent of the frames
- 15 to 30 frames per second for 48 percent of the frames
- Less than 15 frames per second for 2 percent of the frames
- Loading time on the development station of less than 45 seconds

These standards are measurable and are caught quickly by test automation. They might not be stringent enough to ship with, but they are acceptable for the "magazine demo" quality releases.

**Experience**

Decide early what range of phones your mobile game will run well on and test on that range frequently and early. I've seen teams ignore this and lose half their potential market by testing only on the latest phones during development.

### *Staying Within Technical and Asset Budgets Throughout the Project*

The benefits of having the game run at shippable frame rates throughout development are vast. We get a more true experience of the game emerging when it runs "within its means" at all times. However, there is an ongoing give-and-take between iterative discovery and incremental value. For example, developers may want to experiment with having 24 AI characters rush the player in an "AI wave" to find out whether it's fun. Do they have to optimize the entire AI system to handle 24 characters in the experiment? Of course not. If the experiment has shown that the feature *would* add a lot of value to the game, we have only improved our understanding, not the game. We have iterated to improve our knowledge, but we haven't yet incremented the value of the game.

Too often we'll add such a scene to the game without enough optimization. We have created a bit of debt that we have to pay back later. This payback cost could be large. It could be so large that we can't afford it and have to eliminate the mechanic altogether. This could occur for many reasons; here are some examples:

- The AI character models are too complex to afford 24 in the scene.
- Spawning a wave of 24 AI characters causes a one-second pause, which violates a first-party technical requirement (for example, TCR/TRC or App Store).

The list could go on. What can we do to reduce this debt and truly increment the value of the game? We need to do some spikes to determine the optimization debt and influence the Product Backlog to account for it. If a spike reveals these two problems, we could address them in the following ways:

- Plan for simple models with a smaller number of bones to populate characters in the wave.
- Implement an interleaved spawning system (like a round-robin) to spawn the characters one per frame over a second.

Both of these Backlog items enable the Product Owner to measure the cost of the AI wave against the value we learned in the test. This enables cost and value to be the deciding factor rather than the need to ship a game on time.

There are many examples of this type of decision that need to be made early. When these decisions are not made, the optimization debt often becomes overwhelming. This requires an objective eye to watch out for. Too many times we view these features with the "developer's eye." We overlook the flaws that cause frustration to our stakeholders.

## What Good Looks Like

When we started applying Agile principles to our technical practices, the dream was that we could eliminate the alpha and beta project phases. These were usually the worst part of a project due to the stress, crunch, and compromises to quality we endured to get the game out the door.

We weren't able to do that, but we did put an end to the crunch and much of the stress, instead focusing on recon testing[3] and tuning the entire game. This greatly improved the game and the overall experience of making it.

## Summary

This chapter explored technical practices that Agile game developers most frequently benefit from because they move programmers away from separate design, code, and test phases of development into iterative daily practices where these activities are mixed and better serve the other disciplines. They create code that matches emergent requirements, is more maintainable, and has higher quality.

The next several chapters explore the other game team disciplines and how their practices can be adapted for more agility as well.

## Additional Reading

Beck, K. and Andres, C. 2005. *Extreme Programming Explained, Second Edition.* Boston, MA: Addison-Wesley.

Brooks, F. 1996. *The Mythical Man-Month, Second Edition.* Reading, MA: Addison-Wesley.

Kim G., P. Debois, J. Willis, J. Humble, and J. Allspaw. *The DevOps handbook: how to create world-class agility, reliability, and security in technology organizations.* Portland, OR: IT Revolution Press, LLC; 2016.

McConnell, S. 2004. *Code Complete, Second Edition.* Redmond, WA: Microsoft Press.

3. Testing the entire game from start to finish, often with beta testers.

## Chapter 13

# Agile Art and Audio

Computer-based artwork is dynamic and evolving. Art styles transform, and artists explore new meaning in what they create. The medium that they use has undergone as much change in the past few decades, with the advent of powerful and cheap computers, as it had since the caves in Lascaux, France, were painted 16,000 years ago.

Cell animation and pre-rendered computer graphics have enabled artists to add more motion to their work. This has made it possible for the wild imaginations of artists and storytellers to be more deeply shared such as in the movie *Fantasia*.

Video games have added a whole new dimension. Now art has to be interactive, which enables it to be used in ways its creators didn't imagine. The medium is complex and requires the artist to collaborate with designers and programmers to bring their work to life.

This chapter explores the benefits, concerns, and common practices of artists on cross-discipline Agile teams. This chapter covers principles and practices that apply to many artistic disciplines including modeling, texturing, animation, audio, and so on. It refers to the members of every discipline as artists.

## The Solutions in This Chapter

An artist once asked, "Why use Agile for art? When Michelangelo painted the ceiling of the Sistine Chapel, he wasn't using Agile. He had a plan to paint the entire ceiling."

In reality, Michelangelo may have been better off using a more Agile approach to painting the Sistine Chapel. There was a great deal of trial and error and false starts.

He had no idea how to paint images on a curved and segmented ceiling. He signed a fixed-price contract calling for 12 figures to be painted. Four years later he had painted 300. It's no wonder he referred to it as one of the worst experiences of his life.

Video game artists face similar challenges. Translating their vision into reality runs headlong into the challenges of the medium, whether it is fresco or graphics processors. Overcoming these challenges and understanding the limitations of the medium before creating the final product are necessary.

The following are some of the main problems artists encounter. This chapter focuses on their solutions:

- **Artists need to know whether they are creating the right thing and not wasting effort:** Parallel development of assets and technology that the assets depend on is a traditional source of wasted effort. Engine development is often started with optimistic feature sets, performance goals, and schedules. Unfortunately, projects fall short of these goals, and the assets created cannot be used as built and have to be rebuilt. Technical iteration requires an ongoing conversation and experimentation with what looks and works best. Every artist knows that the quality of a complex asset, such as a level, depends on a trade-off between polygon count, texture quality, lighting complexity, and the palette of effects available. None of these is independent of each other. Some levels require more effects than others and require trade-offs. We want to build the knowledge of these trade-offs during engine development before we commit to production. This requires frequent collaboration between the technology creators and the artists who leverage their work.
- **Artists need a stable, working build:** Nothing impacts progress more than a broken build. Graphical defects that impact visual quality prevent an artist from developing the best possible assets. Relying on a separate technology team to solve these problems adds delay. Cross-discipline teams are more likely to have a team member who quickly solves these problems or is able to communicate with someone who can help.
- **Artists need faster tools and pipelines:** Artists are often limited by slow iteration times and therefore can't iterate as much as they like. Less iteration translates to lower-quality art. A common problem is that programming team members, who have control over improving tools and pipelines, are not impacted by the same problems. They don't experience how slow it is to change a texture on a game. They are focused on the tasks that are important to their team. Cross-discipline teams share common goals. Problems that impact individual progress impact the entire team. When this happens, then such problems receive the level of attention they deserve.

## Concerns About Agile

Artists have several common concerns about Agile and Scrum:

- **Scrum is for programmers:** Scrum is used to a great extent on software development projects, but it wasn't created for programmers. In fact, it purposefully has no specific practices for any one discipline. It's as applicable for artists as it is for any other discipline.
- **Art production runs on a schedule. We can't be iterative:** With video games, art and technology have to integrate with the gameplay mechanics to create a fun experience. Teams have to explore how all these components work together. After they discover this, they can schedule the creation of 10 to 12 hours of production content. Exploring in pre-production is necessary. Cross-discipline pre-production teams using by-the-book Scrum thrive. During production, many practices will change but remain Agile. Production issues continue to create unexpected challenges. These challenges wreak havoc on the best-planned schedules. Artists creating assets still need rapid response to technical problems. They need to continually find ways to collaborate (see Chapter 10, "Video Game Project Management").
- **Cross-discipline teams don't work:** On large projects, artists have traditionally been pooled with members of their own discipline, and they've learned to work that way. Once they try cross-discipline teams and experience day-to-day responsiveness from teammates who help them solve problems, they change their minds. Scrum doesn't prevent artists from communicating outside of a Sprint. They can form communities of practice (see Chapter 21, "Scaling Agile Game Teams") and still share ideas and practices with one another.

Like almost any developer, artists need to experience Scrum practices before they'll agree with the benefits. A sense of skepticism is healthy as long as it is paired with an openness to accept what works.

**The Artists Decide to Join**

When High Moon Studios started experimenting with Scrum, our artists were very skeptical of it. Some thought it was a "management fad" or a covert form of micromanagement. They wanted no part of it, and we didn't force it on them.

The programmers decided to try it and formed teams. Their Daily Scrums quickly identified impediments that impacted their progress. Many of these addressed the lack of proper assets to work with. The producers, recruited to be the Scrum Masters, spent much of their time pestering the artists to produce the assets the teams demanded.

After the artists saw the producers focusing their effort on solving Scrum-raised impediments, they wanted to start using Scrum, too.

## Art Leadership

As with all leadership roles, Agile shifts the responsibility of art leadership from daily command and control to mentoring and facilitation. The role of art leadership is to improve the quality of the art being created and to help artists improve their ability to create art. These two must constantly be balanced.

To improve the quality of art, the art lead (or art director) reviews new art in-game and provides feedback. This creates the opportunity to work with the artists directly within a Sprint. This influences some of the daily practices. For example, art assets may need a sign-off or approval by a lead artist or art director, so some teams add a column on their task board called "Pending Approval" before the "Done" column to hold an art task to be approved before it is considered done.

A challenge for many Agile game teams is how to avoid having art direction approval become a bottleneck for progress. Art directors are usually not members of any one team, they do not have the same level of commitment to a Sprint as teams who depend on their feedback. Delayed feedback is often a source of impediments for these teams. Studios develop unique practices, such as highly visible approval Backlogs, to address this.

In addition to asset approval, art leaders must mentor less-experienced artists to improve their art creation workflow. Art cost is as critical as art quality. Without experience or familiarity with all the tools, new artists can waste a lot of time creating assets the hard way.

As the art lead works with artists to improve quality and reduce cost, she will see patterns for improvement that can be shared among all artists or opportunities for improvement that can be championed with the team that supports the pipeline and tools.

**Experience**

In the mid-nineties, many 3D games were a mix of 2D and 3D. One (canceled) game I was working on at Angel Studios took place outdoors. In these outdoor levels, there were trees in the distance that, because of the limited rendering budgets, were tree pictures on billboards (2D cards that always rotate to face the player). One artist made beautiful tree billboards, but he was very slow in making them. This went on for a few months until the lead artist visited him and discovered that he was creating a full three-dimensional tree on the PC modeling tool, taking a picture of it, and using the picture for the billboard! That practice was changed.

## Art on a Cross-Discipline Team

An artist on a cross-discipline team is faced with a number of challenges. Different vocabularies must be understood, and the artists must struggle to make themselves understood as well. They are reminded daily of how their art is used: how it leverages the strengths or exposes the weaknesses of the technology.

For a cross-discipline team that is measured by value added to a working game, the role of an artist shifts to that of a "game developer" who specializes in art. An artist doesn't simply create an asset for someone else to put in the game and make fun. The artist participates in the creation of an experience, where art has an equal value. By having a voice in the discussion about what is being created, artists elevate the value of what they create and minimize the cost of creating it.

### Creative Tension

> When forced to work within a strict framework, the imagination is taxed to its utmost—and will produce the richest ideas. Given total freedom, the work is likely to sprawl.
>
> —*T.S. Eliot*

Creative tension exists between what we *can* do and what we *want to do* in a game. Creative tension is a good thing. It enables us to push the quality of an asset in the game while working within the bounds of technical limits, cost, and schedule. Creative tension puts pressure on our work processes, tools, and practices to find opportunities to eliminate waste.

Some of the best ideas are created from these limitations. When we were developing the game *Midtown Madness*, the shortage of level artists forced us to rely on a tool that procedurally created a city from a simple line map. This tool generated an entire city in an hour and allowed us to iterate hundreds of times whenever we discovered problems such as curb angles interfering with vehicle wheel physics. Had the entire city been modeled by hand, we could not have iterated as many times to improve the game.

Scrum compels teams to improve their performance every Sprint. It forces creative tension to the surface where it belongs.

**95-Mile-Per-Hour Art**

Game art has a function and a form. Its purpose guides its creation. Its function is less apparent when artists are separated from the game. During the development of *Midnight Club*, a city racing game, a group of artists created assets for the streets in a separate room. We were looking forward to seeing their work because we had a city filled with gray cubes. The day finally arrived when the new geometry was placed in the city. It was stunning. The city was truly coming to life. We started driving around and discovered a major problem. Much of the new detailed geometry was at the street level. The actual city we were modeling had a lot of this detail itself, but it was a terrible problem for a racing game. A staircase jutting out from a building could instantly stop a car using the sidewalk. Low planters became uncrossable barriers. Fun transformed into frustration.

Much of this detail had to be removed to eliminate the barriers at street level. From then on, the mantra repeated daily was "Create 95-mile-per-hour art." The art had to look good and function well for players in cars traveling past it at 95 miles per hour. This art can be considerably different from art that looks good standing still in Maya!

## Art QA

Many problems are avoided when the entire team iterates on the game daily. Asset creation tasks aren't considered complete when they are exported but when they are verified in-game on the target platform. Verification not only includes seeing the asset in the game and ensuring that it functions well but also includes verifying that some of the less-apparent aspects of its use are correct. In-game asset verification tools aid in checking the construction of assets in the game in many ways:

- **Physics geometry view:** Does the collision geometry match the visible geometry? Is it aligned properly?
- **Texel density view:** Are the textures properly mapped? Are the textures the right size?
- **Wireframe view:** Is the out-of-view geometry being properly culled? Are the asset visibility flags set properly?
- **Sound volume view:** Are the sound min/max radii properly set? Are the proper sounds triggering at the right time?
- **Asset selection and highlight:** Is an asset lit properly in the game? Is it visible to the player? How often is it instantiated? Rather than searching for an asset, this tool enables the artist to select it from a list and see it highlighted.
- **Target testing:** Does the art look good on all the target phones? Is it too dark for people playing in a well-lit environment?

Artists need to have access to all the target platforms to test their work. Sometimes, equipping every person on the team with platform development kits is too expensive. In those cases, small groups share a development kit in a location that they can all see and control from their own workstation.

When QA is the responsibility of everyone on the team, then everyone needs to examine how assets are being used and make sure that they adhere to the budget requirements.

## Building Art Knowledge

A goal of pre-production is to create knowledge. We want to know how fun the game is, how content will be produced, and how much it is going to cost. Creating this knowledge requires iteration. Unfortunately, teams often focus too much on core mechanics or the fun of the game and not enough on production costs. This result is that many projects exceed their production budgets or schedules. They need to explore production costs more in pre-production.

Level production often costs 50 percent or more of the production budget. Project teams need to refine their understanding of the effort to build levels during pre-production to avoid mechanics that inflate production costs beyond the budget. For example, some shooters have a fantastic feature that makes it possible for every object in the environment to be destructible. Unfortunately, this feature can double level production costs because building destructible geometry requires far more effort. By knowing this cost impact in pre-production, the Product Owner can better judge the return on investment for this feature.

Learning about production cost is an iterative process. It begins with a range of estimates based on existing knowledge (perhaps from a previous title) and is iteratively refined during pre-production. Refinement occurs by iterating on mechanics and building a "vocabulary" of rooms or simpler levels that grow as the team learns more (See Chapter 10).

Building a finished level before a vocabulary of mechanics is established is wasteful. This waste is seen on many milestone-driven projects. Teams often feel compelled to show something that is polished to their publisher when the gameplay is still undetermined. These polished milestone levels are eventually thrown out or require a great deal of rework when the team learns more about the gameplay.

## Overcoming the "Not Done Yet" Syndrome

Teams are often called upon to demonstrate the potential value of a mechanic in a low-cost way. This often requires that stand-in assets, such as low polygon models or roughly blended animations, be used instead of polished assets. These demonstrations are useful tracer bullets to indicate where the game is headed. Although the results might be thrown away, their purpose is to learn more about a feature before deciding to invest more time in it.

> **Tip**
>
> Often level designers create a set of basic level shapes they refer to as **LEGO™ bricks** that allow them to "snap together" a large level very quickly. These levels give a sense of scale for production levels that take many times more effort to create.

Artists often resist showing stand-in assets to the world and want to add more polish for a prototype. There is nothing wrong with doing this as long as it doesn't negatively impact the goal. For example, one project team discovered that its prototype level was running extremely slowly. After exploring the problem, it was discovered that hundreds of the props placed in the level were dynamically lit. The artists had done this because they didn't have enough time to properly pre-light the level and wanted everything to look good.

Iteration often requires showing proof-of-concept work to demonstrate knowledge gained. Stand-in assets are fine to use, but care should be taken to make it obvious they are temporary. Candy-stripe textures or characters that look like "crash-test dummies" allow stakeholders to look beyond the test assets and judge the results.

**Experience**

Be careful of using reference assets. Because they look good, they are often forgotten until there is a problem, such as the time an artist pasted in the eyeball of a character with a photo that was a megabyte in size! Another time, on *Midtown Madness 2*, an artist textured a garbage can with a picture from a real garbage can. The company whose logo was on that can successfully sued for its illegal use!

## Budgets

One of the most frustrating things for artists is seeing their work go to waste. It's not unusual to review the assets created for a game and realize that enough of them were created and discarded to complete *two games*. The majority of the team often consists of artists, so wasting 50 percent of their effort is a tremendous burden.

Much of the waste comes from assets being created when not enough about their requirements and budgets are known. Because a game artist's creation tools are often separate from the game itself, they "get ahead" of the rest of the project and create assets that are based more on speculation rather than the constraints of the emergent game. This is usually driven by schedule and "resource allocation" plans. A schedule might stipulate a certain number of assets created by a specific date, which in turn drives staffing on a project that may not be ready for it.

For example, a project plan and schedule may forecast a date when a set of characters is complete. As a result, a group of character modelers and animators join the project months before this date to start producing the character assets. At this point it's expected that the project has proven character requirements and budgets such as the following:

- The skeletal budgets, such as how many bones are required, and so on
- The model polygon requirements, such as how many characters are on the screen at any one time
- An identified set of behaviors to derive the animation sets
- Character motion needs, such as whether all the animations are identified for characters to "look good" while moving

If character mechanics are not sufficiently developed to the point where these things are known, it leads to waste. The character artists would have to guess about these requirements and, because they have to keep busy, start building assets with them. This usually results in character assets that need a great deal of rework or, worse, have to be used as is.

Cross-discipline teams iterate and refine specific asset budgets and requirements as part of the goal of finding the fun and the cost. As pre-production moves forward, budgets and production tool requirements need to become part of the Definition of Done for asset classes. When these elements become "out of sync," the team identifies it quickly and corrects the problem (such as altering team membership or future Sprint goals).

**Murderous Artists**

When optimization and target integration are late, artists are often the ones to suffer the most.

When we were preparing *Midnight Club* for shipping, we discovered very late that the PlayStation's ability to stream textures into memory wasn't as fast as advertised. As a result, we had to fit all of our cities' textures into memory, which reduced our texture budget by 50 percent. The artists were very unhappy with this news and struggled to minimize texture use where possible, but it was a tough choice for them, and they didn't hit their target soon enough for our technical lead, so he re-exported all the city textures to one quarter of their original size (the engine at the time required square textures) to make them fit. What was worse was he didn't tell anyone he did it. None of the artists saw the result until they received their retail copies months later.

The artists were so furious with the quality of the textures they saw in the game, I became concerned for the technical lead's safety. I wouldn't have been surprised to find him beaten to death with a Wacom tablet in the parking lot.

## Audio at the "End of the Chain"

Adding audio to an otherwise completed asset or mechanic is often the "last step" in a chain of steps (see Chapter 10), even in pre-production. This can lead to audio designers or composers with little to do at the start of a Sprint and then too much to do at the end. Scrum teams often change the assumptions about handing off work and find ways to interleave work on multiple assets and increase collaboration across disciplines.

### Shifting to Kanban

Chapter 10 described the challenge of moving into content production using Sprints. When the less predictable swarm of exploratory work shifts to a more predictable flow of mass-producing assets, then time-boxed Sprints become less useful. Teams should recognize the following symptoms as triggers to shift to Kanban:

- Content completion does not fit cleanly into a Sprint.
- Sprint planning is less useful because the workflow has been established for one or more asset types in previous Sprints.
- Daily emergence of tasks shifts to a repeated hand-off of work in an established flow.

When ready, a team can quickly shift to Kanban practices as described in Chapter 6, "Kanban."

## What Good Looks Like

In Chapter 10, we explored Lean production practices and how cross-discipline teams work together to reduce waste while continually improving what they are creating and how they are creating it. A side effect of these practices is that role boundaries begin to blur. For example, as concept artists shift from handing off drawings to engaging in more collaborative daily conversations with level designers, both begin to learn each other's role and vocabulary. The level designer won't start drawing concept art and the concept artist will not start editing levels, but they learn more about each other's goals and methods. They use this knowledge to modify their practices to better accommodate one another. For example, when working on a racing game that took place in Paris, the concept artist learned about the layout, landmarks, and visual style of Paris, while the level designer focused on what the vehicle was able to do. The two worked closely together to find intersecting areas (landmarks and street styles of Paris that worked well with the vehicle dynamics), and the result improved quality and reduced waste.

**Experience**

When I started creating tools for artists and designers, my understanding of the complete process of creating games grew by a magnitude. It altered my approach to how I developed code and later led teams. A wider view of other disciplines benefits every role and is a natural advantage of cross-discipline teams.

## Summary

Artists face many challenges on game development teams. They are often at the mercy of uncertain technology and impossible schedules that end up forcing them to overproduce assets and compromise quality. As teams grow, these challenges will also grow.

As with the other disciplines, artists need to see themselves as game developers first and artists second. When they work on art teams in isolation, it creates communication barriers between the other disciplines. Players aren't buying just art; they're buying art that does something entertaining. This requires a cross-discipline approach to creating value, which is what Scrum promotes.

## Additional Reading

Austin, R.D., and L. Devin. 2003. *Artful Making: What Managers Need to Know About How Artists Work.*

Catmull, E.E., and A. Wallace. 2014. *Creativity, Inc.: Overcoming the unseen forces that stand in the way of true inspiration.* New York: Random House.

Goldscheider, L. 1953. *Michelangelo: Paintings, Sculpture, Architecture.* London: Phaidon Press.

# Chapter 14

# Agile Design

When I first started working on games professionally in the early nineties, the role of designer was being instituted throughout the industry. Following the mold of prominent designers such as Shigeru Miyamoto and Sid Meier, designers were seen as directors of the game, or at least the people who came up with many of the ideas. The role required communication with the team on a daily basis but not much written documentation.

As technical complexity, team size, and project durations grew, the role of the designer became more delineated. Some projects had teams of designers who specialized in writing stories, scripting, tuning characters, or creating audio. Hierarchies emerged to include lead, senior, associate, or assistant designers, among others.

The overhead of communication with large teams and the cost of longer development efforts led to a demand for certainty from the stakeholders. Large detailed design documents attempted to create that certainty, but at best they only deferred its reckoning.

This chapter examines how Agile can reverse this trend.

**Viewpoint**

"Designers are the chief proponents for the player. This has not changed in 20 years of game development. Though titles and roles have changed, designers look out for gameplay and quality of the product from a player's perspective.

"When teams were small—with ten or less people—this could be done easily; it was a series of conversations while textures were created and code was written. The design was natural and organic as it emerged from the team. 'Horse swaps' could easily occur. For example, trading a very difficult-to-build mechanic for an easy one that still achieved the same gameplay vision was relatively simple.

"However, in the past ten years, teams have begun to balloon, first to the 30- to 50-person teams of the nineties and then finally to the occasional several-hundred-person monstrosities of the 2000s. A single designer could not have all the conversations that needed to happen (even several designers have problems). As a result, documentation began to surface that outlined the product as a whole, from the very high level to the very granular. Although this paints the initial vision of the title, it does away with one of the most important facets of any type of product development: the dialogue.

"Scrum addresses this. Five- to ten-person cross-discipline Scrum teams usually include a designer. Each of these designers is entrusted by the lead designer to understand the key vision elements and speak to the team."

—Rory McGuire, Game Designer

## The Solutions in This Chapter

What are some of the problems that face developers on large projects? The two most common problems are the creation of large detailed plans at the start of a project and the rush at the end of the project to cobble something together to ship. This chapter explores the solutions to these problems.

### Designs Do Not Create Knowledge

Originally when designers were asked to write design documents, they rebelled. Writing a design document seemed like an exercise to placate a publisher or commit the designers to decisions they weren't ready to make. Over time this attitude toward documentation has changed. Writing design documents has become the focus for many designers. It's felt that this is the easiest way to communicate vision to both the stakeholders and a large project team.

Designers need to create a vision, but design documents can go too far beyond this and speculate instead. Once, on a fantasy shooter game I worked on, the designers not only defined all the weapons in the design document but how many clips the player could hold and how many bullets each clip contained! This level of detail didn't help the team. In fact, for a while, it led it in the wrong direction.

**Do they Really Read the Design Document?**

One publisher demanded that our design document be at least 300 pages long. This was a puzzling requirement, but we had to do it to get approval for the rest of the game. As a test, we inserted a paragraph describing how SpongeBob SquarePants would make an appearance in our M-rated game. Our publisher never commented on the inclusion of a licensed character we had no permission for, which confirmed our suspicion that they never read the design document.

It turns out that we didn't invent this practice. Managers for popular rock bands also include ridiculous requirements in the contracts they make with performance venues. The most notorious example was the requirement that the band be provided with a bowl of brown M&Ms before the show. If there were no brown M&Ms, it meant they didn't read the contract and could be held in breach. In reality, no one in the band cared very much about the color of their candy.

## The Game Emerges at the End

At the end of a typical game project, when all the features are being integrated, optimized, and debugged, life becomes complicated for designers. This is the first time they experience a potentially shippable version of the game. At this point it typically bears little resemblance to what was defined in the design document, but it's too late to dwell on that. Marketing and QA staffs are ramping up and marketing campaigns are scheduled.

The true performance of the technology begins to emerge, and it's usually less than what was planned for. This requires that budgets be slashed. For example, waves of enemy characters become trickles, detailed textures are decimated, and props are thinned out.

Because of deadlines, key features that are "at 90 percent" are cut regardless of their value. As a result, the game that emerges at beta is a shadow of what was speculated in the design document. However, it's time to polish what remains for shipping.

## Designing with Scrum

Successful designers collaborate across all disciplines. If an asset doesn't match the needs of a mechanic, they work with an artist to resolve the issue. If a tuning parameter does not exist, they work with a programmer to add it. They also accept that design ideas come from every member of the team at any time. This doesn't mean that every idea is valid. Designers are responsible for a consistent design vision, which requires them to filter or adapt these ideas.

**Cops and Robbers**

In the late nineties, while we were developing *Midtown Madness*, I was playing "capture the flag" after-hours in the game *Team Fortress*. One day it occurred to me that a version of "capture the flag" for our city racing game might be fun. I raised this idea with the game designer, and he suggested a creative variation called "cops and robbers." In it, one group of players were robbers, while the other group were cops. The robbers try to capture gold from a bank and race to return it to their hideout. The cops try to stop the robbers and return the gold. This feature was a big hit with online players and seemed to be even more popular than racing! Good ideas can come from anywhere!

### A Designer for Every Team?

A designer should be part of every cross-discipline Scrum team working on a core gameplay mechanic. He should be selected on the basis of the mechanic and his skills. For example, a senior designer should be part of the team working on the shooting mechanic for a first-person shooter. If the team is responsible for the heads-up display (HUD), then a designer with a good sense of usability should join the team.

### The Role of Documentation

When designers first start using Scrum, they'll often approach a Sprint as a mini-waterfall project; they'll spend a quarter of the Sprint creating a written plan for the work to be done during the remainder. Over time this behavior shifts to daily collaboration and conversation about the emerging goal. This is far more effective.

This doesn't mean that designers shouldn't think beyond a Sprint and never write any documentation. A design document should limit itself to what is known about the game and identify, but not attempt to answer, the unknown. Documenting a design forces designers to think through their vision before presenting it to the rest of the team. However, a working game is the best way to address the unknown.

A goal of a design document is to share the vision about the game with the team and stakeholders. Relying solely on a document for sharing vision has a number of weaknesses:

- **Documents aren't the best form of communication:** Much of the information between an author and reader is lost. Sometimes I've discovered that stakeholders don't read any documentation; it's merely a deliverable to be checked off!
- **Vision changes over time:** Documents are poor databases of change. Don't expect team members to revisit the design document to find modifications. Recall the story of the animal requirement for *Smuggler's Run* from Chapter 7, "The Product Backlog"; that was a case of failed communication about changing vision.

Daily conversation, meaningful Sprint and release planning, and reviews are all places to share vision. Finding the balance between design documentation and conversation and collaboration is the challenge for every designer on an Agile team.

### Conversation Skills are Key

"Being able to have a good conversation is a fundamental part of a game designer's toolkit. Learn how to ask questions, listen openly, and provide considered and informed answers. Just as important: make space for everyone to participate. The loudest voices, intentional or not, can hamper others' contributions and understanding."

—James Everett, Producer, Weta Gameshop

### "Stay the %#&$ Out!"

One designer at High Moon Studios had a difficult time shifting his focus away from documentation when he joined his first Scrum team. At the start of every four-week Sprint, he locked himself in an office for a week to write documentation for the Sprint Goal. The team didn't want to wait and pestered him with questions during this time. The constant interruptions led the designer to post a note on his door that read "Stay the %#&$ out! I'm writing documents!" Eventually, the team performed an "intervention" of sorts with the designer to get him to kick the documentation habit!

## Parts on the Garage Floor

Agile planning practices create a prioritized feature Backlog that can be revised as the game emerges. The value of features added is evaluated every Sprint. However, many core mechanics take more than a single Sprint to demonstrate minimum marketable value. As a result, the team and Product Owner need a certain measure of faith that the vision for such mechanics will prove itself. However, too much faith invested in a vision will lead teams down long, uncertain paths, which results in a pile of functional "parts" that don't mesh well together. I call this the "parts on the garage floor" dysfunction.

We saw one such problem on a project called *Bourne Conspiracy*. In this third-person action-adventure game, the player had to occasionally prowl around areas populated with guards who raise an alarm if they spot the player. This usually resulted in the player being killed. In these areas, the designers placed doors that the player had to open. At one point, an epic in the Product Backlog read as follows:

> As a player, I want the ability to pick locks to get through locked doors and avoid noisy confrontations with the guards.

This is a well-constructed epic story. The problem was that there were no locked doors anywhere. This resulted in another story being created:

> As a level designer, I want to have the ability to make doors locked so the player can't use them without picking the lock.

This story is a little suspect. It represents value to a developer, but it doesn't communicate any ultimate value to the player. Such stories are common, but they can be a symptom of a debt of parts building up.

The parts continued to accumulate as Sprints went by:

> As a player, I want to see a countdown timer on the HUD that represents how much time is remaining until the lock is picked.
>
> As a player, I want to hear lock-picking sounds while I am picking the lock.
>
> As a player, I want to see lock-picking animations on my character while I pick the lock.

This continued Sprint after Sprint; work was being added to the lock-picking mechanic. It was looking more polished every review.

All of these lock-picking stories were building the parts for a mechanic that was still months away from proving itself. The problem was that lock picking made no sense. The player had no choice but to pick the locks. Nothing in the game required the player to choose between picking a lock or taking a longer route. Ultimately, the vision was proven wrong, and lock picking was all but dropped from the game despite all the work dedicated to it.

Figure 14.1 illustrates this problem of "parts on the garage floor."

The figure shows many parts, developed over three Sprints, finally coming together in the fourth. This represents a debt that could waste a lot of work if it doesn't pay off. It also prevents multiple iterations on the mechanic over a release cycle, because the parts are integrated only in the last Sprint.

Ideally, each Sprint iterates on a mechanic's value. Figure 14.2 shows the parts being integrated into a playable mechanic every Sprint or two.

The approach changes the stories on the Product Backlog:

> As a designer, I want doors to have a delay before they open. These doors would delay the player by a tunable amount of time to simulate picking a lock while the danger of being seen increases.

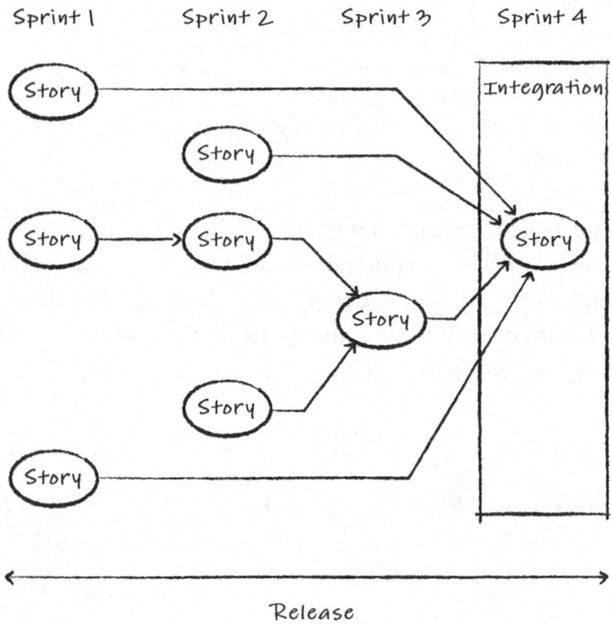


**Figure 14.1** *Integrating a mechanic at the end of a release*

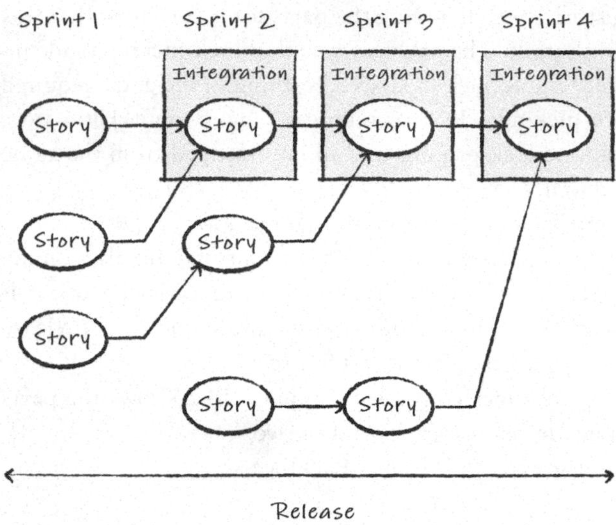

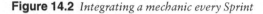

**Figure 14.2** *Integrating a mechanic every Sprint*

Notice that this story expresses some fundamental value to the player, which communicates a vision to both stakeholders and developers.

> As a designer, I want to have guards simulating patrols past the locked doors on a regular basis so the timing opportunity for the player to pick the lock is narrow.
>
> As a player, I want to unlock doors in the time that exists between patrols of armed guards to gain access to areas I need to go.

The first few stories are infrastructure stories, but they describe where the game is headed. They build the experience for the player in increments and explain why. The value emerges quickly and enables the Product Backlog to be adapted to maximize value going forward. This is in stark contrast to building parts that assume a distant destination is the best one. Iterating against a fixed plan is not Agile.

## It Doesn't Stop Here

Integration and discovery aren't limited by a Sprint's timeboxed iteration. Teams can integrate, explore, and even deploy on a daily basis if their teamwork, practices, and tools support it!

**Creating Fun is Iterative and Collaborative by Nature**

One year I took my family to Colorado to spend Christmas in a cabin. After a large snowstorm, my sons wanted to sled on the side of a small hill. So, I went to the local hardware store but could only find a couple of cheap plastic sleds. At first, the snow was too thick and the hill was too small for the sleds, so we packed down a path in the snow and built a starting ramp for speed. The sleds kept running off the track, so we packed snow on the sides. To increase speed, we poured water on the track to ice it—it began to look like a luge track!

After a few hours we had a great track. The boys would speed down on their sleds. They built jumps and curves and even a few branches into the track.

My oldest son said, "It's lucky that you bought the perfect sleds!" I hadn't done that, so we talked about it. The sleds weren't perfect; we had merely iterated on the track to match their characteristics. We added elements, such as the sides to the track, to overcome the sled's lack of control. We added other features, such as the ramp and track ice, to overcome the limitations of the thick snow and low hill. The sleds were the only thing that couldn't be changed.

I couldn't help comparing this to game development. We created an experience by iterating on things we had control over and adapted for things we didn't. In this case, design was entirely constrained to working with the level (the track) and not the player control (the sled), and we were still able to "find the fun"!

## Set-Based Design

When a project begins, the game we imagine is astounding. Players will experience amazing gameplay and explore incredible worlds where every turn reveals a delightful surprise. However, as we develop the game, we start to compromise. Imagination hits the limits of technology, cost, skill, and time. It forces us to make painful decisions. This is a necessary part of creating any product.

Identifying and narrowing down the set of possibilities is part of planning. For example, when we plan to create a real-time strategy game, we eliminate many of the features seen in other genres from consideration (see Figure 14.3).

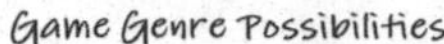


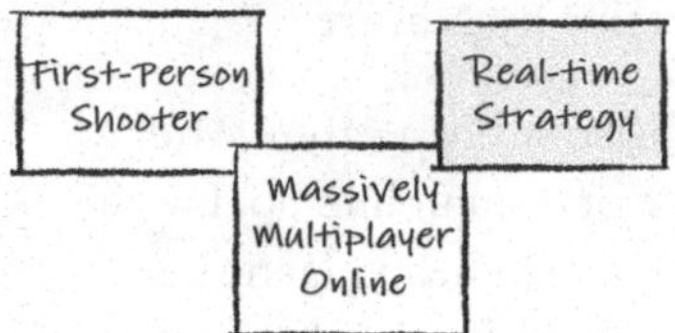


**Figure 14.3** *Narrowing the game to a specific genre*

Planning continues to narrow down the set of possible features. Following a high-level design, many developers refine discipline-centric designs. Designers plan the game design possibilities, programmers plan the technical design possibilities, and artists plan the art design possibilities. These possibilities do not perfectly overlap. For example, the designers may want large cities full of thousands of people, but the technology budget may only allow a dozen characters in linear levels. Figure 14.4 shows how the union of design, art, and technical possibilities overlap to create a set of features that all disciplines agree upon.

As mentioned earlier, the project starts with an area quite large in scope. As time goes by, the project staff gains more knowledge of what is possible, and the range of possibilities shrinks, as shown in Figure 14.5.

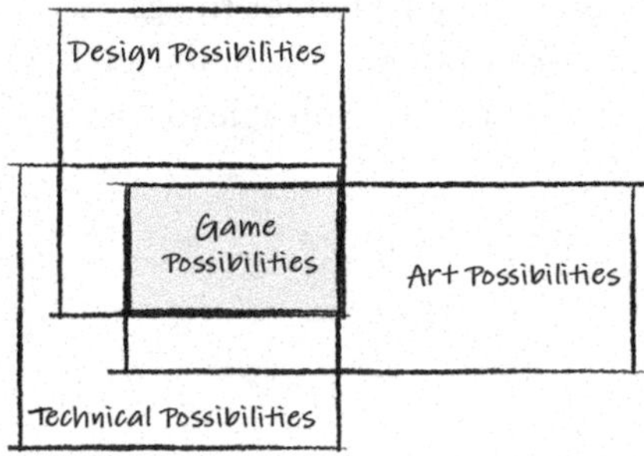


**Figure 14.4** *The set of possibilities at the start of a project*

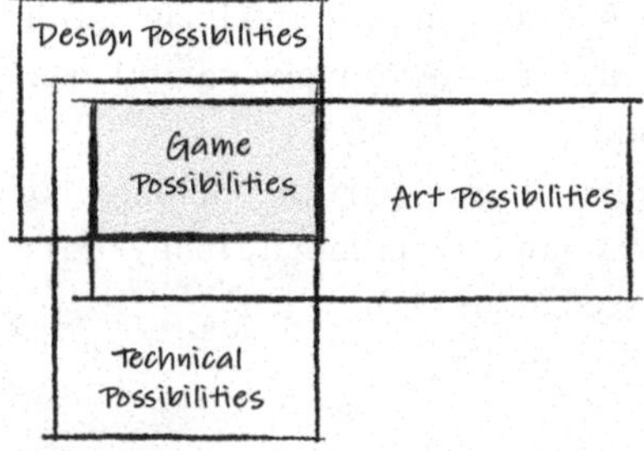


**Figure 14.5** *The set of possibilities as the project progresses*

This refinement of scope slowly happens through iteration and discovery. It requires cross-discipline collaboration to find a common ground so that effort is spent on a rich set of features possible for everyone to succeed.

Problems occur when the disciplines branch off from one another and plan in isolation. If the disciplines refine their set of possibilities too early or in isolation, then it greatly reduces the set of overlapping options for the game. This approach is called **point-based design** in which a single discipline design is refined in isolation (usually the game design). The set of design options have been narrowed so much that the overlapping game feature set has been vastly reduced, as shown in Figure 14.6.

This is the reason for cross-discipline planning. It keeps options open and the union of all sets as large as possible, so when more is learned, the project has a wider range of options.

An example of the problem with a point-based design was with a level-streaming decision made early on a game called *Darkwatch*. Early in development the designers decided that contiguous sections of levels had to be streamed off the game disc in the background during gameplay so that the player felt the game was taking place in one large world. The decision was made although no technical or art tool solutions for such streaming existed.

Entire level designs were created based on the assumption that the technology and tool set would be created and that artists would be able to author the streaming levels efficiently. Unfortunately, these assumptions were proven false. The effort required to implement the full streaming technology left no time to create the tools necessary for the artists to manipulate the levels. As a result, the levels were "chopped up" into small segments, and these segments were loaded while the player waited. The gameplay experience suffered greatly from this.

Another approach to narrowing multidiscipline designs, called **set-based design**, is used to keep design options alive as a number of solutions are explored, and the best design is converged upon. Set-based design has been shown to produce the best solutions in the shortest possible time (Poppendieck and Poppendieck, 2003).

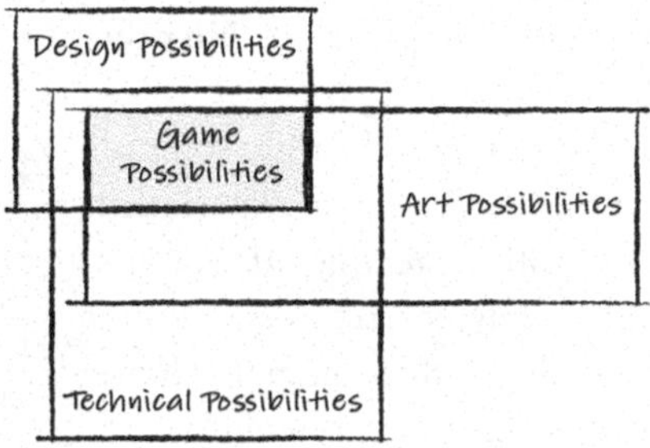


**Figure 14.6** *Narrowing game design too soon*

A set-based design approach to such a problem as the streaming level example is different from a typical point-based design. Instead, a number of options are explored:

- A full level-streaming solution
- A solution that streams portions of the levels (props and textures)
- No streaming at all

As each option matures, knowledge is built to enable a better decision to be made before level production. Potential solutions are dropped as soon as enough is learned about cost, risk, and value to show that they weren't viable. Although developing three solutions sounds more expensive, it is the best way to reduce cost over the course of the project.

Making decisions too early is a source of many costly mistakes. This is difficult to combat because such decisions are often equated with reducing risk or uncertainty. In point of fact, early decisions do not reduce risk or uncertainty. The delay of the level design decision in the set-based design approach is an example of postponing a decision as long as it can be delayed and no longer. This is an essential part of set-based design.

**Learn by Failing Fast**

Imagine we are playing the high/low game, where I have a secret number between 0 and 100 and you must discover that secret number by making a guess and having me tell you whether your guess is higher or lower than my secret number.

What do you usually guess first? The usual answer is "50." How many times is "50" the right answer? Never! So why do you guess it? You guess "50" because it gives you the most information about what range my secret number is in. It eliminates half of the possible numbers with a single guess. No other guess eliminates as many numbers.

The same goes for exploring what is fun. We don't aim for the right solution, but the one that gives us the most knowledge in the set. We set up experiments to provide us with this knowledge as quickly as possible. Creating huge designs up front is like taking 10 minutes to analyze the likely correct answer to the secret number from 0 to 100 and then announcing that "38" is the right choice. It's just as likely to be wrong and gives us less knowledge than guessing "50."

## Lead Designer Role

The lead designer's role is similar to other lead roles; he or she mentors less-experienced designers and ensures that the design role is consistent across multiple Scrum teams. Lead designers meet with the other project designers on a regular basis (often once a week) to discuss design issues across all teams (see Chapter 21, "Scaling Agile Game Teams").

Scrum demonstrates—through Sprint results—whether the project has enough designers. Scrum teams challenge designers who cannot communicate effectively. A benefit of Scrum is in exposing these problems so that a lead designer will step in to mentor less-experienced designers.

## Designer as Product Owner?

Many game development studios using Scrum make the lead designer the Product Owner for a game. This is often a good fit because the Product Owner role creates vision, and when we think of visionaries, we often think of successful designers such as Shigeru Miyamoto, Amy Hennig, Tim Shafer, and Will Wright. Lead designers make excellent Product Owners for the following reasons:

- Designers represent the player more than any other discipline.
- The product vision is driven primarily by design.
- Design is highly collaborative. Experienced designers should be experienced in communicating vision to all disciplines.

On the other hand, designers often lack experience for some Product Owner responsibilities:

- **Responsible for the return on investment:** Most designers I've known often need to be reminded of the cost implications of their designs! A Product Owner needs to carefully evaluate costs against the value for each feature.
- **Project management experience:** Teams accomplish many, but not all, of the duties traditionally assigned to someone in a project manager role. Many requirements or resources that have long lead times require a long-term management view.
- **Avoiding a design bias:** Product owners need to understand the issues and limitations for all disciplines. They cannot assume that everything outside the realm of design "can be handled by others."

For these reasons, having a senior producer or project manager support the "designer as Product Owner" is often beneficial. This support role can be a voice of reason and cost management.

## What Good Looks Like

Working with Shigeru Miyamoto taught me that the best designers are always questioning their designs and can objectively judge what players will enjoy. They don't monopolize the ownership of ideas but actively encourage other disciplines to contribute creatively and to offer feedback based on their deeper knowledge of the opportunities and limitations of their own domains.

When I first learned of Scrum, I felt it was a framework for supporting this type of behavior from all disciplines. Culture and established work patterns slowed its implementation, but as we embraced the principles, we slowly adopted more of the mindset of game designers: thinking of how players might enjoy our game.

## Summary

Agile reverses the trend of isolation of disciplines. This trend sees designers turning more to long-term plans and documentation to communicate with teams that are ever increasing in size. Scrum practices require the designers to collaborate and communicate face-to-face on small, cross-discipline teams.

In reversing this trend, designers need to embrace the benefit of emergent design. Designers do not have a crystal ball about any mechanic. The limitations of what is possible prevent this. Instead, they need to ensure that their vision is communicated and be open to all potential ideas.

## Additional Reading

McGuire, R. 2006. *Paper burns: Game design with Agile methodologies.* http://www.gamasutra.com/view/feature/2742/paper_burns_game_design_with_.php.

Chapter 15

# Agile QA and Production

Part of the role definition for quality assurance and production is the ability to communicate with all disciplines. Because fostering a common language across all disciplines is a principle for Agile game teams, quality assurance (QA) and production have an advantage when Agile is adopted.

At the same time, Agile practices change the role of QA and production the most. Fortunately, the change is for the better. This chapter addresses those changes and how the QA and production roles fit into Agile teams and organizations.

## Agile QA

When my sons were in grammar school, I was invited to parent career day. It was always fun. To the class, "video game developer" was the coolest career imaginable. I could be standing next to the "astronaut/secret agent" dad wearing his space suit, and the kids would climb over him to ask me questions.

An inevitable question was, "How can I be a game tester?" They dreamt that the role of a tester is eight hours a day of the same fun they experience playing games. What could be better than that? Unfortunately, I was forced to destroy this notion. I describe the long hours with games that crash. I described how testers are often very frustrated because they understand what the game is and have very little influence over how it is developed. I don't want to discourage future generations of testers; I just don't want to give the impression that there is this wonderful job waiting for them simply because they are "good at playing games."

As you may guess, the QA role attracts people who are passionate about games. The sheer number of people applying for this role gives the industry the ability to choose from among the best. We need to leverage their passion and experience far more.

## The Solutions in This Chapter

In this chapter, we'll learn how to improve and expand the role of QA on an Agile game team. We'll also explore the role of producers and how their job potentially maps to either a Scrum Master or Product Owner role.

## The Problem with QA

Traditionally, quality assurance is largely performed at the end of the project by a dedicated QA team. Figure 15.1 shows the pattern where most bugs are discovered on such a project after alpha, when all features are considered complete but not debugged.

The reason for this is simple—testing is performed on a potentially shippable game. Because the typical game project does not achieve this state until post-production, most testing has to be compressed between the alpha and ship dates. As a result, armies of testers are hired in hopes of achieving a ship date with a working game. Hiring and properly training a small army quickly is impossible, so testers are minimally trained for each game.

This type of quality assurance doesn't always assure the highest quality. By alpha, the important decisions about the game have been made, and the job of QA is to find and report minor defects. Most major defects are rooted too deep in the design or architecture of the game to be properly addressed. For example, if level

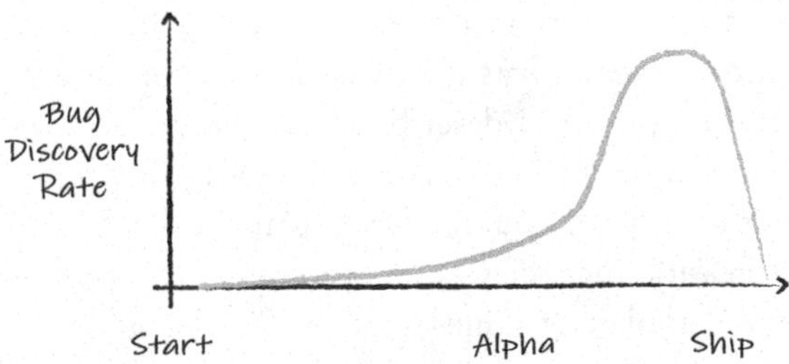


**Figure 15.1** *Bug discovery rate on a traditional project*

pacing isn't fun, it may be too late to correct it. This compromises the quality of the final game.

The other problem with traditional testing practices is that quality becomes the responsibility of remote[1] QA and not the developers. Studio cultures encourage this by basing employee performance evaluations on the pace of feature implementation or asset creation. Bugs that do not stop progress are considered part of making the game and are tolerated before alpha. Adding QA practices during this time slows feature and asset creation in the short term, so it is deferred.

**Black Box and White Box Testing**

Testing can be divided into two types: black-box and white-box.

**Black-box testing** uses a player's perspective to test a game at the highest level. A tester is given a list of expected behaviors and the conditions or input for causing them. The tester then ensures that they occur. It's also meant to ensure the pacing and mechanics are fun and engaging (see the "Play-Testing" section later in this chapter).

**White-box testing** uses an internal perspective to test a game. The components of the game, from code to assets, are examined and tested for standards and functional compliance. This requires skill and experience in the discipline that created the code or asset to be tested.

## Most QA Is Just QC

Over the past decade I've seen a few examples of proper QA being done at studios. Proper quality assurance is a role that focuses on finding ways to improve practices that reduce quality issues. This is opposed to quality control (QC), which is finding quality issues after they've been introduced.

Typical QA practices I've seen are:

- White box testing to ensure unit test coverage
- Writing and managing test scripts to automate gameplay
- Finding ways to automate manual testing tasks

1. Such as a publisher's QA department in another location or a QA service

Sometimes, people in these roles are called "product assurance engineers." This is obviously a more skilled and expensive role than traditional QA role, but the advantages are

- You need far fewer of these people than you would with an army of QC testers.
- Fixing bugs is far more expensive than finding ways not to create a bug in the first place!

## Agile Testing Is Not a Phase

The approach to QA on an Agile project is different from that of a traditional project in a number of ways:

- **Testing takes place on an Agile project throughout its life cycle:** This is a major benefit of creating a potentially deployable version of the game every Sprint. Defects are not deferred or tolerated.
- **Testing is white-box testing:** Testing focuses on the internal components of the game rather than the game as a whole. This requires more skilled product assurance engineers who can specialize in areas such as code reviews and test automation.
- **QA is part of every role:** Each developer performs QA in his work. QA doesn't eliminate this need but catches problems that slip through and helps improve team practices so that similar problems are more likely to be caught by the developer in the future.

Employing this approach evens out bug discovery rate to a consistent level throughout development without the necessary staffing up and down of QA.

**Definition**

The game industry traditionally refers to members of a QA group as **testers**. This title becomes obsolete as a studio adopts Agile. Testing becomes part of everyone's job, and the QA function specializes and overlaps those of other disciplines. However, because everyone uses the term **testers**, I use it here along with **QA**, which defines the role more than the individual.

## The Role of QA on an Agile Game Team

Compared to traditional approaches, Agile projects extract more value from testing. Much of this value comes from each team's goal of delivering a playable and potentially shippable game every Sprint. The QA role shifts to take advantage of this:

- Testers are members of Scrum Teams, rather than gathered in separate QA pools. This increases the speed of feedback on defects to the developers.
- Product Backlog Items (PBIs) require QA action for approval before they are considered done by the development team.[2] This creates a true pace of development, which should include fixing defects and reduces the cost and added risk of fixing them at a later date.
- QA's voice is heard throughout development, not just at the end. This allows its valuable feedback to influence the game.

QA's role on an Agile team grows beyond its traditional role. It starts with QA's participation in Sprint Planning. As each story is discussed, QA needs to understand how that story will be approved, before tasks are estimated. This usually takes the form of how the story and the Acceptance Criteria (AC) are written.

Consider, for example, the following story:

As a player, when I hit the jump button, my character will jump.

The team discusses this story and may ask the following questions:

- Will the character have jump animation? Will it need smooth transitions?
- Can the character jump to a higher level?
- Can the character jump from a moving platform?
- Can the character jump while walking or running?

These questions help the team understand the tasks necessary to implement and test the story to ensure it is done. For example, the answers to the previous questions may define the following AC:

- The character will have a simple stand-in animation that will not be blended.
- The character will jump up to a ledge or down to a lower level.

2. The Product Owner has the final say, however.

- The character is not expected to jump correctly from a moving platform.
- The character can jump from any starting motion, but its momentum will be ignored. It can jump only a fixed distance and height.

Using these AC, both QA and the developers verify that the story is complete before the end of the Sprint.

QA should also locate problems that are not part of specific AC but are part of development. For example, if the test level is missing some physical geometry that enables the player to "fall through the world," QA should identify it as an impediment.

A tester should help to ensure that the team is not impacting other teams. This includes the following:

- **Performing regression tests on areas the team is working on that could break other areas of the game:** For example, if the team is working on character control for jumping, keep an eye on other character motions to ensure that some side effect of the team's changes is not breaking them. Another example would be if every time a player dies, his character assumes the jump pose, then the team working on jumping has probably broken something!
- **Testing tools and pipeline changes that a support team wants to release to the content creators:** This includes testing beta versions of a tool with the content creators to verify changes have not broken a workflow.
- **Finding ways to improve testing:** For example, if bad textures are frequently crashing the game, QA should raise a request to have the texture exporters improved to catch the problem.

Some of QA's time is spent verifying gameplay and offering advice on areas of improvement. This requires an ongoing dialogue with members of the team. Because QA is a voice for the consumer, it needs to keep a "consumer eye" on the game. It should point out any issue that the consumer will notice (such as progression stoppers).

QA will be challenged in this new role. People in this role are required to communicate with every discipline, understand the tools, and stand up and be heard. QA has traditionally been a "gateway role" for other roles in game development, so developing these skills is appropriate to grow their career in game development.

## QA, Embedded or in Pools?

To what degree should testers be spread across teams or located in a QA pool that tests independently? There is no simple answer beyond "It depends." It depends on what the team and project need in order to ensure that quality is built into everything being worked on. It depends on the skill level of the testers and how much white-box testing they can accomplish. It depends on the testing tools, harnesses, and telemetry that are available.

When a game is in early development, the depth of gameplay and limited assets don't need as much separate testing; teams might share testers. As the project progresses, there is more to test. The game may need to run on several platforms. The growth of complexity requires not only more testing of the added features but also more regression testing to ensure that previously added features have not been inadvertently broken. QA pools can even out this workflow, helping team testers in times of need. As a game approaches its ship date, QA may be concentrated in a single pool or in separate pools dedicated to each platform.

A tester embedded within a single team takes on a more expanded role. He can assist the team in addressing impediments and completing tasks. For example, if an artist needs to test an asset on the iPhone, an embedded tester can help by creating an iPhone build, launching it, and calling the artist over when the asset is visible. Embedded testing encourages a tester to build his white-box testing skills and knowledge to overlap his work with the other developers on the team.

## How Many Testers per Team?

A frequent question raised is, "How many testers does a Scrum team need, and when should they be added?" It's the same as asking how many animators or audio designers a team needs; the answer is "as many as you need!"

The number of testers depends on the testing needs of the team. This hinges on the following:

- **The Definition of Done:** As the Definition of Done for Sprints approaches the final shippable state, more testing is required. For example, if a Definition of Done requires the game to be completely playable from start to finish without crashes on any platform, more testers are required than in early development when the game has to run on a development PC for a few minutes at a time.
- **Team testing practices:** If the team uses practices that support higher quality, such as Test-Driven Development (TDD) or thorough export testing, there will be fewer problems that QA is needed to find.

- **Test automation:** It depends on the coverage level of automated test utilities, ranging from simple smoke tests to complex scripting, that allow the game to "play itself" and offload manual testing.
- **Playability testing needs:** The game needs hands-on, in-depth testing from a player's perspective. QA needs to evaluate usability, pacing, and difficulty levels and provide feedback to the team.

Typically, one tester per team is enough for most of the game, but ultimately the team's needs are driven by Sprint results. As the stakeholders raise the Definition of Done, it may put pressure on the team to recruit more testers to help it meet its goals.

## Using a Bug Database

As discussed in Chapter 10, "Video Game Project Management," a debugging stage after the alpha date is unavoidable for many games. For these projects, the QA staff is expanded, and the entire game is tested from beginning to end.

It's dangerous for a project to rely too much on post-production testing and allow significant defects to remain undetected throughout production. When such defects are uncovered after alpha, they can invalidate a great deal of work. For example, discovering that the disc budget has been exceeded by 50 percent in post-production is very bad.

Ideally, post-production efforts should focus on tuning and polishing tasks that are identified and prioritized daily. Even without major flaws, tracking polishing, tuning, and minor bug-fix tasks can overwhelm a Sprint task-board approach.

It's important that there is only one Product Backlog for the game and that the Product Owner prioritizes a single list of work for the team to draw from every Sprint. Before alpha, any bugs that are addressed must either come from the team during the Sprint or come from the Product Backlog. If a bug database is maintained prior to alpha, then any bugs that are to be worked on are moved from there and placed on the Product Backlog to be prioritized by the Product Owner.

At alpha, all unimplemented stories on the Product Backlog are cleared off (they may become part of the Product Backlog for the next version of the game). From here out, only bug fixing and tuning work can be placed on the Product Backlog. The Product Backlog might even be replaced by the bug database.

The Product Owner manages the priority of bugs with QA through frequent triage sessions. As with hardening Sprints, described in Chapter 9, "Agile Release Planning," the team draws a set of tasks to work on daily, without a specific Sprint Goal. The new goal is to burn down all the high-priority bug fixes and tuning work.

### Advanced Practice: The "Done Done" Column

Although quality assurance is every developer's responsibility, the depth, complexity, and interconnectedness of games means that they benefit from someone playing the game during each Sprint to catch unanticipated interactions and behaviors.

The "done done" column is added to the right side of a Sprint task board, after the traditional "done" column. When a PBI in the Sprint Goal meets the Definition of Done, it is placed into that column. This creates a more concrete, visible declaration of which part of the Sprint Goal has been completed.

## Play-Testing

A major benefit of producing a potentially shippable version of the game every Sprint or release is that a game is tested early by potential consumers. **Play-testing** is a practice where consumers are lured in to play a game in development—often with the offer of free pizza—and provide useful feedback about the gameplay experience.

Play-testing can be as informal as a conversation. It can also take a more scientific approach by recording progress metrics or the answers to carefully designed surveys.

Play-testing has substantial, but limited, benefits:

- **It reinforces a Definition of Done:** Developers, who see a game every day, overlook flaws or shortcomings. Play-testing is often a shock when they observe how these problems impact real consumers. For example, that missing piece of collision geometry is always found by play-testers!
- **It won't produce any breakthrough ideas:** Don't expect the play-testers to provide original ideas. That's the developer's job. At best, they provide feedback that can improve Backlog prioritization.
- **It teaches about usability and challenge:** Ever see a player simply run past a painstakingly scripted boss? It's a sobering thing to see. It's also very frustrating to see a player walk against a wall for two minutes until you realize that she is trying to make sense of a HUD map that is too vague!

### Experience

Play-testing is a tool for focusing a team on *done*. We often scheduled play-testing sessions for the end of a Sprint. This made the team look at the game with a different set of eyes and uncovered many polishing and tuning tasks that had previously been invisible to us.

Play-testing is often organized and run by QA or usability specialists. These duties include the following:

- **Recruiting play-testers:** Local universities and game retail shops are teeming with good play-test candidates. Be sure to enlist people who represent the full scale of demographics and skill levels. For example, a hard-core gamer won't provide the same feedback about the tutorial level as a casual gamer. Maintain a database of people, and invite the more valuable play-testers back.
- **Organizing and running the session:** A poorly organized and run session elicits inferior feedback from play-testers. Don't waste their time.
- **Including the developers:** Having the developers see players interacting with their game in ways they did not anticipate is very beneficial. It can lead to improved interfaces and usability (see the sidebar "Damage Meter").
- **Letting play-testers meet the other developers:** Many testers are curious about game development and relish the opportunity to speak with the rest of the team at the end of the session. Encourage this. The conversations can be very fruitful!
- **Publishing the results:** QA's observations of how well the game was received provide many insights. However, care must be taken not to "overinterpret" the results to include subjective bias from QA. A simple compilation of the answers helps the team understand the results. Leave the conclusions to the readers or discuss them together.

Maintaining the playability of the game allows everyone to value the working game over the comprehensive design.

### Damage Meter

During the development of *Midtown Madness*, we needed to find a way to communicate the level of damage to the player's car. This was important because if a car accumulated 100 percent damage, it stalled, and the player lost the race.

We first drew a meter that grew as damage increased. During play-testing, we found that half the players quickly and intuitively understood that a growing meter indicated growing damage, but the other half did not.

We then switched to a health meter that shrank as the car became more damaged and "lost its health." Once again, play-testing showed that half the testers understood it immediately, while the other half did not.

So, we went back to the drawing board. How could we communicate the car's damage level in a way that every player would immediately understand? Someone suggested we communicate a wider range of damage on the car's body. It was a great idea. We already had some body-damage effects, but it wasn't enough. So, we added wobbling tires, broken side mirrors, smashed windows, and smoke that darkened as the car approached destruction. At one point, we even added flames, but the vehicle licensees vetoed that effect!

At the next play-test session, all the players understood the damage level of their cars!

## The Future of QA

As the game industry continues to improve Agile practices, the role of QA continues to transform. As testing becomes more white-box driven, testers require more knowledge about development disciplines, and testing specialties will grow. For example, test engineers in many industries focus on the quality of the code being produced by programmers. These specialists run code-quality scanner tools[3] and measure unit test coverage to ensure that coding practices are being held to a high standard. Is this a testing role or programming role? It's a bit of both, and it represents a typical evolution and blurring of roles in an Agile environment.

The rising importance, skill level, and value of testers on an Agile game project will improve the role and make it a truly desirable career.

# Agile Production

Producers are the most open to adopting Agile but usually with some trepidation. They are the first to foresee its benefits, but they are also concerned about the implications to their role on an Agile game project. The main concern is that as teams become self-organizing and self-managing, then there will be no need for producers. In reality, producers are often the engines of ongoing Agile adoption. As with the discipline lead roles, the production role is divested of many of the mundane tasks with Agile, such as tracking hourly estimates and solving the myriads of small

3. Such as PC-Lint

problems that cross-discipline teams handle themselves. Instead, Agile producers expand their focus on the big picture while helping teams achieve continual improvement in how they create games.

This section identifies the changes in responsibility for traditional producers on a Scrum project and how they can assume the Scrum Master, Product Owner, or Product Owner Support role.

## The Role of a Producer on an Agile Project

Producers are often seen as the person who makes sure everything gets done. This is not the case on a Scrum project. As Scrum teams take responsibility for what is done every Sprint, they relieve the producer of some daily project management tasks:

- **Building and maintaining detailed schedules:** Scrum teams create and estimate their own tasks.
- **Tracking daily tasks for each member of the development staff:** This is managed in the Daily Scrums by the team.
- **Managing dependencies:** Cross-discipline teams manage dependencies daily and in Sprint Planning by selecting goals and team members who avoid external dependencies.

Instead, the producer should focus on the larger project management challenges:

- **Tracking external dependencies:** Will the outsourced cinematics be delivered on time?
- **Publisher collaboration:** Are the stakeholders playing the game if they can't attend a review?
- **Outsourcing support:** What does the outsourced level art team need to complete its work?
- **First-party (platform) support:** When are we scheduled for acceptance testing, and what are the requirements?
- **Risk management:** What are the external schedule and resource risks for obtaining licensee approval or assets?
- **Critical chain management:** What are the resource schedule needs for the production assets?

Most of these responsibilities are best described in a number of good game production books (see the "Additional Reading" section at the end of the chapter).

## Producer as Scrum Master

Many studios adopting Agile struggle with identifying people to best fill the Scrum Master role. It's often assumed that the producer is natural for the role, and many times this is true. There are benefits and potential drawbacks with a producer taking on the Scrum Master role.

A benefit seen with producers in the Scrum Master role is the ability to communicate equally well with all the disciplines. This is essential for a cross-discipline team. This allows him to remain unbiased toward issues or unconflicted about what he needs to do. For example, programmers who become Scrum Masters often see issues through a filter that says most problems are best solved with code. This leaves the other disciplines feeling less supported.

Another benefit is that producers usually have fewer tasks to commit to every Sprint. This prevents them from having to choose between completing critical tasks and supporting the team. Depending on the team, the Scrum Master role can take anywhere from 33 percent to 100 percent of a person's time.

A common drawback with a producer taking the Scrum Master role derives from his past duties on more preplanned projects. These duties required producers to lead individuals toward task completion. However, Scrum teams manage their own tasks to achieve a Sprint Goal as a team. The Scrum Master does not interfere with the team by creating, estimating, assigning, and tracking tasks for them. Unfortunately, some producers assume, out of habit, that the Scrum Master role continues to focus on tasks. This prevents teams from achieving all the benefits associated with self-management. The transformation of a producer-as-task-manager to a team coach is a challenging transformation, but one that results in a far more interesting and satisfying role. Chapter 19, "Coaching Teams for Greatness," explores this coaching role.

### QA as Scrum Master

We often found good Scrum Masters by recruiting and training them from our pool of testers. My theory is that testers are not biased by any one discipline and aren't seen coming from a management or authority position by the team.

## Producer as Product Owner Support

On large game projects, the demands of a Product Owner's time has led to hierarchies of Product Owners (see Chapter 11, "Faster Iterations"). Similarly, the long-term demands of production planning, resource requirements, marketing, licensing, and first-party hardware support have led Product Owners to seek production support.

As a result, pairing a Product Owner with a senior producer is a common practice. The Product Owner manages vision while the senior producer attends to many project management details. This support enables the Product Owner to make better decisions based on license, franchise, budget, and schedule limitations.

License and franchise details are usually managed by the Product Owner, but there are details that need to be handled on a day-by-day basis. For example, providing sample assets or seeking approval on the use of brands or likenesses can be very time-consuming.

The most important schedule and budget limitations are those that define the production requirements and dates. Pre-production creates cost and schedule debt that is paid off in production. The Product Owner needs to monitor this debt to ensure it doesn't grow beyond the limits of schedule and cost defined by the stakeholders. For example, before defining the number of characters to produce, the cost for a single shippable character needs to be understood.

A Product Owner and senior producer make an effective pair to create the best game at the right cost and schedule.

## Producer as Product Owner

Many successful games have been led by a senior producer who provides project management and vision for the game. As with lead designers who have strong project management skills, a senior producer with a strong vision of what the market wants is rare and invaluable.

When a studio has such a producer, the Product Owner role is ideal for him or her. The role leverages vision and project management strengths like no other (see Chapter 3, "Scrum").

### By Any Other Name

I often visit EA studios where the traditional production role is filled by people who have the title of "Development Director" and where the responsibility of people who have the Producer title is similar to that of Product Owners.

It doesn't matter so much what the titles are. Identifying responsibilities and discussing how those might best map to the Scrum roles are more useful. Most game teams find that the responsibilities of producers don't completely disappear when adopting Scrum. There are plenty of things left for them to still do!

### The Future of Production

As the industry becomes more Agile, the producer role will include specialized and team roles.

Teams no longer need the ubiquitous "gopher" but will need the support of the following specialists:

- Outsourcing/insourcing
- Licensing
- Franchise management
- Production planning and support
- Technical production (including first-party communication)

Producers can successfully assume the Scrum Master and Product Owner roles as well. Production will not disappear from Agile studios but flourish.

## What Good Looks Like

Roles don't change overnight, nor should they. Change requires some stumbling and exploration that takes a while to adjust to. QA department managers don't easily surrender their testers to work on teams, and producers don't usually hand off task tracking to teams immediately. This is a transformation that takes time.

The same willingness to surrender applies to producers. Control through task management and detailed process rules rarely leads to optimal results. At best, one gets compliance and not engagement

QA that transforms to true "Quality Assurance" and producers who have the courage to relinquish the illusion of control and transform from task manager to coach are at the heart of successful Agile teams.

## Summary

Agile QA and production will continue to draw people who have these primary strengths:

- A deep passion for video games
- Great organizational skills
- Great communication skills

These strengths are in demand in every industry, and the game industry has to compete for them like any other. By leveraging them, Agile organizations reap major benefits from QA and production, while testers and producers receive greater challenges in which to rise.

## Additional Reading

Chandler, H. 2008. *The Game Production Handbook, Second Edition*. Sudbury, MA: Jones and Bartlett Publishers.

Crispin, L., and J. Gregory. 2009. *Agile Testing: A Practical Guide for Testers and Agile Teams*. Boston, MA: Addison-Wesley.

Hight, J., and J. Novak. 2007. *Game Development Essentials: Game Project Management*. Clifton Park, NY: Delmar Cengage Learning.

Irish, D. 2005. *The Game Producer's Handbook*. Boston: Course Technology PTR.

Isbister, K., and N. Schaffer. 2008. *Game Usability*. San Diego: Morgan Kaufmann.

Laramee, F. D. 2003. *Secrets of the Game Business*. Boston: Charles River Media.

PART V

# Getting Started

# Chapter 16

# The Myths and Challenges of Scrum

A studio's development process is a reflection of its culture, and cultures change slowly. Change usually has to overcome resistance, but change happens—especially in the game industry—whether we like it or not.

Change requires commitment from a studio. It should avoid quick-fix solutions or ritual adherence to defined practices. With Agile adoption, both of these extremes are often seen. Some fall in love with the values and principles and dive into adoption with the illusion that the only possible outcome is success. Others sabotage Agile adoption from the start. Saboteurs repeat "urban legends of Agile failure" or label Agile as "the latest management fad." This is referred to as spreading fear, uncertainty, and doubt and is addressed later in the chapter.

## The Solutions in This Chapter

There is a kernel of truth to many of the myths. This chapter identifies the major ones. It looks behind the myths and explores the truths and falsehoods that they rely upon. It also explores many of the barriers to Scrum adoption. Exposing these facts enables a studio to better judge the value of Agile because the best possible path for adopting it is to understand the reasons behind every practice and leave little to faith. This is the benefit of an empirical system: to base what we do on what we know rather than on theory or conjecture.

## Silver Bullet Myths

Common to the tales of vampire slayers, silver bullets possess magical properties that give the hero an advantage when facing certain disaster.

Often the adoption of Scrum is motivated by a disaster. A studio ships a game that is a financial failure or has a project canceled because of budget, schedule, or quality problems. During these times, studio management is more open to change. This isn't necessarily bad, but desperation often leads them to seek a project management silver bullet.

The problem is that Scrum doesn't work miracles. It has no magical properties. Improvements in development by using it require an understanding of the underlying principles, not blind faith. Scrum is a framework to build a process that supports talent, great teams, and leaders. It does not replace them.

By avoiding the following silver bullet myths, you avoid falling into the trap of thinking a process can solve all your problems.

### Scrum Will Solve All of Your Problems for You

Sometimes we have grand assumptions about what a process can accomplish. Perhaps if we create enough rules, then everyone will follow them, and problems will disappear. The truth is that if there are underlying problems, Scrum will only expose those problems. It doesn't solve them.

**Experience**

A former California studio adopted Scrum following another project failure. From the start, the Daily Scrums unleashed a flood of complaints about studio operations. Management quickly decided that Scrum was the source of these problems and immediately halted its use. As expected, the level of complaints fell off, and management felt that they had averted a disaster.

The best that can be asked of Scrum is to facilitate problem-solving through transparency. What is done with this transparency depends on a studio's culture. This studio closed because it ignored the problems that existed for years.

### Fear, Uncertainty, and Doubt

Some myths fall under the category of fear, uncertainty, and doubt (FUD). FUD myths are like urban legends; they are exaggerated stories that have a kernel of truth that make them stick.

There are many reasons people use FUD to sabotage Agile adoption. The main reason is that change alone creates FUD. Change threatens the status quo and therefore a person's security in his or her position. Sometimes the memory of past successes creates the belief that the practices used then will continue to apply equally as well in the future. Problems are seen not with the process, which has proven itself, but with the developers using it now.

This section addresses some of the common FUD myths about Agile. Chapter 17, "Working with Stakeholders," shares strategies of overcoming the status quo, which can be the greatest obstacle to adopting Agile.

### *Endless Development*

> Agile teams never plan. They just iterate without a goal.

Sometimes a team new to Scrum assumes that being Agile means it doesn't need to plan. It starts by iterating to discover the game that emerges. Eventually the urgency to ship intrudes, and the team has to scramble, often with enforced overtime, to finish something. This isn't Agile. It's an iterative and incremental death march. It's a danger for Agile teams that don't sufficiently plan.

Having a shared vision for any project is also essential, whether it is Agile or not. If the Product Owner on a Scrum team does not provide a vision, the team cannot be sure that its work creates the greatest stakeholder value.

> **Experience**
>
> I once knew a team that had no Product Owner. It was working on a first-person shooter. The Product Backlog was prioritized by the lead programmer. Because he was focused on physics, each Sprint would show increasingly impressive physical effects. After the first release, buoyant rag-doll bodies were seen floating down a stream in front of the player. When we asked to see how enemies were shot and fell into the stream, we were told that shooting wasn't implemented yet.
>
> A few months later, the stakeholders canceled the project.

### *Management Fad*

> Scrum is just another management fad. It will be replaced by something else next month.

Someone investigating Agile will encounter labels such as Scrum, Extreme Programming, Evo, RUP, Scrum-#, Scrum Type-C, Lean, feature-driven development (FDD), Kanban, and so on. It's a confusing process landscape. This was one motivation behind the Agile Manifesto. Decades of discovery about how people best work together to create new products are embodied in its simple values and principles. It is an umbrella "brand" name for any number of processes and frameworks that embrace them.

The expanding list of labels represents the various practices that are constantly emerging as Agile becomes more common and accepted. This book has described numerous practices for game development that lie outside the core definition of Scrum. We could label them (perhaps *Scrum-G*), but the point is for each studio to evolve and adopt its own practices to best fit its needs. There will never be a single template for game development that applies to even a majority of game types or studios!

Scrum is a great starting place. For almost a decade, people such as Mike Cohn and Ken Schwaber have fought to keep it a simple framework for each team to adapt for the needs of their products:

> Agile will go away, but it will most likely go away in the same way discussing the merits of object-oriented development went away. Agile will eventually become the accepted way of doing things, and it will just be what we do. In the same way no one says, "Gotta run, I'm late for the object-oriented design meeting" (they just say "design meeting"), we will stop talking about Agile development but only after it is the norm.
>
> —*Mike Cohn*

## *The Double Standard*

> We hear one of two things about Scrum. Either Scrum was successful, or if the project using it failed, it did so because the teams weren't using Scrum correctly.

Scrum can't be blamed for failure or even credited with success. Teams succeed or fail because of many factors: technology, capability, vision, communication, collaboration, talent, or even the underlying idea of the game. Scrum creates transparency into how well these elements are working, often in a measurable way, but that's all. It doesn't prescribe what to do when Sprints repeatedly show the game isn't fun or the velocity of the team is low.

### *Change Is Bad*

> Our process has worked in the past. If we change things, we'll fail.

Studios have a certain level of resistance to change in the process they use to create games. This is not necessarily a bad thing. A studio's process evolves over many years. It's reinforced by its strengths and successes.

However, processes also embed cultural weaknesses. For example, many studios institute a one- or two-week "lockdown" before a milestone date. The lockdown ensures that no new features are allowed into the build that can destabilize it while the build is debugged and polished. This is a concession to a development culture that allows too many defects into the game during development.

Lockdowns slow development because the cost of fixing bugs increases the longer you wait. When developers are aware that there is a period of time being set aside for dealing with quality problems later on, they're less likely to address those problems up front. Also, the entire project staff is usually not engaged in bug fixing during a lockdown, and therefore they have to find other things to do. Lockdowns also end up becoming a dumping ground for checking in bug-ridden code or unpolished assets under the assumption that they will be fixed later. This creates a vicious cycle that can inflate the duration of future lockdowns!

Changing core practices, such as introducing unit testing to improve code quality, is more challenging than adding a quick fix, such as a lockdown. The problem is that quick-fix practices become a normal part of a development.

Over months and years, such quick fixes build up. Each of them adds a bit of drag to development. Resistance to change prevents corrections to the process until there is a catastrophic failure (such as a project cancellation over high cost or slow progress).

#### Normalization of Deviance

Two examples of how ignoring problems can lead to tragedy are the Challenger and Columbia space shuttle disasters that took the lives of 14 astronauts. Both incidents involved problems that were well known and documented with the shuttle system. These problems had occurred frequently but had not resulted in the loss of a shuttle. As a result, they became an acceptable part of operations until there was an accident.

Following the Challenger accident review, the phrase *normalization of deviance* was coined (Vaughan, 1996) to describe how the attitude toward defects in the shuttle system resulted in its loss. Unfortunately, identifying this problem with NASA's culture was not enough to prevent it from contributing to the loss of the Columbia years later.

## *Endless Meetings*

> Scrum consists of nothing but meetings!

As previously described, the meetings defined by Scrum within a Sprint cycle are as follows:

- Daily Scrum
- Sprint Review
- Sprint Planning
- Sprint Retrospective

All of these meetings, except for the Daily Scrum, occur once a Sprint. Many teams find that for a three-week Sprint, these once-a-Sprint meetings can be conducted in a single day. This represents one day of meetings for a 15-working-day Sprint, or 7 percent of the available time. The Daily Scrum meeting is a 15-minute, timeboxed daily meeting. This uses about 3 percent of the working day. Totaling these percentages results in 10 percent of a team's time, or a little more than four hours of meetings each week average.

**Eliminating the Daily Scrum?**

One sign of Agile adoption failure is when teams new to Scrum abandon the Daily Scrum. The typical reason is that they don't see the value in talking to each other or that the meeting is run in an ineffective way (for example, it's just a task-reporting exercise).

However, I've noticed that some of the most effective teams abandon the Daily Scrum. The reason for it is different: They've co-located themselves and communicate throughout the day, so they no longer need the ceremony to improve communication.

Scrum meetings are optimized to create the highest bandwidth of necessary communication. A 15-minute Daily Scrum will often identify issues that are easily solved within a day. If not identified, the issue might grow to waste days and require hours of meetings to address weeks later.

The details in this book will help teams run these meetings as effectively as possible without losing their benefits. If any of these meetings do not engage everyone attending nearly 100 percent of the time, then there is room for improvement. The goal isn't to reduce meeting time, but to optimize communication effectiveness.

**Note**

Shorter Sprints will use a greater percentage of time in meetings. For example, the Sprint Review, Planning, and Retrospectives might take six hours to complete for a two-week Sprint rather than the eight that a three-week Sprint might require. See Chapter 4, "Sprints."

## Scrum Challenges

The only thing harder than starting something new is stopping something old.

—*Russell L. Ackoff*

Scrum is not a "one-size-fits-all" solution for developers. A goal in adopting Scrum is to initiate a never-ending cycle of continual improvement customized to the needs of a studio's culture, people, and games. Before this goal can be realized, a studio or team has to start practicing the fundamentals and navigating early challenges. This section describes a few of these challenges and some of the ways of navigating them.

### Scrum as a Tool for Process and Culture Change

Any process can be used to make games, but no process is perfect. Even if we were to identify a perfect process, the constant change in our industry would quickly make it obsolete. This is a major motive for using Scrum. Scrum is not a process; it's a framework for creating and evolving your own process. It can help any organization create transparency, which enables commonsense change.

Scrum will influence every part of your studio. Scrum pressures leaders to focus on mentoring and coaching. It involves buy-in from departments such as human resources (HR), which can resist the emphasis on team performance over individual performance. It demands people take ownership in areas in which they had no ownership and give up ownership in areas they once ruled over. It challenges marketing to participate with development far earlier in a project. It even puts pressure on facilities to provide open team areas, wall space. and shared spaces for privacy, when needed.

Scrum adoption starts with creating transparency to expose cultural weaknesses and strengths. An example of this was a studio dominated by technology; games were seen as platforms to demonstrate technical achievement. Tools and pipelines to improve productivity for artists and designers were lower on the list of priorities because the programmers were always trying to accomplish nearly impossible challenges. The build was rarely working because of all the bugs left along the way, so the time it took to iterate on an asset change was very long.

How did Scrum influence change? First, it made the high iteration costs visible. Requiring a potentially deployable version of the game every two to three weeks exposed a lot of problems. At first, the teams spent half their Sprints trying to cobble together a working build. Because velocity was measured by the value of the features working in the game, their initial velocity was low.

This simple measurement of velocity is important. Teams need clear performance measurements to evaluate themselves and make changes to improve that measurement. Our example team did this. They started to come up with ways to improve the reliability of the build. Because velocity derives from what is seen in the game, which includes art and design, they formed cross-discipline teams. They co-located to reduce the overhead of communication. Programmers focused on improving tools and pipelines. All of these things improved their velocity.

Before they adopted Scrum, they would have thought that such change was only possible through great technical effort. Scrum allowed cultural change, which resulted in huge performance gains.

**Experience**

"After research into methodologies, we were drawn to the advantages of Agile software development and decided to adopt Scrum. Within the first few months of *Brütal Legend* development, the team was practicing Scrum, and the initial payoffs were impressive. Because of Scrum's emphasis on features over systems, on rapid prototyping and iteration, on cross-disciplinary teams, on people over process, and on the creation of a potentially deployable piece of software, every Sprint/milestone made the game playable at a very early stage in development."

—Caroline Esmurdoc, Executive Producer and COO,
Double Fine Productions, Inc.

## Scrum Is About Adding Value, Not Task Tracking

Running a Daily Scrum is easy. Prioritizing a list of features to be implemented is straightforward. Creating a task board and burndown chart takes minutes. So, why do some teams struggle adopting Scrum?

One reason is that many studios that adopt Scrum come from a task-centric culture. Progress is measured against how well individuals complete their work against estimates. Task tracking is an important tool in Scrum, but value creation takes precedence. If value isn't maximized, then the tasks were wrong.

Have you ever heard someone report "All the tasks for feature X are completed" only to see that feature X is nowhere near being done? In Scrum, the conversation shifts to discuss a feature's emerging value and the impact on the tasks for that feature. If this shift doesn't occur, then the value of Scrum practices is greatly diminished. For example, in a task-centric culture, the Daily Scrum is seen as a task-reporting meeting that is easily replaced. In a culture focused on value and team commitment, the Daily Scrum takes on greater importance.

Cultural change is hard. The status quo will often fight tooth and nail against it. Scrum is a framework for this change, but it comes from real leadership, not from a book or a fixed set of practices.

**Experience**

"One of the first things I did when starting to work with my current team was this: 'We're going to try this Scrum thing. We're going to start with Scrum, but our goal is to end up with a process that fits this team and the work it does. I will never say no to a change proposed by the team, but I insist on one thing. We will try Scrum by the book for at least two Sprints (one to learn the process and one to figure out what you don't like about it) before we start making adjustments.' From day one, it was *their* process. We were just starting from a template called Scrum."

—Bruce Rennie, Independent Developer

## Status Quo Versus Continual Improvement

Building a culture of "continual improvement" is one of the ultimate goals of Scrum. Scrum practitioners use empirical measures to assess benefits of all practices. If, for example, a practice change improves velocity, then it's a beneficial change.

This is a simple idea to introduce, but it can be challenging to embed. The status quo, or groundless resistance to change, is often a tremendous barrier to continual improvement.

Fear of change is not always baseless. Management fears that introducing profound change gambles a studio's future. Introducing change requires bravery. For example, changing a process that may have worked for a PlayStation game paints a big target on the person who changed the process for a live mobile game. There is enough risk in changing platforms alone to cause someone to hesitate over changing one more variable.

This is why it often takes utter project failure and crisis to usher in significant change. This isn't ideal either because it often leads to the "silver bullet" adoption pattern described previously. Ideally, any method for introducing change needs to do it in ways that

- Make small, reversible steps
- Are measurable to ensure that any perceived improvement is real

Scrum supports change in this manner. At worst, a change in practices will impact a single Sprint of one to three weeks. Metrics, such as task burndown slope, user story point velocity, or any number of metrics that the team has introduced, provide frequent measurement of the value of changes.

This change of culture can't happen only from the bottom up. It has to be supported by company leadership. Management needs to understand the tools that Scrum provides them to ensure that teams are making progress and that leadership, vision, and commitment exist.

Lack of management commitment to Scrum and Agile principles is a major challenge for studios attempting to adopt Scrum. Under pressure, a manager might find it easier to alter a team's goal mid-Sprint rather than fight to preserve the team's commitment to the Sprint Goal. Educating management about the benefits of Scrum—especially for them—is an ongoing effort.

## Cargo Cult Scrum

When teams first start using Scrum, they are encouraged to follow the practices "by the book." This enables them to become accustomed to the practices while the principles sink in. After the team experiences the initial benefits, it begins altering practices to improve upon those benefits, but it's important that changes to the practices still preserve the principles behind them.

However, some teams stick to the "out-of-the-book" practices and resist changing anything. These teams end up practicing what I call **Cargo Cult Scrum**. This refers to the infamous cargo cults of the Pacific.

Until World War II, many Pacific Islanders were never exposed to Westerners or their technology. This changed drastically during the war when the Navy arrived to occupy the islands and construct airfields. When the airfields were complete, cargo planes would land and bring in supplies. These planes carried many things including simple trinkets that were shared with the islanders to promote goodwill. The islanders loved these objects (such as steel knives and mirrors) and gathered around the airfield every time a large aircraft landed seeking further gifts.

When the war ended, most of these airfields were abandoned, and the cargo planes stopped coming. The islanders once again found themselves isolated from the Western world, but they did not forget the cargo planes and their treasures. They wanted them to return. Out of desperation, they tried to draw the cargo planes back by replicating the practices they saw at airfields during the war.

They constructed bamboo towers and manned them with natives wearing coconut headphones who spoke into pineapple microphones. They built bamboo mock-ups of small planes, lit fires next to the runway, and waved flags of cloth in the air. But the cargo planes did not return. The practices weren't enough to bring them back.

This approach is similar to what is done on Cargo Cult Scrum teams. Following the practices isn't enough to bring the full benefits of highly productive teams. Teams need to understand the principles behind the practices and improve those practices to best fit their product, people, and culture.

### Consistency and Monkeys

Consistency is a hard-coded survival trait. Change is resisted. It's a primal instinct. I never fully appreciated this fact until I read about the following experiment (Stephenson, 1967)[1].

Five monkeys were placed in a room with a banana tree at the center. Whenever a monkey attempted to climb the tree to pick a banana, a sprinkler system sprayed all the monkeys with water until the hungry monkey retreated from the tree. They repeated this until all the monkeys learned to avoid the tree.

The next stage of the experiment involved replacing one of the monkeys with one who had never been sprayed with water. The new monkey soon approached the banana tree. However, before it could reach the tree, the other

1. There is some debate as to this study being apocryphal. In any case it's a useful metaphor for what goes on with the methodologies we apply.

monkeys jumped into action and beat the new monkey until it drew back from the banana tree. This was repeated every time until the new monkey learned not to approach the tree.

The researchers continued to replace original monkeys who had been sprayed with water one by one with fresh monkeys. Eventually none of the monkeys in the room had ever been sprayed with water for climbing the banana tree. The monkeys still continued to beat up any monkey who approached the banana tree, but none of them knew why. They just knew that it was off limits.

Sometimes we developers exhibit similar behavior. A company's culture becomes intertwined with "best practices" that aren't questioned and never replaced. Personally, I did this for many years pursuing waterfall methodologies. I wrote big documents and schedules that attempted to address every detail of the project. Even after those projects shipped—following months of crunch and despair—I would start the next project the same way.

## Scrum Is Not for Everyone

One of the challenges of Scrum adoption is that Scrum is not for everyone. The initial challenge will be that some people refuse to work in an Agile environment and leave. Some of these people will be valuable. They leave because they are not comfortable with the change in their position.

Some developers reject participation in any team activity (such as a Daily Scrum). Some have grown comfortable from a career of working in relative isolation and being called upon to be heroes during crunch times. Others find a niche in a lax management environment where they are given a great deal of freedom to create technology or assets on their own. Joining a Scrum team and making daily commitments to a team of peers limits these individual freedoms.

Most studios find ways to accommodate these individuals, perhaps creating special "R&D" roles for them, but in some cases they eventually leave. The transparency Scrum introduces to a studio makes such positions stand out and not easily justifiable.

The benefits greatly outweigh the losses. Scrum grows leaders and outstanding contributors at a far greater rate than those who are lost.

## Overtime

Scrum doesn't limit teams to working 40-hour weeks. Its practices enable teams to find a sustainable pace of work. This pace is discovered as they commit to Sprint goals and learn how much they can achieve Sprint after Sprint without overextending themselves.

**Note**

In everyday vocabulary, a Sprint is something that isn't sustainable. Calling it a **jog** might have been more accurate but less appealing.

A Sprint can have many uncertainties. Unanticipated problems or unforeseen work slows progress. When this happens, teams sometimes put in a bit of overtime to fulfill their goal.

How much overtime should Scrum teams work? It's up to them. If they find that they are working overtime too often, they need to address the problems that are causing it. Common examples for this are late commits or handoffs at the end of a Sprint or committing to extra polishing and tuning work on the last Sprint of a release.

When management doesn't tell teams to work overtime, their attitude about it changes. When a team decides to work overtime, it does it as a team. Occasionally working a few extra hours shoulder to shoulder with your teammates is a team-building experience.

## Crunch

Extended periods of enforced overtime are called **crunch**. Many studios that are new to Scrum continue to practice it until the empirical measure of velocity demonstrates its futility.

Studies have shown the impact of crunch on productivity and quality of life.[2] For High Moon Studios, the proof came when management enforced companywide overtime early in our adoption of Scrum. The teams were told to work 10 hours a day for 6 days a week on a troubled project. The subsequent burndown charts told an interesting story. Figure 16.1 shows the hours the average team burned down per week from their Sprint Backlogs.

Week 1 was a normal workweek, before overtime. Weeks 2 to 5 were crunch weeks of 60 hours each. In the first week of crunch (week 2), velocity greatly increased; more work was being done because of the 50 percent overtime. However, as weeks passed, the velocity decreased until week 5, when the velocity was less than it was before crunch started!

2. https://igda.org/resources-archive/quality-of-life-in-the-game-industry-challenges-and-best-practices-2004/

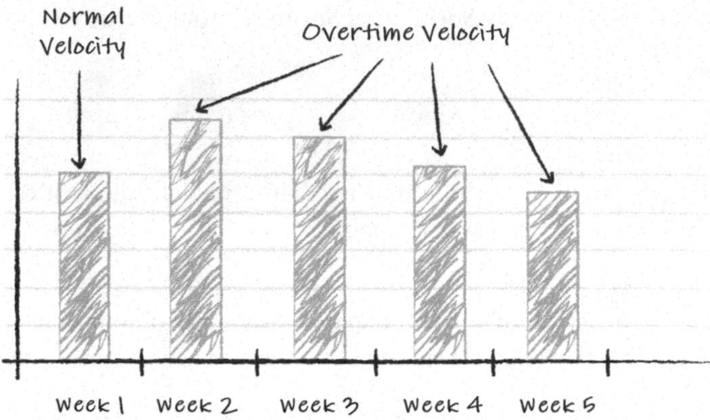


**Figure 16.1** *Burndown during crunch*

How is this possible? The reasons are simple. People were tired. They made more mistakes. They lost their concentration.

This realization represented a huge benefit of Scrum for High Moon, providing simple empirical evidence about what works and what doesn't. This is why there is no rule about overtime in Scrum. There doesn't need to be a rule. If your teams are using Scrum to find the best way to work, they'll quickly discover that after several weeks of overtime, any benefit from it is lost. It becomes common sense to maintain a sustainable pace.

### Velocity in Hours

Although the term *velocity* usually refers to the measure of scope (for example, story points) accomplished per Sprint, the velocity, or change, in hours of work remaining in a Sprint per day or week provides interesting, though less stable, feedback about a team.

### Experience: Counting Cars in the Parking Lot

We first started using Scrum at Sammy Studios. Sammy was owned by a Japanese Pachinko manufacturing company called Sammy Corporation. Although we had gotten off to a slow start, Scrum was helping us get back on track and demonstrate good progress. However, good progress wasn't enough for Sammy Corporation. A source of concern from them was based on the opinion that American game developers don't dedicate as much overtime as

Japanese developers. They felt the lack of crunch meant a lack of commitment to the success of the studio.

Sammy Corporation eventually merged with Sega to accelerate its transition into game development and publishing. During this time, Sega debated about whether to retain Sammy Studios. To help in the debate, it had someone drive past the studio late at night and count the number of cars in the parking lot. The count was low, which to Sega meant that our commitment to success was also low.

Fortunately for us, there was a newspaper distribution warehouse next door. They were quite busy between midnight and six a.m., so we asked the workers to park in our lot, which wasn't an inconvenience. This satisfied Sega for a while.

Eventually, though, Sega informed us that it was closing the studio. Fortunately, we were able to acquire the studio, which was renamed as High Moon Studios.

Managers often confuse overtime with commitment. They think that forcing people to work overtime demonstrates commitment to the success of a project. In reality, this is like forcing someone to smile to prove they are happy. It just doesn't work that way.

## What Good Looks Like

The most successful Agile adoptions have a few things in common. One of them is having a leader who is knowledgeable and curious about methodologies, leadership, teaming, and various project management approaches. In other words, having a "process nerd" in a leadership position is essential.

I was the process nerd for High Moon Studios. At first, I read books on methodologies in an attempt to find the perfect one, but after a while I came to realize two things:

- Rather than being the latest "buzzword," Agile is the evolving result of decades of slow change away from the discredited scientific methodology introduced more than a century ago (and still being widely applied as "waterfall").
- The focus of methodology has shifted from process and practices to a focus on people. Growing people, teams, and culture is now recognized as the biggest factors of success.

Desperation and self-survival instincts[3] led me to be a process nerd, but having encountered them at thriving studios has led me to realize this position is critical.

## Summary

The best way to adopt Scrum is to do it with eyes wide open. Establishing useful metrics and establishing practices such as the Daily Scrum provide immediate demonstration of its value.

Scrum is a framework. It doesn't include practices to optimize code, create better art, or tune a mechanic. Those come from each studio's development practices and culture. In this light, there is less to fear about the change Scrum introduces.

Keep the myths and challenges from this chapter in mind as you read the next chapter on launching Scrum, which continues to introduce challenges and describes how to meet them and what to expect in a studio as Scrum principles take hold.

## Additional Reading

Heath, C., and D. Heath. 2007. *Made to Stick: Why Some Ideas Survive and Others Die*. New York: Random House.

Pascale, R. T., M. Milleman, and L. Gioja. 2001. *Surfing the Edge of Chaos: The Laws of Nature and the New Laws of Business*. New York: Three Rivers Press.

3. Motivated by a Sega executive described in Chapter 20, "Self-Organization and Leadership"

# Chapter 17

# Working with Stakeholders

As a member of the Nintendo Ultra-64[1] Dream Team in the mid-nineties, Angel Studios was exposed to a very collaborative publishing model. Nintendo and Angel discussed a game idea, and we were asked to "find the fun" with it. Nintendo funded the project for three months and then visited to see the results. Occasionally, the legendary Shigeru Miyamoto—creator of *Mario*, *Donkey Kong*, *Legend of Zelda*, *Nintendogs*, and many other hit games—visited as well!

Nintendo had no interest in any documents we had prepared; it only wanted to see the game. If the game was making progress and demonstrating fun, Nintendo funded another three months and left us with the instructions to "find more fun." If not, the game was abandoned, and another idea was discussed.

This iterative approach, which gauges progress based on the game alone, is very Agile, but few stakeholders pursue development in such an Agile way. In fact, there's a polarization of views about Agile approaches such as Scrum within the publishing community. Some have mandated that all their first-party developers use it, while others have allowed it, but enforce fixed and detailed project management approaches that eliminate most of the benefits. Those that use Scrum have found challenges in establishing the best level of collaboration.

Establishing an Agile relationship between stakeholders and developers is challenging. Publishers don't simply hand out money to developers who offer nothing more than a promise to try to "find the fun." There usually has to be a more formal arrangement. Outside of our industry, there are plenty of examples of Agile contracts between stakeholders, such as publishers, and developers that work and could form the model for the game industry.

1. This was the code name for the Nintendo 64.

## The Solutions in This Chapter

This chapter examines the typical issues with stakeholders, the challenges with establishing a more Agile model, and a range of solutions to becoming more Agile.

## Who Are the Stakeholders?

A stakeholder is someone who has an interest or concern in the outcome of the game. Scrum differentiates the Scrum Team from the stakeholders to highlight the communication and transparency inside and outside of the Sprint. Scrum Teams and stakeholders will have a high level of transparency and communication in Sprint Planning and Reviews, but Scrum Teams are left alone during Sprints to focus on the agreed-upon Sprint Goals.

Stakeholders are in one of two categories:

- **Internal stakeholders:** These are leads, directors, producers, studio executives, and so on who are usually part of the studio developing the game.
- **External stakeholders:** These are remote stakeholders, typically publisher employees such publisher producers, marketing, sales, or someone funding the game.

Due to the challenges of their remoteness, this chapter focuses on external stakeholders. Chapter 20, "Self-Organization and Leadership," focuses on the role of internal stakeholders. For brevity, they are referred to as "publishers" in the text from here out.

### The Law of Stakeholders

The main rule I've learned about stakeholders is the longer they go without hearing or seeing anything, the more they think things are going wrong. Communication is key.

## The Challenges

When I was working in the defense industry, documentation was king. For every week of actual development (writing code, testing, and so on), I spent two weeks writing documentation. Everyone's cubicle had an overhead shelf filled with binders that demonstrated the amount of documentation each of us had written for their current project. Our performance was measured primarily by the amount of documentation we generated.

The last defense industry project I was on was to design an avionics architecture for a new fighter jet. It represented hundreds of millions of dollars of work that our company was desperate to secure.

My job was to compile hundreds of various requirement and specification documents into a single document to deliver to the Air Force within a few months. After a couple of weeks, it became apparent to me that I could not create a comprehensive, organized, and readable document from all of these separate documents. I approached the project manager with my concern. "Oh, don't worry about that," he told me. "The Air Force just weighs these documents; they don't actually read them!"

I was shocked at this revelation. I finished compiling the master document with an eye toward maximizing the weight. When completed, the printed version weighed 20 pounds and filled one of those boxes that copier paper comes in. It was truly massive. The document was delivered, and I was given a pat on the back for a "job well done." Shortly after, I resigned.

One of the main reasons that game development has become less iterative is the increasing requirement for detailed, up-front plans from publishers. This has resulted from the rising cost of project failures. Publishers desire more certainty from developers and want to be sure they are "thinking things through" before creating code and assets. Publisher-side producers are encouraged to demand a detailed plan and schedule, tied to a contract, because it places much of the responsibility for project uncertainty in the hands of the developer.

Developers are encouraged to create these documents and schedules because the false sense of security they provide gives them time to explore the game, fund their studio, and (ideally) ensure that the publisher's long-term financial commitment is established.

Although design documents have not reached the size of those on major government weapons systems, most publishers and developers are realizing that there is no correlation between the size of the design documents and the success of a game. The illusion of certainty and the ulterior motives that drive these bad practices have to end. The business model won't support it for much longer.

## Focus Comes Too Late

Most games demonstrate significant increases in gameplay value after alpha, when integration, debugging, optimization, and polishing begin in earnest. This is often a stressful time between the publisher and the developer because the publisher finally has a potentially deployable game to provide feedback on, but the definition of alpha usually means that all features are implemented and so it is too late to consider many of the suggestions.

The pressure to add these last-minute changes is often too much. Teams succumb to adding late features because they know the game needs them, and they don't want to deliver a bad game after all the effort put into it. Unfortunately, the delivery dates are not changed to reflect this added work, or if they are changed, it involves a performance penalty for the studio or damage to their relationship with the publisher.

## Milestone Payments and Collaboration

Publishers usually hold the upper hand in a development agreement. Contracts often allow them to terminate a project at their convenience. Given this leverage, they can usually dictate new features, which result in "feature creep."

Milestone payment delays and threats of termination are blunt tools. The pressure they create results in milestone builds that lack fun and also lack consistency with and adherence to a vision. They might satisfy a milestone deliverable checklist, but they don't move the game toward market success as much as they should.

Contracts negotiated between a publisher and developer usually cover the full development cycle of the game from concept to gold master. Given this liability, publishers prefer to have some guarantees of performance. These typically take the form of milestone schedules linked to payments. Milestones usually occur every three months and have specific testable conditions in them such as the following:

- Three playable levels.
- The AI characters navigate environments and attack the player.
- Players can join other players for online gameplay.

These seem like reasonable milestone deliverables, but they highlight a few problems:

- **Quality cannot be defined in a contract:** Development studios are highly dependent on milestone payments, so if the choice comes down to providing two great levels of gameplay or three mediocre levels, as defined by a milestone the developer may choose the latter simply to be paid. There is no way to contractually define a quality bar unless the developer allows the publisher to subjectively judge the quality of deliverables, which it would be negligent to allow.
- **Collaboration is discouraged:** In the event that a publisher or developer identifies a change to the game that alters future milestone deliverables, introducing such a change into the contract is usually difficult, especially if it impacts

the budget or delivery date. As a result, game-improving changes are inhibited at many levels.

- **Problems are hidden, and trust is destroyed:** Developers try to load as much of the development fees from a publisher into early milestones as possible and define the deliverables in a way that avoids exposing problems until late in the project (see the "Examples of Milestone Definitions That Hide Problems" sidebar), when the cost of cancellation is too high.
- **Developers don't want to expose problems to the publisher early because they think they will overreact and cancel a project:** Publishers think that developers won't openly share the bad news, so they end up assuming the worst. These attitudes destroy trust.

**Examples of Milestone Definitions that Hide Problems**

The following are milestone definitions I have seen in contracts, which help the developer avoid hard questions from the publisher after a milestone is delivered:

- **"The AI is 60 percent complete":** I have no idea what "60 percent complete" means. It could mean that everything is broken and the AI does nothing.
- **"First-pass at the main character model":** First out of how many passes? Two or one hundred?

## Limited Iteration

Many publishers see the need to iterate planning and development. One common practice used is to allow "rolling milestone" definitions. These enable the detailed definition of a milestone to be fleshed out during the preceding one. Although this enables details to emerge, it doesn't permit changes to major deliverable dates or much flexibility within the milestone being worked on. Like an Oreo™ cookie, it sandwiches the flexible part between two inflexible lumps.

## First-Party Problems

The issues of contracts and payments largely disappear when a studio—acquired by a publisher—becomes a first-party developer. This seems like a relief to a studio that has struggled to survive, but it raises different challenges.

A publisher that owns a studio has more freedom to control it. For example, if a project is late, the publisher might transfer developers from another project over to help, which rarely does (see the discussion of "Brook's Law" in the "Fixed Ship Dates" section later in this chapter). It might decide that it doesn't trust some of the design decisions being made and dictate them remotely, which destroys morale.

Some studios with a track record of success erect barriers with their parent publisher to avoid these problems, going so far—in one case—as to bar them from entering the premises!

Keeping publishers entirely in the dark doesn't help because they have a role to play in the success of a game. For example, this success depends not only on the quality of the game but also on the publisher's responsibility in marketing it. A talented marketing group can help the developers fine-tune the game to deliver what the market wants.

**The Eye of Sauron**

Marketing often is the area of publishing that is the hardest to adopt Agile practices to as they are often accustomed, and staffed, to only pay attention to the game at the beginning of development and when the delivery date is approaching. The problem with this is that they are often surprised at what the studio is going to deliver and ask for many late changes, which usually cannot be accommodated without missing the delivery date.

We likened this behavior to "The Eye of Sauron" after the *Lord of the Rings* movies, where the evil Sauron and his giant magical flaming eye would focus on the poor hobbit protagonist at the worst possible time. We felt the same as that horrified hobbit when the marketing group would turn its focus on us when we were struggling to finish a game.

Practices such as those described in the book *Innovation Games: Creating Breakthrough Products Through Collaborative Play* (Hohmann, 2015) are effective at engaging marketing throughout development with an Agile team and improving the chances for shipping a successful game.

## Portfolios Drive Dates

Market forces often compel publishers to promise delivery dates and even projected sales figures for a game. The demands of large retail chains, licensing deadlines, long-term portfolio plans, and the desire to please shareholders pressure publishers to commit to very uncertain and optimistic product flow and ironclad delivery dates.

This compels a publisher to ask the improbable of their developers, even after many failures demonstrate the futility of this. It's not that publishers are unaware of the development realities. They simply can't resist the pressure from retailers and shareholders.

Perhaps as the market changes and as new distribution channels appear, this problem may be alleviated, but it won't happen soon. One solution is to increase the level of collaboration between the publisher and the developer to make them partners in the goals of the game. This requires a higher level of trust that has to be slowly built to overcome long-established fears.

## Building Trust, Allaying Fear

The common root of all these problems is a lack of trust and collaboration between a developer and publisher. Trust takes a long time to build. Building it through iteration, transparency, and collaboration are Agile principles.

The first step is to deliver value regularly. When a publisher receives Sprint builds with significant incremental improvements to the game, it builds confidence and trust.

The second step is welcoming collaboration with the publisher. Observations from publishers contain valuable feedback about the marketable value of the game. When this feedback is reflected in the game within the next few Sprints, it builds trust. Publishers and developers become true collaborators, rather than rivals trying to manipulate one another.

These steps lead to greater trust in the developer's ability and decision making. It enables honest discussions of project goals whenever scope, schedule, and cost start to conflict as they invariably do on most projects. By having these discussions earlier, when there are more options for addressing problems, the relationship and product benefit.

First, the fears that publishers have of releasing the "Agile genie" must be overcome.

### The Fears

Publishers have a great deal of fear about Agile. Some of these fears are as follows:

- "We would have no idea where the project is headed. They could iterate forever!"
- "If the scope is flexible, developers won't work very hard. We'll get half the game for our money!"

Developers have fears about an Agile relationship with a publisher as well:

- "The publishers will micromanage the Product Backlog, and we'll have no creative control."
- "Allowing publishers to always change the scope will lead to a death march!"

These fears aren't groundless. A misunderstanding of Agile or Scrum practices and principles makes it possible for any of these problems to be realized.

**"Take all that Scrum Stuff off the Walls!"**

When Activision merged with Vivendi, who owned our studio, it evaluated every studio to determine which to keep or close down. Just before our evaluation, we were told by an Activision manager to "take all that Scrum stuff off the walls!" because its CEO didn't like Scrum. When we asked why, he told us that another studio had used Scrum and had failed to ship a game on time. Someone had the impression that Scrum falsely promised success rather than merely transparency.

This warning was the first sign that I needed to leave. Fortunately, High Moon survived the day. Since then, I have taught Scrum at various Activision studios; the CEO's attitude must have changed.

## Understanding Agile

Teams slowly absorb the principles of Agile development as they iterate, deliver working builds that demonstrate value, and receive stakeholder and customer feedback. Publishers are not faced with the daily lessons of Agile and can't absorb these principles as quickly. As a result, they may not understand the importance of Scrum practices and their role as a stakeholder, which leads to the following dysfunctions:

- Not playing Sprint builds
- Not attending reviews or planning sessions
- Ignoring the Product Backlog
- Demanding detailed schedules and documents up front and ignoring the need to revisit them based on actual progress
- Making urgent requests in the middle of a Sprint

These are typical actions of publishers who are accustomed to traditional projects that hide uncertainty and don't demonstrate real value until post-production. Agile developers need to reinforce the principles and benefits of Agile development with their publishers. One method is to establish a publisher-side Scrum advocate or even a publisher-side Product Owner.

## Publisher-Side Product Owners

A Product Owner is usually a member of the project development team. Video game Product Owners need to provide frequent and subjective feedback. Does the control of the player feel right? Is a mechanic fun enough? This feedback requires daily engagement with the team. Product Owners are the single voice for all the customers and stakeholders of the game.

Unfortunately, many stakeholders reside with a publisher who is based thousands of miles away. This challenges the Product Owner's capacity to create a shared vision with them. One solution is to delegate a portion of the Product Ownership role by creating a publisher-side Product Owner. This person represents the publisher-side stakeholders to the developer. Figure 17.1 shows the arrangement between both Product Owners.

The publisher-side Product Owner communicates with the developer-side Product Owner as frequently as necessary.

The publisher-side Product Owner has the following responsibilities:

- Review each Sprint build
- Participate in as many Sprint Review and Planning meetings as possible

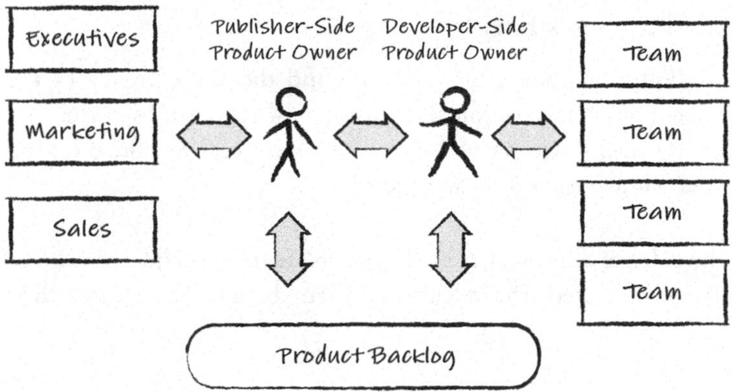


**Figure 17.1** *The Product Owner roles*

- Attend the Release Planning and Review meetings
- For first-party developers, ensure that the developer-side Product Owner is tracking return on investment (ROI) and general project cost dependencies
- Represent the developer-side Product Owner to publisher-side stakeholders such as executives, marketing, and sales groups
- Ensure that all the publisher-side stakeholders are aware of the current status of development

The two Product Owners should communicate about every aspect of the game and clearly define the limits of ownership. For example, the publisher-side Product Owner might own the release goals (epic-level stories) while the developer-side Product Owner owns the release plan (the stories that fit within the release). This is different for every studio, publisher, and game. For example, some externally licensed games require strong publisher-side Product Ownership, whereas intellectual property being developed at the studio must have stronger developer-side Product Ownership.

Third-party (independent) developers usually maintain more ownership because they have sole responsibility for maintaining their own financial stability.

Together, the two Product Owners manage the Product Backlog. This includes discussing the addition, removal, and prioritization of features. The publisher-side Product Owner must understand that new features are always welcome on the Product Backlog, but the Product Backlog itself is not a promise of what will deploy with the game. He or she needs to understand what velocity means and how to use it to avoid feature creep and allow collaboration to exist between the publisher and developer.

## Meeting Project Challenges Early

Scrum's empirical measure of development velocity and the transparency of the Product Backlog enable honest and continual discussions of scope and schedule. By developing a potentially deployable set of ordered features every Sprint, the team and publisher have the following controls over the project:

- **Control of the release date:** If the velocity of the features being introduced is different from predicted, the release date can be earlier or later than planned.

- **Control of the scope:** Scope is the easiest factor to manipulate as long as value emerges during development, rather than emerging all at once after alpha, which is often the case.
- **Control of the budget:** The Product Owner continually measures ROI based on value, velocity, and cost. This gives greater visibility into whether the budget being spent on the project is generating sufficient return in value seen.

Most publishers are used to waiting until after alpha for the state and quality of the game to emerge, which is usually too late to apply these controls without expensive consequences. Thus, they are not accustomed to having them available. Agile projects give more stakeholders more visibility and control.

As Chapter 9, "Agile Release Planning," described, these controls are similar to those applied during a cross-country drive. Experienced drivers won't rely on a map, or plan, as the only source of information about the trip. They fine-tune the plan based on the reality emerging, such as miles driven per day or—if there is enough time—side trips taken to add value to the trip.

## Managing the Production Plan

Chapter 10, "Video Game Project Management," described how production debt is impacted by decisions made in pre-production and how the estimation of this debt is continually refined.

Production plans are critically important to publishers and developers. They represent major cost and resource obligations. The date that teams start production is a signal that the gameplay is more certain and that they are in the home stretch. Unfortunately, the desire to reach the state of production often overshadows the reality of whether the game and team are truly prepared to enter it. Often the date, or the need, to transition production resources takes precedence over whether the game is ready to enter production.

Developers and publishers need to clearly establish the goals a game must meet before it enters production. Metrics need to be established in pre-production that demonstrate the production plan is still viable. These metrics, such as the number of people-days to produce each level, continually measure the cost of completing assets in pre-production as they approach production quality. Without them, production schedules remain highly speculative and optimistic.

Production forecasts and metrics should be part of every release deliverable. Given these forecasts and metrics, the publisher and developer plan coming releases to ensure that production dates are met or to update planning to match reality.

### Allaying the Fears

Given the tools described earlier, developers and publishers begin to allay the fears that were identified at the start of this section.

> We have no idea where the project is in development. Developers can iterate forever!

Agile methods require close participation between the stakeholders and the developers on a regular basis. Without a shared vision, a game easily strays off course and becomes something the publisher did not want.

With development projects that cost $40 million becoming common, publishers must have the games prove their value along the way, regardless of the methodology used. Scrum creates a framework for close collaboration and iteration that allows this.

> If the scope is flexible, developers won't work very hard. We'll get half the game for our money!

Publishers should be impressed with the velocity of features introduced by Scrum developers. If not, the project should be canceled. Agile contracts give both parties an opportunity to identify when a game idea is bad or a team is not a good match for a project. Neither party should wait two years or spend $40 million to discover that all the hard work won't provide a sufficient return on the investment.

> The publishers will micromanage the Product Backlog, and we'll have little creative control.
>
> Allowing publishers to change the scope will lead to a death march!

A first-party developer without a Product Owner owning the vision is in the greatest danger of this happening. The developer needs to establish the roles on both sides in terms of Product Ownership. The practices of Scrum reinforce this every Sprint.

## Agile Contracts

With the emergence of mobile games and digital distribution platforms, there are many examples of Agile contracts that are flexible and iterative. These enable clients and developers to work with a series of short-term contracts. Rather than committing to years of promised effort involving large sums of money, the smaller contracts each cover an incremental released version of the game and provide much more certainty and far less risk.

Because Agile game development provides a more incremental delivery of value, it gives publishers and studios the potential to build relationships where progress is measured on a regular basis to determine whether the project is worth pursuing further, much as Nintendo and Miyamoto did with Angel Studios. Developers can now "test the waters" with early demos and "Minimally Playable Games" that provide valuable feedback from players.

The benefits of this approach are significant. Not all ideas result in great games. Some teams are not well matched to a game they are tasked to develop. Abandoning those efforts early is better than spending years following a bad path.

While frightening to consider at first, it is actually a measure of success for projects to "fail early" rather than to "fail late." Failing early reduces the possibility of harming the relationship between a publisher and developer. On the other hand, spending $10 million for a game that never sees the shelf creates a lot of bad feelings and destroys careers. Besides, no one wants to spend years of their career working away on a mediocre game.

Many AAA games still have one "big-bang" deployment followed by a small number of patches. There is greater risk in funding these large projects, which leads to detailed, ironclad contracts.

Although developers might prefer the security of a long-term contract, the reality is that the "termination for convenience" clause in most contracts allows a project to be canceled at any time, for any reason.

### No Burrito in the Contract

Very late in the development of *Midtown Madness*, I received a call from our producer at Microsoft. "I've got good news!" he proclaimed. This worried me, as it only meant that he had a feature idea he wanted to creep in.

He went on: "We just made a deal with Taco Bell, and we want you to put some Taco Bell restaurants in the game. Players will then be able to drive up to the take-out window and order burritos."

"Why would we want players, who are either racing other vehicles or evading police to do that?" I asked.

"Because then the game would then give them a one-time coupon for a free burrito at a real-world Taco Bell!" he exclaimed.

I immediately rejected the request, not because it was a bad idea, but because I was focused on finishing the game. Because the feature wasn't in the original design document, I could do that.

However, I later regretted that decision when it occurred to me that offering free burritos to our target demographic would have likely been a desirable feature.

This illustrates the problem with inflexible contracts. They create a resistance to change and collaboration between the development teams and the stakeholders.

## Iterating Against a Plan

Huge design documents and schedules are like a woolen security blanket in the rain; they give comfort for only a short amount of time. Despite up-front planning's poor track record, publishers and project managers demand it because the only alternative they see—no planning at all—leads to chaos and ruin. They're not wrong.

### True Fixed Ship Dates

Some games will fail if they don't hit a fixed ship date, such as games that ship the same day the movie they are tied with is released and sports titles that must ship at the start of a season. Chapter 10 discusses the management of such titles in more detail.

When faced with this, the challenge for Agile developers is to gradually introduce Agile planning practices and to find the cracks in the big bang process that always exist—such as rolling milestone definitions—and exploit them for the benefit of the project.

What does an Agile team do when a publisher demands all-embracing design documents and schedules? The first thing is to determine how much flexibility exists within the publisher's process. It's rare to find a publisher that does not allow some form of rolling milestones described earlier. If these are allowed, such milestones are managed the same as releases. When the publisher requests an upcoming milestone definition, hold a Release Planning meeting for it, and invite a representative from the publisher who can make decisions.

Over time, a developer builds trust by allowing some change from the publisher. Care must be taken to not give a blank check for changes. If a fixed scope list exists, rather than a Backlog, each change must be accompanied by the deferral of other work from it.

Most long-term deliverables are tied to the minimum required feature set. As described in Chapter 10, the greatest threat to schedules and resources is an excessive amount of advance speculation about the details for these features. They paint teams into death-march corners.

If—in the worst case—no flexibility or trust exists and the developer cannot refuse the work, what can be done? Although teams benefit from some practices such as Sprints and Daily Scrum meetings, they will be limited in how they may react to the emerging game. They should attempt to insert meetings in the schedule that require stakeholders to review progress and make decisions about the course of the project. Another useful tool is to enumerate all known and potential risks and identify how they will be addressed (see the "Experience" sidebar). Transparency is still encouraged; hiding problems only creates debt that the team pays back with a death march.

**Experience**

For our first game on the latest PlayStation, we drew upon the memory of all the problems we encountered with the previous PlayStation and enumerated them as risks (see Chapter 7, "The Product Backlog"). These included broken tools, buggy libraries, poor documentation, and delayed test hardware. We highlighted all the potential impacts to the productivity and schedule that would occur if any of these problems were realized. As it turned out, all of them were. Although we couldn't mitigate the impact to the project, we worked together with the publisher to address the issues. As a result, it became partners with us in finding a solution, and this prevented us from being blamed for something we had little control over.

## Fixed Ship Dates

A common impression about Agile is that it does not allow games that use it to deliver on a fixed schedule. The impression is based on the idea that Agile teams don't plan but simply iterate with a very short horizon—they just don't know when the project will end!

Although most games have a delivery date, many of these are considered "firm" rather than "fixed." Firm delivery dates are established by publishers to fit portfolio or budget projections. A firm delivery date will drive the project, but if it desperately needs another month or so of work to achieve far better results, slipping the date won't be a disaster. Fixed delivery dates, on the other hand, are critical for the success of some games. Examples of games with fixed delivery dates are those that must deploy simultaneously with a movie release or games like *Madden Football* that must be on shelves by the start of each NFL season. The penalty in lost sales for missing these dates is major.

How is a project with a fixed delivery date managed differently from one that is not? Mainly, it is the way risk is handled. Risk is uncertainty about what a team is creating and how it is going to build it. For example, if we want to dedicate 20 percent of our project budget to creating a cooperative online death-match mode with AI opponents for our game, a few of the uncertainties might be the following:

- Will the AI work online?
- Is 20 percent of the budget enough to create a fun and complete experience?
- Will problems in other areas delay work or take people away?

The list can go on. Any one of these can threaten the project's schedule and result in the feature being dropped after almost 20 percent of the project's budget has been spent on it.

So, how is risk handled? Developers often try to plan and schedule their way out of risk by creating exceedingly detailed plans that attempt to identify the solution to every foreseeable problem. Unfortunately, because the danger lies in what a team does not know, it's certain that the tasks required to overcome risk will not be identified up front. The best way to handle risk is to focus on answering the unknown; in other words, creating knowledge.

Creating knowledge and value is important for any project, regardless of the delivery date. For projects with fixed delivery dates, the prioritization of work to reduce risk is a bit higher. For example, if a movie-based shooter game with a fixed delivery date has to decide between shipping six months after the movie's release or dropping online gameplay, they will be more likely to drop online. A game that is not based on such a license, which instead has a firm delivery date, is more likely to be delayed to ensure the feature is included.

So, let's return to the original question: Does Agile aid or impede a project's ability to achieve a fixed delivery date? Executed properly, an Agile project has significant advantages over other methods. Two core principles are behind this advantage:

- **Prioritizing to create knowledge and reduce risk:** Focus on delivering high value and addressing risk early. Fixed delivery dates only enable a project's staff or the scope to vary. Increasing the number of developers on a troubled project usually doesn't help. Brook's Law[2] says that "adding manpower to a

2. https://study.com/academy/lesson/brooks-law-in-project-management-definition-formula.html

late software project makes it later." The law also applies to game development. The best option is varying the scope, or feature set, of the project. Identifying the best features that fit within the schedule is critical to the success of a game with a fixed delivery date.

- **Not postponing debt:** Frequent integration, immediate defect correction, and maintaining target performance (for example, keeping the game potentially deployable) will prevent late surprises that require rework and delay. When projects with fixed delivery dates postpone critical work to post-production, they often meet with disastrous results.

Two tools for applying these principles are the Product Backlog and the Definition of Done. Stories that address schedule risk must often be prioritized over others on a project with a fixed deployment date. An example of this is a spike to mock up a full level. This would create early knowledge about the level dimensions to better refine the production schedule and risk. Doing this constrains some of the options for emergent gameplay, but it might be necessary to know this information sooner than later.

Elevating the Definition of Done (see Chapter 7) enables risk to be addressed earlier. For example, if a game must deploy on all platforms, a Product Owner might require stories to run on all the platforms earlier in the project than they normally would. Although this additional Definition of Done may slow teams down, especially if the platform technology isn't fully mature, it accelerates improvements and creates more knowledge about the risks of those platforms earlier.

As described in Chapter 7, Agile methods don't attempt to plan away uncertainty with large documents, but they also don't ignore uncertainty. They simply tailor the practices to the different level of uncertainty over time. Planning for short-term goals, such as Sprint goals, is done at a high level of detail. Planning for medium-range goals, such as release plans, is less detailed but receives continual refinement. Long-range planning for things such as delivery dates, production scheduling, and so on, is also continually refined and influences short-term planning. For example, an Agile plan won't say, "Production will start on September 14" a year in advance. It will refine a range of times over the course of pre-production. The reason is that not only will we gain knowledge about production in pre-production, but the debt itself will change. By acknowledging uncertainty and working to refine it, Agile planning will increasingly match the reality that is emerging rather than drifting further away from the big document written at the start of a project.

Too many times fixed delivery dates result in little innovation or a poor game that must be shipped before it has been properly polished. Games released along with the release of movies have long had a reputation for low quality. This doesn't need to be the case. Eliminating the waste of dropping features at the eleventh hour after months of working on them is a good place to start.

Sometimes a fixed delivery date is impossible to achieve. A risk-based approach for developing completed features will not work miracles, but it will expose the bad news sooner than later.

## Agile Pre-Production

Publishers aren't deaf to the Agile message. They understand that fun cannot be defined in a document. They've seen detailed plans and schedules fail projects again and again. However, most publishers exist as publicly traded companies that must be able to forecast budgets and delivery dates for their games. As a compromise to this reality, publishers are more readily engaging developers to be more Agile in pre-production alone. This involves small teams taking longer to iteratively explore potential features, creating knowledge about production costs, and defining the quality and fun of the game. Because production is more expensive and amenable to predictive schedules, this is a reasonable compromise.

**Note**

Chapter 10 describes Lean production and the benefit of Agile thinking during production.

## The Stage-Gate Model

With a "big-bang" release model, a contract that covers the entire development cycle is a rather large gamble, especially for an original idea. For these games, publishers may require decision points, called **green lights**, often at the juncture of two stages to decide whether to continue funding the game. Two of the most common green-light junctures are the following:

- **Concept green light:** The publisher decides whether to let a game enter the pre-production stage after reviewing project concepts, an initial plan, and a prototype.
- **Production green light:** The publisher decides whether to let a game enter the production stage after reviewing the gameplay, the production-representative assets, and the resource plan and schedule for production.

Publishers fund a number of game ideas and use green lights to funnel them down to a select a few of the best. This is called a **stage-gate model**. It gives a larger number of innovative ideas a chance to be proven.

Figure 17.2 shows a stage-gate being used to winnow four games down to the one that demonstrates the best value.

The stage-gate model creates a clear advantage for an Agile developer. It aligns the principles of Agile with the goals of the model: to judge the game itself rather than the plan for it.

> **Stage Gates and Green Lights**
>
> Some large games are required to go through several gates between stages. These stage gates require a green light for the team to proceed to the next stage (for example, concept to pre-production). Although this is a good way to discuss progress and risk with the stakeholders, it has drawbacks as well. The main problem is that it batches up decisions such as concept into one gate that locks in those decisions for subsequent stages.
>
> Experience has shown that concepts need to be proven out and build upon each other in an emergent way. A less risky approach uses iteration and interleaving stages as much as possible throughout development. It requires frequent engagement with the stakeholders, which is a primary barrier to doing it.

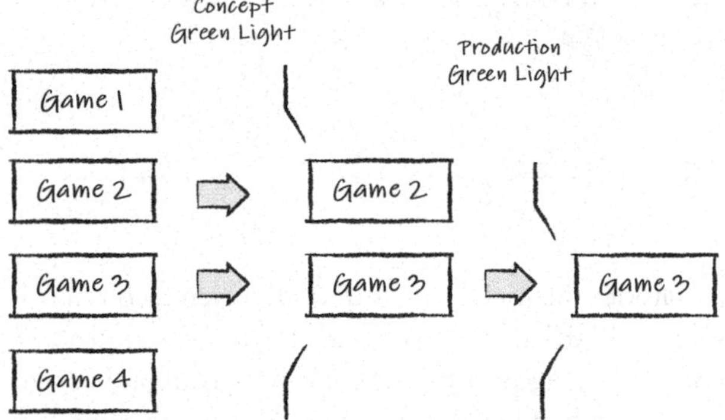


**Figure 17.2** *A stage-gate in action*

The stage-gate model can also establish the boundary between a longer pre-production stage that is largely exploratory and the production stage that is far more predictable.

**Note**

Mark Cerny's method (2002) is an example of a stage-gate process that focuses on exploring game value before entering production.

## What Good Looks Like

Teams and publishers effectively using an Agile approach together exhibit the following:

- There is frequent communication between the two.
- The Product Backlog is shared.
- Risk identification is ordered high on the Product Backlog and mitigation plans are in place in the event risk triggers.
- Bad news is not hidden and not punished.
- The build is reviewed every Sprint by the publisher and feedback is sent quickly.
- A representative from the publisher visits the team at least once every release.
- Areas of publishing such as marketing, sales, and QA are involved early and frequently.

## Summary

Although publishers may not consider themselves Agile and may even recoil in fear at the term, they have been trying to find ways to be more Agile for more than a decade. Iterative practices have been creeping into the way business is done between them and developers. By continuing to build an Agile vocabulary and trust through applying Agile principles, this trend will continue and allow game development and publishing to remain a viable and even lucrative business model.

## Additional Reading

Cook, D. *Rockets, cars and gardens: Visualizing waterfall, Agile and stage gate*. https://lostgarden.home.blog/2007/02/19/rockets-cars-and-gardens-visualizing-waterfall-agile-and-stage-gate/.

Cooper, R. 2001. *Winning at New Products: Accelerating the Process from Idea to Launch, Third Edition*. Cambridge, MA: Basic Books.

Hohmann L. *Innovation games: creating breakthrough products through collaborative play*. 2007. Boston, MA: Addison-Wesley.

# Chapter 18

# Team Transformations

Although Agile practices are simple and easy to learn, its adoption challenges organizations, processes, and cultures. It can take years to overcome those challenges. Although each studio and team has its own pace of adoption and challenges, there are enough common ones to establish a rough road map.

## The Solutions in This Chapter

This chapter reviews some of the team challenges presented by a move to Agile and discusses some strategies for helping organizations and teams adapt. These strategies apply to all Agile teams regardless of whether they are using Scrum or Kanban.

## The Three Stages of Team Transformation

In the movie *The Karate Kid*, a boy wants to learn karate from an old master. The master agrees but only on the condition that the boy does what he is told. The master begins by having him wash and wax his cars, paint his fence, and sand his patio floor. The only constraint he imposes is that the boy uses exact motions for each chore. For example, when waxing the car, wax is applied in a clockwise motion with the right hand and removed in a counterclockwise motion with the left hand.

After days of effort, the boy is exasperated. He expected to be taught karate, not perform chores. When he complains, the master has him repeat the motions he was shown for the tasks as he throws punches and kicks. The movements used for the chores are the exact motions used to block such attacks; the chores were meant to teach them subconsciously.

The movie illustrates the first stage of martial arts competence: the apprentice stage. In the apprentice stage, the student focuses on the proper forms; in other words, he is learning the basics. The second stage is the journeyman stage. Here the student modifies the motions to leverage his strengths and offset his weaknesses. The third stage of martial arts competence is the master stage. Masters create their moves. They reinvent the art because they know the underlying principles.

> **Note**
>
> In martial arts, this progression is known as Shu, Ha, and Ri.

A similar progression of stages is seen with teams adopting Agile principles. Teams cannot master self-organization and continual improvement from the start. They need to establish muscle memory with basic practices in the apprentice stage; expand, add, and change them in the journeyman stage; and then take full control of how they organize and achieve their goals in the master stage.

Figure 18.1 shows the three stages of Agile adoption.

> **Note**
>
> Apprentice, journeyman, and master stages are not guidelines but convenient labels that help identify typical milestones of progress with Scrum. Different teams have different pacing and will improve in different orders than what is represented by the road map.

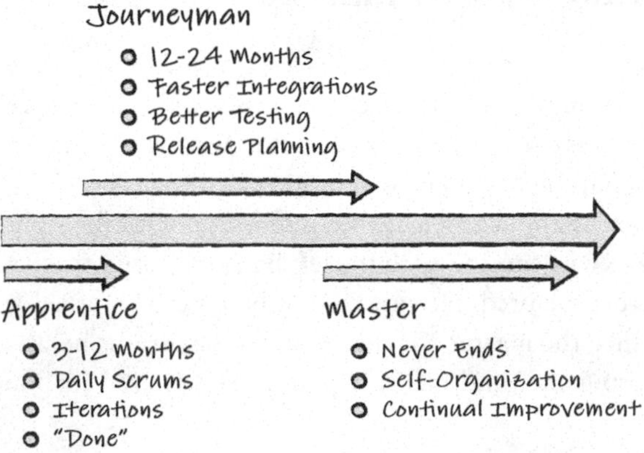


**Figure 18.1** *The road map of Agile adoption*

## The Apprentice Stage

In the apprentice stage, teams become accustomed to iterating on features and committing to their goals. They are challenged to deliver an improved version of the game that requires cross-discipline collaboration. They learn to step up every day as a member of a team committed to the goals and to report any impediments.

The team establishes a shared Definition of Done between it and the stakeholders. Adopting a shared Definition of Done puts pressure on individual skills, fundamental development practices, and the communal build process and pipeline. The new Definition of Done will almost certainly force changes and improvements. These improvements appear quickly and demonstrate the benefits of Agile.

### *Adjusting to Sprint Pacing*

Many traditional teams don't need to demonstrate their game to stakeholders very frequently. Often a demonstration is given every several months when a milestone is due. The work required to integrate changes made since the last milestone to fix errors and polish the game often requires the final few weeks before the milestone date.

When teams transition to Agile, the pace of producing a working game for demonstration to the stakeholders is accelerated. Now they need to show something at a more frequent cadence. The immediate problem is that creating a build now occupies a more substantial fraction of time. Teams can spend 50 percent of their time maintaining a working build. This overhead puts pressure on the practices used to commit and test changes to the game. Rather than abandoning Agile because iterating is costly, an Agile team finds ways to drive down the cost of iterating. Chapter 11, "Faster Iterations," covers this topic.

### *Defining "Done"*

Traditional project management does not fully burden developers with the responsibility of judging when a feature is complete. They merely need to accomplish tasks assigned to them on time. Agile requires teams and stakeholders to develop a Definition of Done that they agree upon. Establishing this definition challenges the apprentice team.

At first, this definition might only require a game to run without crashing. Later, a feature may be expected to run on a target platform at 30 frames per second. The challenge with the Definition of Done is that it causes new tasks to emerge during development. At first, teams might ignore these tasks; they think a successful iteration means that all the estimated tasks are completed at the end. It comes as a shock to them to learn that the working game is considered more important than task completion alone.

As the Definition of Done is refined and understood by teams, they will factor an amount of uncertainty into planning. If past efforts required 20 percent additional time for work not reckoned for, teams would leave that much slack in future planning sessions. This is covered in detail in Chapter 7, "The Product Backlog."

## Daily Scrum Challenges

The Daily Scrum is an essential practice of an effective team. Without it, teams would find it more challenging to manage their progress toward the best possible iteration. The Daily Scrum is a discussion among teammates ensuring they understand the state of the game, their progress towards their goal, and what is to be worked on next.

Daily Scrums are hard to get right from the start. Dysfunctions or misunderstandings about the purpose of this practice can prevent teams from achieving its full benefit. This section describes some of the common dysfunctions and ways to alleviate them.

### *Reporting to the Scrum Master*

When the team members report to the Scrum Master in a Daily Scrum, rather than the team, it indicates that they view the Scrum Master as a manager, which creates a barrier to ownership and commitment. Team members may think it's the Scrum Master's job to solve all of their problems and tell them what to do. This is common with an apprentice team. The reason for this behavior is that people need to overcome a career history that allowed far less ownership. They don't yet fathom or trust that their team takes ownership of the goal and controls the means to achieve it.

The Scrum Master can subtly discourage this behavior through several practices. For example, he can avoid eye contact with the person speaking in the Daily Scrum, which encourages the person to address the entire team. The Scrum Master should also pose critical questions such as "What problems could we have with achieving our goal?" or "What do you think we should look at next?" These questions drive teams to come up with solutions they own.

> **Tip**
>
> Sometimes not talking at all is the Scrum Master's best tool. A few moments of uncomfortable silence will often produce some creative ideas. Silently counting to 10 or more gives his or her mind something to do while waiting for the team.

The Scrum Master can inadvertently reinforce this dysfunction. One way is by taking notes at the meeting. Excessive note-taking creates the impression that the task information the team is reporting is being recorded and tracked, which can create distrust. If the Scrum Master needs to record task hours to produce the up-to-date burndown chart, he or she should explain this to the team.

*Not Reporting Impediments*

Teams not reporting impediments either have none or don't have a sense of ownership or commitment to their Sprint Goal. The latter is more likely.

The Scrum Master can do a few things to encourage problem reporting during the Scrum. One is to help teams understand that if they weren't able to achieve the progress they had set for themselves at the previous day's Daily Scrum, then they ought to report the impediments that caused this to the team.

Key questions help. For example, occasionally adding a fourth question such as "What threatens our achieving the goal?" at the Daily Scrum can help. The team members will begin to speak up, not for themselves, but for the team when they realize that their problems threaten the team's success and therefore belong to the team.

*Micromanaging the Sprint Backlog in Scrum*

One of the most common areas where apprentice teams struggle is in learning to self-manage their work. A barrier to doing this is the insistence of the Scrum Master to use an electronic tool to do the job.

These tools are used to

- Build the Sprint Backlog
- Update the estimates during the Sprint
- Display Sprint Backlog details during the Daily Scrum
- Spit out the Sprint burndown

Apart from distributed teams, which may benefit from these tools, I rarely see them as positive for new teams. The tools are not at fault, but how they are used.

One of the primary benefits of Scrum is in the boost of productivity seen with teams that have a sense of ownership in how they run their Sprints. Teams with ownership are accountable for their shared commitment to the Sprint Goal. They enjoy their work more and continually explore ways to improve.

Sprint tracking tools can get in the way of that by

- Not allowing an "all hands" approach to managing the Sprint Backlog: one mouse, one keyboard, one operator.

- The practice of only bringing the data in the tool out once a day because there are not enough licenses, developers don't want to learn the tool, or the extra effort isn't worth it.
- Limiting the team's ability to customize the artifacts (task board, burn down, and so on).
- Management monitoring the metrics of the Sprint (Sprint velocity, burndown), and even individual developer progress. Guess what happens when a developer or team is asked why their burndown is not diagonal enough?
- Making the Daily Standup a status reporting meeting by focusing on individuals.

Even if the tool is used in benevolent ways, the team can suspect otherwise. In organizations that are trying to grow trust, this can be a subtle barrier.

Teams also need their Sprint Backlog to be "radiated" to them. Tools "refrigerate" the Backlog by storing it in the cloud or on a server.

When I point this out, I often hear from Scrum Masters that the tool makes it easier for them to do their job: tracking the Sprint and producing the burndown. I remind them that their job is to help the team build ownership and trust, not to manage them.

The Sprint Backlog is owned by the developers to help them organize and manage their shared commitment and forecast for achieving the Sprint goal. It serves no purpose external to the team.

### Tracking a Kanban

The same advice applies to Kanban boards (see Chapter 6, "Kanban"). Having physical boards and cards that a co-located team manages usually gives better results than using an electronic version.

*Lack of Focus on the Goal*

Sometimes teams focus too much on finishing the tasks they estimated in the planning meeting and not enough on what shows up in the game. As a result, all the tasks are accomplished, but the value of what was added to the game is limited: Progression stoppers prevent the player from completing a level, annoying bugs are not fixed, assets are missing, and so on.

The main goal of Agile is to add value to the game, but "finding the fun" can't always be predicted. A lot of trial and error occurs during development. Tasks are volatile when the goal is as subjective as "finding the fun." For example, an initial Sprint Backlog based on a goal to allow the player to navigate a complex environment may not anticipate all the character control issues that will typically arise. That doesn't mean the team should avoid responsibility for them. Even if unforeseen work threatens lower-priority stories, the team should add the emergent tasks that the Definition of Done requires.

Scrum Masters encourage this behavior in several ways. One example is to embolden the team to change the Daily Scrum to focus more on the goal. Instead of going around the room to answer the three questions, the team could visit each story on the board and address the progress and issues for them, which focuses the work more on the stories themselves. Another useful practice is to conduct a short play-through of the game before a Daily Scrum, which focuses the team on the value added to a running game rather than progress against estimated tasks.

The team should be creative in exploring the practices of the Daily Scrum to improve the chances of achieving the goal.

*Replacing the Daily Scrum with a Tool*

I'm often asked by teams starting Agile, "Can we replace the Daily Scrum with a software tool?" My answer is always an emphatic, "No!"

As described earlier, the Daily Scrum is not merely a meeting to update task hours. The Daily Scrum's purpose is for the team members to inspect their progress and make commitments to each other about the work needed to achieve their shared goal.

Understanding the purpose of the Daily Scrum takes a while for teams new to Agile. In the past, tasks were estimated and assigned to them by managers. How the tasks came together to fulfill larger goals was not their responsibility. Scrum turns that upside down. Teams are given total responsibility for the tasks and how to accomplish the larger goal, which requires a different mindset for the new Scrum team. It's not a simple challenge; years of muscle memory must be overcome. This is why the Daily Scrum might seem wasteful at first. New teams think it's all about the tasks and their estimates.

Tasks and estimates are critically important, but experienced teams don't focus entirely on them. Their Daily Scrum is a beehive of activity that focuses on what everyone is doing to achieve *Done* and the emergent challenges to their shared goal.

## The Journeyman Stage

The journeyman stage of adoption occurs as teams improve how they iterate and deliver value. Iterations are no longer mini-waterfalls with a design phase at the start and a test-and-fix phase at the end. These activities take place daily.

Journeyman teams take more ownership of their practices and process, identifying and solving impediments and examining the underlying assumptions of how disciplines work together. These changes focus on improving their craft and team velocity.

An example of such an improvement was with a team that created characters. The last stage of creating a character was to supply sounds at particular animation trigger points, such as a footstep sound during the walk cycle. One problem was that the animators were checking in all their animations to revision control late in the Sprint, which caused the composers to rush their changes in so the team could achieve its Sprint Goal. This rush didn't lead to the best sounds added. The solution the team originally applied in their apprentice stage was to create a cutoff rule that all animations had to be checked in five days before the end of the Sprint. This allowed plenty of time to add the triggered audio, but it forced the animators to work on animations that might be needed for the next Sprint after the cutoff. Although this solved the immediate problem, it was a resource-based solution that didn't improve velocity.

As the team's experience with Scrum increased, it found a better solution, which required the animators to deliver each unpolished animation as it was created to the composers and then polish the animation after the composer attached audio. Although this might seem like a simple fix, it violated a deep-rooted artistic preference not to share an asset until its completion. In this case, and many others like it, a discipline's bias was overcome to improve the team's velocity. Journeyman teams build cross-disciplined trust and find ways of optimizing the entire cycle of development rather than parts of it.

### Experience

Apprentice teams often create work to prepare for future Sprints such as writing small design documents or creating partial assets. Journeyman teams eliminate most of this by reducing handoffs and by chopping work into smaller batches of discovery. These changes arise as the barriers between disciplines are broken down.

Journeyman teams also use more long-term Agile estimating and planning practices such as release planning and story point estimation as described in Chapter 9, "Agile Release Planning." They also introduce change to discipline practices, such as test-driven development as described in Part IV, "Agile Disciplines."

### *Release Cycles*

Journeyman teams improve releases, planning, and execution. As an apprentice team, they were challenged by the Sprint, but journeyman teams are accustomed to the pace of Sprints. They work with the Product Owner to plan and monitor releases (for example, they might use story point estimation; see Chapter 9). This gives them better tools for forecasting how much they can accomplish over a longer period than just a Sprint.

### *Team Co-location*

Agile principles emphasize face-to-face communication whenever possible. The benefits of this are demonstrated best at the team level. When a team is spread across a studio, the overhead and problems that arise from a lack of easy communication are seen daily. Studies have shown that when teams reduce the physical distance between themselves, their performance increases in many ways (Van Den Bulte and Moenaert, 1998). Eventually, teams realize this and rearrange themselves to improve communication.

#### Experience

Often a studio's physical arrangements greatly influence their culture. I typically see this in studios that are based on a number of floors in a building. When game teams or even disciplines are separated across floors, it can create a rivalry that significantly impacts collaboration and work.

*Physical Arrangement*

Teams that want to co-locate can have limited options. Sometimes an office is arranged with small cubicles that cannot easily be removed because of power and data wiring limitations. Team rooms or "bullpens" are less expensive to create than cubicle farms or separate office spaces, so teams lucky enough to influence the initial office space build-out can create an ideal location for themselves. Otherwise, they may need to adapt their current space by slowly remodeling it. Usually, having one team co-locate to judge the cost and benefit is best before a studio will allow all of them to co-locate.

What makes an ideal team space? There is no single solution. Sometimes teams can't even agree among themselves about what makes the best space. On a cross-discipline team, the programmers might want windows while the artists don't want light from the outside. It's up to the team to work this out. These are some of the other issues teams need to consider when defining their area:

- Is there enough wall space for a task board, information radiators (see the note "Information Radiators"), and whiteboards? Teams can never have enough wall space!

- Is there enough "slack" in the space so that developers can pair up or gather around a monitor? For example, can a programmer sit with an artist to discuss a problem?
- Is there space for meetings, such as the Daily Scrum or a play-through? Is there a development station available to conduct a play-through with the entire team?
- Is the room off the beaten path? Will traffic through the area from people outside the team create disruption?
- Are there rooms where people can have private conversations, conduct interviews, or read their e-mail?

### Tip

Furniture is also an important consideration. My opinion is that mobile, modular, and adjustable furniture like that built by Anthro[1] is best. Teams change and improve over time. The ability to regularly rearrange their space creates a big benefit.

### Information Radiators

An **information radiator** displays information in a place where those passing by can see it. With information radiators, those passing by do not need to ask questions; the information simply hits them as they pass (Cockburn, 2007).

*Concerns About Co-Locations*

Before teams co-locate, members often raise concerns about the potential problems of co-location. Two of the more common concerns are covered in this section.

> The first is that programmers (artists, designers, and so on) need to work in quiet isolation to focus and be effective. We can't do this in a noisy team room with constant interruptions.

There are certainly more interruptions in a team room. Most of these are the point of the team room. When developers are trying to achieve individual goals, such

1. www.anthro.com

as writing some code or creating an asset, interruptions often impede them from achieving that goal as quickly. However, Agile emphasizes the delivery of value integrated into the game, not the value of finishing "parts" that should join flawlessly because a document or Gantt chart states they will.

When a team is focused on achieving a common goal that requires everyone's participation, fast access to other team members who can help progress is essential. For example, having an animation programmer build an animation system apart from the animators doesn't make sense. They should be solving the problem together.

Noise and interruptions from outside the team are usually a source of unnecessary disruption. Teams should strive to eliminate things that distract them from their goals, such as public-address systems (DeMarco and Lister, 1999).

**Experience**

Every team that I have seen co-locate doesn't want to return to isolation.

> If I am not sitting with a group from the same discipline, then I won't learn and collaborate with them as much.

This argument creates a barrier for teams who want to co-locate, but it does have some validity. One example of this was in a large studio where half a dozen AI programmers were spread out across three teams. This led to three incompatible AI solutions, each duplicating the effort of the others. Although having an AI programmer close to the designers and animators was beneficial, there still needed to be communication that occurred with the other AI programmers. Communities of practice, described in Chapter 21, "Scaling Agile Game Teams," enabled this to happen. The AI community of practice met as frequently as necessary to share knowledge that benefited all their teams needing AI.

### *Release Dysfunctions*

Teams can encounter some common dysfunctions as they start using releases, rather than Sprints alone. These are usually caused by the longer time frame and the difference between the Definition of Done for a Sprint and the more demanding Definition of Done for a release. Also, the release cycle can bring out vestigial waterfall behaviors that cause problems.

This section identifies symptoms of release dysfunctions and identifies ways to help the team cure them.

*Hardening Sprint Used as a Dumping Ground*
Hardening Sprints, described in Chapter 9, are a practice that teams should strive to minimize or even eliminate. The danger from hardening Sprints is that they become a dumping ground for work that should be completed during regular Sprints. Left undone, unfinished work interferes with progress and reduces team productivity.

Here are some warning signs that hardening Sprints are being abused:

- Artists are postponing asset completion and leaving too many stand-in or missing assets in the game each Sprint.
- Programmers are deferring bug fixes.
- Designers are not tuning features for gameplay value.

Every Sprint should achieve a level of *Done* that includes much of this work. If this isn't happening, then the Definition of Done needs to be improved to include it.

**Tip**

Frequent play-throughs during the Sprint can help the team focus on making sure its work is done.

*Postponed Value*
Apprentice teams often divide Sprints into phases, treating them like mini-waterfall projects. A similar problem can affect teams during releases. Early Sprints are considered "design Sprints," whereas later Sprints are focused on debugging, tuning, and polishing for the release.

Velocity is used to measure the progress of a release and forecast its completion (see Chapter 9). This forecast assumes that the velocity trend will be a straight line through the remainder of the release. However, teams might experience a velocity drop-off toward the end. This is often accompanied by overtime, as teams compel themselves to achieve their goals. Teams are working harder, yet velocity seems to be dropping!

Figure 18.2 illustrates this happening over a four-Sprint release. The solid line shows the total story points accomplished during the release. The dotted line shows a subjective value of the game (the fun) from the Product Owner's perspective (there's no practical or easy way to measure this; it's meant to illustrate a point).

Ideally, because work is being prioritized by value, it should grow faster than story points. In the figure, story point velocity (slope of the dark line) increases quickly at first and then slows down at the end of the release. Value grows slowly at first—there isn't much "fun" being added to the game in the first few Sprints—but the game becomes a great deal more fun in the last few Sprints.

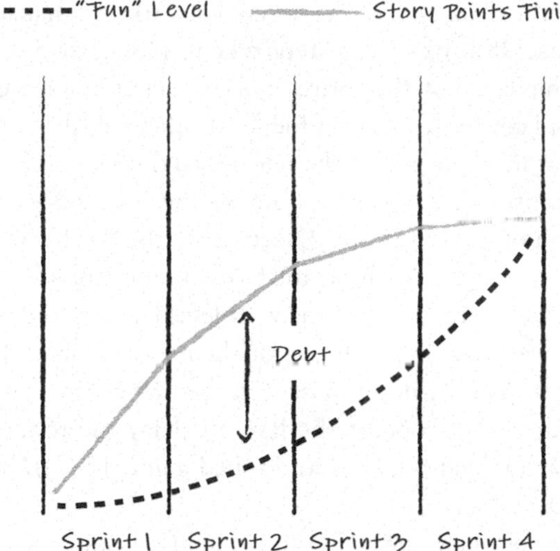


**Figure 18.2** *Velocity and fun in a release*

What happened is that the team used a waterfall approach in the release, treating it as a single-phased iteration of the game with integration, debugging, and polishing at the end. This builds up unfinished work in the release, called **debt**.

Debt consists of the following:

- Polishing or tuning work
- Assets that are left out or built before the team knows what works best
- Bugs that aren't fixed
- Developing large assets in parallel

Debt postpones the actualization of value toward the end of the release, much like a waterfall project defers it until post-production. Teams need to prevent this debt from growing so as to build value continually.

For example, consider a team with a release plan of creating a level that explores various mechanics. This level has many rooms that are each meant to offer different challenges to the player. A team might build the entire level using a phased approach. In the first Sprint, untextured modular parts are used for prototyping the level. In the next Sprint, design places AI and triggered events. Finally, in the third Sprint, detailed geometry is added. Polishing, debugging, and sound design are done in the final Sprint.

By creating a large level this way, the team is building a debt of work that has to be "paid off" by the end of the release. If any of these steps take too long, then the deadline drives the team to rush completion of the entire level or delay the release. This often leads to stressed teams and concerned stakeholders. Another drawback is that a polished experience won't exist until the end of the release, so the value is not seen until the end. This allows for almost no gameplay iteration on the polished level.

A better approach is to create a polished and tuned section of the level every Sprint. If there are four Sprints in the release, each Sprint Goal might attempt to complete a quarter of the level each Sprint. For example, if your level has a medieval village, castle, forest, and fair, your team would finish one of them every Sprint. If the level is too large for the release, the team will discover it in the first Sprint, and the Product Owner could either reduce the scope of the level or delay the release date. Another benefit of this approach is that polished and tuned gameplay can be iterated on for almost the entire release.

Existing gameplay, tool technology, or rendering technology might not support an approach of vertical slices every Sprint, but this is a further argument for not risking an entire release to such uncertainties.

### The Limits of Velocity

There's been a lot of talk about abandoning the concept of velocity and the practice of using story points among coaches and trainers. Much of this comes from its abuse. Velocity is meant to be used to measure what a team has accomplished that meets a Definition of Done and to use that metric to roughly forecast what *might* be achieved in the future.

Unfortunately, velocity has been used to set fixed goals for teams, even on a Sprint-to-Sprint basis, and to compare teams to one another. Because velocity is based on relative estimation techniques, it isn't accurate enough to do either, so teams end up cutting corners to achieve velocity-based goals, usually at the expense of quality.

I usually recommend that, outside of story-point estimation at the epic Product Backlog Item (PBI) level, that developers not be exposed to story points.

I've found that most teams that have reached the mastery level have abandoned the use of velocity for feature forecasting because they are better at managing debt and delivering value first.

### *Improving Iteration*

Journeyman teams begin to accelerate the cycle of continuous improvement by altering practices. To do this, they must measure their velocity and focus on improving it.

Journeyman teams will introduce significant new practices such as test-driven development to improve the quality of code or continuous integration, which allows change to be propagated more safely and quickly (see Chapter 12, "Agile Technology"). The team will seek to improve iteration times in every area of development, through automated testing, improved tools, or team practices that move QA closer to the developers (see Chapter 15, "Agile QA and Production").

Measuring velocity is critical for this to occur. Velocity and other measures of value create the empirical control system at the core of Scrum. Without empiricism, a process is like alchemy, where teams try to transmute work into success through paradoxical practices.

## The Master Stage

The master stage is the final stage of Scrum adoption and is the goal of every Scrum team to achieve. Such teams do the following:

- **Self-organize:** Master teams work well together. Great teams are based on chemistry and motivation. They trust one another and achieve a high level of communication. The team decides who joins or leaves.
- **Drive continual improvement:** They take control of the rules. Management merely has to support their needs. These teams take ownership of their own performance.
- **Enjoy their work immensely:** Work is a commitment to their teammates. They are all in it together, and everyone's contribution and creativity are valued and leveraged.
- **Deliver the highest level of value:** Master teams are often referred to as **great teams** (see Chapter 5, "Great Teams"), far outpacing other teams.

#### Experience

Developers on great teams have referred to their experience as a highlight of their career. I've been on two such teams in 20 years and have always sought to return to that state.

Master teams are hard to define, but easy to recognize. There is no formula to create them, but I have observed the following:

- **Independence and a sense of ownership:** The team needs to feel that it contributes creatively and has control over how it works.
- **Leadership:** There is often a natural leader on the team who communicates a vision between the team and the stakeholders and helps keep the team focused. This isn't a lead position defined by a role but by actions.
- **A core expert:** Not everyone on the team needs to be an expert, but on a master team there is often at least one core expert. This person supports the vision with brilliance that the team can rally around with confidence.
- **Team collaboration:** Teams become great organically and evolve together based on chemistry and experience.
- **Proper studio culture:** Studio cultures can either nourish such teams or prevent them from taking root and flourishing. Sometimes great teams will form in a highly dysfunctional culture, but they don't last.

Great teams form independently of process. However, Scrum assists them based on the mastery of its principles. Team self-organization, Sprint Goal ownership, commitment, and a daily dose of visibility cultivate them.

### *Team Organization and Membership*

Collaboration is a necessary element for master teams. A team of highly skilled developers who cannot collaborate cannot assume success.

Teams need to form carefully and have the ability to adjust their membership to enable them to improve collaboration and chances of success. At first, teams can't do this on their own. Team formation needs to be facilitated by studio leadership early on by mentoring and encouraging the team to slowly take control and make the best decisions for themselves. Eventually, these teams become self-organizing and make decisions on their own.

Let's examine how self-organizing teams adjust their membership.

Teams don't change membership mid-Sprint. They hold off on such changes until after the Sprint Review but before Sprint Planning. There are two reasons for changing members. The first is to match the team to its goals. For example, if a team needs animation support for a coming Sprint but does not have an animator, it needs to have one join the team before it plans the Sprint.

The second reason for changing membership is to improve collaboration and commitment. This involves adding or removing a member to make it easier for the team to work effectively. Removing team members is challenging but sometimes necessary. Often, it's a simple lack of chemistry or personality conflict. Chapter 20, "Self-Organization and Leadership," explores this topic further.

At the start of a new release, a master team might substantially change its membership to accomplish a specific release goal. Usually, these teams retain a core of individuals. Building a chemistry of personalities that are effective together is far more difficult and rewarding than simply gathering individuals with the necessary skills. After a working chemistry is found, it should be protected and supported.

### *Major Practice Change*

A characteristic of master teams is its ability to abandon or modify any practice while preserving the underlying values and principles of Agile development. Some master teams have varied their methods so much that what they are doing is barely recognizable as Scrum on the surface.

An example of this is the introduction of Lean practices as described in Chapter 10, "Video Game Project Management." These practices eliminate Sprint Planning and Sprint Goals for teams creating production assets. These may seem like a gross violation of Scrum rules, but they aren't. The Scrum principles of empiricism, emergence, timeboxing, prioritization, and self-organization described in Chapter 3, "Scrum," still hold true.

Master teams make these changes relying on empirical measures, a sense of ownership, freedom, and a deeply embedded understanding of what the Scrum and Agile principles mean.

**Experience**

I've noticed over the past decade that the teams most successful in adopting Agile/Lean change a majority of practices over several years, but still maintain the principles. Teams that maintain the same practices "by the book" see minimal benefit beyond those seen in the apprentice stage.

## What Good Looks Like

The benefits of master teams are unmistakable:

- They have more creative input that is aligned with the game's vision.
- They are far more productive.

- They enjoy working together.
- They solve problems rather than expect someone outside the team to solve them.

Chapters 19 and 20 explore how coaches help teams grow and how leadership can spread that culture through an entire studio.

## Summary

Every studio that adopts Scrum has a unique experience. The path from apprentice through journeyman to master is different. Some take a few years, others stall.

## Additional Reading

Cockburn, A. 2007. *Agile Software Development: The Cooperative Game, Second Edition*. Boston, MA: Addison-Wesley.

Cohn, M. 2010. *Succeeding with Agile*. Boston, MA: Addison-Wesley.

Hackman, J. R. 2002. *Leading Teams: Setting the Stage for Great Performances*. Boston: Harvard Business School Press.

PART VI

# Growing Beyond

# Chapter 19

# Coaching Teams for Greatness

One of the main lessons I've learned from decades of game development is that you don't remember the games you shipped so much as the people you worked with making them. The teams I most fondly remember are the ones that enjoyed the work and the camaraderie. Coincidentally (or not), these teams made the most successful games.

In 2012, Google launched project "Aristotle" in a quest to identify what made its greatest teams great. For Google, a great team, as Aristotle famously said, is one in which "the whole is greater than the sum of its parts." The study eventually found that, other than intelligence or skill, what differentiated high-performing teams from dysfunctional ones was the level of emotional intelligence: how team members treated one another and responded to problems.

## What Is a "Great Team"?

Almost every game development veteran I've asked has been on at least one **great team** in his or her career. A great team is often described as being:

- **Productive:** Able to accomplish an exceptional amount of useful work almost every day
- **Engaging:** Very interested in where the work was headed, and members felt they were valuable contributors
- **Successful:** Able to provide the result of what was usually a good game
- **Enjoyable:** Able to take pleasure in the work and the people they worked with

Game development teams are fortunate to work in a field where the best work comes from teams that enjoy doing that work.

I've been on a few such teams in my career and when I learned about Scrum, I felt that the framework supported the creation and nurturing of great teams by separating the typical role of project management into the Product Owner role and the Scrum Master role. These roles are in place to balance the pressures of "building the right game" and "building it the right way."

## Why Coaching?

In sports, coaching is often the most critical factor of a team's success, despite the fact that a coach isn't the best at any position. Coaches create team cohesiveness and build a sense of teamwork. They keep the team focused on the big goal and reflect what they are seeing back to the team.

It's the same for game teams. A coach isn't the best artist or programmer. He or she helps the team be better by helping it grow and focus on its goals.

## The Solutions in This Chapter

This chapter explores coaching, facilitation, and tools that can be used to help teams grow their maturity and reach higher levels of productivity and engagement with their work.

## Coaching Skills

A good parent focuses not on solving every problem for their children but on helping them grow to be self-sufficient adults who can solve their own problems. It's the same for coaching, and it's the biggest challenge a coach can face: not taking the easy path to solve someone's problems but to help them grow as problem solvers.

This section describes the "stance" that coaches take with those they are coaching, techniques for how to facilitate conversation and agreement among groups, and some fundamental tools a coach can use along the way.

### My Path to Coaching

After decades of making games as a hobby, I finally landed my dream job at Angel Studios in the early nineties. Shifting careers from defense work to video game development was a shock. The work environment was less formal, and the level of technology and innovation involved with making games far exceeded that in the defense industry.

Given my experience managing small defense projects, I found myself leading game teams within a year. I wasn't promoted for my leadership ability, however. I wasn't a good leader. I didn't inspire people. I led by anger and intimidation, which was driven by my well-founded insecurity as someone thrown into a position he had no experience or training for.

As any such leader soon learns, the stress and burden of micromanagement became overwhelming. People didn't take initiative in solving problems when there was little upside but lots of downside. A mistake means an angry leader. I ended up attempting to solve hundreds of problems per week that an engaged team should solve on its own.

As a result, the burnout of the role almost led me to leave the industry. Instead I disengaged and started letting people solve problems and even make mistakes. I worked on unlearning how to micromanage and how to coach. This eventually led me to my current role as a professional coach and trainer.

### Scrum Master as Coach

Scrum created the role of the Scrum Master specifically to be a team coach. So, if you are using Scrum, when I talk about a "coach" in this chapter, I'm referring to the Scrum Master.

## The Coaching Stance

A coaching stance is the mental or emotional disposition coaches adopt when assisting others. It helps them position themselves in relation to what a person or team truly needs, and will most benefit from, to foster growth.

**"It's like Coaching Soccer"**

"I've actually been teaching Scrum here to our IT department and adapting it for their needs. The approach I have been taking is the same one they taught us at the national coaching school for soccer: Start simple and work toward complex. When coaching kids' soccer, you start with the basics and the individual, then progress to 1 versus 1, then 2 versus 2, then 6 versus 6 etc., until

> you work your way up to a very complex, full-sided game. I took the same approach with the IT guys, starting with the basics and just worrying about the Fibonacci sequence or goal language in a vacuum. Eventually we did relative sizing and goal language together and worked our way up to full-fledged Scrum with Stand Ups in our first Sprint. We had good success with it."
>
> —Erik Theisz, Certified Scrum Professional and Scrum Master

**Definition**

*Client* refers to the person you are coaching (I prefer client to "coachee").

The following sections cover specific ways in which successful coaches can be most effective in supporting their teams and helping them grow.

### *Maintain Neutrality*

When helping a client with a problem, you usually have a solution in mind. Trying to force your solution creates barriers and gets you emotionally invested in seeing your suggestion adopted.

Maintaining neutrality means keeping that opinion to ourselves and helping those we're coaching create their own solution—and then helping them implement it, even if we believe it might fail. Owning a solution, even a failed one, helps clients grow. We also have to have the humility to acknowledge the possibility that the client will see solutions we do not. Note that asking powerful questions (described later in this chapter) along the way can help others make better decisions and avoid failure while learning.

### *Serve the Client's Agenda*

As a new Agile coach, my initial goal was to "help" people "be Agile," even if it wasn't what they were ready for or even wanted. I was doing them a disservice.

A coach needs to discover the true agenda from the developer to the studio executives who invite your coaching. Sometimes it's just the need to open up communication between layers of the studio. Whatever that true agenda is, you need to serve it and not your own. Trust your clients. They know what they need better than you.

### *Maintain Your Principles*

One time, I visited a studio that excelled at its effective micromanagement of developers. The developers were miserable and their productivity reflected that. The studio's agenda was to find ways to increase that micromanagement. I wasn't about to coach that agenda.

This sounds like it violates the two stances previously described, but a coach has to have principles and the integrity to follow them. You don't simply want to assist in building dysfunction. You also don't want to shame clients into behaving differently. You want to treat them with compassion and be clear about how the principles can help them, but also be honest with what you observe happening, without judgment.

### *Have Compassion*

You have to truly care for your clients and their journey. You have to assume they have the best intentions. When you start to think you know better and that they are in some way lacking for not seeing what you do, you have lost.

Treat them like family members who are on a journey they are leading themselves along. They will make their own decisions that will lead beyond their current job or role in the future. You only want the best for them along that journey.

That attitude will clearly come through to them.

## Facilitation

The most basic skill for a coach is group facilitation, which is the skill of helping groups of people reach consensus. This section explores a pattern of doing that and reviews tools to help you facilitate, rather than direct, your team.

### *The Diamond of Participatory Decision-Making*

A useful pattern to help in group facilitation is called **the Diamond of Participatory Decision-Making** (Kaner, 2014). The diamond is a guide for facilitating collaborative group decisions through the following three stages:

- **Divergent zone:** In the divergent zone, people are exploring ideas and sharing possibilities. Here the facilitator helps participants explore more options and avoid stopping at familiar ideas or opinions. Also called *ideation*, this is where all ideas are brought forward without judgment or evaluation.
- **Groan zone:** This is the period in the middle where those with different frames of reference attempt to understand others' ideas. A facilitator's role here is help build the shared context and strengthen relationships.
- **Convergent zone:** Having created a shared understanding or frame of reference, the group narrows down ideas/opinions to converge on a decision.

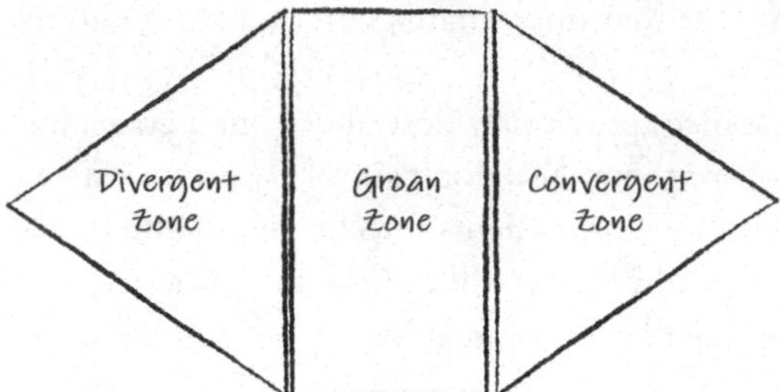


**Figure 19.1** *The Diamond of Participatory Decision-Making*

The diamond pattern, shown in Figure 19.1, applies to almost any group collaboration you can imagine.

Here's an example of how the diamond pattern can be used to guide Retrospectives:

- **Divergent zone:** Each member of the team records specific events or situations that occurred since the last Retrospective that helped or hindered his or her progress. Each of these is recorded on self-stick notes that are randomly placed on a whiteboard or flip chart.
- **Groan zone:** The group arranges the self-stick notes using affinity mapping (described later in the section, "Affinity Mapping") to find common patterns.
- **Convergent zone:** Using root cause analysis (described below), the team finds the root cause of what went right or wrong and some practices to try that will improve teamwork.

The reason to separate these zones is that most often group efforts dive into problem solving too quickly. As a result, only the loudest voices or "HiPPOs"[1] get the attention.

## *Other Facilitation Tools*

The following are other facilitation tools that I find most useful.

### *Planning Poker*

As described in Chapter 9, "Agile Release Planning," planning poker is a useful facilitation tool for estimating story points. It can also be used for estimating tasks and evaluating value, priority, or anything else you can assign a number to.

1. Highest Paid Person's Opinion

*Rank Ordering*
As described in Chapter 7, "The Product Backlog," rank ordering is a collaborative tool that allows groups to create a linear rank of things relative to one another. We've used this practice to even rank local restaurants!

*Affinity Mapping*
One of my favorite tools, affinity mapping groups sets of items into categories to elicit patterns. The most common use is to ask a group to create a list independently with one item per self-stick note and to place these notes on a flip chart. Team members then move the notes around to place items that are related to one another close together. Following this, we can discuss those patterns.

**Example**

Our family would occasionally create affinity maps about things we like to do in our spare time. When we grouped them and explored the patterns, we came up with a set of things we could plan our vacation around that we all could enjoy.

## Coaching Tools

This section describes a number of coaching tools that I've found most useful for team coaching in the past. Many other tools can be found in the coaching books listed at the end of this chapter.

### *Count Silently*

A good practice for coaches and leaders is to ask questions and wait for the answer, even if they think they might know the answer. The practice is to silently count to 10 after you have asked the question. Don't be surprised if it takes six to seven seconds before someone responds. Long silences can be uncomfortable for a developer who may know the answer but is just a bit shy to speak up.

### *Listen Actively*

The practice of active listening is merely a set of techniques that you can practice to achieve higher levels of comprehension when communicating with others. Actively listening means doing the following:

- **Stay focused on what they are saying:** Avoid distractions like coming up with the quickest possible answer and waiting to tell them about it. Also, do your best to avoid judgment.

- **Ask relevant questions:** Ask powerful questions (see the following section) that are relevant to what they are saying to elicit more potential solutions they will own.
- **Allow for silence:** Don't jump in when there is a pause. Practice a silent count, and then ask them a prompting question such as, "What else might you be able to do?"
- **Paraphrase or mirror key phrases you hear verbatim:** Occasionally paraphrase what is being said in your own words to ensure you understand what is being said.
- **Practice the SOFTEN method[2] to show your engagement:** The acronym stands for Smile, Open posture, Forward lean, Taking notes, Eye contact, Nodding.

You can try these techniques out of the studio as well or merely listen to others having conversations to hear where these techniques might help them.

### *Ask Powerful Questions*

Powerful questions are impactful and drive thought and conversation. They also avoid evasive or short responses.

Asking powerful questions takes practice, and the following basic rules can help you get the results you are looking for:

- Keep questions short.
- Avoid questions that have a yes-or-no answer.
- Don't ask rhetorical questions.
- Use the silent count practice waiting for answers. They require thought.

Here are some examples of powerful questions:

- What is hindering us from reaching the Sprint Goal?
- What are you enjoying about the game right now?
- What do you feel about the game we are making?
- If you could fix one thing about the way we work, what would it be?
- How else could you have solved that problem?

2. https://tinyurl.com/y2vod8vo

**It's all about Communication**

"The most important thing is your communication skills. You have to be able to communicate with people at their level and in their language. I recommend that everyone learn a bit about what their teams do; you don't have to be an expert, but have an understanding of how they work and how they communicate is vital."

—Grant Shonkwiler, Commander & Shonk, Shonkventures

## Coaching Teams to Higher Performance

Opposed to the traditional approach of pressuring teams to higher performance through metrics-driven goals, coaches pursue improved team performance by exploring personal and team motivational factors in the areas described in the following sections.

### Psychological Safety

According to Amy Edmondson, Harvard Business School professor and author of *The Fearless Organization: Creating Psychological Safety in the Workplace for Learning, Innovation, and Growth* (Edmondson, 2018), psychological safety is a "shared belief held by members of a team that the team is safe for interpersonal risk-taking."[3] She defines psychological safety as having "a sense of confidence that the team will not embarrass, reject or punish someone for speaking up," and that it "describes a team climate characterized by interpersonal trust and mutual respect in which people are comfortable being themselves."

**Observation**

The Daily Scrum and Retrospectives are common times to observe and improve psychological safety. If team members can't speak their mind during these events, they won't serve their purpose.

3. https://hbr.org/ideacast/2019/01/creating-psychological-safety-in-the-workplace

## Common Goals

High-performance teams have common goals they focus on that integrate all disciplines. For example, a goal of a boss character and its behaviors requires modelling, animation, AI, audio, and state machines. Lacking a common goal (for example, a goal that has separate tasks for each discipline) can lead a team to have divergent interests and behavior.

## Shared Accountability

In Scrum, teams have a shared accountability for their Sprint Goal (which should be a common goal). For example, if a Sprint Goal describes a "class of enemy character that can walk on walls," shared accountability means all team members accept responsibility for achieving the goal, regardless of their role or position. It doesn't matter if the code is working, but the animations aren't done. The entire team is accountable for the goal.

Shared accountability drives higher team collaboration. For example, if the animators are unable to get their animations in the game, shared accountability will motivate a programmer to help them.

## Working Agreement

A working agreement is a set of protocols that the team defines to establish how members work together. These are not rules established by management, but defined by the teams themselves and refined over time (usually in Retrospectives).

**A Team is Greater than the Sum of its Parts**

Focusing on team membership and performance gives you great insight into the value of a team's chemistry and the variation of performance that comes from that chemistry.

On one occasion, as an experiment, we gathered eight of the most talented people in the studio together in hopes of creating a "super team" that would demonstrate the highest possible performance.

What we got instead was the most dysfunctional team imaginable. The members argued constantly and produced less value than most other teams. After a few Sprints, the Product Owner disbanded them.

Great teams need skill and leadership, but they also need members willing to be followers.

## Root Cause Analysis

Most problems don't manifest themselves immediately. Often there are two or more layers of cause and effect before you or your team are impacted. For example, if texture artists keep applying unnecessarily large textures to their models because an exporter doesn't prevent them from doing so, it may take months before the accumulated impact of those textures slows the game down considerably.

Root cause analysis is a method of backtracking through these layers of cause and effect to get to the root cause of a problem. This allows one to address the true cause (in our example, the exporter) rather than the cause we'd see on the surface (blaming the texture artists instead).

My favorite practice for root cause analysis is the "Five Whys."

### *The Five Whys*

This practice, usually held during a Retrospective, helps teams focus on actionable solutions. A retrospective starts with an ideation phase where the issues and impediments encountered over the previous iteration are collected. Following this, the teams generate insights into why these problems occurred. Often, the root cause of a problem is several layers deep and must be dug out.

The Five Whys practice starts by dividing the team into small groups of two to four people. For each problem, one person asks the other(s) "Why did this problem occur?" For each answer, they ask "why" again. After no more than five answers, the group arrives at the root cause of the problem, which lends itself to a solution. The root cause is recorded and the group moves on to the next question. When the groups reconvene, the root causes are discussed and solutions are generated in the next phase of the retrospective.

**Example of a Five Whys Discussion**

- "We waste a lot of time every morning."
- "Why?"
- "The build is always broken in the morning."
- "Why?"

- "Commits are made late during the previous day that are not sufficiently tested."
- "Why"
- "There are no target machines to test on at the end of the day."
- "Why"
- "QA does all their regression testing at the end of the day."

## Team Maturity Models

As Project Aristotle confirmed, team maturity and chemistry are major factors in team performance. Many team maturity models exist that can help guide a leader or coach in growing teams. This section briefly describes a few that have proven useful.

### The Five Dysfunctions of a Team

*The Five Dysfunctions of a Team* (Lencioni, 2005) describes a hierarchy of dysfunctions that need to be addressed for teams to mature. That hierarchy, from the most basic on, is:

- **Absence of trust:** Having an unwillingness to be vulnerable to each other or management
- **Fear of conflict:** Avoiding constructive debate out of fear that it might lead to disagreement
- **Lack of commitment:** Having an unwillingness to commit to a shared goal
- **Avoidance of accountability:** Evading responsibility on quality issues
- **Inattention to results:** Putting personal goals ahead of team goals

Addressing these dysfunctions in order is often necessary for new Agile teams. Trust is usually the first to address among team members and between the team and the studio. With trust established, teams can move on to eliminating fear of conflict and so on.

## The Tuckman Model

The Tuckman model,[4] illustrated in Figure 19.2, describes the typical phases that are all necessary for the team to mature:

- **Forming:** The team first forms and establishes its initial goals. Members operate independently and are on their "best behavior." Often little trust is established.
- **Storming:** Teams struggle to establish trust and norms as they get used to working with one another. Conflict often arises as power relationships are established and personalities clash. Teams sometimes get stuck in this phase
- **Norming:** Personality and power conflicts are ironed out and teammates establish closer ties allowing more honest debate.

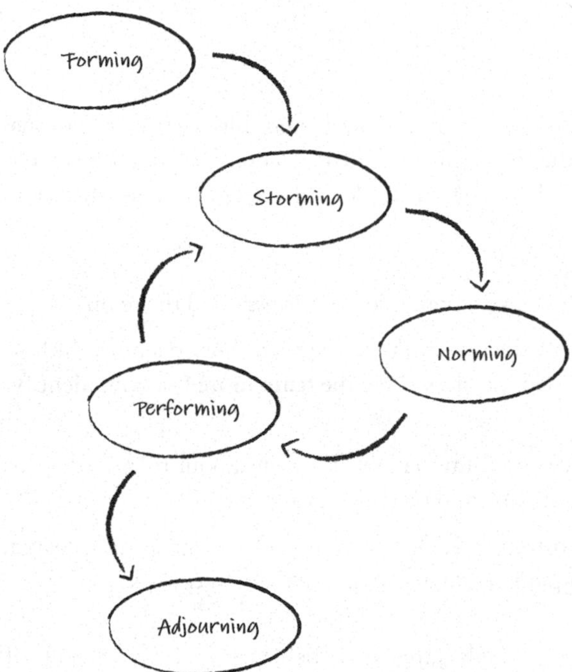


**Figure 19.2** *The Tuckman model*

4. https://www.mindtools.com/pages/article/newLDR_86.htm

- **Performing:** Teams start to focus on shared goals and commitments and work across boundaries to achieve them. Team accountability becomes paramount, and self-organization emerges.
- **Adjourning:** Unfortunately, teams cannot stay together forever and eventually disband. Teams should still take the time to celebrate their success and capture the practices and behaviors that helped in their success to hopefully carry to new teams.

The Tuckman model and the five dysfunctions are complementary. A lack of trust and a fear of conflict will keep teams from moving into the norming and performing stages. Also, due to the division of specialties on game teams, there is always a danger when losing one or two teammates between Sprints, of slipping back into storming. This is also a reason behind the "Scrum Master as sheepdog" metaphor. A Scrum Master always protects the team from the "predators" outside the team that can disrupt it back into storming.

## Situational Leadership

Developed in the late 1970s by Paul Hershey and Ken Blanchard, situational leadership is a set of principles that help guide how leadership is applied to teams of differing maturity levels. They defined four leadership categories, as shown in Figure 19.3.

- **Directing:** A leader defines roles and tasks for developers and the team.
- **Coaching:** A leader still sets the direction for the team but coaches it in how roles and tasks are determined. Leaders allow the team more freedom identifying and tracking its work.
- **Supporting:** A leader allows the team to make decisions about roles and tasks, but still shares in decision-making and progress monitoring.
- **Delegating:** A leader is involved in decision making and progress monitoring, but the team is fully self-organizing in its roles, practices, and work.

Scrum teams usually start in the "high supportive behavior" side (top half of Figure 19.3). Often a studio's culture will be more directive going in, and you'll find teams reporting to the Scrum Master. Over time, a good Scrum Master will improve his or her facilitation skills and support (upper-left quadrant) the team as an equal member, standing as a part of the team's circle.

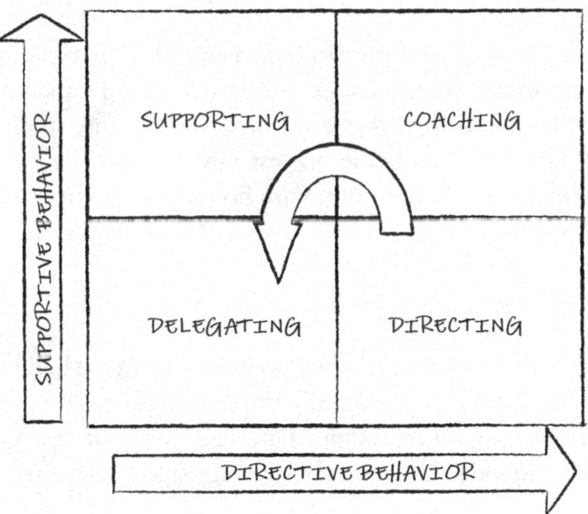


**Figure 19.3** *Situational leadership*

As a Scrum Team matures and becomes more self-organizing, the Scrum Master will delegate more of the team's day-to-day duties, but always observe and support the team (lower-left quadrant).

## Coaching Tools and Practices

The section describes a few tools and practices a coach can use to help transition teams to higher levels of maturity. For a larger set of practices, see the book *Gear Up!: 100+ Ways to Grow Your Studio Culture*, 2nd Edition (Keith C., Shonkwiler G., 2018).

### Lighten the Mood

Some cultures don't tolerate mistakes very well, and someone who makes a mistake can become a target for blame. This results in fear that can stifle learning and innovation. People end up "playing it safe" and only do what they are told to, and if they make a mistake, they try to hide it.

### *The Practice*

Communicating that making mistakes is part of the process when developing games (as well as being a human), is important. Studios and teams have done a number of things to "lighten the mood" when someone makes a mistake. In fact, one studio gave a small trophy to the developer who made the biggest mistake over the past month. This "Biggest goof-up award" was handed out, with honorable mentions to runners-up, to thunderous applause.

> **Experience**
>
> One studio had a life-sized cutout of Justin Bieber. When someone broke the build for the first time, Justin stood beside that person's desk; the second time, he was on his desk, and the third time Justin went with him wherever he went. It was a silly gesture, but one that kept the mood light and in that way managed to inspire.

### *Tip*

These "awards" or celebrations are never meant to be humiliating. I've seen some of them used with teams that were not getting along very well and the humor was lost, so use this practice with care.

## Love Card Wall

Build team culture by sharing moments of respect and appreciation visually.

### *The Practice*

Team members identify moments of appreciation, goodwill, and respect throughout the Sprint by writing a brief note of what happened on a self-stick note. The notes are posted in a team open space (possibly the war room) for all to see.

### *Tips*

Here are some tips for using a love card wall:

- You can find heart-shaped sticky notes for sale online.
- Anyone can write a love card for any instance encountered, even if it's between two co-workers.
- The coach (or Scrum Master) encourages these notes to be written throughout the Sprint.

## Notes of Encouragement

When someone does something great it's valuable to bring attention to what they have done, but sometimes it is more meaningful (and depending on the person's personality type, more desirable) to be thanked quietly with a note.

### *The Practice*

Writing an encouraging note is a simple process:

- Get some simple (but colorful) 3x5 cards and a pen or marker.
- Identify the person you want to thank or encourage and write a personal heartfelt message.
- Leave it on his desk when he isn't around so he can come back to it.

### *Tips*

Here are some tips for using notes of encouragement:

- Don't limit these notes to just the people doing big great things: include notes for people doing simple but necessary work.
- Aim to write at least one note a week.
- Get creative and decorate the notes.

## PechaKucha Introductions

When forming a new team there are many ways to assist people in bonding quickly. One of the quickest ways is by gaining a shared understanding of each other and focusing on commonalities through personal PechaKucha introductions. A PechaKucha introduction is a timed slide presentation where the presenter shows ten slides describing themselves, with each slide being shown for only ten seconds each. This results in a 100-second introduction of the presenter.

### *The Practice*

As a fun exercise have everyone create a slideshow about themselves that consists of

- 10 slides per person
- 10 seconds per slide (auto advance)
- Nothing about their professional life (except schooling) and what inspired them to make games

Have a fun event with food and drinks where everyone has a chance to go through their slideshow. The goal is to encourage cohesion by getting people to learn about similarities they share or interesting facts about each other.

### *Tips*

Here are some tips for using PechaKucha introductions:

- If your team is larger than 10 people, consider having multiple meetings.
- Create a slide deck/template with the auto advancing rules in Google Slides, PowerPoint, or Keynote and have people contribute to them.
- You can also do this informally using index cards.
- Set aside a time for people to work on their slideshow during work.
- It's important to show only pictures: no text.

## Socialize the Team

Building a new team can be challenging and adding team members can also be a challenge. One of the easiest ways to improve how teams work together is by helping them to get to know each other better. One easy way to accomplish this without making it feel like a "trust fall" exercise is to encourage the team to socialize both at work and outside the office.

### *The Practice*

This practice is simple: Come up with fun things that the team can do that will allow them to socialize often. Ideas for in the office include (for big companies, do once a month) birthday celebrations, holiday celebrations, team happy hour, playing board games together, and team dinners.

Ideas for outside of the office include laser tag, go karts, Whirlyball, arcade rental, picnics, museum outings, sports outings, dinners, mini Olympics, and bowling.

### *Tips*

Here are some tips for socializing teams:

- Schedule these events during office hours.
- Ensure these events are company sponsored.
- If you offer alcohol at any event, make sure team members have a safe option to get home.

- Make sure your leadership team is present and participates in these events.
- To discourage cliques, find ways for the team to mix with new people at these events.
- Select events that encourage collaboration and competition.

## Measure Team Health

The best way to determine the health of your project is by knowing the health of the working teams. When discussing your team's health and progress at a high level, having a common language and quick visual way to review all the teams is best.

### *The Practice*

Create a spreadsheet or board with each team listed by name with a space to include a color-coded cell or card. Each time your Scrum Masters meet, have them update each of their team's health indicators, such as the following:

- **Red:** Something is wrong and it should be addressed immediately (examples the team is impeded, a team member is sick, internal dysfunction exists).
- **Yellow:** The team is getting work done but might be running into some small problems. These should be monitored and addressed when possible (for example, excessive off-team communication is occurring or requests are being missed).
- **Green:** The team is progressing well on its Sprint and is in good overall health.

### *Tip*

Have the Scrum Master regularly ask team members questions to assess how the team members feel things are.

## Group Confession

Allowing a safe place for people to learn from each other's mistakes and how to handle them when they arise is important. This practice is for helping create that place.

### *The Practice*

Once a month, have the team meet in an informal space and allow everyone to "confess" some mistakes that they have made in the last month. Have them explain what they did wrong and how they either fixed it or tried to fix it. This isn't supposed to be a place to judge but to discuss and learn. This helps a lot with openness, trust, and creating that "safe to fail" culture.

### *Tips*

Here are some tips for using group confessions:

- Keep the mood light and fun.
- Make sure everyone has at least one story to share.
- The story doesn't have to be from the last month, but it helps if it is from the same project.
- Try to meet in a less formal space than a meeting room.
- Try the "failure bow," which is a deep bow, after a confession. When done spontaneously, it can lighten the mood.

## 360 Reviews

Have teams review themselves on a regular basis. One way to do this is through 360 reviews. These reviews are dramatically more impactful than yearly performance reviews. They provide direct feedback from peers and happen often enough to engender improvements.

### *The Practice*

At least once every three months, have each member of a team (less than 10 people) review the other team members. The typical review format is to rate others on a simple scale of one (needs improvement) to five (is a strength) on characteristics such as collaboration, technical skills, leadership, initiative, and so on. The results are gathered, averaged, and handed out. Often, the results are reviewed with a discipline lead to discuss and compare with previous results.

### *Tips*

Here are some tips for doing360 reviews:

- Avoid doing these reviews by hand as they are time consuming. Great software packages are available for conducting 360 reviews through a web page.
- Having a field for gathering comments can be useful, but comments often have to be reviewed and filtered manually, and therefore take up valuable time.

- Avoid collecting and sharing comments for newly formed teams until they've had time to settle in and work with one another for at least a month.

## What Good Looks Like

Great teams encompass the attributes described in the previous chapter, but don't imagine that they'll always be singing Kumbaya while holding hands in the moonlight. Great teams can be like any big family. Individuals can argue, compete, endlessly debate, and have mood swings. Passion does that. But like any family, the bonds created on a great team overcome the occasional chaos.

Imagine not being able to wait to go to work on a game with a group of people you trust and enjoy working with. Imagine being excited about the game you are working on, with new ideas flowing constantly that build the game towards success. This does happen, and it can happen to your team.

## Summary

Becoming a coach is a major challenge if you have spent your career managing tasks. Your transformation is as challenging as that of any team's. You learn more about yourself during the journey than you would imagine.

The career of a coach is one of human psychology and life-long learning. A coach must be a student of people and relationships. Coaching individuals and teams is only the start. The coach's role expands to the entire studio and beyond.

## Additional Reading

Edmondson, Amy. 2018. *The Fearless Organization: Creating Psychological Safety in the Workplace for Learning, Innovation, and Growth*. Wiley.

Kaner, Sam. 2014. *Facilitator's Guide to Participatory Decision-Making, Third Edition*. Jossey-Bass.

Keith, C., and G. Shonkwiler. 2018. *Gear Up!: 100+ ways to grow your studio culture, Second Edition*. CreateSpace Independent Publishing Platform.

Kimsey-House H, Kimsey-House K, Sandahl P, et al. 2018. *Co-active coaching: the proven framework for transformative conversations at work and in life*. Boston, MA: Nicholas Brealey Publishing.

Lencioni, Patrick. 2015. *The Five Dysfunctions of a Team: a Leadership Fable*. Jossey-Bass A Wiley Imprint.

Stanier MB. 2016. *The Coaching Habit*. Toronto: Box of Crayons Press.

Tabaka J. 2006. *Collaboration explained: facilitation skills for software project leaders*. Boston, MA: Addison-Wesley.

## Chapter 20

# Self-Organization and Leadership

*"At Supercell we celebrate success with beer and failure with champagne."*
—Ilkka Paanenen, CEO (Lappalainen, 2015)

In 2004, my life was threatened by a publishing executive. Our parent company had acquired Sega, who would now control our studio, and a group of us who led High Moon were meeting some of their executives for dinner in San Diego. None of them spoke English, so they brought a translator. At one point during the meal, we were being reprimanded for being late on our first game by a very scary Sega executive and, in mid-yell he drew his finger across his neck. We immediately turned towards the translator for clarification of the gesture, hoping that it implied something more benign in Japan.

Unfortunately, the translator was attempting to soften the message and merely said the executive was "encouraging" us to hit our deadlines, but we didn't buy that. This became a significant impulse to explore new ways of working. Threats to your life will do that.

But much credit for our transformation goes to our CEO, John Rowe. He recognized the need for radical change and merely told us to do whatever was necessary. He gave us his full trust to succeed or fail. That trust was exceptionally motivating. We didn't want to let him down and we didn't.

That was a great lesson for me. Giving people the trust and authority, while setting the vision for where we want to go, engages people in their work. This can be expanded to every level of the studio.

## The Solutions in This Chapter

Motivating creative workers can be a challenge. The book, *Drive: The Surprising Truth About What Motivates Us,* by Dan Pink (Pink, 2013) summarizes three factors, which decades of study revealed motivated creative workers:

- **Autonomy:** A desire to be self-directed
- **Mastery:** The longing to improve skills
- **Purpose:** The impulse to work on something important

This chapter focuses on the autonomous factor. Self-organization is the principle of exploring the boundaries of what we can allow developers to decide on their own. By growing autonomy, we grow responsibility and engagement.

This chapter demonstrates that self-organization has benefits, but that there is no formula and that every studio must find what works for it. The chapter also describes what leadership in an Agile organization encompasses and how coaching, at the studio level, can help.

## Self-Organization

The Scrum Guide says:

- "Self-organizing teams choose how best to accomplish their work, rather than being directed by others outside the team."
- "Development Teams are structured and empowered by the organization to organize and manage their own work."

Self-organization is the most culturally challenging aspect of Scrum. It requires a lot of trust and team maturity to grow. Despite the sound of it, it still requires leadership.

Many organizations outside the game industry have embraced self-organization. The book *Reinventing Organizations* (Laloux, 2014) describes the benefits and challenges those organizations have faced.

In the game industry, we've seen a few self-organizing studios emerge. These studios have the following attributes in common:

- Their leadership hierarchies are far flatter, with fewer layers between studio leadership and development.
- Individual teams are given a great deal of freedom to guide the course of their games and even decide when to abandon them.
- They were formed self-organizing from the start, hiring only those people they felt could work in such an environment.

A decade ago, when the discussion of self-organization arose, most felt that the idea was suspect. However, the studios that have formed using flat, self-organized structures have shown that it is possible. Studios such as Valve and Supercell have not only shown that self-organization is possible, but that such organizations can achieve levels of success that most other studios only dream of.

Note that the goal isn't to transform your studio to the level of self-organization that these studios enjoy—I personally believe that that level of transformation is near impossible—but to use these examples as proof of the benefit that increased levels of team ownership, grown slowly over time, can provide a studio.

## Valve Software

In 2012 Valve Software published its new employee handbook.[1] The handbook's release has led to a number of discussions about the merit of the Cabal (what Valve calls its process) and its self-organizing work environment.

Since first reading about the Cabal in 1999 and attending a few Game Developer Conference sessions since, I've been inspired. That inspiration was one of the threads that connected Agile thinking to game development. I felt that Valve was the kind of place where I would enjoy working and one of the main reasons for that was the connection to Agile thinking and values, a place where rigid process and hierarchies were considered a barrier to creative development.

Valve's handbook states this belief near the start:

> "Hierarchy is great for maintaining predictability and repeatability. It simplifies planning and makes it easier to control a large group of people from the top down, which is why military organizations rely on it so heavily.
>
> "But when you're an entertainment company that's spent the last decade going out of its way to recruit the most intelligent, innovative, talented people on Earth, telling them to sit at a desk and do what they're told obliterates 99 percent of their value. We want innovators, and that means maintaining an environment where they'll flourish."

1. At the time of this writing, the handbook is located at www.AgileGameDevelopment.com/ValveHandbook.pdf.

The handbook goes on to describe the role of an employee in this environment. The criticisms I've heard about the Cabal often say, "You need the right kind of people for this to work." I agree, but I think that the potential pool of such people is larger if you provide mentoring to help the transition into such an environment. The handbook acknowledges this as a challenge:

> "There are a number of things we wish we were better at:
>
> - Helping new people find their way. We wrote this book to help, but as we said above, a book can only go so far.
> - Mentoring people. Not just helping new people figure things out, but proactively helping people to grow in areas where they need help is something we're organizationally *not great at. Peer reviews help, but they can only go so far.*"

This is a common challenge in any studio that is attempting to increase self-organization. People have to unlearn a lifetime pattern first imposed in our public education systems, which train children how to work in a task-driven top-down hierarchical organization. It's an even greater challenge for a studio that has been hierarchical, because it threatens the status quo.

Self-organization and leadership aren't mutually exclusive. Gabe Newell leads Valve; it's not a pure democracy, but Valve doesn't have many layers between him and an artist creating texture maps. Nor does the artist being handed a list of texture maps he or she is assigned to create during the week. What self-organization does is to flatten hierarchies and reduce the number of lines of communication between people that need to communicate.

## Supercell

Formed in 2010, Supercell's mobile games lead it to a billion-dollar valuation in 2014 and in 2016, Tencent acquired 84.3 percent of Supercell for $8.6 billion. With a staff of around 200 and yearly revenues of more than $1.5 to $2 billion,[2] Supercell outperforms other mobile publishers 10 times its size.

Founder and CEO Ilkka Paananen credits the success of the studio to the culture of self-organization. "At Supercell I'm just the team coach and the players score the goals," he said (Lappalainen, 2015).

As with Valve, Supercell has a flat organizational hierarchy. Small teams, usually less than 10 developers, spend up to a year exploring a potential game before deciding, as a team, whether to deploy it for limited testing or abandon it. Nintendo takes a similar approach: cancelling games that haven't "found the fun" to focus on those that have.

2. https://venturebeat.com/2019/02/12/supercell-revenues-take-a-big-dip-in-2018-to-1-6-billion-and-profits-of-635-million/

### *Why Is Self-Organization So Hard?*

So why do few companies ever achieve similar cultures? Why is it so challenging for organizations that adopt the Scrum framework to adopt more self-organization?

Why do few diets work? Why do most people who join gyms after their New Year's resolution to work out soon quit? Habits are hard to change. It's the same for studio cultures. As mentioned earlier, an organization that grows in a hierarchical pattern resists the adoption of self-organization.

> **Observation**
>
> Some leaders resist change even when their studio is failing. It always seems to me like the passengers with the best rooms on *Titanic* refusing to board the lifeboat!

Resistance comes from developers as well, who focus on their tasks and discipline and leave responsibility for solving problems and upholding quality to their bosses. This feels safe, despite evidence that this behavior frequently comes back to haunt those same developers in the form of late-project crunch time and death marches.

Valve and Supercell had the benefit of being founded with the principles of self-organization. Both also have very high standards for hiring. Often new hires won't make it through a probationary period or simply quit because the environment isn't a good match for them. Studios that already have a full staff don't have this option.

### *Self-Organization Is Not Perfect and It's not the Goal*

Valve and Supercell's organization demonstrate that self-organization is not impossible and, in the right context, can work quite well. However, examples of working cultures should never be taken as blueprints to model your own culture after.[3] Valve and Supercell's culture were organically grown based on their founding principles. If you impose their practices on your people, I guarantee you that half will quit.

That said, pushing the limit of self-organization and growing your culture toward more team ownership and engagement is beneficial. The next section explores more options.

## Growing Teams

Team self-organization is a challenging area for teams and studios. Self-organizing teams select their members based on who they believe can help them achieve the best results.

3. As Spotify's example has shown, as well

### *Flattening Hierarchies*

With the adoption of cross-functional teams that manage their own work, the need for multiple layers of management decreases. When an artist can just turn in her chair and ask for help from a nearby programmer, it reduces need for intermediate management and tools that might have been needed in the past. This is the Agile value of "individuals and interactions over processes and tools" in action. It's far more effective.

"Flattening" doesn't mean "eliminating." Studios slowly explore how teams can organize themselves and realign their hierarchies based on what the teams need. Flattened hierarchies are often the result of, not the cause of, self-organization.

### *Self-Selecting Membership*

Teams that select their own members exhibit greater levels of accountability. When people are assigned to a team built by management, it's something that they have no control over, and a lack of control prevents full commitment.

Teams are allowed to change their membership between Sprints, but usually they only make changes at the start of a release cycle. Shortly after a release plan is discussed with the project staff, they negotiate among themselves to exchange members. The teams take the following into account when self-organizing:

- **What are the release goals and initial release plan?** Sometimes release goals require a reorganization of the teams. For example, a game might be transitioning to content production with fewer programmers providing more support to the artists.
- **What disciplines and skills are required to implement the release goals?** For example, if a team that has been implementing a shooting mechanic is now being called upon to create AI characters that shoot back, it needs to bring an AI programmer on board. If some simple changes need to be made to the codebase, perhaps a junior programmer is the best fit.
- **What are the priorities of the release goals?** If teams compete for people, the higher-priority release goal determines where people go. For example, if both a shooting and driving team need AI and there is only one experienced AI programmer, the higher-priority goal determines that the AI programmer first goes to the shooting mechanic team.
- **Do the team members have chemistry?** Although it is often ignored, the chemistry of people working together on a team has as much impact as any of the practices. For example, teams often benefit from having one outspoken member but suffer from having two. Both might be equally talented, but

together they just don't work well. Teams recognize this and should be able to control their membership to avoid it.

Like other Scrum practices, a team isn't expected to master self-organization from the start. Most studios starting Scrum avoid introducing self-organization at first and over time allow the team a greater degree of influence over who is added and removed from the team. Eventually, the team will make the decisions on its own, with leadership providing help with conflicts and problems that exceed the team's authority.

The rewards are profound. Self-organizing teams deliver unequalled levels of performance and enjoy their work far more than conventionally managed teams (Takeuchi and Nonaka, 1986).

**Dealing with Skepticism**

When people first hear about self-organization, they are skeptical. It reminds them of painful childhood memories of not being chosen for a sports team. Indeed, inexperienced teams can treat this practice as a popularity contest. They will need the assistance of management to help them make the best choices. Experienced teams, which understand team commitment, end up making better choices that benefit the game and their teamwork.

**When Someone is Kicked off a Team**

Occasionally, teams remove a member who is not a great fit. It's pretty rare for a team to unanimously eject someone from the team. Usually the person ejected has ignored months of Scrum Master coaching and team and leadership feedback about his or her poor performance or lack of teamwork. However, being ejected from a team cannot be ignored. It is a strong statement from a group of peers.

After this occurs, another team willing to take this person has to be found. The new team has to be made aware of the issues that led to that person's ejection from the last team. Teams cannot be forced to accept people they don't want.

If it's the first time this person has been ejected and several other teams are around, the person will likely be able to join another team easily. Most of time this person corrects the issues and becomes a valuable member of another team, or the person simply finds a team where the chemistry is better.

On rare occasions, a person doesn't work well on the next team either. After a few ejections, it's common to find that no other team will accept this person. It then becomes management's duty to release this person from the studio. Sometimes the person gets the message and leaves before this happens.

I've only seen this happen a few times. It's unfortunate, but it makes a statement to the teams: They control their destiny. They are responsible *and* have the necessary authority to make changes to improve their performance. When this authority doesn't exist, it doesn't allow a team to achieve its potential. Teams that can't self-organize will feel that they are stuck with the members on their team, and there is nothing they can do about it. They feel helpless to make the change they need and don't make the same level of commitment they possibly could.

When you see the performance of teams that achieve their potential, you stop questioning the value of these practices. Allowing them into your studios does take a leap of faith. Unfortunately, some don't reach this point and don't see the potential of great teams realized.

### *Selecting Practices*

After every Sprint, Scrum Teams hold a Retrospective to discuss changes to their practices that would improve their performance and teamwork. This practice leads to one of the major benefits of Scrum: continuous improvement.

To continuously improve, teams must have the ability to change their practices. This is a challenge for many studios. Many studios have very prescriptive methodologies that list a practice for every foreseeable element of work, and any new issue that may arise must be addressed by someone in management.

This creates a bottleneck of decisions and accountability. As a result, outnumbered managers cannot keep up with the daily demands of addressing the impediments of all teams. Small problems are ignored until they become large.

By giving teams permission to solve problems and emboldening them to do so, your organization becomes far more responsive. As it turns out, the people who are closest to the work see the issues far sooner and often have better ideas on how to solve them. They also become more accountable for addressing problems.

### *Growing Self-Organization*

The transformation toward self-organization doesn't happen overnight. The role of the Scrum Master is to help the team and the studio grow the trust and maturity to take on more ownership and accountability. This is an area where studio culture, which eats strategy for breakfast, can put the hard brakes on self-organization.

**Drawing the Line**

At High Moon Studios, we established some "laws" that were meant to describe the practices and rules that projects and their teams had the authority over and others that they did not. We referred to these laws as the "state laws" that defined project and team authority and "federal laws" that defined decisions that were made for them.

For international readers, in the United States federal laws govern the entire country, while state laws govern those within a state. If the two conflict, federal laws take precedence.

One example of a federal law was the use of a studio-wide engine and pipeline technology. Studio management didn't want the teams creating significantly different engines and pipelines for their own games. We wanted the benefits that came from individuals understanding a shared technology as they moved from one project to another. An example of a state law was how the project members organized themselves into individual teams and implemented items from the Product Backlog.

## Leadership

When I was a child, my father decided to teach me to swim as his father had taught him: by tossing me into a lake where the water was over my head. After watching the bubbles come up for half a minute, he dove in and pulled me out. I didn't learn to swim that day. In fact, I learned to avoid even trying for the rest of the summer. With my children, we have adopted a more gradual approach of coaching them to take on greater swimming challenges from a few seconds of dog paddling through the point where they can swim back and forth across an Olympic-sized swimming pool.

Leadership in an Agile organization has a similar challenge. Agile organizations need to grow leadership at every level but find the approach between micromanaging teams and throwing them in over their head that will bring about success. Both of those extremes will lead to failure.

### Agile Leadership

In my work, I'm frequently asked to revisit studios I've worked with in the past. The visits fall into two categories. The first category is where the studio wants to expand training and coaching for new or promoted employees. The second is where the studio wants a primer as another attempt at adopting Agile.

It's a bit discouraging to revisit a studio where a previous Agile adoption failed, but there is usually a consistent reason for the failure. The reason is usually in the area of leadership support. An Agile transformation begins and survives only with that support. Leadership can support or destroy an Agile transformation in a number of ways.

### *Growing Trust and Transparency*

Trust and transparency go hand in hand. When no trust exists between leadership and development, then there is no motivation to be transparent. Developers will hide bad news to avoid blame.

To grow transparency, to better react to emerging problems and value, we have to grow trust. Growing trust takes time, but destroying trust can take minutes.

### *Sticking to Values and Principles*

When pressure builds to hit an untenable schedule, a common practice is to abandon doing things "the right way" and go back to what was done in the past, such as

- Reduce testing and validating that Product Backlog Items (PBIs) meet a Definition of Done
- Impose crunch time
- Assign scope to teams instead of letting them commit
- Abandoning refactoring and other practices that maintain quality

Leaders can be judged based on how they adhere to their principles and values under pressure. Do they protect the team and do the right thing for the game, or do they bend to the pressure of certain stakeholders?

Anyone leading an Agile transformation needs to understand the principles and values of Agile and lead based on those and their own principles. This doesn't mean following practices by the book, but understanding the reasons why those practices exist.

## Studio Leadership

Studio leaders such as Gabe Newell, Ilkka Paananen, and John Rowe demonstrate the attributes of good studio leadership:

- They create the vision and strategy of the studio and establish its culture.

- They live the values they extoll; for example, growing trust from the top down by demonstrating it.
- They clearly set the limits of how much authority is given to their teams.
- They provide mentoring studio leadership.
- They engage with developers, understand their challenges and how they work, and inspire them.

**Experience**

One of the signals of whether a studio will successfully adopt a change is how much leadership engages with the necessary work. I've seen the founders of studios attend a full week of training and be the most engaged people in the room. I've also seen studio leaders completely ignore the investment. It seems logical that if you're going to invest in changing how every developer works in your studio, you should know about it.

## Discipline Leadership

The responsibilities of game development leaders (lead programmers, lead artists, lead designers, and so on) change as teams adopt Agile:

- **Design and planning:** Leads still guide the design (gameplay, technical, concept, and so on) for their discipline in concert with the other disciplines and oversee how the design is implemented.
- **Development allocation:** Leads will estimate how many people in their discipline are needed on the project, what areas they will work on, and approximately when they will work on them, but these will only be forecasts. The teams will slowly take over the responsibility of identifying areas of need on a per-Sprint and even Release basis.
- **Task creation and management:** Leads no longer break down work into tasks that they estimate, assign, and track. Teams manage this themselves. Leads still participate in Sprint Planning and helping members of their discipline improve their task identification and estimating skills.
- **Review and promotion:** Although leads may continue to review every member of their discipline on a regular, usually annual, basis, the performance of the team becomes a more important part of their information for the review (see the "Reviews" section in this chapter).

- **Mentoring:** Leads work with less experienced developers to improve their quality and productivity. The lead role shifts from managing primarily through project management tools to one where they "go and see" what is occurring with each developer as frequently as possible (see the later "Mentoring" section).

Team self-management and organization challenges the lead role definition. It's difficult for many leads to give up making detailed decisions for teams on a daily basis and allow them to risk failure, even for smaller challenges. However, the benefits of growing self-management becomes apparent as some of the more mundane management duties of a lead, such as task creation, estimation, and tracking, are taken over by the team.

For example, a project staff of 80 developers generates and tracks approximately 1,200 tasks during a three-week Sprint (10 teams × 8 people × one task per day × 20 days per Sprint). This is an overwhelming volume of detail for any group lead to manage and draws her time away from the more valuable leadership duties of her role.

**Promotion or Punishment?**

I've often felt that promoting someone to a lead role was part reward and part punishment. We want to reward artists who create assets quickly, so we promote them to lead artist with a salary increase. At the same time, we tell them they can't make much art anymore, but must now estimate and track the work of other artists, a job they don't enjoy as much.

Instead, I would rather have the lead artist continue to make art and teach other artists how to make better art faster, too. For example, using a "verification column" on a task board (see Chapter 8, "User Stories") is a useful way to create frequent opportunities for mentoring.

## Director Roles

The game industry is filled with director roles, such as art directors, technical directors, and so on. Usually these roles are given to members of a discipline who show the greatest level of craftsmanship but who also have authority over the work, rather than a group of people. Often these roles exist to oversee and approve or disapprove of the work being done in their area. Scrum Teams need to adjust their practices to meet the needs of these roles, such as described in Chapter 13, "Agile Art and Audio."

## Mentors

The most important role of the lead is to mentor developers to improve how they work. An example is when lead programmers pair with associate programmers to teach them how to improve their coding and design practices.

> **Note**
>
> Junior programmers often implement simulation solutions that are far too expensive in the CPU resources they consume. I recall one new programmer who was tasked with implementing a wind effect. He started implementing a complex fluid dynamic engine that used 90 percent of the CPU time to simulate thousands of air particles. A lead programmer intervened and showed him a few tricks to introduce a good effect in a few hours that required hardly any CPU time.

Scrum creates opportunities for leads to continue working on games and lead by way of example instead of through a spreadsheet. Rather than spending half a day with a tool creating and tracking tasks, he or she interacts with people working one on one.

## Reviews

Another critical role of leadership is to provide career support for the developers in their discipline. In studios that employ a matrix management structure, this takes the form of a yearly management and salary review. This reinforces discipline-centric performance over team-centric performance.

For example, if artists are evaluated on how productive they were creating assets over the past year, then they focus on faster asset creation to improve this metric. As a result, when a teammate interrupts the artist about a game problem, it reduces the number of assets that person creates; the artist then tries to isolate him- or herself to reduce these interruptions for the benefit of a better review. This is not a good dynamic.

Leads in Agile environments have introduced frequent team-based peer reviews to supplement, if not replace, the yearly review process (see "360 Reviews" in Chapter 19, "Coaching Teams for Greatness"). This allows feedback about teamwork and cross-discipline collaboration to be introduced. Individual lead roles for each discipline are described in greater detail in coming chapters.

## Servant Leadership

Robert K. Greenleaf (Greenleaf, 2002), who coined the term "Servant Leadership" wrote:

> "The servant-leader is servant first. It begins with the natural feeling that one wants to serve. Then conscious choice brings one to aspire to lead. The best test is: do those served grow as persons: do they, while being served, become healthier, wiser, freer, more autonomous, more likely themselves to become servants? And, what is the effect on the least privileged in society; will they benefit, or, at least, not be further deprived?"

Servant leadership can seem like the antithesis of what leadership is to new leaders like I was 25 years ago. The promotion to leadership can be seen as receiving power over people, but, in fact, it's the reception of responsibility to empower others. There are many attributes of servant leaders. The following six have stood out for me in the past:

- **Listen:** Servant leaders need to hear the group and to clarify its needs. They often need to silence their own inner voice (agenda) first.
- **Are systems thinkers:** W. Edwards Deming said, "A bad system will beat a good person every time." This is true. Servant leaders should start with finding what led the system to beat someone, rather than blame them. They need to be a student of system thinking and to continually explore better ways of working.
- **Care for people:** No one will give their best creative selves to a leader who doesn't care about them. Servant leaders know about the lives and drives of their people and stay connected to them. They care about the growth of their people, even going so far as to mentor their own replacements.
- **Expect greatness and mistakes:** Bill Gates was quoted as saying he tried to hire people smarter than him and get out of their way. I've always found this to be a formula for success, but it doesn't happen unless you allow people to make mistakes along the way. There is no better teacher than failure.
- **Have foresight:** Servant leaders have enough experience and the focus to look into the future and help their team avoid the potholes through coaching and powerful questions. This teaches their teams to develop their own foresight.
- **Build community:** Servant leaders help grow the chemistry of the team and facilitate independent interactions (rather than jealously guarding their role as the communication hub). Steve Jobs famously designed the Pixar workplace to force the various disciplines to cross paths and interact as frequently as possible. This philosophy went so far as to include the placement of bathrooms.

**People First**

"Understand that people are people, and that people are ultimately our job. Our job is people first. Focus on people and make sure they have everything they need."

—Grant Shonkwiler, Commander & Shonk, Shonkventures

## Systems Thinking

In any organization, many interrelated and interdependent parts all influence each other, often creating feedback loops that build in a positive (virtuous cycle) or negative way (vicious cycle).

An example of a vicious cycle is when we stop practices of testing and refactoring when schedule pressures build. As shown earlier, this leads to debt, which grows in time and causes additional delays and further stress.

Taking these interconnected relationships into account is part of systems thinking, which is a useful tool in building virtuous cycles that build quality, speed, and engagement.

### Turning a Vicious Cycle into a Virtuous Cycle

Sketching out feedback loops is very useful when approaching a systems thinking model. For example, I often see the cycle occurring in Figure 20.1.

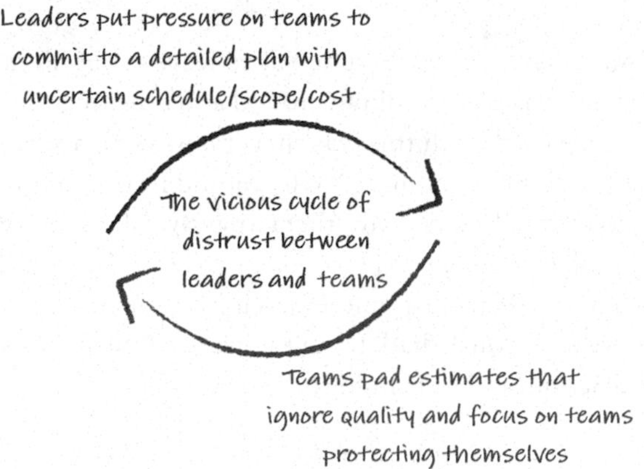
Leaders put pressure on teams to commit to a detailed plan with uncertain schedule/scope/cost
The vicious cycle of distrust between leaders and teams
Teams pad estimates that ignore quality and focus on teams protecting themselves

**Figure 20.1** *The vicious cycle of distrust*

This vicious cycle increases distrust between management and development as each side games the other to protect itself. Less work gets done, and quality suffers.

A significant role of leadership is to identify these vicious cycles and find ways to turn them into virtuous cycles. We do this by changing the vicious cycle of distrust into a virtuous cycle of trust. The greatest opportunity to begin this is in the Sprint Planning and Review meetings and to reinforce it during the Sprint.

### *Building Trust in Sprint Planning*

Building trust in Sprint Planning is simple enough: Let the team refine the Sprint Goal by selecting the work it feels it can accomplish. Leaders must resist the temptation to push more work on the team because they distrust the team and fear they are padding. The team might be padding the schedule because it distrusts the leaders and expects the push. Building trust takes time and courage.

Teams build trust by challenging themselves. As mentioned in previous chapters, teams that achieve their Sprint Goals every Sprint usually are protecting themselves. Planning even two weeks of work can be uncertain. Teams and leaders that trust one another don't worry about the occasional overcommitment.

### *Building Trust in Sprint Review*

Leaders must trust that the team has done its best to accomplish what it has in the Sprint. If a team has run into problems, focus on solving those problems or improving practices, not blaming the team.

Teams build trust with leaders through transparency. By sharing not only what went right, but what went wrong and being accountable for their work, they build trust with the leaders.

### *Building Trust During the Sprint*

As a leader, the hardest thing for me when adopting Scrum was to leave teams alone during a Sprint. Previously, half my day was spent walking around and directing people and solving their problems. The problem with this was that it destroyed a sense of responsibility at the development level. They thought, "Why should I worry about solving problems if Clint is going to tell me how to solve them anyway?" It put a lot of stress on me and disengaged a lot of developers.

After we adopted Scrum, I forced myself to stop micromanaging people. It was hard at first, and, lacking the purpose I previously had, I spent more time surfing. For a while, people thought I promoted Scrum so that I could surf more.[4]

---

4. We even made a video mocking this: https://youtu.be/UT4giM9mxHk.

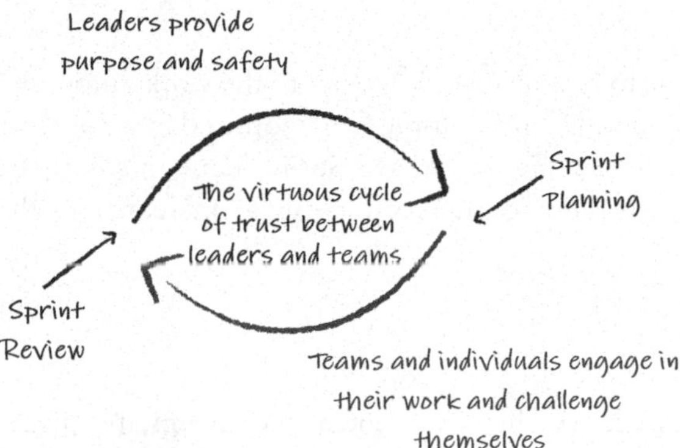


**Figure 20.2** *The virtuous cycle of trust*

As trust builds, developers will seek out leadership as needed for technical and dependency issues and questions. Leadership becomes more of a support structure. The vicious cycle then becomes a virtuous cycle, as illustrated in Figure 20.2.

### Seeking Out Systems

Systems exist throughout the studio: production feedback loops, departmental issues, stakeholder communications, and so on. Books such as *The Fifth Discipline* (Senge, 1990) are a great resource to explore them further.

## Intrinsic Motivation

In 2009, the book *Drive* by Dan Pink was published. The book summarized research demonstrating that creative workers are not motivated so much by financial incentives or other such explicit motivations, but by intrinsic factors.

The three primary intrinsic factors identified in the book are

- **Autonomy:** The urge to direct our own lives
- **Mastery:** The desire to get better at something that matters
- **Purpose:** The yearning to do what we do in service of something larger than ourselves

We want motivated teams. We want to be on motivated teams. We want to be motivated ourselves, but a studio's culture and process can often prohibit it. The following sections cover each item in the preceding list in more detail and how Agile values and Scrum practices support them.

### Autonomy

The purpose of self-organization is to give the people closest to the work autonomy in taking greater ownership, as they become ready for it, over more and more of their work. At first, it might be how they plan and track their Sprint. Later, it's how the team manages its membership and the practices it uses to create an increment of the game.

### Mastery

By allowing the team the freedom to decide "how" it implements a Sprint, it explores better ways of working. When our level artists had the freedom to explore new ways of creating levels, they eventually found methods that reduced level creation time in half.

### Purpose

Teams that are formed around the skills necessary for a feature area are far better connected to the purpose of their work. When your Sprint Goal is to demonstrate an improved game and everyone essential to accomplish it shares that goal, there is no confusion about your purpose.

Leaders cannot force developers to be motivated. They must find it within. The role of leadership is to help create the conditions for intrinsic motivation to flourish. Game development leaders should always be asking themselves, "How can I help improve upon these intrinsic motivators?" A core part of this practice is improving the feedback loops so that increases in autonomy, mastery, and purpose are reinforced quickly and that mistakes are not punished but initiate a conversation to highlight what valuable thing we learned from the experience.

## Flow

I discovered computers when I was 14 years old. That might make me sound like a late bloomer, but back then, there was only one computer in our high school.[5] This big, noisy, slow clunker of a machine sat alone after school hours, and I was allowed to play with it. Rather than a screen, it had a teletype that shook while it slowly pounded out text. I hunched over that teletype working on my first game for hours every day.

5. And I had to walk uphill in the snow to use it.

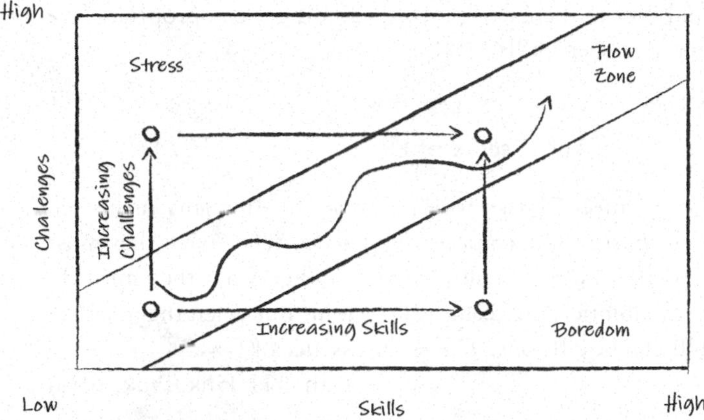


**Figure 20.3** *The flow zone*

For the next few decades, the focus of writing code addicted me. I loved it. I lived for it. What I was feeling was later coined *flow*.

The concept of *flow* was originated by psychologist Mihaly Csikszentmihalyi, who wrote in 1990 that "I developed a theory of optimal experience based on the concept of flow—the state in which people are so involved in an activity that nothing else seems to matter; the experience itself is so enjoyable that people will do it even at great cost, for the sheer sake of doing it" (Csikszentmihalyi, 1990).

What Csikszentmihalyi's research showed was that the state of flow is not only enjoyable, but also extremely productive. Most game developers have experienced it.

It turns out that flow can be created and sustained (in the "zone") by working on things that challenge one's level of skill, but not too much. Figure 20-3 illustrates this zone of flow.

When challenges are too high for our skill, we get anxious and stressed. We get out of flow until our skills rise to meet those challenges or the challenges are offloaded. When the challenges fall below our level of expertise, we get bored and need a greater challenge to get back into the flow.

### Internet Filters

Studios often install filters on Internet traffic to limit access to social media or other sources of distraction on the Internet. This is done because managers see developers spending time on the Internet, rather than working on a game.

These filters are another case of treating the symptom instead of the cause. A typical cause is that the developers are either bored or frustrated: They are not in flow. Finding ways to challenge them at the appropriate level is a better solution.

Helping developers find flow in their work involves finding the appropriate level of challenge while they increase their skills.

**The Essence of Flow**

"One source of frustration in the workplace is the frequent mismatch between *what people must do* and *what people can do*. When what they must do exceeds their capabilities, the result is anxiety. When what they must do falls short of their capabilities, the result is boredom. But when the match is just right, the results can be glorious. This is the essence of flow."

—Daniel H. Pink (Pink, 2013)

The following sections provide tips for helping creatives find flow.

## Finding the Right Challenge

The earlier "Intrinsic Motivation" section describes how mastery, autonomy, and purpose motivate creative people. Developers want to improve their skills and have a vision for what they are working on.

Rather than trying to discover the appropriate level of challenge for each developer, leverage autonomy to let them, with their team, discover it for themselves. By establishing a vision with teams, they find purpose. As a team, they support one another to find the right challenge. When a team member's challenge is too great, the team supports that person. When a developer, for example, is challenged too little, he or she can help another or the team can take on more challenging work in its next Sprint.

## Increasing Skills

Mastery, as another intrinsic motivation, is the desire to improve one's skills. The best studio cultures are the ones that embrace learning. They spend time and money to grow knowledge. Rather than worrying about investing in people who may leave, they create a culture where people thrive in an environment they don't want to leave.

**Practice: Wednesday Pizza Topic**

Growing knowledge and skills should be an essential part of being a game developer. Unfortunately, the pace and urgency of work can make that growth less of a priority. A great practice is to set aside time for learning. Sometimes it can be done for just the cost of several pizzas.

Wednesday Pizza Topic is a practice where a developer presents a topic to a group of other developers every Wednesday night, over pizza. The format can be whatever the presenter wants, but interactivity and demonstration are always encouraged. The only overhead is to have someone facilitate the practice by

- Scheduling the space
- Organizing and promoting the future presentations
- Ordering the pizza

Here are some tips for these types of learning sessions:

- Sessions don't have to be on Wednesdays or after work. Lunch sessions work, too.
- We found Wednesday to be the best day because it breaks up the week, and more people can attend during this less busy time.
- Sessions can focus on a single discipline such as technical topics for programmers or art topics for artists or cross-discipline topics, which are excellent.
- They don't have to apply to game development directly. A designer who had a film background ran sessions where he analyzed popular films.

What used to challenge a developer will no longer be a challenge as his or her skills increase. Helping developers find greater challenges and grow is an essential part of leadership.

## Studio Coaches

A useful practice outside the game industry is to hire Agile coaches (full time or consultants) to come in and work with teams and leaders to help improve their Agile adoption. Having a good coach help an organization navigate its transformation can be very valuable and save years of effort exploring better ways to work and grow self-organization.

Studio coaches

- Coach at every level of the organization from development to CEO
- Coach Scrum Masters and Product Owners

- Coach developers on improved practices that other teams have explored
- Coach leadership on their role in improving self-organization
- Are relentless in learning more about improved practices and coaching techniques from outside the studio

This practice has a number of challenges, as well. I've found that the ratio of good coaches to people who call themselves coaches (anyone can) is low. Coaches with experience and training (such as a Certified Scrum Coach) are usually booked for a year or more. Also, someone who comes from the outside of your organization doesn't know your culture very well and isn't trusted at first by the people he or she is coaching.

This practice is more of a problem in the game industry because very few coaches have made a game in the past. As earlier chapters have discussed, Agile game development best borrows from a set of different frameworks. Many coaches prefer their own "brand" of Agile.

The best approach I've seen is to "grow your own" coach. Very often a team Scrum Master demonstrates good potential to increase his or her role into a studio coach, working with all teams and helping the studio improve as a whole. This doesn't have to be a full-time role at first. It requires an investment to train this person by having him or her attend courses that focus on coaching.[6]

### Exception to the Rule

Often when an external coach visits, people give that person more weight than an internal coach. I saw this when Mike Cohn coached us and see it when I visit studios. An external coach can use the same words said before, and people will treat it as a new revelation.

## Shifting Roles

Coaching a newly formed team that isn't familiar with Agile can be a full-time job. As teams grow, discovering ways to improve their performance and self-organize, their need for a coach diminishes. However, this doesn't mean the Scrum Master's job is done.

One of my favorite images is this one (see Figure 20.4) from the book *Large-Scale Scrum: More with LeSS* (Larman, Vodde, 2017), which illustrates the shift.

6. I recommend the Advanced Scrum Master (A-CSM) courses through the Scrum Alliance, which I also teach.

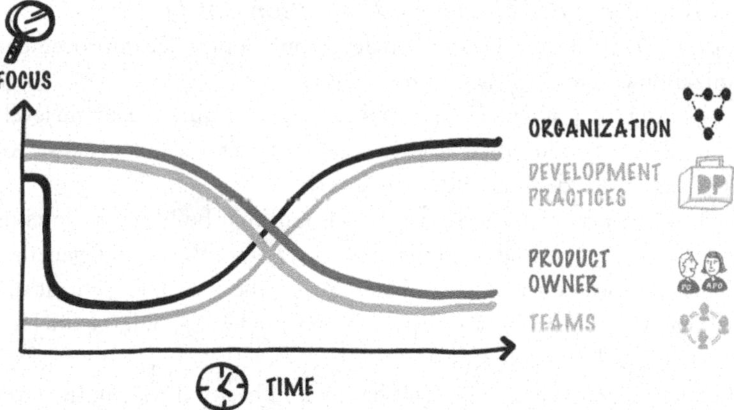

**Figure 20.4** *The focus shift (from* Large-Scale Scrum: More with LeSS *(Larman, Vodde, 2017)*

The figure illustrates the shift of focus for the Scrum Master over time. When teams first form, a Scrum Master's focus is on the role of the Product Owner and the team practices. Over time, as the team becomes more self-organizing, the Scrum Master's focus will shift to coaching the team on improved development practices and the organizational issues that are impacting team performance.

## Large-Scale Scrum: More with LeSS

As teams improve, impediments from outside the team become more pronounced and impactful. For example, upper management might be behaving in a way that impacts team commitments and the quality of their work by interrupting them mid-Sprint. As a result, the Scrum Master focuses more on coaching the organization outside the team and on development practices used at every level.

### Experience

I compare a Scrum Master to a soccer coach. Professional soccer coaches don't do much during a game. I compare this to my son's soccer coach. He worked like crazy running along the sidelines yelling "kick and run!" A new Scrum team, like a team of little kids playing soccer, needs a fulltime coach, but over time the team learns how to coach itself through many situations. If after years of doing Scrum, a team needs a fulltime Scrum Master, it either has the wrong person in that role, or a whole lot of studio impediments aren't being resolved.

### *Organizational Impediments: The Level Production Battle*

One impediment example illustrates the focus on development practice improvement and how an organization can resist those improvements.

Our team was working on a side mechanic for a game that required a single level. All other levels were being produced by a level production team, but because we required a unique level, we decided to build it ourselves.

After a few weeks of production, our level artists found that building the level in the Unreal Editor, rather than the studio standard of Maya, gave them huge benefits. While Maya is a fantastic tool, it wasn't a good match with the Unreal Engine (at the time). Our level designers were at least twice as fast creating level geometry (including iteration time) than the designers using Maya.

However, the lead artist for the game wasn't happy and began directing the level designers on our team to return to using Maya. When our designers pushed back, their jobs were even threatened!

We (the Scrum Master and I, as the Product Owner) took the problem away from the team and to studio management. We used the production metrics and demonstrated that the quality of the level produced using the Unreal Editor was just as good. It wasn't easy to convince everyone, but we did. Eventually, the entire studio went over to using the Unreal Editor.

### *Impediments Caused by Studio Culture*

Studio culture can often impede improvements. There are many reasons, including the following:

- Leads can feel their authority or position is threatened by change at the development level.
- Process is considered written in stone, and change is not welcome.
- Developers don't feel they have permission or the responsibility to suggest change. Most game developers play games and have great ideas about how to improve the game they are working on.
- Executives can override development on a whim and destroy trust.

Scrum Masters, who usually have little authority at this level in the studio, must use their organizational coaching skills to overcome these obstacles.

## Adoption Strategies

The strategy for rolling out Agile to your project or studio has to be carefully considered. Transitioning an entire project is challenging. A bottom-up or beachhead approach proves that Agile practices introduce beneficial change with less risk. However, this approach takes more time.

This section addresses strategies and specific tools and practices for studios to use to manage adoption.

## Beachhead Teams

During World War I, the major combatants fought battles on vast front lines. Offensives were launched along these fronts in massive attacks. Because of the ever-increasing lethality of twentieth-century weaponry, these attacks were often ineffectual and resulted in nothing more than heavy losses in the attacking force. The war became a series of deadly stalemates and attrition. Eventual victory came to the side that could withstand more losses than the other.

Battles in World War II were different. They were often marked by the penetration of a small area of the front by a focused attack. Large units poured into the breach, taking advantage of the confusion and disarray of the opposing army. Offensives such as the Battle of France and D-Day are examples of this strategy.

A similar approach of introducing Agile provides an effective way of overcoming the well-founded concern about large-scale change. Small teams first experiment with iterations to increase studio knowledge about its benefits before it is rolled out to a larger group. These teams are often referred to as **beachhead teams**. If a beachhead team is able to establish a foothold and find success with Agile practices, it encourages other teams to adopt them.

Beachhead teams have an improved chance of success for a number of reasons:

- They can be staffed with people who are open-minded about trying it.
- One team is more easily coached than a dozen. Teams new to Agile will have many questions.
- They can take on noncritical features at first, which puts less pressure on them to get it perfect the first time.

This seems like stacking the deck in Agile's favor, and it is. It's similar to planting a seed in a garden; its germination period is when it is most vulnerable. Conditions have to be carefully monitored during this time. Even if everything is done right, the plant might not grow. If the soil is the wrong type or if there is not enough sunlight or moisture, no amount of care will allow it to grow.

The same idea applies to the beachhead effort. Agile may not "take" in the studio. The soil (culture, management style, and so on) might not be fertile for it. In this case, it's better to see the experiment fail with one team than a dozen.

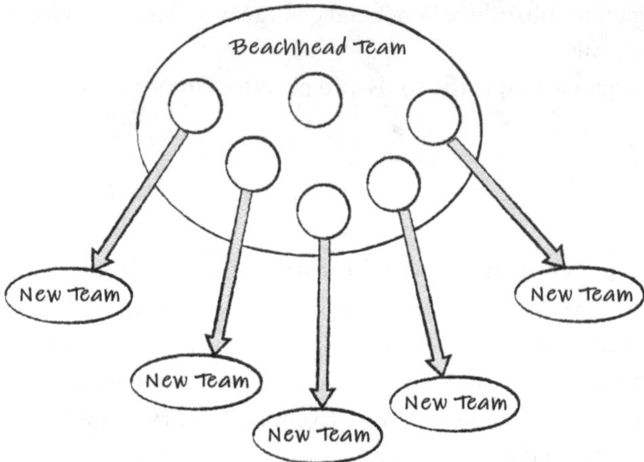


**Figure 20.5** *Split-and-seed strategy*

If a beachhead team is successful employing Agile and the studio wants to increase its use, there are three methods to use: split and seed, split and reform, or cross-team coaching.

## *Split and Seed*

In the **split-and-seed** method, a successful beachhead team is split up to "seed" other teams that are starting Agile. This enables the most rapid deployment of Agile experience throughout the studio. About eight teams can be seeded this way. Figure 20.5 shows what this looks like.

The drawback of this approach is that a successful team is broken up. Breaking up such a team is likely discouraging to the members. When random people are grouped, it takes time for them to form a strong team, if it happens at all. The other disadvantage is that not all the members of the original team will be effective coaches for the newly formed teams.

As a result, a good team might be replaced by half a dozen or more that aren't nearly as effective. It can make the beachhead result look like a fluke. Therefore, this approach is not recommended if a more gradual adoption of Scrum is possible.

## *Split and Reform*

In the **split-and-reform** strategy, the beachhead team splits into two, and each team brings in new members. This results in a slower adoption speed than the split-and-seed approach, but it enables each half of the original team to stay together.

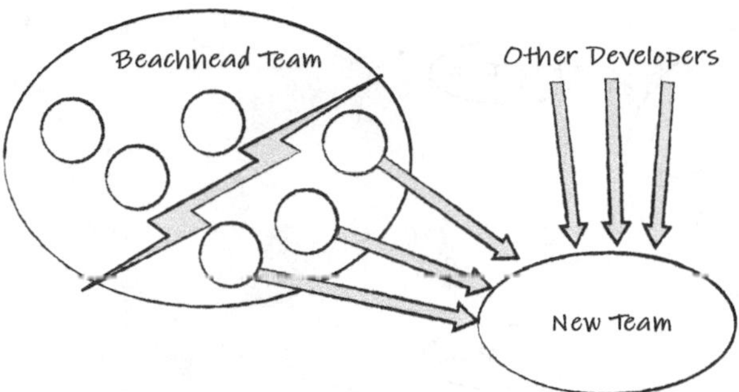


**Figure 20.6** *Splitting the beachhead team into two teams*

This strategy, illustrated in Figure 20.6, is a compromise between the number of teams created and the desire to allow teams to remain together.

Although not as traumatic as split and seed, this approach still splits up a successful team and can result in dysfunctional teams. The old guard from the original beachhead team might exert more ownership of the process, which inhibits ownership and commitment from the new recruits.

### *Cross-Team Coaching*

A third solution is to leave the beachhead team in place and have it coach other teams transitioning in a number of ways:

- A member of the beachhead team serves as a part-time member of a new team. He commits 50 percent or less of his time to each team.
- A member of the beachhead team becomes the Scrum Master on one or more new teams.
- A member of the beachhead team attends a new team's Daily Scrum, Sprint Planning, Review, and Retrospective meetings, offering advice and coaching whenever the team has questions about Scrum practices.

This **cross-team** solution, illustrated in Figure 20.7, will subtract some time from the beachhead team's Sprints, but the team will recover it over the following several Sprints as the new teams come up to speed on the practices, needs less of members' time, and eventually replaces them.

The number of new teams transitioned to Agile this way is limited to how many members of the beachhead team are suitable coaches and how much time they can spare.

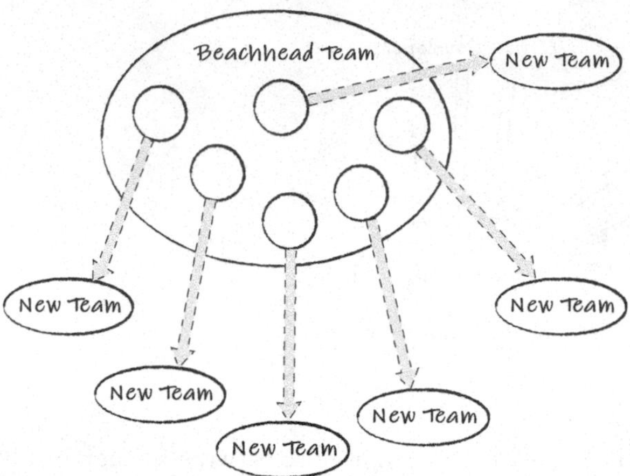


**Figure 20.7** *Cross-team coaching*

In most cases, cross-team coaching is the best method of deploying multiple Agile teams from the beachhead team. It enables members to retain a successful team and deploys Scrum quickly throughout a project or studio.

> **Coaching Lesson: Don't Adopt Major Changes Before the First Deployment**
>
> When a studio contacts me to schedule training or coaching teams on new practices, I ask it where the team is in development. If the team is close to deploying the first version of a game (within six months), I suggest the studio defer the training until after the team has deployed and things have settled down. The reason is that teams under pressure tend to revert to the "old ways" of working and the time spent training is wasted.

## Full-Scale Deployment

Some studios desire a companywide or projectwide deployment of Agile. This presents more risk to the studio, as any major process change would, but if done properly is the fastest way to roll out Scrum. This section discusses the areas of risk and an overall strategy to reduce it.

### *Transition Planning*

Full-scale deployment has to be planned more carefully than the beachhead team experiment. The larger the number of people transitioning, the more challenging it is to communicate and sustain the vision for why change is taking place and to create the conditions that enable them to start using Scrum quickly. This is the goal of transition planning.

> **Note**
>
> Transition planning is also needed after a beachhead team has proven successful and a larger number of teams are deployed from it.

First, a **transition team** is formed to establish the initial team organization, federal and state laws, and a Product Backlog.

A transition team should consist of the following:

- Product Owner
- Scrum Masters
- Studio executives
- Discipline leads

Have at least one person become a Certified Scrum Master (CSM).[7] This provides an exposure to Scrum practices and principles to ensure the team starts on the right path.

The next step is to establish roles and definitions. This is best done in a meeting with all the executives, stakeholders, Scrum Masters, and project leads that form the transition team that is responsible for the transition. The CSM or a Scrum coach facilitates this meeting.

The Product Owner and stakeholders for the project and Scrum Masters for the teams are identified. They must all be well versed in the duties and responsibilities of the Product Owner role.

> **Note**
>
> Product Owners should be considered fulltime on any project of three or more Scrum teams. Ideally, they should attend a Certified Product Owner (CPO) course.

7. www.ScrumAlliance.org

The studio executives discuss their expectations and roles with the group. They must be aware of the principle that teams are committed to work during the Sprint and that all changes in priorities to the project should occur outside the Sprints themselves.

This transition team should help the Product Owner create an initial Definition of Done. Does it mean that each story must run at a minimum frame rate on the target platform? Does it have to run on the development platform? The transition team needs to establish the baseline definition with the expectation that it will improve over time.

### *The First Release and Sprint*

The next step for full-scale Scrum deployment is to prepare for the first release for each project. This begins with establishing an initial Product Backlog, Release goals, and a Release plan created in a Release Planning meeting (see Chapter 9). This meeting is conducted by the transition team or with the entire project staff, if it's not too large.

After a Release plan is ready, the transition team will meet with the entire project staff to discuss the goals of the release. Leading up to this there should be a number of meetings with the teams to educate them about the practices and goals of Scrum.

The goals of the first Sprint should be modest to establish a cycle of success. The first Sprint will reveal a lot of problems with the existing studio practices and the team's adoption of Scrum.

**Tip**

Management should be careful not to go too far promoting Scrum. The team will be sold by the results. Overselling Scrum will turn some developers off. The best thing for management to do during a Sprint is to support the teams by helping them address every impediment they can't solve themselves. There will be many at first. When the teams see management being facilitative, it will sell them on Scrum more than any entreaty about its benefits.

The following are the principles and practices that team members need to understand in preparation for their first Sprint:

- They are committing to Sprint goals as a team, not as individuals committing to their own tasks. The entire team will succeed or fail on this basis. Overcommitting is not a great danger, because they can renegotiate with the Product Owner during the Sprint. Teams new to Scrum are more likely to underestimate their work.

- Commitment is reciprocal. Management will not change their goals or the Sprint review date without a Sprint reset.
- The Definition of Done must be clearly understood between the team and the Product Owner. The functionality delivered at the end of the Sprint must reflect this definition.
- The rules of the Daily Scrum are understood.
- The purpose and utility of the burndown chart are understood.

**Experience**

Iterating on *any* change within one to three weeks is challenge enough for some teams!

Following the first Sprint, the Scrum Masters will need to set aside several hours to run Retrospectives for the teams and then meet with the transition team to discuss the results.

### *Establishing the Product Backlog*

A goal for the first release should be to refine the Product Backlog. This usually includes the following:

- Discussions with the publisher and license holders to establish a vision for the game
- Concept and design work to refine the vision
- Infrastructure work and risk identification

All of these elements are used to create a backlog and prioritize the stories within it.

**Tip**

It's easy to go too far and create a Product Backlog that is too finely detailed and unwieldy. The Product Backlog should be large enough to support several releases of stories, with detail decreasing with priority, yet not so large that the burden of maintaining it is too great. For a console game, 300 to 500 stories on the Product Backlog is a good target. For an iPhone game, probably 100 to 200 stories are enough, but your mileage may vary.

## What Good Looks Like

The chapter started with describing what good looks like at the extreme end of self-organization: Studios built on the principle of self-organization have dominated their sectors. But they are merely examples that self-organization is not impossible, not patterns to be duplicated.

Self-organization can benefit at every level of adoption:

- Teams that organize and manage their own Sprint Backlog usually do a better job than teams that are handed a set of tasks estimated by leads.[8]
- Teams that have some control over their membership usually do a better job than teams that are organized by a resource plan.
- Developers who have some creative input over their work are usually more engaged in that work than developers who do not have input.

Leaders are necessary to grow self-organization. They exist to serve the teams and get out of the way, when necessary, extending trust and understanding that failure is a necessary part of making something that's never been made before.

## Summary

Exploring roles and team structures is an ongoing process. Teams must use the retrospective practice to find ways to improve how they work together and with the leaders of the studio. Allowing teams to take ownership and authority over some of the daily aspects of their life leads to their being more likely to take responsibility for their work. This doesn't happen overnight. It takes years in many cases and will create head-on collisions with studio leadership culture. The results are worth the effort.

## Additional Reading

DeMarco, T., and T. Lister. 1999. *Peopleware: Productive Projects and Teams, Second Edition*. New York, NY: Dorset House Publishing.

8. https://docs.broadcom.com/doc/the-impact-of-agile-quantified

Greenleaf, R. K. (2002). *Servant Leadership: A Journey into the Nature of Legitimate Power and Greatness* (25th anniversary ed.). New York: Paulist Press.

Katzenbach, J. R., and D. K. Smith. 2003. *The Wisdom of Teams: Creating the High-Performance Organization.* Cambridge, MA: Harvard Business School Press.

Laloux F. 2014 .*Reinventing organizations: a guide to creating organizations inspired by the next stage of human consciousness.* Brussels, Belgium: Nelson Parker.

Lappalainen, E. 2015. *The Realm of Games.* Jyväskylä Finland: Atena Publishing.

Larman C. and Vodde B. 2017. *Large-Scale Scrum: More with LeSS.* Boston, MA: Addison-Wesley.

Pink D. 2013. Drive: *The Surprising Truth About What Motivates Us.* New York: Riverhead Books, U.S.

Senge PM. *The Fifth Discipline: The Art and Practice of the Learning Organization.* New York: Doubleday, 1990.

Takeuchi, H., Nonaka, I. 1986 *The New New Product Development Game, Harvard Business Review*, pp. 137–146, January–February.

The Greenleaf Center for Servant Leadership; rev Edition (September 30, 2015).

# Chapter 21

# Scaling Agile Game Teams

Although the ideal Scrum team size is five to nine people, modern game development efforts typically require far more developers (see Chapter 1, "The Crisis Facing Game Development"). Sometimes these developers are distributed across multiple locations. Although Scrum is designed to be scalable, large teams need to add practices, realign roles, and take precautions in how they organize teams and foster communication so that the increasing challenge of getting large groups of humans to align can be overcome.

## The Solutions in This Chapter

This chapter explores a framework of scaling that is unique to game development. The main areas of focus are

- Product Backlog organization
- Team formation
- Product ownership
- Release and Sprint practices
- Managing dependencies
- The practices of distributed and dispersed teams

Together, the practices described here have been successfully used with game teams of more than 1,000 developers spread across dozens of studios.

## Challenges to Scaling

The development of the avionics for the F-22 jet was done in secrecy. Every one of the hundreds of developers, including myself, had to have security clearance to even enter the building we worked in. The greatest impediment in developing the avionics was that the work was spread over as many congressional districts as possible. This was done to ensure ongoing support for a project costing tens of billions of dollars.

As a result, when I had to have a conversation about solving a software problem with a remote person who wrote a library or piece of hardware my software depended on, I had to schedule a call to be held in a soundproofed room on a scrambled phone with a security agent present, which usually took a week to arrange.

Those phone calls were nearly useless because the scrambling and descrambling degraded sound quality, and the security agent wouldn't allow us to speak in great detail. I would merely end up yelling something like "Something you're doing isn't working with something I'm doing."

I believe this kind of communication overhead was a major reason why the F-22 was years late and tens of billions of dollars over budget.

Communication is the biggest challenge for large teams. Although teams might not face as critical a problem as we did on the F-22, the results are similar.

This section describes some of the significant challenges seen with large games.

### Loss of Vision

Maintaining a shared vision with more than 100 developers is a significant challenge. It's easy for individual developers to lose connection between what they are working on and the overall vision for the game. Because developers make many decisions each day based on their vision of the game, the impact of a splintered vision can be very costly.

A main ingredient in creating a shared vision is frequent conversations with stakeholders and the Product Owner.

**Advanced Practice: The Feature Box**

"Feature Box" is a useful practice for creating and reinforcing a shared vision.

After the Release goals are debated (BHAGs), the game development group gathers, and each team mocks up a prototype box that their feature would theoretically ship in, using a large flip chart sheet and markers to sketch art and marketing blurbs. The goal is to present their feature in a way that would encourage players to buy it off of a shelf. After the box art is created, a team representative presents it to the rest of the group. The marketing bullet points that teams create for their features usually make great epic stories for the Release!

Here are some things to keep in mind for using Feature Boxes:

- This is a useful practice to implement at the start of every Release.
- During the presentations, the Lead Product Owner can clarify or correct a divergence of vision. For example, if a team's box lists "online gameplay" as a feature and that epic is not in the Product Backlog, the Product Owner can address the reasons for its exclusion.
- If the Release is a live update, give the team the option to create a web page instead.

## Adding People Late

Very often, when stakeholders are unhappy with the progress of a team, they'll "move resources from one project to another" to "speed things up." I've had this happen with games I've worked on, and many of us have heard the stories of beleaguered studios being sent busloads of developers from a sister studio to help them meet a ship date.

The problem is that it never works. As the old saying goes, "Nine women can't make a baby in a month."

This has been known for decades, most famously by Fred Brooks' law: "Adding human resources to a late software project makes it later." (Brooks, 1975).

The problem is that people aren't interchangeable resources. As we add new people, not only does the overhead of communication burden the flow of communication, but those new people have to be brought up to speed on doing the work, usually by the people who were already doing the work! This ends up further slowing the effort. By the time we start seeing the benefits of the additional people, the game is also behind schedule and with an even higher burn rate, which will often result in additional busloads of "resources" sent.

## Communication Among Large Teams

Project staff sizes for many console and PC games have grown steadily from the "good old days" of the lone developer who designed, coded, illustrated, scored, and

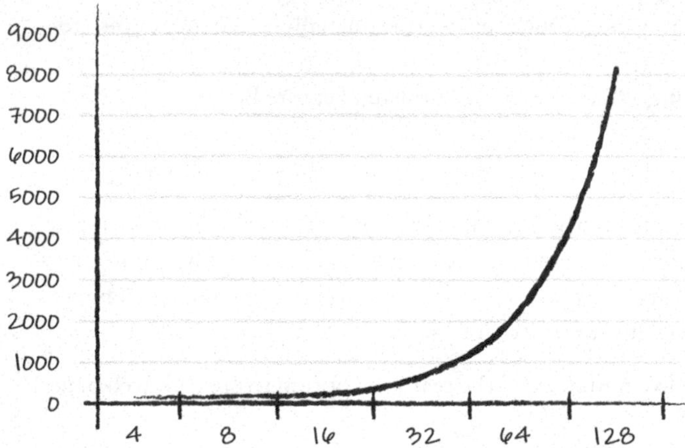


**Figure 21.1** *Team size and lines of communication*

tested the game on his or her own to project team sizes that now often exceed 100 people. Unfortunately, the effectiveness of a 100-person project is usually not 100 times that of a one-person project. This loss of effectiveness has many sources, the main one being the overhead of communication.

Consider the combinations of any two people who may need to communicate on a project. These "lines of communication" grow much faster than the number of people on the project (see Figure 21.1). For example, a project with 100 people has 4,950 possible lines of communication between members (the formula for lines of communication is $n*(n-1)/2$, where $n$ is the number of people on the project), which is far too many connections for teams to manage on their own. As a result, hierarchies of management were created to oversee this complexity.

## Dunbar Numbers

Anthropologist Robin Dunbar theorized, and research has supported, the idea that there are thresholds of group communication effectiveness based on the number of individuals in the group. For thousands of years in the past, armies have organized themselves around similar size limits (for example, squad, platoon, and company) based on an intuitive sense of these thresholds as well.

## Should You Scale Up?

No scaling framework has any magic that can overcome the overhead of larger groups. Work that takes 30 people a year can likely be done by 10 in two years, but we often don't have that much time. We can still apply questions such as, "Can we do the most important features with 10 people and still make a great game?" or "Can we find ways to do more with 10 people?"

Scaling up should often be the last choice made of all the options we have, but sometimes it's a necessary one. Although eight developers might be able to make a AAA game most efficiently, the market for a game that takes 10 years to make might not be the same.

## Scaling the Wrong Process

The main problem with scaling is that we usually scale the wrong approach. Consider a small team with a producer, some programmers, artists, and designers that are iterating on a game. When studios scale that team up, they often do it by "scaling resources," that is, by focusing on scaling the number of people in each discipline and organizing the scaling by creating hierarchies of control. For example, if they triple the number of programmers, they'll end up hiring someone to manage them.

When all the disciplines do this, then a layer above them is created to manage the dependencies between them. Tools such as task management databases are installed to keep track of the dependent work.

When an issue arises, for example, when an artist is unable to export an asset into the game, they'll turn to their lead, who will report it to the producer. The producer then creates a work order for a fix placed into a task database. In the future, a lead programmer will assign the task to fix the exporter to a programmer. Figure 21.2 shows the flow of this issue.

This is a widespread approach seen with big games, but it includes the following issues:

- The delay between recognizing a problem and fixing it creates other issues. If it turns out the asset doesn't work, then the artist could have created many other defective assets in the meantime.
- The number of lines of communication that transpired between the artist and the programmer could have introduced an error. The programmer may end up implementing something that doesn't address the problem.

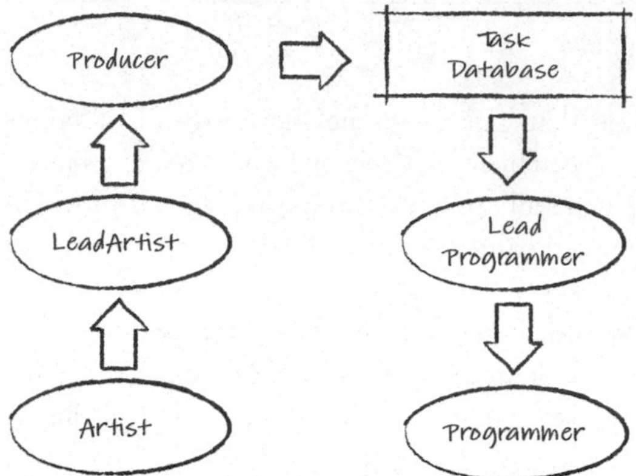


**Figure 21.2** *An example flow of a problem from art to programming*

- The issue could be lost in the shuffle and the problem not solved until it becomes urgent, leading to crunch.

Scrum teams avoid these problems by being cross-disciplined and addressing these problems on a day-by-day basis. When scaling Scrum, we need to apply the same principle of scaling the practices that allow teams to solve as many of their problems on their own without creating a bureaucracy.

## The MAGE Framework

Over the past decade, many scaled Agile frameworks have emerged. Each has its approach to how Agile can be scaled up for IT projects. Game development presents unique challenges for scaling. Fifteen years of experience dealing with these challenges has driven me to produce my own framework that I've christened MAGE, or Massively Agile Game Environment.[1]

MAGE, like Scrum itself, is a framework based on lessons learned with many large-scale games. Its practices are meant to be inspected regularly and adapted to your unique challenges.

MAGE encompasses team formations, roles, planning, execution, practices, and tools that have proven useful for large game development teams. It applies Agile and lean principles and it duplicates many of the principles at the large scale seen at the team level.

1. I leaned in the aerospace industry that sometimes you have to mangle a phrase to produce a catchy acronym.

## Whole Game Focus

Large game projects must still maintain a focus for the entire game. Every Sprint demonstrates one build, not a build from every team. We focus teams and practices towards this.

## Communication, Purpose, and Autonomy

Often, developers working on massive games complain that they have little idea of what they are working on or what their part in the game is. This creates an impact on development by leading to disengagement and a lack of ownership (http://www.melconway.com/Home/Conways_Law.html).

By preserving the principles of Scrum while scaling, we can keep lines of communication short and ensure that developers maintain a sense of purpose and autonomy in their work.

## Systems Thinking

We continuously apply systems thinking, Lean thinking, and Scrum patterns to continually improve the flow of work, reduce overhead, and address every aspect of studio organization to enhance the flow of communication and the output of value to the game.

**Conway's Law**

In 1967, Melvin Conway wrote a paper that described how "any organization that designs a system (defined broadly) will produce a design whose structure is a copy of the organization's communication structure."

This adage is known as "Conway's Law" and it is in games that studios make.

I've seen this in every game I've made or studio I've worked with:

- Studios organized around a technological focus will make games with impressive technology but with weak art and design.
- I've seen large games that have development split across half a dozen studios that each own a feature area feel like six different games packaged into one.

- Teams with separate quality assurance (QA) groups and discipline silos release games with many quality issues.

Conway's law is unavoidable, but it's a useful tool when applying systems thinking to your studio and game organization.

### Scaling the Right Way

At its core, MAGE is still Scrum:

- Teams of five to nine developers that commit to Sprint Goals.
- Potentially shippable game increment is demoed every Sprint.
- Each team has a Scrum Master and a Product Owner.

MAGE scales Scrum by organizing around "teams of teams" that reflect a hierarchical Product Backlog with a similar hierarchy of Product Ownership to ensure a vision is being shared, in both directions, between all stakeholders and developers.

## The Product Backlog

A game starts with a Product Backlog organized as a hierarchy. This hierarchy will reflect the team and Product Owner organization. This hierarchy will also change over time as the game emerges, and our knowledge grows.

Figure 21.3 shows a starting hierarchical mind map of major epics for a game. Initially, the game staff will be smaller and focus on the camera, character, and hand-to-hand combat epics. They might consist of a single small team or three teams, depending on how many developers are working on the game.

Later releases might reorganize into single-player and multi-player teams that build upon these core mechanics.

### Tools and Mind Maps

Most tools for a Product Backlog support hierarchies, but I prefer the ones that can visualize the Product Backlog as a mind map. A mind map of a Product Backlog

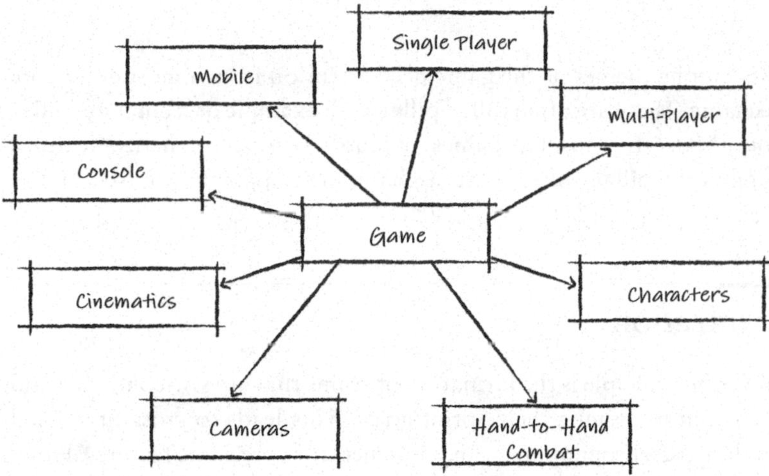


**Figure 21.3** *A basic mind map of the game epics*

should represent the team structures as well as the hierarchy of features. Mind maps have some benefits:

- Mind Maps better serve how we think of a set of features.
- Mind Maps can be quickly reorganized as teams reorganize, usually on a release-to-release basis.
- It's easier to allow teams to take over a branch of a mind map and will enable the Lead Product Owner to focus on the trunk.

## Pooling Functions and Dispersing Components

It might seem logical for every branch to have audio. A feature isn't "done" until it has audio, right?

The problem is that you might only have two audio composers for a dozen teams that each need only 10 percent of a composer's time. We don't want an audio composer spread across six teams, so we'll pool the composers into an audio support team (see the later "Pool Teams" section).

Conversely, we might have a team of AI programmers create the architecture for basic AI (pathfinding, senses, character and animation control, and so on) before dispersing across teams to better support the needs of AI for all characters in the game (see "Component Teams" below).

The changing needs of the game and team organization should be reflected in the organization of the Product Backlog.

### Pillars

Sometimes cross-cutting themes of the game need attention from almost every core feature and mechanic. These are often called **pillars**. An example of a common pillar is monetization. Many free-to-play games explore ways to monetize features throughout. Significant pillars often have a champion supporting it (see "Pillar Champions" below).

## Team Organization

A fundamental Scrum principle is the formation of teams that are self-contained and can genuinely commit to owning their Sprint goals. This leads to cross-functional teams that include artists, programmers, and designers for core game features. However, some self-contained teams might need fewer disciplines, perhaps even one, to accomplish something of value.

This section lists a variety of team types used for Agile game development. Not all of these team types are necessary for your game.

### Feature Teams

Feature teams are cross-disciplined teams that develop core game features. For example, the small cross-disciplined team shown in Figure 21.4 could take full responsibility for a driving mechanic.

| DISCIPLINE | ROLE |
|---|---|
| Designer | Tune drivingcontrols andlayout test levels |
| Designer | |
| Artist | Create vehicles and props andtest levelgeometry |
| Artist | |
| Programmer | Program vehicle drive-train, physics, and artificialintelligence for opponent vehicles |
| Programmer | |
| Programmer | |
| AudioDesigner | Sound support for vehicles, level, and gameplay |

**Figure 21.4** *An example driving mechanics team*

A significant benefit of feature teams is the sense of ownership they experience. Participating in the full development of a few mechanics is far more satisfying to most developers than attending part-time on many. For many developers, this gives a greater sense of accomplishment.

A feature team should have everyone it needs to build the mechanics. In practice, this is difficult to accomplish. Sometimes teams need to share disciplines in short supply. An example of this is an effects (FX) artist who is utilized 25 percent of the time by any single team. Often this person is shared among multiple teams.

**Experience: All Feature Teams?**

On one of our first Agile games, we used features teams for all the core mechanics and ran into problems. The main problem was that each mechanic ended up having a different look and feel, which made the whole game more confusing and harder to play.

## Component Teams

Component teams are composed of developers who work on a component of the game, such as a rendering engine or content area. Although less common than feature teams on an Agile project, component teams have their benefits. One example is a platform team comprised mostly of programmers. These programmers are experts in optimizing performance for a particular platform such as the iPhone or Android. Concentrating these individuals on a single team focuses effort on challenging problems that are wasteful for feature teams to solve on their own. For example, if the iPhone programmers are spread across multiple teams, then their efforts creating a working iPhone build are diluted.

Component teams are typically used only for foundational or services work. Using component teams for work that impacts multiple mechanics often leads to less suitable solutions for the game. For example, a component team was formed to create the character AI for a game. This team consisted of AI programmers who wanted to develop the best-architected AI possible. Unfortunately, their efforts led to AI functionality that was handed off to other teams that neither understood how the AI worked nor benefitted from many of the features designed into it. Ultimately this team broke up, and the AI programmers scattered across the project to implement AI needed by various teams.

## Production Teams

Production teams are cross-discipline teams used for game development projects that have a production phase. These teams have a more defined pipeline of work for creating specific content and applying some of the Lean and Kanban practices described in Chapter 6. Production teams are also less bound by the five-to-nine-member team sizes due to the more predictable flow of work.

Production teams may exchange members as needed with other production teams to maintain a steady flow of asset creation. Production teams often form from feature teams as a mechanic transitions from pre-production to production. For example, most of the programmers might leave the level pre-production team as it enters production and be replaced with more modelers, texture artists, and audio designers. Example production teams include:

- Level production
- Character production
- Cinematics
- Community website

## Support Teams

A frequently asked question is how support teams should organize themselves in an Agile project environment. Because they support multiple teams, they receive requests for features that cannot be as easily ordered as they are for a single team, which can create confusion and conflict between the support team and its "customers," the games that depend upon them.

A support team requires their own Backlog and Product Owner. Having more than one Backlog and one Product Owner for a support team is a recipe for disaster. The team should have every benefit that other Agile teams have in an understandable Backlog and single vision. Customer teams should identify priorities during Release Planning and include the support team (or at least its lead and Product Owner) in their Release Planning.

### *Support Kanbans*

Support teams often benefit from using Kanban over Sprints, which allows them to be more responsive to urgent requests for bug fixes or other impediments to teams that use their services. Figure 21.5 shows a simple Kanban board for a support team.

One of the most critical metrics is the average amount of time it takes between a support request to be received and when it is deployed. Support teams always try to find a way to reduce this response time.

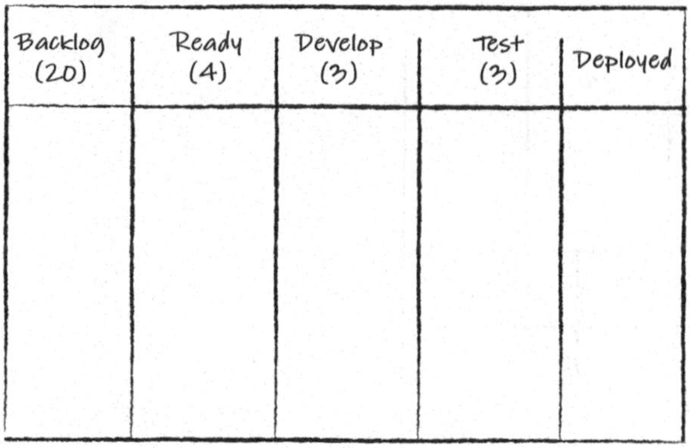

| Backlog (20) | Ready (4) | Develop (3) | Test (3) | Deployed |
|---|---|---|---|---|
| | | | | |

**Figure 21.5** *A Kanban board example for a support team*

Note that even the Backlog has a work in progress (WiP) limit, which is meant to force the Product Owner to refine the Backlog from time to time so older requests don't pile up and reduce response times. This also helps the teams asking for support to refine and prioritize their requests continually.

The ready state on the board represents the requests that the team has tasked out and are ready to be worked on. When the last request is pulled into the develop column by the team, the empty state of the column signals the members to have a planning session soon and to fill up that column with four new features, tasked out, as indicated by the WiP number.

**Tip**

If a support team is a dependency for the deployment of multiple games, its Product Owner should ideally be at the executive level (or in frequent contact with executives) to arbitrate conflicting game priorities. Deciding to support one game over the other is a company-level (strategic) decision and should have input from the people who run the studio.

### *Support Team Iteration Goals*

Support teams can also have iteration goals. This is common with engine and tools teams, which have research and development (R&D) goals of their own. In these circumstances, a Sprint swim lane (see Figure 21.6) can be added below a Kanban lane. The team would determine how much time it could dedicate to each lane per Sprint and judge how much of a goal to forecast in Sprint Planning.

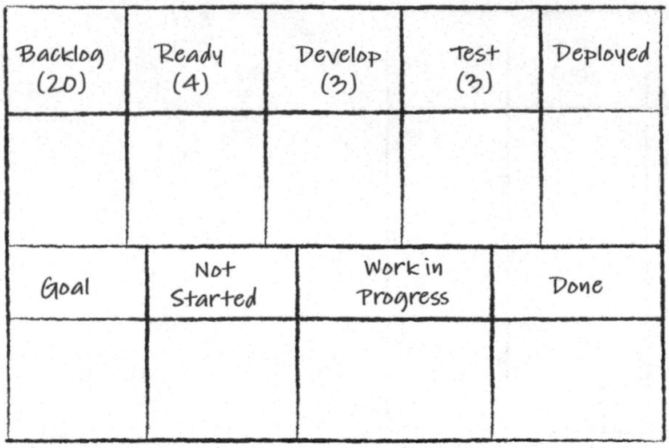

| Backlog (20) | Ready (4) | Develop (3) | Test (3) | Deployed |
|---|---|---|---|---|
| | | | | |

| Goal | Not Started | Work in Progress | Done |
|---|---|---|---|
| | | | |

**Figure 21.6** *An example Kanban board with a Sprint swim lane*

### *Managing Maintenance and Quality Issues*

Support teams should factor in emergent support work. Setting aside a certain percentage of your bandwidth for unexpected maintenance is critical. It's easy to track how much time is being spent addressed on maintenance work every Sprint and subtract that from your planning capacity.

> **Tip**
>
> Loaning support team members out to another team for a Sprint is okay, but it should be identified in Release Planning. Having support team members see how their "product" is used is valuable.

## Tool Teams

A tool team consists of tool creators (programmers, technical artists, QA) whose customers are users of a common toolset and pipeline.

Like a support team, a tool team often supports multiple projects and has its own Product Backlog.

Tool teams have the added benefit of releasing tools to customers who are in the same building, not just stakeholders who represent them. Having tool users who can participate in Backlog definition, prioritization, planning, and reviews is a significant benefit to the tool developers. Tool development can be even more exploratory than game development and benefits substantially from using an Agile approach.

## Pool Teams

A pool team is a collection of developers from a single discipline. Unlike other teams, they don't have their own Sprint Goals. They exist to support teams that do. Examples of this are a pool of animators that could support a feature team that needs a large number of animations in a single Sprint.

Another benefit of a pool team is to provide a service center for art production, also referred to as **insourcing**. Environment artists and animators are in higher demand during production, and pool teams help level the developer requirements in a larger development studio.

Pool teams require more planning and management during a release to ensure that they are fully utilized. Pool teams are commonly used in late pre-production or production.

## Integration Teams

Sharing a vision on larger projects that contain more than 40 developers is challenging. The vision among separate teams can drift, even with a hierarchy of Product Owners. As a result, some projects have "integration teams" that integrate mechanics, developed initially by feature teams, into a unified experience.

These teams are similar in structure to feature teams. The difference is that they are responsible for the overall theme of the game. For example, in an action racing game, eventually the core team takes over the driving mechanics from the team that developed it after it is mature enough. From this point forward, the core team modifies and maintains the mechanic to seamlessly work with the other mechanics.

## Feature Area Teams

Feature area teams are a blend of feature teams and component teams that create base features in a specific area for integration teams to assimilate into the game. An example of this is a physics feature team that would create vehicles, destructibles, cloth, and many other physics-based features for a game, but not bring them to a deployable state.

There were two reasons we introduced these teams. First, on large projects, having many feature teams make deployable features led to a divergent feel across those features. Handing the final polish off to an integration team led to a more cohesive look and feel to the game. Second, this allowed these teams to stay together longer. After this, they were able to stay together and move on to another physics-based feature.

Feature area teams are still cross-discipline, needing artists, designers, programmers, and so on to achieve their goals.

### Objection: Component, Pool, and Core Teams—These Don't Sound Very "Scrum" at All

Ideally, every team should be a functional team, but the sheer number of specialties required for game development leads to pool and core teams. If every team needs 10 percent audio support and you have two composers supporting 16–20 teams, you can't have them be part of 8–10 teams each. When I've described pool teams to Agile consultants outside the game industry, I've been accused of blasphemy. One time, I asked one of the authors of the Agile Manifesto what his solution would be, and he said, "just have every developer learn how to compose audio"!

Scrum is more about teams finding ways to perform best rather than "following the rules out of the book."

## Communities of Practice

Another challenge created by large Scrum projects is the potential loss of communication caused by the separation of discipline, or functional expertise, across multiple cross-discipline teams. For example, if all the graphics programmers are spread across various teams, what is to prevent them from solving the same graphics problems in different ways?

### Note

We had this problem when all the AI programmers were split up across three feature teams. Each team implemented a unique AI state machine. One team implemented a script-based system, another implemented a C++-based system, and the third team developed one that was manipulated with a graphical interface.

The solution is to establish **communities of practice** that can share knowledge and eliminate the duplication of effort. Figure 21.7 shows how the AI programmers from across multiple Scrum teams can form an AI community of practice.

Each community can decide how frequently it needs to meet and address the issues it is facing. The AI community might discuss common solutions it could implement. The Scrum Masters can form a community to share improvements to their team's practices. The designers could create a community to complain about everyone else.[2]

Communities of practice do not have their own Sprint Goals or assign work outside their teams. Their only purpose is to share information.

2. One design group I knew did this; they were able to keep it mostly constructive!

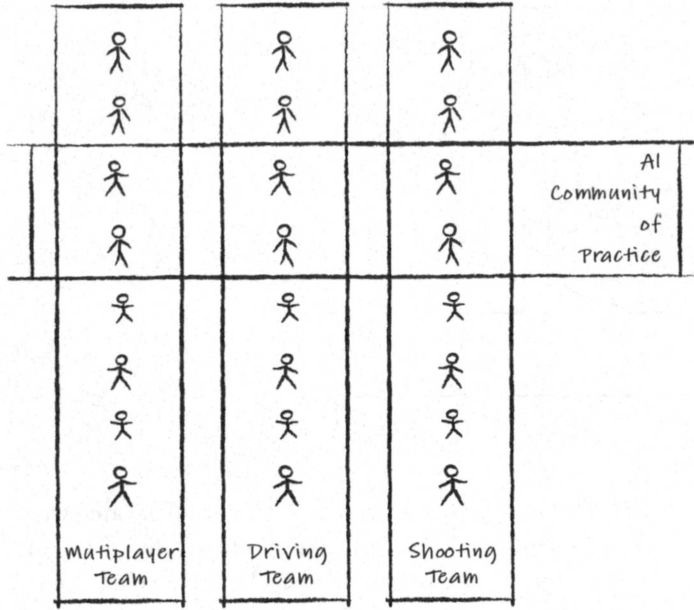


**Figure 21.7** *An AI community of practice*

> **Example: Spotify**
>
> Spotify has explored several different orthogonal group structures such as tribes, chapters, and guilds that are worth reading about (Kniberg, Ivarsson, 2012). They are great examples that game teams can try out themselves.

## Product Ownership

The demand for a Product Owner's time on game teams can be greater than the demand for Product Owners in other industries. Teams are challenged with knowing if the "fun" they are creating is the "fun" the Product Owner wants. Questions such as how "bouncy" a physics response should be or how "snappy" an animation transition needs to be are subjective and may need daily feedback from the person who owns the vision for the game: the Product Owner.

For large projects with a dozen or more teams, this creates a challenge. The Product Owner's time becomes spread too thin, and he or she cannot adequately maintain a shared vision for the game across all teams. Without a shared vision, each mechanic will drift from the original vision as it evolves, and the game becomes less consistent and appealing.

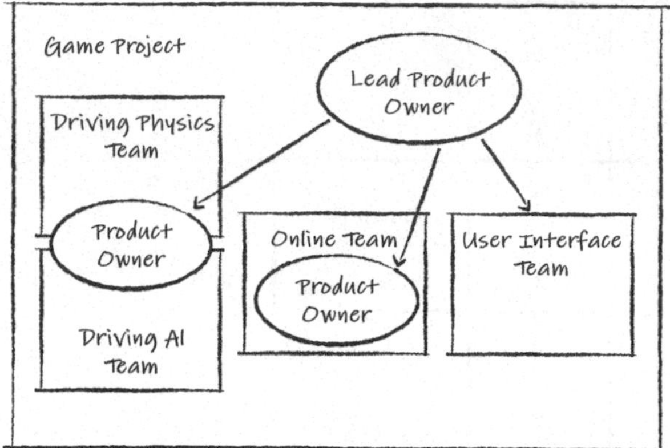


**Figure 21.8** *An example Product Owner hierarchy*

A useful practice is for the Product Owner for a large project to delegate ownership of feature areas. One way of doing this is to establish a hierarchy of Product Owners. A lead Product Owner guides the project, and each core mechanic has a Product Owner. Figure 21.8 shows an example of such a Product Owner hierarchy.

### Definition: Feature Areas

Feature areas are sets of features that are related by an underlying component and usually supported by a team. For example, a physics feature area could encompass cloth, destructibles, vehicles, and anything else that might require a team that is familiar with the technical and asset limitations of a physics engine.

The Lead Product Owner oversees the two Product Owners who work with one or two Scrum teams. The Lead Product Owner continues to work with teams directly, such as the user interface team, but he or she delegates Sprint responsibilities to the teams that have their own Product Owner.

The Product Owners work with their teams during the Sprint, helping them plan the Sprint and working with them daily to ensure that they achieve the Sprint Goal. For example, as a Product Owner on a team implementing a driving mechanic, my role included educating the team about the shared vision for the mechanic. These often required conversations about the balance between a "sim" versus "arcade" feel for the controls, vehicle physics, and the environment.

The Product Owners need to ensure that a shared vision exists for the entire project. This includes frequent meetings among them all, including the Scrum-of-Scrums meetings (see the later section, "The Scrum of Scrums"), to address any questions about the game's vision.

Product owners take direction from the Lead Product Owner between Sprints and Release Planning. A difference of opinion often exists on the best path to achieve release goals between the Product Owners. The insight of a team's Product Owner is invaluable in finding the best way, but the lead Product Owner is responsible for safeguarding a consistent vision for the game across all mechanics and features.

A Product Owner team creates a shared vision on a large project and ensures consistency of vision everywhere.

**Team Product Owners?**

There is disagreement among the scaled Agile frameworks as to whether each team or feature area should have a Product Owner or whether there should be just one for the entire game.

In my experience, one Product Owner for a big game is not enough, unless the teams are sufficiently self-organized to replace the role (see "Ditching Product Owners" in Chapter 7, "The Product Backlog.").

However, Team Product Owners can often become "output owners" who have little authority to guide the vision of their feature area and merely focus on having the team create as much output as possible.

## Additional Roles

Larger groups of people and projects invoke extra work and roles that help overcome problems of scale. This section describes some I've found useful.

### Project Management Support

Due to the enormous production debt of a large game development project, pairing a Lead Product Owner with someone who can help him manage that debt is often beneficial. That role is often a "senior producer" or "development director" in studios. This role will support the Lead Product Owner to prioritize work that helps refine the content production plan to ensure work is ordered to meet schedules (for example, making sure we are ready with tool pipeline functionality when motion capture actors arrive).

### Supplemental Roles

The book *Scaling Lean and Agile Development: Thinking and Organizational Tools for Large-Scale Scrum* (Larman and Vodde, 2014) describes several additional roles outside of teams that I've found useful for game development:

**Travelers** are team members on one or two teams that only stay for an iteration or two to provide assistance and to teach developers. An example is the physics expert who works with a team to set up a cloth effect and also pairs with another programmer to write the code. After the cloth is working the traveler leaves, and the programmer remains to support the cloth effect.

**Scouts** attend as many of the Daily Scrums as possible and provide a progress report to the Lead Product Owner. They also take part in Release Planning and Backlog refinement meetings helping large teams to be more synchronized.

**Component mentors** are members of a feature team who reserve spare time to mentor other teams on their component (such as multiplayer online) or discipline (for example, animation or programming). They teach techniques and help advise teams on the best way to implement features related to their component or area of expertise.

### Pillar Champions

Pillars (described previously) benefit from having a champion that, like a Component Mentor, work with every team to help support its pillar, such as monetization or ways to connect the game to social media platforms such as Facebook.

## Releases

For large games, Releases establish a cadence that

- Enable distant stakeholders to gather and discuss the progress
- Enable teams to realign around upcoming Release goals
- Provide regular checks on debt and the "shippability" of the game itself

As teams and studios improve, this cadence improves to the point where these things can occur far more frequently than once a release.

## Release Planning

Chapter 9, "Agile Release Planning" describes Release Planning as

- Establishing Big Hairy Audacious Goals (BHAGs) for the Release in an initial planning session
- Capturing those goals in epic stories
- Breaking out upcoming Sprint Goals from those epics (the Release plan) in regular Backlog refinement/Release Planning sessions

**Tip**

Try to limit the initial Release Planning session to fewer than 20 people.

Larger teams use the same approach, but with the following changes:

- The BHAGs and epic creation are not created by the entire team, but a subset of the team consisting of leads, stakeholders, and the Product Owner group.
- The BHAGs are presented to the entire game group.
- The breakout of the Release plan occurs at the team level.

These changes still allow each team to participate in the creation of the Release plan at the team level, which is great for building and evolving a shared vision.

### A Global Game Release Story

CCP Games, the developer and publisher of EVE Online, was founded in 1997 with development split between studios in Reykjavík, Iceland; Atlanta, United States; and Shanghai, China. It has grown to have more than 400 employees and to host more than 300,000 active subscribers in a single online world.

In the fall of 2008, CCP undertook the development of its tenth expansion pack called *Apocrypha*. *Apocrypha* was the most ambitious expansion of the EVE universe. It added major technical features and significantly extended the size of the EVE world. The goal of the company was to release the expansion pack within six months following a four-month development cycle (see Figure 21.9).

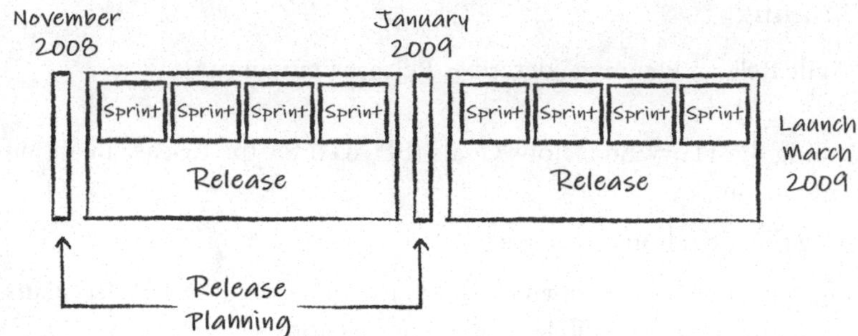


**Figure 21.9** *The Apocrypha timeline*

This ambitious goal required CCP's worldwide development studios to work in parallel. Features and content developed simultaneously across three continents had to come together to achieve their goal seamlessly. Usually, this would be the introduction to a disaster story, but CCP pulled it off. CCP is a longtime adopter of Agile methods, specifically Scrum.

In the case of *Apocrypha*, with more than 120 developers in 13 Scrum teams spread across three continents, nine Product Owners were required. These Product Owners took their direction for the game from a project management group in Iceland.

**Release Planning**

The stakeholders identified two release cycles of development to release the expansion pack in March 2009. Ideally, Release Planning should gather every developer, but it was nearly impossible to collect 120 people from around the world in one location, so CCP had to create some innovative practices to perform Release Planning.

*Apocrypha* Release Planning meetings took place over a single 12-hour period. A high-definition video conferencing network facilitated this meeting and allowed every developer to take part.

Because most of the development staff, including the project management group, was in Reykjavík, the meeting was focused there. It started at 9 a.m. Because of the time difference, it was far too early for the developers in Atlanta to attend. It was the end of the day for the developers in Shanghai, so they and the Reykjavík group met first. Hours later, the Shanghai team would leave, and the Atlanta team would join to discuss the Release (see Figure 21.10).

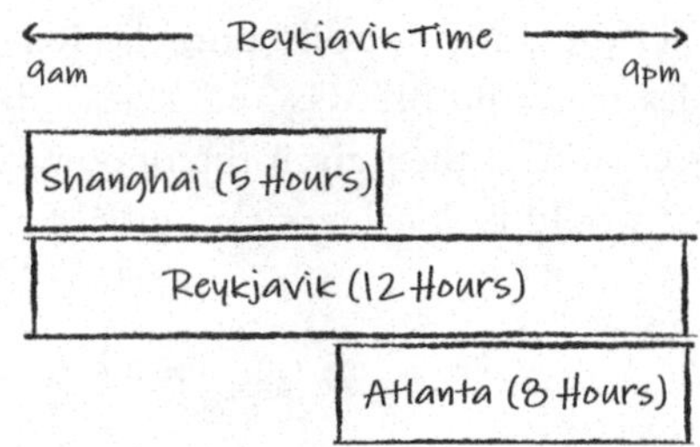


**Figure 21.10** *Overlapping meeting times*

You can see a time-lapse video of this fantastic meeting in Reykjavík on YouTube.[3]

It's important to note that the time zone limitations and the limitations of video conferencing allowed only two teams to meet at one time. In this case, Atlanta and Shanghai could not attend together. To avoid potential problems, two developers from Shanghai flew to Reykjavík to participate at the core meeting and to represent the Shanghai teams.

Each pair of locations would discuss the Release goals and begin breaking them down into smaller goals that were reasonably sized to fit into a Sprint. The conferencing network enabled multiple simultaneous meetings to occur. This was necessary because many questions raised during this process required a great deal of lively conversation among the entire staff or individual teams.

The goal of the Release Planning meeting was to generate a set of potential Sprint Goals for each of the 13 teams that would fulfill the Release BHAGs. This wouldn't be the last time that the teams would communicate. Daily issues were discussed, and a build of the game was demonstrated every two weeks at the Sprint Review. Changes to the Release plan were made every Sprint to adjust for the realities of development.

After two releases, *Apocrypha* was ready to do final testing and polishing, and on March 10, 2009, it shipped on schedule.

3. http://www.youtube.com/watch?v=gMtv1zDUxvo

## Rolling Out the Release Plan

On larger projects, having the entire project staff attend the Release Planning meeting is sometimes impractical. In this case, only the Product Owner, domain experts, and discipline leads attend.

After Release Planning, the Product Owner presents, or **rolls out,** the Release plan to the entire project staff. The owner describes the BHAGs and Release plan and answers any questions raised. The project staff is then given the opportunity to organize themselves into Scrum teams that would best achieve the initial Sprint Goals in the plan.

## Forming Teams

The creation and conversation about the Release plan is an excellent place to examine the best team formations for achieving release goals. Depending on what level of self-organization the team practices, one of the following occurs:

- Managers make team assignments from the available staff.
- Senior team members have conversations about team makeup and recruit members of the team.
- The entire game's staff gathers and, after the Release is described, decides team formation on their own.

Between Sprints, teams can swap members as needed. Although keeping good teams together is best, you have to acknowledge reality. If you don't plan any animation work in the next Sprint, let your animator help a team that does!

> **Note**
>
> As mentioned earlier, limiting any one developer to being on no more than two teams is best.

## Updating the Release Plan

Large teams will often have two meetings to update the Release plan after each Sprint. The first meeting is among the members of the group that established the BHAGs to review the general direction of the game's progress and any reprioritizations or respond to dependencies that have arisen.

The second Release Planning session is among the team and its Product Owner to refine their portion of the Release plan.

> **Should Teams Own their Release Plan?**
>
> A Release plan is just the top of the Product Backlog that we're forecasting we can accomplish by the end of the Release. However, when you have multiple teams working on their own Release plan, there are benefits to having shared and separate Release plans.
>
> The benefit of having a shared Release plan is that teams can share stories. For example, if two teams need the same particle effect, they don't need to decide at the start of the Release which team will take it on. A shared Release plan makes that easier.
>
> The benefit of having separate Release plans is that each team can decide what kind of tool it wants to use to manage it. For us, a big mind map poster worked best.

## Using Project Boards

On larger teams, having a "big picture" view of the current progress is a useful tool. The project board shown in Figure 21.11 is an example of such a tool.

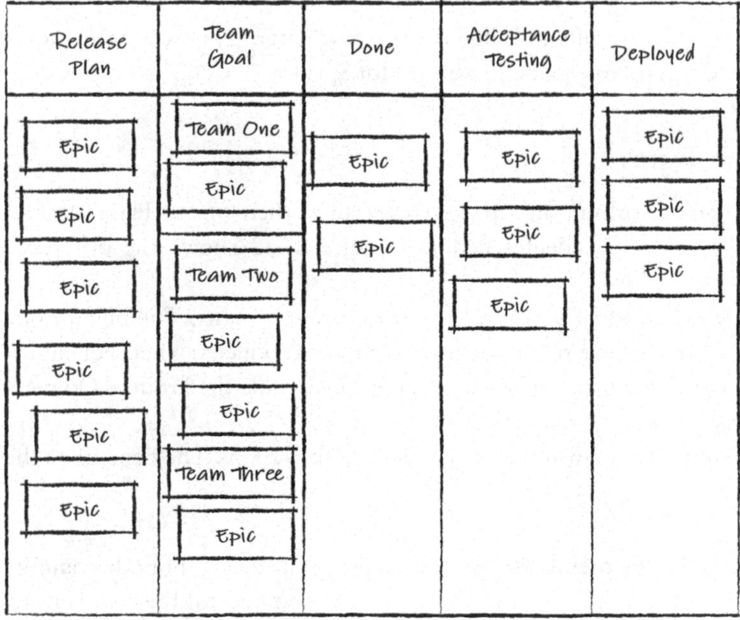


**Figure 21.11** *A project board*

The board shows a 6- to 12-week Release plan, which consists of epic Product Backlog Items (PBIs) being worked on by three teams. Each team area shows the epics each team is currently working on, but not the task details. Each team manages that level of detail on its own board. The board also shows the current progress of the features going through acceptance testing and the ones deployed in the current Release.

A project board can be used to gather all teams working on the game or for a Scrum-of-Scrums meeting at whatever frequency they need to.

## Sprints

Ideally, for each team, a Sprint for large games should be the same as a Sprint for a small game. Unfortunately, there is an overhead cost with larger games that must be paid by each team. These mainly come from

- Unforeseen dependencies
- Planning coordination with other teams
- Managing shared specialists
- The overhead of merging changes for a single review build
- Scrum of Scrums and community of practice meetings

Avoiding any of these results in a higher cost paid later. This section explores some of the practices that large games have used for Sprints.

### Aligning Sprint Dates

Separate Scrum teams working on a project may align their Sprint Planning and Review dates or have independent schedules. Figure 21.12 shows the difference between the two dispositions.

For teams with independent schedules, there are some benefits. The biggest one is that each team doesn't have to vie for time with the Product Owner. For multiple teams with aligned dates, it can be challenging to schedule the Product Owner's time, especially for planning the next Sprint.

Nonetheless, aligning the Sprints is usually best (Cohn, 2009). The benefits to the game are as follow:

- **Teams can exchange members:** Following the Sprint Review, nobody commits to any Sprint Goal, so it is easy for teams to trade members for the next Sprint.

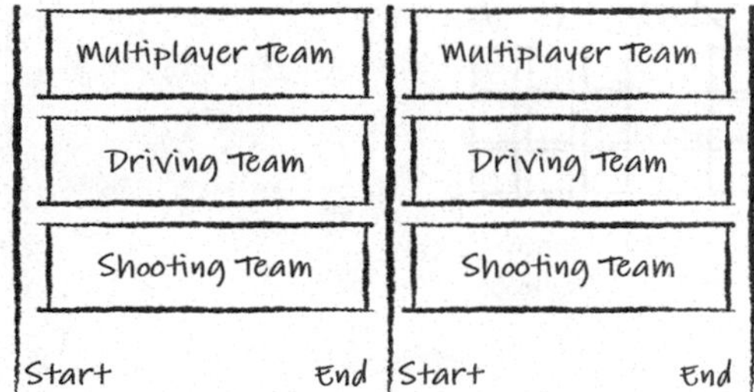

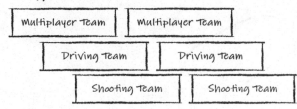

**Figure 21.12** *Independent and synchronized Sprints*

- **An integrated view of the game is encouraged:** Teams with the same Sprint Review date can integrate all work into a single build so that the entire game is reviewed. This encourages more cross-team collaboration and an integrated view of the game.

A hierarchy of Product Owners on larger teams avoids spreading the Lead Product Owner too thin when teams need to plan the next Sprint.

## The Scrum of Scrums

The central practice for scaling Scrum is the Scrum-of-Scrums meeting. Figure 21.13 shows how a larger project could divide into sub-teams and how each team sends a member of their team to the Scrum of Scrums.

This meeting enables one or more representatives from every team to gather to inform other teams about their progress and impediments. Who attends the meeting often depends on what needs reporting. It's very useful for identifying shared or potential problems that one team can solve for all the others.

For example, an engine technology team often works with multiple teams to improve the engine technology. Changes to this technology often create impediments

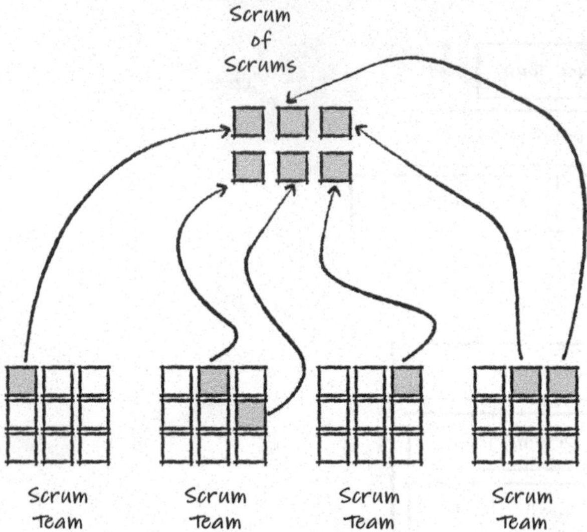


**Figure 21.13** *The Scrum-of-Scrums meeting*

for teams when rolled out because of unforeseen bugs. Imminent changes to the shared technology are described at the Scrum of Scrums, so any resulting problems are quickly identified and resolved. In this case, a technical lead from the shared technology team attends the meeting to report the pending changes.

The Scrum-of-Scrums meeting is different from a team's Daily Scrum meetings:

- **It doesn't have to be daily:** It can be weekly or semiweekly. The group that meets should decide on the best frequency for it.
- **It is for problem-solving:** The meeting is not timeboxed to 15 minutes. Potential solutions are addressed in the meeting. This meeting may be the only time when these individuals meet during the week, and the problems they discuss have a larger impact on the project.
- **The questions are different:** The meeting starts with everyone answering slightly different questions:
    - **What did the team do since we last met?** Each team's representative describes, in general terms, what their team has accomplished since the last Scrum-of-Scrums meeting.
    - **What will the team do next?** The representatives discuss what their team will accomplish next.

- **What is getting in the team's way?** What impediments are causing problems for each team? These are usually issues that the team cannot solve on their own or communicate with other teams.
- **What is a team about to throw in the other team's way?** Like the previous engine example, teams often commit changes that may impact other teams. Perhaps a team is committing a change to the animation engine, which every other team uses, later that day. If characters start moving strangely shortly after this commit, then knowing about the change can save a lot of time tracking down the problem.

### Don't Name Individuals

It's important to discuss a whole team's progress and not the progress of each individual on each team when answering the first two questions at the Scrum of Scrums. Otherwise, the meeting takes far longer!

The Scrum of Scrums doesn't have a Product Backlog, but it creates a short Backlog of shared impediments addressed at every meeting. An example of a shared impediment is when the one FX artist for the studio is out sick, and it impacts multiple teams. Many impediments identified take days to resolve, so tracking them is beneficial.

A Scrum Master for the Scrum of Scrums isn't necessary, but teams often assign one of their members to the role to help keep the meeting on track.

### Alternatives to the Scrum of Scrums

As teams mature, they often see the Scrum of Scrums as a bottleneck. For example, if the meeting is once a week, then almost a full week can pass before a necessary conversation occurs. Some alternatives to the Scrum of Scrums are

- An integration team (described previously) can be a hub of communication for any problems that arise at any time
- Problem-solving "travelers" who float around between teams solving problems the team can't solve on their own
- Have closely related teams meet in Daily Scrums

## Sprint Planning

Each team on a big game will plan Sprints the same as small teams do, except that it can benefit them to invite representatives from other teams that have similar Sprint Goals. For example, if two teams have a goal that involves path-finding, then they can coordinate to find ways to share solutions.

## Sprint Reviews

A Sprint Review for a large project team occurs in an area that accommodates the entire project staff and all the stakeholders. This will require an ample space. On projects with more than one team, one of the Scrum Masters or the Lead Product Owner becomes the emcee and describes the results of the past Sprint. These results include the overall goals and the major impediments of the Sprint. The meeting is handed over, in turn, to a member of each team that contributed features. Each person describes his or her team's progress and shows an aspect of the build that demonstrates where the team added value.

**Rule: Demo a Single Build**

Regardless of the number of teams on the game, there should only be a single build used in the Sprint Review. When you allow each team to demo their build, it hides a great deal of debt that will emerge when code and assets are eventually merged.

A single build consists of the current executables and exported assets that make up the running game. The source code and assets for the current build are also considered part of the build as they are used to create it.

A Q&A session follows the presentations to allow comments about the game and discussion about its future direction. The benefits of a full project Review are as follows:

- The entire project staff can see the progress of the whole game.
- Showing only one build encourages cross-team integration and improved build practices.
- The overhead in time for the stakeholders is minimized. The entire Review should take place in an hour or two.

The drawbacks of a project Review are as follow:

- The teams often require more time to prepare. Large reviews are often treated more as ceremonies rather than quick demonstrations for the stakeholder.
- They diminish the time for one-on-one stakeholder-to-developer communication that occurs in team reviews.

If the project staff is large (more than 50 people), then a smaller follow-up meeting may take place between the stakeholders, leads, and the Scrum Team. The reason for this meeting is that larger Reviews inhibit some of the critical and detailed conversations that need to occur. For example, discussions about the quality of animation across the entire game need to include the animation and technical leads for the project. In a large team setting, this conversation might be muted to avoid coming across as too critical of the animators when the animation technology could cause the problem.

**Practice: The Review Bazaar**

For large groups making a game, a review of the integrated changes made at each iteration in one demo is beneficial. The downside is that there is less exposure to the details of what each team is doing. Occasionally, giving the entire group a chance to get a detailed view of what other teams are doing can give them new insights into the big picture and also reinforce cross-team collaboration.

A Review bazaar is a good approach for multi-team reviews.

The Review bazaar is usually conducted in the middle of a Release where there is likely to be more divergence of mechanics or epics in various stages of progress. Ideally, it's run in a single open space with a table running the game for each team. One or more representatives from each team staffs the table and everyone else has a chance to walk around, view the builds, and ask questions.

## Sprint Retrospectives

After every Sprint, each team will hold its Retrospective. Following this, there is a shared Retrospective among representatives from each team (like the Scrum of

Scrums). This Retrospective will explore the following areas and create a start, stop, and continue list that will guide improvements in how teams work together how they work together:

- Revisions to the shared Definition of Done
- Changes to the format or frequency of the Scrum of Scrums
- Improved methods of interteam communication
- Areas where the studio and stakeholders can support teams and the overall project better

**Sharing a Definition of Done**

Having a shared Definition of Done is essential for large projects (see Chapter 7). This doesn't mean that individual teams shouldn't explore ways to improve their own. Each team should expand on a shared DoD, and over time, the shared DoD will be enhanced based on what is found to benefit individual teams.

## Managing Dependencies

Interteam dependencies inside a Sprint can prevent teams from achieving their goals. Consider a team whose Sprint Goal is to implement a wall-climbing mechanic, but it has to rely on another team to provide the animation. Because of the separation of teams and goals, the mechanic team will likely hand off its work to the animation team near the end of the Sprint rather than collaborating daily. At best, this limits the number of iterations that can occur with the mechanic. At worst, the goals that the animation team has for its Sprint might prevent it from handing back the wall-climbing animation in time.

When projects begin using Scrum, these dependencies are quite common, and they are the source of many impediments and failures to achieve Sprint Goals. Over time, teams change their membership to reduce dependencies and establish other practices to prevent their impact.

The goal isn't to find ways to utilize everyone's time fully. To respond to work that couldn't be planned for, there has to be a certain amount of "slack" available. Ultimately this slack, which allows everyone to respond quickly to problems, is more effective than attempting to plan it all away.

## Team Formation

Changing membership to create more self-contained teams is a valuable solution. If the team implementing a new mechanic needs full-time animation work throughout the Sprint, having an animator join them is best.

In many cases, there isn't enough work to justify a specialist joining one team full time. In these situations, teams can share specialists within a Sprint or trade them between Sprints. Doing this requires a bit more planning and foresight to avoid overlapping demands for a specialist's time. There are two places where this is done: at Release Planning meetings and Backlog refinement meetings.

## Release Planning

In Release Planning, teams identify potential Sprint Goals for the next several Sprints. Using these goals, they identify Sprints where part-time specialists or a concentration of disciplines (such as a bunch of texture artists) might be needed. Often these will uncover conflicting needs among teams. The best way to resolve these is to raise or lower the priorities of PBIs creating the conflicts. For example, if two teams require the same FX artist full time during the same Sprint, then the Product Owner changes the priority of one of the PBIs requiring FX work enough to shift the Sprint for one team to remove the overlap.

**Borrowing an Audio Engineer**

Our team was working on a driving mechanic. We were able to implement much of the simple audio ourselves. However, the Sprint Goal of adding complex audio behavior for the drivetrain was approaching. This required engine sounds that would be realistic throughout the entire RPM range and blend between gears. This was a difficult problem to solve, primarily because our vehicle was licensed, and the drivetrain physics (revolutions per minute [RPM] and torque curve) didn't match those of the actual vehicle. We asked the audio pool team if we could borrow one of its audio engineers for the Sprint. We moved our goals around a bit with the Product Owner to accommodate a Sprint where that team could free him up. This worked out well for both teams.

Problems occur with little warning on a day-to-day basis that require a specialist on another team to help out. For example, one of our projects had one UI scripter who could implement UI changes rapidly. Almost every day he was requested to help another team for an hour or so. Because of the demand for his time, his team would allow him to commit to only half the available hours during a Sprint.

Requests like these can be handled in the Scrum-of-Scrums meeting described earlier. Whether or not a specialist can help another team within a Sprint lies with the current team to which the specialist belongs.

**Note**

Scrum doesn't solve the problem of specialists who become bottlenecks, but it makes such issues transparent and, therefore, easier to solve. In the case of the UI scripter, the solution might be to hire more people who can script or cross-train others to be able to write UI scripts. The ideal solution depends on the project and the studio's needs.

## Team Dependency Management

Although a goal in an Agile transformation is to eliminate all dependencies, some will slip through from time to time. Relying on teams to identify upcoming dependencies in Sprint Planning and even the Daily Scrum can mitigate many of those that emerge.

I've seen two tools used by teams to help visualize and track emergent dependencies:

- **Project Board Lines:** If the teams are using a project board to visualize the Release plan, connecting dependent PBIs with string on the board can highlight dependencies. I've even seen teams use colored yarn to identify the urgency of a dependency.
- **Dependency Sheet:** This is a single spreadsheet that is updated by teams and posted in the area the Scrum-of-Scrums meeting occurs. Each row identifies a dependency and a column or color rates its urgency. The list is discussed during the Scrum of Scrums (Kniberg, Ivarsson, 2012).

## Reducing Expert Dependencies

Most project managers are afraid of a proverbial bus that's seeking to run over one of their expert developers. These developers are the ones who are the most productive or are the only ones who know how a part of the code works.

These experts are indeed hard to replace, but they are often bottlenecks that teams and games depend on. One useful practice to is apprentice someone to work with them and learn how to offload some of the less challenging parts of their work or to deal with issues that would frequently interrupt the expert.

**Experience**

Our physics library was written and maintained by a single programmer. This programmer was a bit temperamental, didn't welcome interruptions, and refused to join a Scrum team. As a solution we had a junior programmer apprenticed to him and learn how to solve the more frequent physics problems, such as rigid body issues, for the teams that needed help.

## Distributed and Dispersed Development

To reduce costs and help balance staffing demands, studios frequently spread the development of games across multiple locations. With this model, teams or team members spread across two or more locations develop core mechanics and features of a game in parallel. This is different from outsourcing, which typically focuses on distributing certain types of production work, such as asset creation or technical support.

### Distributed Versus Dispersed

Distributed development is characterized by multiple teams for a single game that is separated across various locations. For example, a space-based role-playing game might have a core team in San Francisco, while another team works on space ships and their functions in London, and another builds planet levels in Seoul.

A dispersed team has each of its members in separate locations. The COVID-19 pandemic of 2020 saw a massive increase of dispersed teams due to many developers transitioning to working from home, where they could be physically isolated from one another.

Distributed teams have the advantage of co-location for each team. With proper inter-team management, such teams can overcome most challenges described in the next section.

Dispersed teams, on the other hand, have a much more significant challenge. The daily communication within the team is constrained by members' physical separation and the tools they use. Very often, such teams lose the cohesion necessary for a good team and simply become a "group of individuals" with far less engagement and productivity.

## Challenges to Distributed Development

Two common challenges affect distributed teams:

- **They lack a shared vision:** It's more common for distributed teams to experience their visions "drifting apart" because of physical separation. This divergence leads to conflicting or incompatible efforts from the teams.
- **Iteration and dependencies can destroy the benefits:** The potential savings in cost for distributed teams is quickly lost when time and effort is wasted through iteration delays and dependencies between teams.

### *Applying Agile Values and Principles*

Many of the Agile practices discussed help distributed teams overcome the aforementioned challenges. They allow teams to maintain a shared vision, increase collaboration, and avoid going down separate paths.

#### *Align Scrum Teams with Location*

Usually each distributed team is a separate Scrum team. Occasions occur when having members of a Scrum team distributed to share knowledge and create bonds between locations is beneficial (Cohn, 2009), but for the most part, having each Scrum team co-located is best.

When each Scrum team is co-located, they can more effectively collaborate on a shared Sprint Goal. Such teams need a local Product Owner but should find ways to hold Sprint Review and Planning meetings with other teams and the lead Product Owner either in person or through a video-conferencing system.

#### *Shared Scrum of Scrums*

A video- or phone-conferenced Scrum-of-Scrums meeting is essential for distributed teams. These don't have to occur every day, but they should be held at least once a week. If teams are spread across many time zones, the time of the conference call should not be fixed so as to impose a constant burden on one team more than the others. The meeting time is changed on a regular basis so that attendees from different locations have to come in early or stay late.

*Shared Release Planning*

It's critical for a Release plan to be developed and shared to the greatest degree possible among the teams. Often this will include flying one or more members from each location to a central place where the planning occurs. This necessary cost should not be avoided with distributed teams. You either spend money on airfares and hotels or spend much more on the costs incurred by divergent goals. See the earlier sidebar "A Global Game Release Story."

*Improved Sharing of Builds, Assets, and Code*

A problem with large games is how to share the vast number of changes that occur. Frequent small changes can perpetually break the build, and bulk changes committed weeks apart can bring teams to a halt for days at a time. With co-located teams, this problem is bad enough. With distributed teams, defects passed across in shared builds, assets, and code can be disastrous. When a single question can take a day for an answer, tracking down a problem and the necessary expertise to solve it consumes days rather than hours or minutes. Extra care must be taken to protect distributed teams from external defects. This requires a focus on improved commit practices and testing described in Chapter 11, "Faster Iterations."

## *Solving the Problems*

A globally distributed development team can be successful in creating a high-quality product within budget and within the schedule limits. To summarize the raw ingredients for this success:

- **Local vision and ownership:** Scrum enables individual cross-disciplined teams to take ownership of their Sprint Goal and achieve it independently. Having a team Product Owner on-site who is responsible for the vision of what the team is creating is essential.
- **Iterative development methodology:** Creating an integrated, potentially deployable version of the game every two weeks from work done around the world forces problems to the surface and demonstrates real progress. Without this, critical issues can remain submerged until late in the project, when it is too late to avoid delays and cost overruns.
- **High-bandwidth communication:** Communication on large co-located teams is stressful enough. On large distributed teams, it can be the main challenge. Teams must have the tools to communicate effectively, such as a networked conferencing system, reliable and ubiquitous, as well as a methodology that creates transparency, such as Scrum.

Distributed teams have barriers that co-located teams don't have. Conference calls cannot make up what is lost, but they can come close enough to ensure that the teams are productive.

## Challenges to Dispersed Development

A dispersed team shares the same challenges as a distributed team. Additionally, it is challenged with maintaining transparency, collaboration, self-organization, and the need to leverage the tools available in the best way possible.

This section explores ways that dispersed teams can overcome these challenges.

### *Transparency*

Transparency is expressed in the artifacts a team uses to maintain a shared understanding of their progress and impediments. For example, many online tools provide an analog to a Sprint task board, where each team member can visualize the Sprint backlog the same way a physical board allows.

Dispersed teams must avoid the abuses of transparency. A common example is with managers reacting to daily progress shown in the Sprint backlog. This behavior often reflects the lack of trust that managers often experience with dispersed team members and results in team members focused on the daily task estimates to the detriment of the Sprint goal.

Scrum Masters must work with such stakeholders and their teams to build the trust necessary for high performance teams (see Chapter 19, "Coaching Teams for Greatness").

### *Collaboration*

Collaboration is the act of working together to achieve a goal. Many online tools support collaborative behavior. Such tools have the following characteristics:

- **They are graphical:** They embody information on objects, such as stickies and various shapes and lines
- **They allow everyone to manipulate objects simultaneously:** They do not create bottlenecks by limiting input to only one user in a host position. Objects can be placed and moved around, just as in the real world.
- **They support facilitation and modification:** The team can adapt the tool to improve the flow of activities and process improvements as self-organization requires.

### *Self-Organization*

Dispersed teams must have the ability to adjust their practices and working agreements to meet their challenges and needs. No two dispersed teams are alike, so their Sprint practices cannot be entirely standardized. Areas of team self-organization include:

- Deciding core hours where communication is assured among every team member.
- Determining which online tools to use to plan, track, share, and communicate Sprint work.
- Deciding what to share and what not to share with stakeholders within a Sprint (see "Transparency" above).

### *Processes and Tools*

Agile methods value "individuals and interactions over processes and tools," but a dispersed team is forced to place more weight on processes and tools to overcome limited interactions and physical separation. Dispersed teams use more tools to plan, track, and display Sprint progress and Product Backlogs and share knowledge. Some of these tools can support personal interactions better than others.

**Remote Teamwork Tools**

Over the past several years, the tools available to remote teams have vastly improved. The number of tools and the practices emerging to help dispersed teams are too numerous and changing to capture here. As a result, Grant Shonkwiler and I have collected them in the book *Remote Teamwork Tools* (Keith, Shonkwiler 2020). Visit the website www.RemoteTeamworkTools.com to learn more.

### *Solving the Problems*

Addressing the challenges of dispersed teams requires more explicit communication than with colocated teams. It's easy to assume that quiet team members have no problems. On the contrary, it's often more difficult to extract information from them.

When a dispersed team is forming, it's valuable to hold daily Retrospectives to help them adjust. Be aware that they will not be very effective at first, and it will take a bit longer for a team to "norm" (see "The Tuckman Model" in Chapter 19).

Avoid focusing primarily on progress (checking out) but on the mindset of the solitary developers (checking in). The coaching tools from Chapter 19 will be especially useful in coaching dispersed teams.

## What Good Looks Like

At the developer level, a MAGE team experience should be minimally different from that of a small Scrum team. There will be more time spent:

- Addressing dependencies
- Merging changes for a single review build
- Scrum of Scrums and community of practice meetings

Over time, improved practices and Backlog and team formations will reduce this overhead. However, the main benefit of MAGE is avoiding the typical dysfunctions introduced by large game projects. MAGE teams and developers should

- Have a shared vision across the entire game
- Have autonomy at the feature level to introduce improved practices and allow creative input
- Be engaged in their work and understand how their work contributes to the whole
- Allow stakeholders to have transparency of the progress of the game, eliminating the need to react by "dumping resources" or imposing end-of-project crunch because of late emergence

## Summary

There is no single formula for scaling Agile on a game project. Scrum scales up to projects of any size but drives changes in team structure, roles, and practices. The place where most scaling frameworks fail is in creating massive overhead, process, and layers of communication that undermine the Agile and Scrum principles, which are the reason we adopted them in the first place.

Scaling is hard. No matter what you do you will encounter obstacles and challenges. The organization and the teams must use the built-in Scrum inspect-and-adapt loop to improve how they work together in order to succeed.

## Additional Reading

Brooks, F. 1975. *The Mythical Man-Month: Essays on Software Engineering*. Reading, MA: Addison-Wesley.

Brooks, F. 1995. *The Mythical Man-Month, Second Edition*. Reading, MA: Addison-Wesley.

DeMarco, T., and T. Lister. 1999. *Peopleware: Productive Projects and Teams, Second Edition*. New York: Dorset House Publishing.

Katzenbach, J. R., and D. K. Smith. 2003. *The Wisdom of Teams: Creating the High-Performance Organization*. Cambridge, MA: Harvard Business School Press.

Kniberg, H., and Ivarsson A. 2012. *Scaling Agile @ Spotify with Tribes, Squads, Chapters & Guilds*.

Kniberg H. 2012. *Lean from the Trenches*. O'Reilly Media.

Larman, C., and B. Vodde. 2017. *Large-Scale Scrum: More with LeSS*. Boston, MA: Addison-Wesley.

Schwaber, K. 2007. *The Enterprise and Scrum*. Redmond, WA: Microsoft Press.

Keith, C., and G. Shonkwiler. 2020. *Remote Teamwork Tools*.

## Chapter 22

# Live Game Development

Since the first edition of this book was written, the mobile game market has exploded in size. This market brings many challenges to the traditional model of game development, which aims for a single major release. It also brings significant advantages to studios that have an Agile mindset.

On the last AAA console game I worked on, we were weeks away from alpha, after years of development, when we had a visit from our publisher's CEO. This CEO was very excited about another game he had recently played, which featured using an AC-130 gunship against enemy artificial intelligence (AI) players. AC-130 gunships are large military cargo planes that have had large-caliber machine guns and cannons built in. They are very impressive and a fun feature to add to games, where appropriate.

The CEO was determined to have us put an AC-130 in our game as well. We argued that our third person action-adventure game didn't have a place in the story for an AC-130 to be useful because most of the gameplay took place in cities or inside buildings. He insisted that our players would love it. We had little data to support our side of the argument, and the CEO had all the power. So we put an AC-130 into the game. The result? Players never cared for it, and many reviewers thought the addition was stupid.

This highlights one thing I like about live games: You can ask the players what they like. You never have to be so speculative as you do with AAA games, but many live game developers still plan and execute like AAA games developers.

## The Solutions in This Chapter

This chapter explores the application of Agile and Lean practices to live games and the teams that support them. It discusses how feedback loops are used to pace development and optimize the delivery of value to the player and how metrics are used to drive the game going forward. The main solutions are to

- Speed up the feature pipeline; that is, how to get feature ideas into players' hands before the competition
- Rapidly respond to issues that disrupt the player experience and causes the game to lose players
- Use metrics to grow gameplay instead of making big gambles

## Games As a Service

Over the past decade, more and more games have shifted to a live model of development, where significant features are continually added to a game already in players' hands. Mobile games are the most exceptional example, exploring freemium and other various models that monetize the game beyond (or instead of) the initial game purchase.

Subscription models have been around for decades, charging players a fixed price every month to continue to play and build their online character or world. MMOs such as *World of Warcraft* are examples of games that were very successful in this space.

Lately, even AAA console games have been shifting to this model, often referred to as Games as a Service (GAAS). This approach is especially useful to sports games that, because of their fixed ship dates, can ship a game with the necessary roster and rule changes for the start of the season, but also offer features throughout the rest of the year that improve the player experience.

GAAS will continue to grow with cloud gaming, microtransactions, and season passes. This opens the door for further agility in game development.

**"Are You Two Crazy?"**

During a conference around 2006, I was approached by two young men who had a bunch of questions about Agile game development. They had started their studio and were building an MMO.

An MMO is probably the most challenging game to build. The complexity of the technology alone can number into millions of lines of code, more than even the most advanced fighter jet. It is a very risky game to take on, especially for a new studio.

But what they said next went beyond that challenge: They told me they were going to give the game away and rely on microtransactions. I wished them luck, and privately hoped they wouldn't suffer too much with their crazy idea.

The two of them, Marc Merrill and Brandon Beck, the founders of Riot Games, went on to release *League of Legends* a few years later, which went on to become one of the most successful MMOs.

## Why Agility for Live Games?

Live games and markets have created more opportunities for game developers, but have also introduced challenges:

- **More competition:** App stores now offer more than a million titles. Compare this to a decade ago when a console or PC gamer had only a few hundred titles to choose from.
- **Increased pressure to respond:** There are many examples of successful titles being edged out by similar games with faster development cycles.
- **Slow to grow, fast to shrink:** It takes time to build active player communities, and one broken or ill-conceived build can drive many of them into the arms of competitors.

Agile practices offer a response to these challenges by increasing response time to player metrics and focusing the team on deploying rock-solid quality.

## DevOps and Lean Startup

Readers familiar with DevOps and Lean Startup will recognize some of the approaches in this chapter. Both DevOps and Lean Startup have emerged from Agile and Lean practices over the past decade to address the challenges of live product support. If you are not familiar with these approaches, I highly recommend reading the *Dev Ops Handbook* (Kim, et al., 2016) and *The Lean Startup* (Ries, 2011) for more detail on specific practices as well as reviewing the practices presented in Chapter 11, "Faster Iterations," and Chapter 12, "Agile Technology."

## Feedback Loops

A feedback loop is part of a system where an output is fed back into the input of the system, which further influences the output. Feedback loops are important not only for gameplay mechanics, but also for the development of games. Using player reaction to a game, teams can shift their focus toward adding features that players prefer.

For AAA games that are many months away from their first deployment, there is no feedback loop with players. The reaction from stakeholders, who represent the potential player, after every Sprint is still a guess of what will succeed in the market, such as our ill-fated AC-130. Traditionally, AAA games have a single, major feedback with players when they ship.

Live games have a continuous feedback loop, which is a major advantage. They can deploy a minimally viable game at lower cost and, based on player response, deploy features that have the highest return on investment.

### Live Games and Fighter Aircraft

Early in my career, working on fighter aircraft, I learned about John Boyd. A former fighter pilot and military strategist, Boyd was instrumental in the design of the highly successful F-16 aircraft. Unlike other heavier fighters that were stuffed with too many requirements, these aircraft were far lighter and built around a philosophy called the "OODA loop."

The OODA loop is a decision cycle used to defeat enemy aircraft in a dogfight. *OODA* stands for

- **Observation:** The collection of data
- **Orientation:** The analysis and synthesis of that data to form a current perspective
- **Decision:** Determining a course of action based on the current perspective
- **Action:** The playing-out of decisions

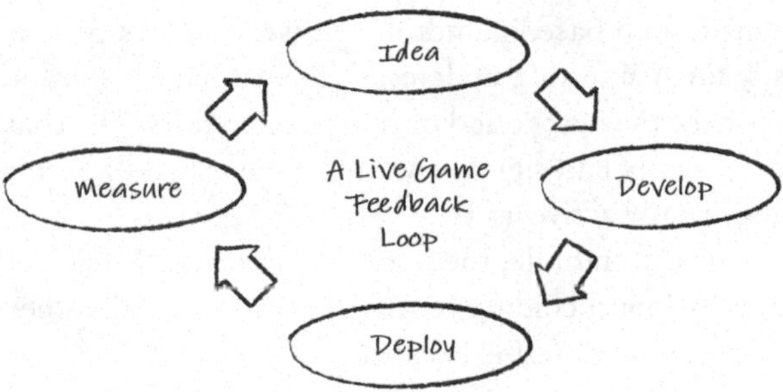


**Figure 22.1** *A live game feedback loop*

The focus of the OODA loop was to get "inside the decision cycle" of the enemy to gain an advantage. The superiority and low cost of the F-16 proved this philosophy.

Boyd later applied this philosophy to business, and it applies directly to live game development. In many cases we've seen that the approach of slowly deploying a complete feature set isn't as critical as quickly deploying individual features that the market desires. As a result, small upstarts can upstage more established teams whose process overhead drags them down.

## Live Game Feedback Loops

Rather than killing enemy pilots, the measurable goal for live game development is to grow the number of players who are enjoying the game as expressed through metrics, often referred to as Key Performance Indicators (KPIs). To execute and measure these metrics, live games implement a short feedback loop.

The most straightforward live game feedback loop is shown in Figure 22.1.

This chapter describes each step of this feedback loop:

- **Part One: Plan**—What players might want from your game and how you would measure their response to what you give them
- **Part Two: Develop**—The next set of features at the highest speed and quality
- **Part Three: Deploy and Support**—The game
- **Part Four: Measure and Learn**—How the players respond to the game and what that means to the next set of deployments

### *How Fast Should Our Feedback Loop Be?*

Studios often struggle with how frequently they can and should release updates to a live game.

I once visited a studio that made web-based games. It released updates once or twice a week, which were mostly for A/B testing updates: minimal changes that the studio could measure and use to make the next round of updates and tests. The challenge it faced was that the updates rarely had significant improvements. As a result, the games suffered a slow decline in daily active users.

Later on, after the studio transited to mobile, the opposite occurred. It released only once every three to six months (not including patches to fix bugs and vulnerabilities). As a result, the games were now suffering because

- The studio couldn't respond to the competition quickly enough.
- The players were impatient waiting for improvements.
- The prominent new features that were eventually rolled out weren't always what the players wanted.

### *U-Curves Help You Decide*

I am a fan of Donald Reinertsen's writings (Reinertsen, 2009). He puts Lean and Agile practices under an analytical lens that helps visualize the big picture and examine measurable trade-offs.

One of the tools he frequently uses is the U-curve. Figure 22.2 demonstrates the two costs (transaction cost and holding costs) measured over a batch size (the size of new features released at once), which produces the total cost.

The goal of the tool is to help you find the ideal batch size where the total cost is at a minimum.

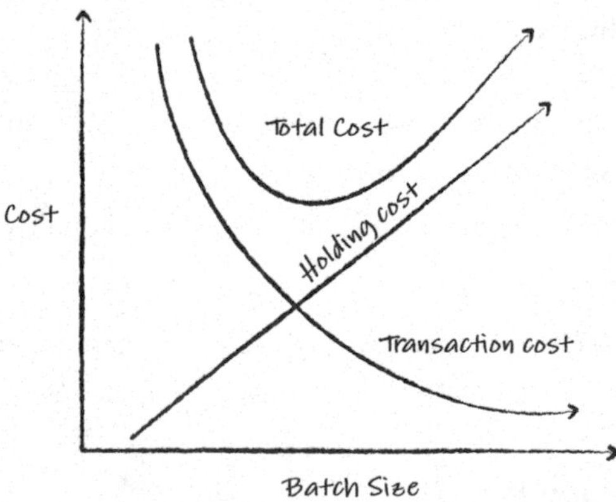


**Figure 22.2** *Cost versus batch size U-curve*

U-curves can be applied anywhere! My favorite example refers to the question of how often you should wash your dishes. There is a transaction cost of washing dishes that is independent of the number of dishes you wash. For instance, you could fill the sink, pour detergent in and wash and dry a single dish every time you use it, but that's a lot of effort for each dish. Alternatively, you could let them pile up for a week or two, but the holding cost (running out of plates and having a messy kitchen) would be too much. Most of us find a happy medium, perhaps once a day, where we batch up the daily dishes and wash them in one go. (Ironically, most studios I visit have a kitchen with a sign reminding people to increase the frequency of washing their dishes (that is, reduce the batch size).

Back to an example of live games, U-curves are applied in the following way:

- **Batch size:** The number of new features and content in the game
- **Transaction cost:** The amount of cost, proportional to the batch size of testing, fixing, and submitting a build that is successfully released, including the time for first party (for example, app store) approval
- **Holding cost:** The cost to your game in the market from holding back the features ready for releases (impatient players and the competition beating you to market)

When the studio mentioned earlier was releasing updates once or twice a week, most of the cost of development was invested in getting a build prepared for deployment. For example, a test might involve changing the behavior of some UI elements in the game. The actual change took an hour, but submitting the changes for review/approval, creating the build, doing regression testing, deploying the build, and addressing any deployment problems took days. That's a 90 percent overhead! The fixed cost of deploying so frequently also took time away from implementing the features players cared about. This is the transaction cost. Transaction costs shrink proportionally as the deployment frequency drops.

For the holding cost, delaying the delivery of larger features will increase the chance that players will shift their attention to another game, which is especially impactful when you have a free-to-play game that derives its income from the average revenue per daily active users (ARPDAU). Holding cost can also come from technical debt that accumulates over time. If a team is allowing debt to grow (for example, by dumping bugs into a database instead of resolving them), then the cost of fixing those before a large deployment increases.

So how often should you release a new version of the game? Reinertsen describes how this is determined by adding the transaction and holding costs. Because these costs move in opposite directions, then there results a minimum (the low point of the

'U' in Figure 22.2) in the total costs, which defines the ideal "batch size" or amount of new scope that is released. Because the rate of new scope is relatively constant, this can be fed into a predicted time frame, like every two to three Sprints.

Holding cost is fixed, so instead we focus on reducing the transaction cost by speeding up the planning-development-deployment pipeline and by reducing the batch size of new features.

**Reducing Transaction Costs**

Many of the development and test automation tools we'll discuss are like adding a dishwasher to the dishwashing analogy: It reduces the transaction costs and allows us to speed up the feedback loop.

### Measuring the Feedback Loop

As Peter Drucker said, "You can't manage what you can't measure."

There are many things we can measure with live games. Most of them are useless and lead to the Cobra effect as described in Chapter 9, "Agile Release Planning." This is often exhibited with games that focus primarily on monetization.

The primary metric for a live game feedback loop is the lead time between when an idea is proposed and when we've learned the player's reaction to it. This is more important than just the internal metrics of how fast the development team is or the amount of scope it can deploy per month. If it takes many months to learn how players are reacting to the new scope or we aren't measuring the entire loop, then we don't learn as much as we could.

## Part One: Plan

Many live game teams struggle to plan further out than a few deployments. Part of the problem is with the gap between KPI-driven short-term focus and the goals for the longer term. The business side still needs long-term vision for where the game is headed (portfolio, Backlog, product canvas, and so on), but the connection between long-term vision and developmental goals for live games is often poorly defined with long-term goals for player retention and growth merely being guesses.

Figure 22.3 shows the flow of connecting the vision and goals of the game with the model we have of the player to identify the next steps for development and how we are going to test the results of those steps.

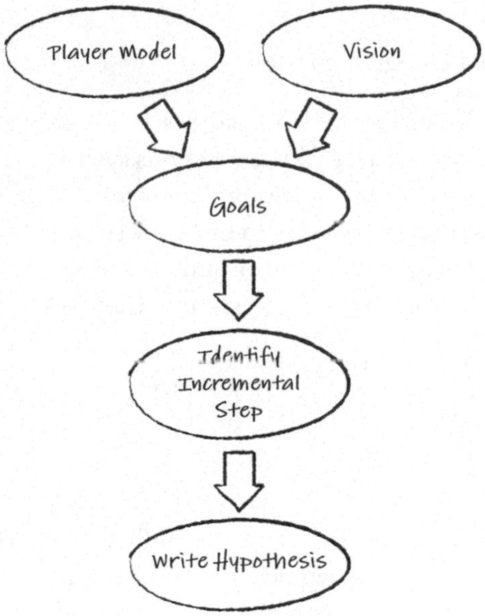


**Figure 22.3** *Flow of planning*

## Have a Vision

A game needs a strong vision. Without a vision, there is no focus. A vision should define the major pillars of the game and a backlog of feature goals. As with AAA games, it's easy to define too much detail here, which is speculative, which is even less necessary with live games.

An example vision would be to grow the social aspect of a single player puzzle game.

## Model the Players

Who plays your game? What do they want to do with it? What frustrates them? What problems are they trying to solve? What is the competition doing or not doing? What are your strengths?

These are typical questions that live games allow us to measure and experiment with. The goal of planning is not only to answer such questions but to learn more about our players and what the market wants so that we can grow that community of players.

Our model might reveal that players want to demonstrate their skill against other players rather than sharing techniques for how to improve solving puzzles.

**Lean Startup, UX, and Design Thinking**

The feedback loop we're using reflects Lean startup, UX, and design thinking, which focus on the users' needs and experience, asking questions such as "Who are our users?" and "Why would they use our software?" and creates a fast feedback loop of experimentation to provide answers to those questions.

As with DevOps, exploring all of these practices are outside the scope of the book. The books in the later "Additional Reading" section are good resources for further information.

## Establish the Goals

Goals could be epic stories, which would take multiple iterations to fully deploy. A goal example, given the vision and model of the player, would be tournament gameplay, where players could complete in head-to-head competitions over a weekend with the victory in each category winning a cash prize.

## Identify an Incremental Step

Instead of designing the entire tournament with ladders and player ranking systems, start with an epic story and split out some initial incremental steps to prove or disprove the assumptions of each goal.

For the tournament goal example, we want to identify a first step that will provide the most information. In this case, the tournament goal will succeed or fail based on the core head-to-head gameplay. If players don't care for that, then there is no reason to waste any more time on that goal, so that would be the step we want to test.

## Develop the Hypothesis

As in scientific research, a hypothesis is a guess that we have which we then use to design experiments around to either prove or disprove it. Ideally, these experiments should be able to produce answers quickly so that we can build on success or learn from failure and move on to the next hypothesis.

Adding anticipated KPIs to a PBI can better connect the two. A typical format would be to add the hypothesis to a user story in the form:

> We believe that <doing something> will <result in this measurable change> <within a constraint>.

How are we going to measure whether players like the new mechanic? Measuring how many players try the mechanic versus how many keep playing it after trying it is an excellent place to start.

**Note**

Keep in mind that raw numbers might not tell the full story. If the mechanic is hard to find or the interface for playing it is confusing, then the retention numbers might be too low. Player interviews and subjective analysis can be as useful as data in getting answers.

Depending on how "experimental" the mechanic is, consider a canary deployment (see the later section, "Canary Deployments") to a limited audience. Throwing many experiments at players may confuse them over time.

Here is an example of a hypothesis:

> "We believe that head-to-head play will be used by 25 percent of our daily active users within a week of its deployment and 50 percent of those players will play multiple times."

Constraints are usually time-based and short (one to three weeks) to allow for sufficient iteration if we want to try a few iterations.

This hypothesis would be fed into the development pipeline (see "Part Two: Develop").

### Refining the Backlog of Goals

A Product Backlog for a game that hasn't yet deployed has a lot of flexibility. We can keep adding features to it and not worry too much about how big it's getting (within reason).

For live games, constraining the size of the Product Backlog is essential. Its size impacts how long feature ideas linger and potentially miss their market window. Therefore, it's more important for the Product Owner to do two things:

- Say "no" more often
- Retire PBIs from the Product Backlog that are no longer relevant or valuable

These are typically done during Backlog Refinement sessions that should occur every few weeks.

## Part Two: Develop

For live games, simply improving development speed isn't enough. To better compete, live games have to be improved along the entire pipeline, from the point a feature idea is generated to the time the player can actually use that feature in game. Figure 22.4 shows the feedback loop for mapping, measuring, and improving the development flow.

### Map and Measure the Entire Pipeline

The first step in improving a live game development pipeline is to visualize and measure the **value stream**. A value stream is similar to the production stream discussed in Chapter 10, "Video Game Project Management." Figure 22.5 shows an example.

A value stream shows all the major stages of development for features, including the time between stages of work (that is, "waiting"), when a specification, code, or assets are waiting for the next stage.

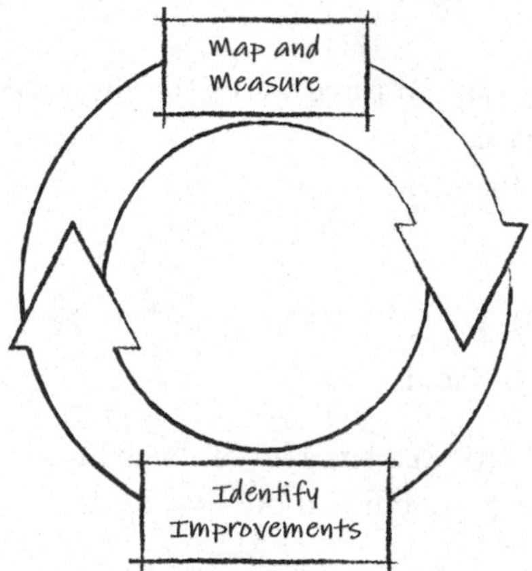


**Figure 22.4** *Development feedback loop*

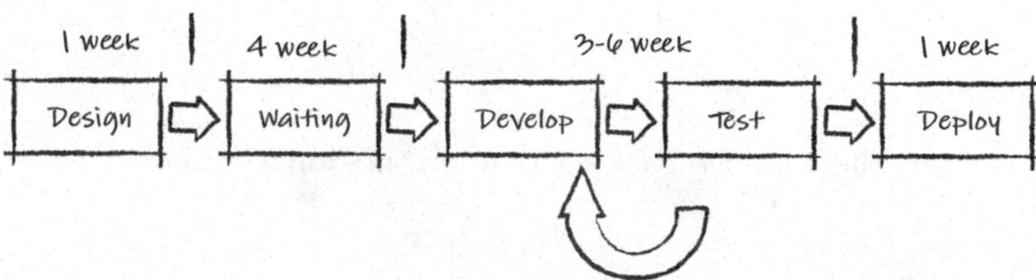


**Figure 22.5** *Simple feature pipeline value stream*

## Identify Ways to Improve the Pipeline

The total time to deploy a new feature, from idea to delivery, is commonly referred to as *lead time*. Lead time includes all the time between start and finish, including the time the feature spends simply sitting around waiting to be released. Lead time represents just how responsive we can be to our players and market.

### *Lead Time Versus Cycle Time*

In contrast to lead time, cycle time is the time between when work actually begins on a feature and when it is deployed (see Figure 22.6). Lead time also includes the time between when a feature is identified and when it is deployed. As a result, lead time is impacted by the length of features in a backlog that are waiting around.

It doesn't matter if we can develop and deploy a game in two weeks if the idea has been languishing in a list for over a year. That means that we've given the competition a year to come up with the same idea and beat us to market.

To reduce the lead time, we can do several things:

- Reduce the batch size of features through the pipeline. Instead of shipping an update with 10 features, deploy each feature as it's ready.
- Reduce the amount of time features are waiting around. This is done by pruning the list from time to time and prioritizing the features that players want (see "Refining the Backlog" later in this chapter).
- Improve development and testing practices. Both this chapter and the methods described in Part IV, "Agile Disciplines," describe how to reduce development time and measure how the players respond to them to build up to epic features, as described in the following case study.

### *Case Study: Speeding Up a Feature Pipeline*

A mobile studio I worked with had a live single-player puzzle game that had been very successful. Money from in-game purchases had been pouring in for years, but the competition had been heating up, and revenues were slowly falling. The major

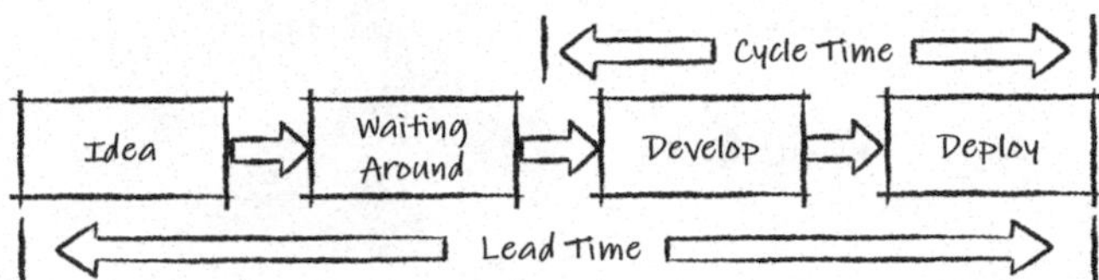


**Figure 22.6** *Lead versus cycle time*

problem was that it was taking six months to implement significant new features. Although the team was using Scrum to implement features, it needed to eliminate a lot of waste outside of Sprints.

The first thing to do was to map the value stream for a new feature from concept to player delivery. Figure 22.7 shows the results.

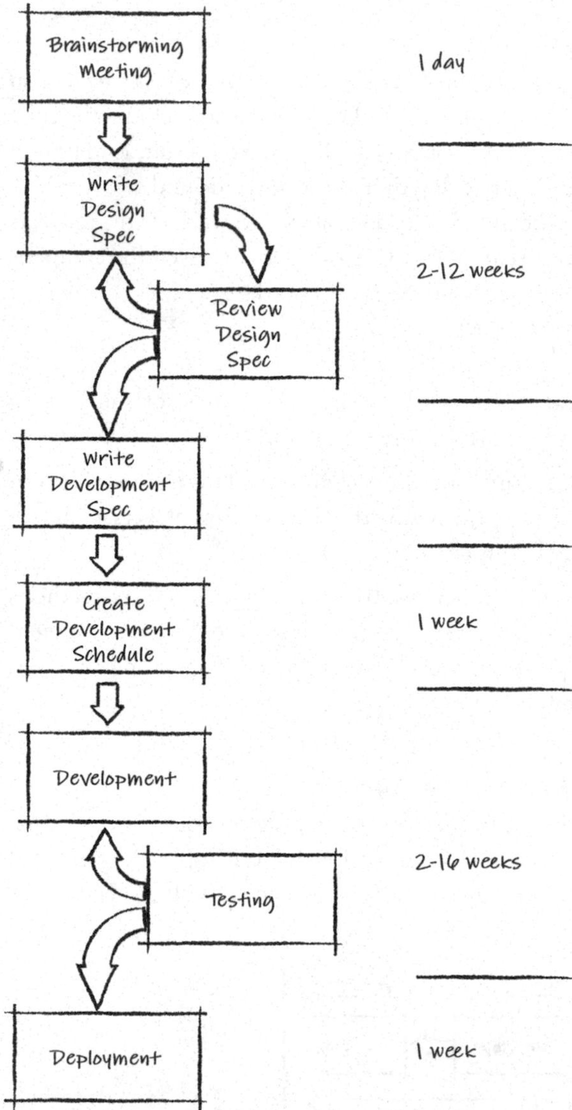


**Figure 22.7** *Feature pipeline before*

This exposed the following:

- New feature ideas were enormous; they were captured in 20–30 page documents.
- Because features were so significant, they went through numerous revisions and reviews that took one to two months.
- Shooting down a revision was easier than approving it due to its risk and cost.
- Gathering all the principles for a review (at best, twice a month) took time.
- The Sprints were not addressing debt as well as they could have, which resulted in a lot of rework in subsequent Sprints after a quality assurance (QA) team found problems trying to validate builds for submission.

To address this, we implemented two main changes, one hard, one harder:

- **The hard change:** Improving the Definition of Done with the Scrum teams to address debt, which required some automated testing, QA joining the teams, and improved practices such as test-driven development. Implementing these changes was difficult because it asked developers to change how they worked and required fundamental reorganization at the team level.
- **The harder change:** Weaning management off of their need to make big gambles with major features, which led to the big design documents. The new approach was to create smaller experiments that could be tested with players and could inform product ownership.

This change in design culture took a while to optimize, but seeing the metrics of the flow proved motivational for the leads, and they embraced being part of the solution.

Ultimately, the business metrics saw a benefit from this new approach. The throughput of new features (albeit smaller, incremental features) increased from one every three to six months to one every four to six weeks (see Figure 22.8). As a result, revenues started growing again.

## Reduce the Batch Size

The larger the plan, the more massive the gamble you take on its success. When the risk is large, stakeholders very often get nervous and want assurances that it will pay off. These assurances are usually offered in the form of large documents or very detailed task plans, which seem assuring, but are just wild guesses that diminish exploration.

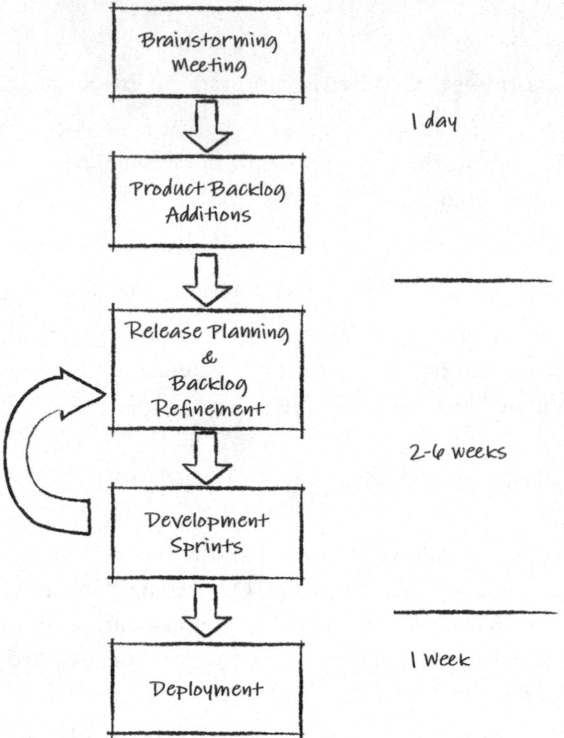


**Figure 22.8** *Feature pipeline after*

The impact on the lead time is tremendous due to three factors:

- Larger designs take longer to write.
- Stakeholders are more likely to reject a part of the plan, which leads to more iteration.
- Stakeholders can also rubber-stamp a larger design without fully comprehending the outcome, which can lead to late rejections and rework.

As shown in the case study, smaller features developed for live games avoid these problems by

- Being faster to describe
- Being easy to comprehend and approve or provide fast feedback
- Allowing early deployment and player feedback and measurement

## QA for Live Games

Live games with quality issues can die very quickly. Although building up daily active user counts might take months, losing them can take days if a problem-filled build is deployed.

This highlights the need to ensure that quality is foremost in everyone's mind throughout the development pipeline. Due to the risks, live game development tends to demand even greater investments in quality practices and test automation than more traditional game models.

### QA Engineering at IMVU

"Most features go through some level of manual testing. Minimally, the engineer who pushes code verifies the functionality in production. In many cases, features get dedicated testing time from a QA engineer. By the time a feature is ready for QA testing, our QA engineers can focus on using the feature much like a customer would. They expose bugs by doing complex, multidimensional manual testing based on more complicated use cases. People are good at this work, which is more difficult to cover with automated testing.

"Our teams are always reviewing QA priorities to see which features get attention. In some cases, there is so much important QA work needed that we organize group tests, either with the team or the entire company, to quickly find and fix issues. Our software engineers are also becoming skilled in carrying out manual testing and following our QA test plans. When this happens, it is more akin to classic Scrum, where all tasks (including QA tasks) are shared among the team.

"From a process standpoint, we integrate QA engineers into our product design process as early as possible. They provide a unique and valuable point of view for developing customer use cases and exposing potential issues before engineering begins work. The collaboration between our product owners and QA engineers adds tremendous value."

—James Birchler, Engineering Director, IMVU

## Part Three: Deploy and Support

I'm slightly embarrassed to admit that the mobile game I play the most is Solitaire. Solitaire is a great game to play when you are waiting to board an airplane or when trying to fall asleep in a hotel. I do both of those things quite often.

The first mobile Solitaire game I played had great graphics and some useful features. It also did a few things that annoyed me such as having slow animations when "undoing" moves and not having a feature that quickly completed the hand after all cards were exposed (a Solitaire hand is "solved" once all cards are face up).

Then one day, after Apple upgraded iOS, the game began crashing on startup. This kept up for a few days. Because I was traveling that week, I was having some withdrawal symptoms. I ended up trying a few competitive Solitaire games and found one that not only worked with the latest iOS, but also had fast undo animations and the autocomplete feature. I ended up buying that game and never going back.

By chance, I started working with the studio that made the Solitaire game that had all those crashes. It was a bit upset to hear that I had switched to their main competitor's game. This act was being mirrored by many of its players, and it was losing market share.

It was an eye-opening experience that such a simple game could suffer from the problems that larger games could as well. The mobile game market can be very fickle. Crashes, exploits, or the emergence of a similar game: Doing something better can change your market overnight.

This section explores support teams and how live support can help address emergent issues quickly and avoid losing players.

## Continuous Delivery

Chapter 12 discussed the benefits of continuous integration meant to reduce the number of team and feature branches into one development branch. The advantage of this is to shorten change merge cycles and reduce the number of problems that large merges create.

This is the same principle of reducing batch sizes in Lean thinking. Smaller batches of change mean that we can respond to problems more quickly and have a higher rate of iteration on improving practices.

This section extends the idea of continuous integration to **continuous delivery**. Continuous delivery is an approach of frequently creating a deployable build through automation, sometimes throughout the day.

### Continuous Deployment

Continuous deployment is the actual delivery of new features to players through automation. Because most live games have to go through first-party approval such as a console or phone app store, continuous deployment is less applicable than continuous delivery for games.

### *Feature Toggles*

Feature toggles are a technique for hiding, enabling, or disabling a feature during runtime, which is an alternative to code branching that allows a feature not ready for deployment to be turned off.

Feature toggles shouldn't be overused or abused. Things to watch out for include the following:

- **Toggle debt:** Having a lot of incomplete features toggled off.
- **Building large features before the player sees them toggled on:** Releasing smaller features to the player that build up over time is a better practice.
- **Toggles can be hacked:** The most famous feature toggle hack was the "Hot Coffee Mod" in *Grand Theft Auto: San Andreas* that players found and toggled on.[1] This exposed an X-rated feature that was never meant to be shipped with the game, which led to a massive product recall and an initial rerating of the game.

### *Canary Deployments*

Sometimes you want to deploy a version of the game to a much smaller audience to measure how they respond. A canary deployment is a way to do that. It can be used in conjunction with feature toggles to target specific sets of player and feature combinations. For example:

- We only want players in Tasmania to fight the zombie wallabies.
- We want to disable the red blood in Germany.
- We want to try out the new tournament mode with our most active players.

**"We Can't Use Scrum Because of Valentine's Day!"**

One of the most unusual reasons I've heard for not adopting Agile practices was from a mobile game developer who claimed that Scrum only allowed deployments at the end of a Sprint.

The game in question would release specific features aimed at holidays and the next holiday on the calendar was Valentine's Day.

There is nothing inherent in Scrum or iterative development in an Agile practice that prevents teams from deploying any time during a Sprint. It turns out that this team didn't have any integration, test, or deployment automation and that it needed at least three weeks to harden and test a build to deploy manually.

1. https://www.theverge.com/2012/5/6/3001204/hot-coffee-game

> Because its Sprint didn't end precisely three weeks before Valentine's Day, the team concluded that Scrum didn't work for it. I suggested that the team have the build ready four weeks early when the previous Sprint ended or have a shorter Sprint and work on improving its tools, but it had made up its mind that the current set of practices, with all the manual overhead cost for deployment, shouldn't be changed.

## Live Support Tools

A live support team is a form of a support team, described in Chapter 21, "Scaling Agile Game Teams," that focuses on addressing issues with a live game. Instead of a backlog of feature requests from development teams, a live support team handles problems that come up with a deployed game. Typical issues are

- Fixing client or service crashes
- Dealing with emerging exploits
- Collecting live game metrics
- Working with teams to improve deployment quality

Our first support team was focused on promoting practices throughout the studio to improve build stability. It became such an important part of their job that members renamed themselves the "Stability Team." The team's job wasn't to fix the problems being caused by other teams, but to capture the patterns of failure and to promote practices that eliminated their repetition.

Tools were key to doing this work. One tool team members used was to have a crashing build send an email containing stack dumps and other debug data to an email address that was constantly monitored. Having a Stability Team member visit you within minutes of a build crashing to ask you what you were doing at the time was not unusual.

Another tool was used to measure, on a day-to-day basis, the average stability of builds. This would show the trend of build stability over time (see Figure 22.9).

Many tools are available that live support teams can use. The recommended books describe hundreds of them. This section lists a few that are more commonly used.

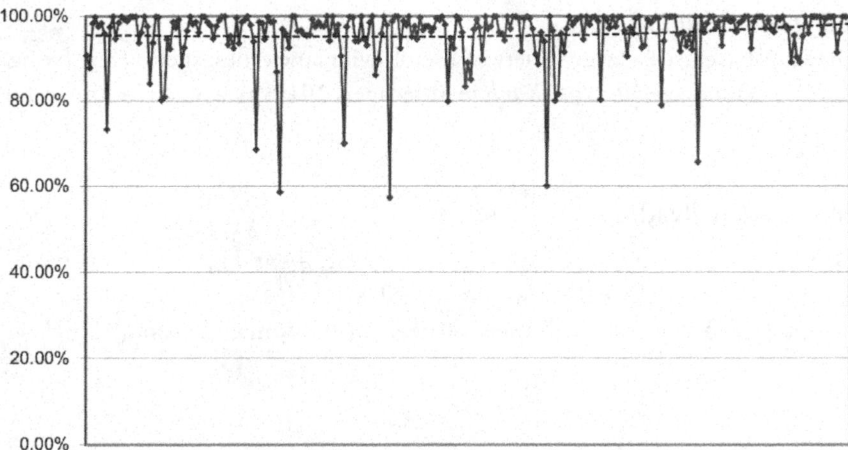


**Figure 22.9** *A stability trend chart example*

## *Emergency Swim Lanes*

The last thing you want to tell a live MMO team you support is, "We'll put 'fix the server crash' on the Backlog and deliver the fix two weeks later"!

Instead, a useful practice for addressing emergencies is to have an emergency swim lane (or emergency lane). When a request is in the emergency lane, it signals the team members just downstream to suspend their current work and focus on pulling the request further downstream. Figure 22.10 illustrates the emergency lane. In it, a crash bug has been placed in the lane by the Product Owner. This is the only person allowed to do that. This signals the developers to stop what they are doing and pull the request, called "Crash!" into the ready column by planning the work needed to address it. After it is done, they'll pull it into the develop column. When it's ready to be tested, the testers will pull it into the test column and verify the crash is resolved before deploying it.

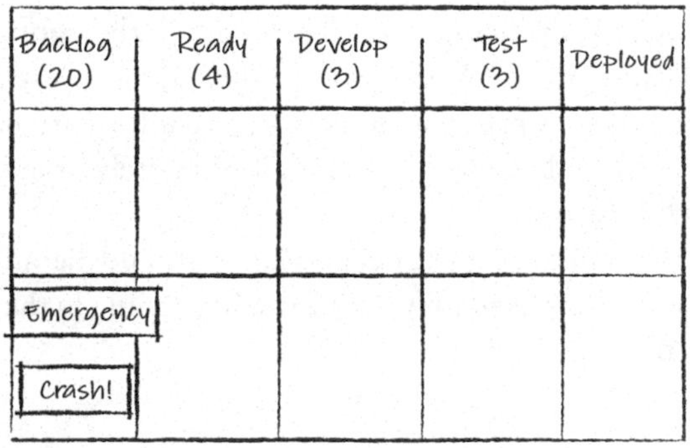

Backlog (20)
Ready (4)
Develop (3)
Test (3)
Deployed
Emergency
Crash!

**Figure 22.10** *An emergency swim lane*

### *Other Types of Swim Lanes*

Kanban teams have used a large variety of useful swim lane types, such as bug fixing. *Agile Project Management with Kanban* (Brechner, 2015) is a great resource for examples of these.

> **Recommended Reading**
>
> My favorite book on Kanban is *Agile Project Management with Kanban* (Brechner, 2015), written by the person who managed Xbox live services at Microsoft. This chapter cannot possibly cover the 160 pages of wisdom in this book. I highly recommend it.

### *Amplify Failure Signals*

I recently visited a studio that had a live action-adventure multiplayer game that was doing well in the market. Halfway through the training session, a number of attendees started to race out of the room looking panicked. It turns out that players had suddenly discovered a way to hack administrative access for their accounts, which gave their characters unlimited powers in the game. By the time it was discovered a large percentage of the players had this hack, and the impact to the entire audience was significant. Removing the access didn't take long, but the damage was done.

Finding ways to identify problems as early as possible can be more important than their fix. Instead of burying the signals for failures in a log file, finding ways to amplify them at the appropriate level (such as sending an email about a crash as mentioned earlier) can avoid catastrophic consequences.

Of course, you don't want support teams bombarded with hundreds of signals a day, so a system for prioritization and triage is useful.

### *Incident Retrospectives*

Whenever a launch failure occurs at NASA, the flight controller orders all the doors in launch control to be locked. Following this, all telemetry data is saved, and everyone is interviewed. The purpose of this is to capture the most accurate information possible to help the failure investigation find the root cause and, ultimately, some measures to prevent its recurrence in future missions.

Similarly, when a crisis such as the Solitaire crash occurs, there should be an immediate discussion on the causes and practices to prevent it from happening in the future. This is where an **incident retrospective** comes in.

An incident retrospective is a Retrospective held immediately after a problem is fixed. The steps taken in the retrospective are

- Construct a timeline of the problem and gather the contributing details leading up to it.
- Identify root causes and new practices to avoid them in the future.
- Identify signals for future failures and ways they can be amplified for the earliest possible detection.

These meetings need to be open and blameless as possible.[2] When blame is assigned, communication gets hampered, and facts are hidden.[3]

### *Blue-Green Deployment*

Blue-Green Deployment[4] is a practice of having multiple instances of a deployed version running in parallel. The production environment can fail over to the "last good version" when a problem occurs.

For live apps that must be approved by a first party (for example, App Store), this switchover is not immediate, but having a known good version of a client app that is ready to go can save time when addressing a major incident.

### *Chaos Engineering*

After Netflix moved its streaming services to Amazon Web Services, it created a tool called the Chaos Monkey to test system stability by triggering failures within Netflix's architecture. This tool identified many shortcomings in the architecture before its customers did, which led to significant improvements.

Live app developers have expanded on this idea, which has led to the discipline of **chaos engineering**, which is useful for live games as well.

Chaos engineering can be used by games to discover how they react to

- High latency
- Loss of connectivity

---

2. https://codeascraft.com/2012/05/22/blameless-postmortems/
3. The deaths of the astronauts on both the Challenger and Columbia were attributed to cultural and communication issues at NASA. None of the root causes of the accidents were unknown.
4. https://martinfowler.com/bliki/BlueGreenDeployment.html

- App crashes
- App server downtime

All of these issues and others can be tested before your customers encounter them.

### *Measuring Incidence Response Time*

The most critical metric for live support teams is the time it takes between an incident being reported to when it is addressed in the live game. This time, called the **Incidence Response Time**, should improve as the team introduces better practices and tools.

Because there are separate types of incidents classified by their urgency, live support teams will often have a few response times to track.

> **Nothing is New**
>
> In the late eighties, I used to play an online air combat game called *Air Warrior*. This game allowed more than 100 players from around the world to dogfight in World War II planes and locations.
>
> Kesmai, the game's developers, were kept on their toes fixing exploits we pilots were always discovering. One time, we discovered that by dropping dozens of AI paratroopers from high altitude bombers over their territory, we could overwhelm the enemy's radar and defeat them.

# Part Four: Measure and Learn

After the game is deployed with the new feature, we gather the data identified with the hypothesis. In addition to the subjective metrics, we can gather other data as well.

## Measure Results

A wide range of approaches exist for evaluating player engagement with features implemented in the game. Some games use a complex statistical analysis,[5] whereas

5. https://www.youtube.com/watch?v=-OfmPhYXrxY

others use a less formal subjective approach, communicating with players directly using forums and other social media channels. Some use a combination of both. Under certain circumstances each approach can work.

### Do Retrospective Actuals and Update Your Vision

After reaching the constraint, hold a Retrospective to review the collected data and discuss the next steps. Include the team and stakeholders.

Remember the lessons from Nintendo and Atari from decades ago, described in Chapter 1. Focus on finding the fun first. If a mechanic fails early, it's still a win. You've avoided the cost of developing a major feature that would have failed!

**Aiming for Failure**

I worked with a team that was trying to create an algorithm to solve a tricky augmented reality device problem. There were dozens of potential approaches to use, and the team had spent months trying one approach at a time before giving up after spending one or two months trying to make each work.

A Retrospective revealed that although proving an approach would work took a long time, proving it wouldn't work was far quicker. As a result, the team shifted its efforts to eliminate as many of the potential approaches as possible and quickly narrowed them down to a remaining few that eventually worked for its device.

## What Good Looks Like

In 2012, Supercell released *Hay Day*, a farm simulation game, on iOS. By releasing a minimally viable game to mobile, it was able to beat the existing market leader to mobile by almost two years. Its strategy of subsequently growing the game's features based on player feedback resulted in *Hay Day* becoming the fourth-highest game in revenue generated in 2013.[6]

6. https://qz.com/172349/why-free-games-are-increasingly-the-most-profitable-apps/

## Summary

Games as a Service is the future of the industry. Even large AAA franchises are transitioning to shipping minimal games that they can use to grow through live support over time.

This transition requires a rethinking of how we plan. Many live developers are stuck between executing on large speculative designs that are large gambles and short-term KPIs that lead to short term gains but long-term extinction.

It's a fertile ground for exploring and innovating in the Agile space, and next decade will see even more new practices emerge than the last.

## Additional Reading

Brechner, E., and J. Waletzky. 2015. *Agile Project Management with Kanban*. Redmond, WA: Microsoft Press.

Garrett, J. 2011. *The elements of user experience*. Berkeley, Calif.: New Riders.

Gothelf, Jeff, and Josh Seiden. 2016. *Lean UX: Designing Great Products with Agile*. O'Reilly.

Ideo Tools. https://www.ideo.com/tools.

Keith, C., and G. Shonkwiler. 2018. *Gear Up!: 100+ ways to grow your studio culture, Second Edition*.

Kim, A.J. 2018. *Game thinking: innovate smarter & drive deep engagement with design techniques from hit games*. Burlingame, CA: Gamethinking.io.

Kim, G., P. Debois, J. Willis, J. Humble, and J. Allspaw. 2016. *The DevOps handbook: how to create world-class agility, reliability, and security in technology organizations*. Portland, OR: IT Revolution Press, LLC.

Reinertsen, Donald G. 2009. *The Principles of Product Development Flow: Second Generation Lean Product Development*. Celeritas.

Ries, Eric. 2011. *The Lean Startup: How Today's Entrepreneurs Use Continuous Innovation to Create Radically Successful Businesses* , NY: Crown Publishing.

# Chapter 23

# There Are No "Best" Practices

I'm often asked, "What are the best Agile practices for doing [X]?"

My stock reply is to ask what they've tried. There are no best practices for Agile teams. The "best practices" we used to make Nintendo 64 games would make it impossible to create games of the scale and complexity we see today.

"Best" implies a static landscape. Technology and gamers' tastes and entertainment choices are anything but.

Over the past decade and a half of Agile adoption, many innovative practices have been applied in the game development community.

## The Solutions in This Chapter

This chapter describes some of the practices and techniques I've seen that are less common, but are highly effective.

> **Innovative Practices**
>
> Grant Shonkwiler and I have been collecting sets of innovative practices from across the game development community in our book, *Gear Up!: 100+ ways to grow your studio culture*. We update the book once a year with new practices.

As emphasized throughout this book, Agility is characterized by continual experimentation and inspection of what we are making and how we're making it, followed by an adaptation of practices. This chapter contains examples of that experimentation and how Agile applies in areas such as indie game development and games developed for novel platforms.

## Visualizing Your Work

An underappreciated aspect of Agile is the value placed on visualizing your work. Task boards, cards on the wall, burndown charts, flashing lights warning of build failures, and so on are all encouraged.

These so-called "information radiators" are hard to ignore. They don't sit on some server, requiring licensed software to access (these are sometimes referred to as "information refrigerators"). They are easily customizable and adapt to changing practices.

A more important aspect of visualizing your work is in choosing how it's presented. The two examples that follow (feature boards and story maps) have led to teams adapting their practices to focus on the outcomes in a game, rather than the output of their individual tasks. Both examples were chosen because they led, through the simple application of practices to better organize and visualize work, to dramatic improvements in the outcomes (time and quality).

### Feature Boards

A benefit of physical task boards is that the team owns them. A physical task board is always visible, requires no licenses and little training to use, and is endlessly customizable as teams inspect and adapt their work. The only limitations are that it requires wall space and team co-location.

A common problem encountered with task boards is a lack of visibility of cross-discipline dependencies. For example, let's say a team is working on several player mechanics, such as jumping, crawling, and ducking. There are three programmers, a modeler, and an animator on the team. Halfway through the Sprint, the programmers have the code working, but can't thoroughly test it because the animator is backed up with too much work or is waiting for a model rig to be fixed. Perhaps the animator is trying to work on all three mechanics at once, or the task of modeling one character is more laborious than expected, or there is a problem with an export.

Creating awareness of these problems is one of the functions of the Daily Scrum meeting, and a seasoned team will address them, but sometimes issues like these don't surface until it's too late in the Sprint to do anything about them. This is one instance where a feature board can help.

#### *What Is a Feature Board?*

A simple feature board is shown in Figure 23.1.

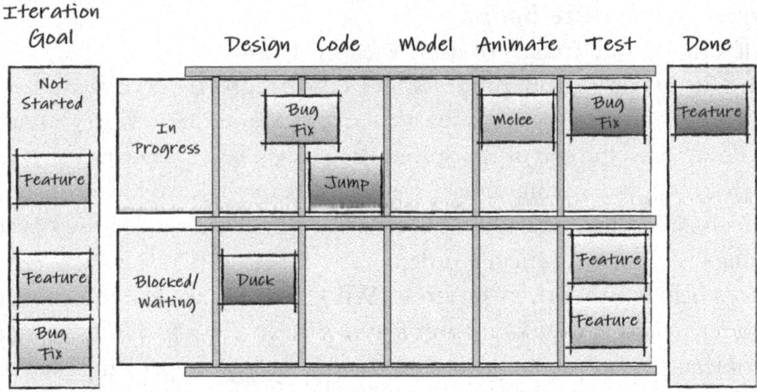


**Figure 23.1** *A feature board*

Instead of tracking tasks, a feature board visualizes a feature's development state. The Sprint Goal is in the left column and contains cards identifying features the team committed to implementing. Cards move around the board (not just left to right) during the Sprint, depending on the work being done. Each column on the board indicates the type of work done on the feature at the moment. The rows show which features are in progress and which features are waiting for work to finish. As features complete, they exit to the right of the board into the "Done" column. In this particular example, the features are prioritized in value. Red features are the most important. Green features are the least important, and yellow are in between.

## *How Is a Feature Board Used?*

A feature board serves the team. It shows members the state of each feature daily and leads to conversations that are necessary for a cross-discipline game team.

Take a look at the board in Figure 23.1. The board shows that the jump feature is being coded, while melee is being animated. A few bug fixes are needed: One of them is being worked on by both a designer and programmer, and another is in test.

The board also raises questions. For example:

- Are the testers overwhelmed? It looks like they have test work piling up.
- What are the modelers doing? Have they run out of work?
- Why are lower priority features ready for testing? Why are they ahead of higher priority features?

The board won't answer those questions, but quickly highlight them for the team to address.

### *The Advantages of a Feature Board*

The following describe the advantages of using a feature board.

**Feature boards focus on feature progress, not task progress.** Too many times, teams focus on completing tasks in any particular order and don't worry about features being "done" until the end of the Sprint. Postponing "done" means features don't get enough polish and tuning time. As a result, teams release lower quality features. Feature boards focus the team on completing prioritized features over merely completing tasks in any particular order.

**Feature boards help limit work-in-progress (WiP).** To complete features sooner in an iteration, a team needs to work on fewer features in parallel and address issues or workflow problems that are stalling work or wasting time. By separating the "In Progress" features from the "Waiting/Blocked" features, a team will see where work is piling up quickly enough to be able to do something about it. Teams can even institute "WiP Limits" on the columns or rows to stop any new features being added when work is piling up too much. This leads to different behaviors. For example, when the team sees that testing work is piling up, others in the team can help out. No law of nature says, "Only testers can test." By embodying WiP limits, feature boards can be a tool for encouraging such "out-of-the-box" thinking.

**Feature boards help balance cross-discipline teams.** Unlike software-only teams, a cross-discipline team of game developers can't share as much of their work (for example, you really wouldn't want me creating a texture or a sound for your game). Quickly identifying problems with the flow of work is essential. Task boards don't do this well; they don't visualize stalls in the flow. As a result, individuals end up solving problems by working on more things in parallel, leading to late integration, testing, and tuning. Feature boards show, dramatically and frequently, where the stalls are occurring, or soon to occur, which focuses a team's response.

**"This Looks Like Kanban!"**

Some of these ideas come from Kanban (like WiP limits), but it's not Kanban by the book. While Kanban by the book is excellent for some work—work that is less exploratory or that follows a predictable flow of hand-offs from one discipline to the next—the feature board is better for teams that are working on unpredictable new features and "first-time" content. Feature boards fit best within a timeboxed Sprint, which has a lot of "swarming." *Swarming* means that an unpredictable flow of work exists between disciplines to create a feature, and the feature will bounce around or iterate unpredictably before the fun is discovered.

## Story Mapping

Story mapping is a technique pioneered by Jeff Patton (Patton, 2014) for creating a two-dimensional map of stories, usually arranged by priority or a narrative of player activity, on the horizontal axis and by time (as forecasted Sprint Goals) on the vertical axis.

The advantage of arranging stories on a two-dimensional map is that it creates a narrative of the Release goal directly mapped to the Release plan. It also encourages teams to execute Sprints as an emergent narrative rather than focusing on the parts of a Release that will someday be integrated. See Figure 23.2 for an example.

### *A Story Map Example*

Creating a map for each Release is useful. In a typical Release, we'll usually start with a "Big Hairy Audacious Goal" or BHAG (see Chapter 9, "Agile Release Planning"). For our example, let's use a BHAG for a hypothetical car racing game:

> "You are a fugitive driver, being chased, avoiding traffic, and using your driving skills to escape Chicago!"

This is a good goal and a sizable chunk of work. The first step in Release Planning is to break the BHAG down into some smaller epic stories (stories still too big to fit into a Sprint).

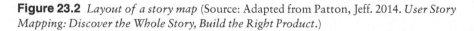

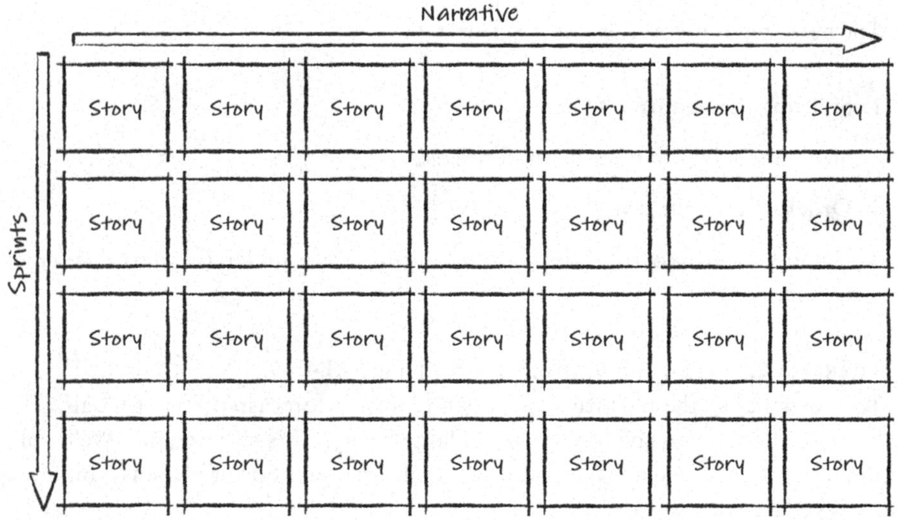

**Figure 23.2** *Layout of a story map* (Source: Adapted from Patton, Jeff. 2014. *User Story Mapping: Discover the Whole Story, Build the Right Product.*)

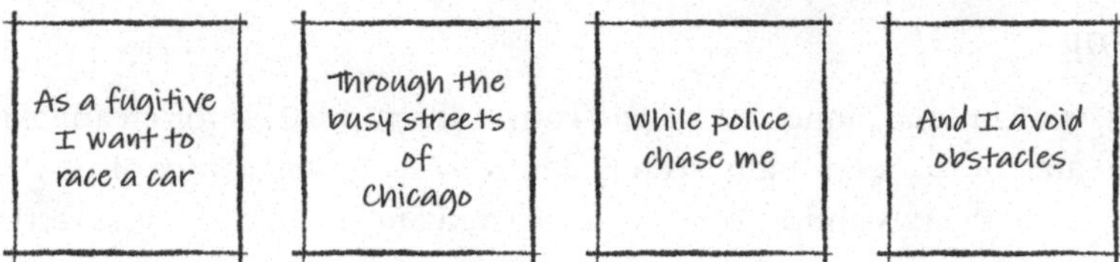


**Figure 23.3** *A narrative backbone*

For our example, we have the following epics:

- As a fugitive, I want to drive a car fast to evade the police.
- As a fugitive, I want to avoid obstacles so I can stay ahead of the police.
- As a fugitive, I want to use the busy streets of Chicago to lose the police.

With a bit of prioritization and refinement based on team structures, we can recreate the BHAG as a narrative backbone made up of the epic stories. The backbone is still a set of epics, but now ordered by importance, as shown in Figure 23.3.

Driving the car is the most important feature. It won't be much fun if you can't evade the police. Avoiding obstacles would be nice but is less important than the city and police.

Also, note that the narrative isn't a set of stories following the user story template. The reason is that we want the narrative to be read as a whole tightly coupled story. The template can get in the way of doing that.

The next step is to forecast some Sprints by

1. Splitting the narrative "epics"
2. Sizing them by whatever method you use
3. Ordering the split stories
4. Placing them into their appropriate Sprint (row) under the narrative epics (column).

In the example, the map might then look like Figure 23.4.

The rows below the narrative backbone represent forecasted Sprint Goals. The ambient traffic item on the lower right is large because it's still an epic. We'll split that up after the spike (experimental work) in the previous Sprint gives us a bit more knowledge about the work involved.

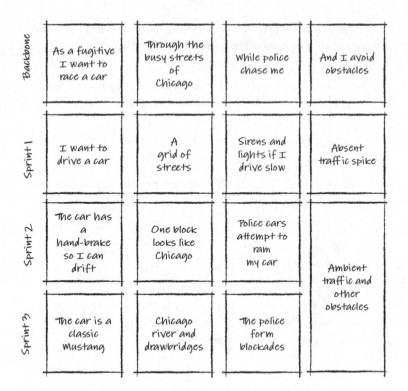

| Backbone | As a fugitive I want to race a car | Through the busy streets of Chicago | While police chase me | And I avoid obstacles |
|---|---|---|---|---|
| Sprint 1 | I want to drive a car | A grid of streets | Sirens and lights if I drive slow | Absent traffic spike |
| Sprint 2 | The car has a hand-brake so I can drift | One block looks like Chicago | Police cars attempt to ram my car | Ambient traffic and other obstacles |
| Sprint 3 | The car is a classic Mustang | Chicago river and drawbridges | The police form blockades | |

**Figure 23.4** *A full story map*

## Note

The example application of story mapping maps Sprints on the vertical axis, where Jeff Patton describes the vertical axis as a prioritized breakdown of the story above it, in the backbone. Mapping to Sprints was just how we applied story maps.

### *Why Use Story Maps?*

Some advantages of story mapping include the following:

- They visually organize the work for a release. I love the big-picture view. They can be even be used on games with a hundred people to give everyone a clear picture of the shared goal and progress.

- The narrative communicates "why" we are working on the stories. I've noticed that teams using a map will respond to emergence better because they understand the big picture.
- They are two-dimensional. The one-dimensional view of a traditional Product Backlog is limiting. Having multiple dimensions is better at handling the order of the work.
- They are *very* customizable. For example, some teams map dependencies by connecting dependent stories with colored string.
- They respond well to change. You can shift stories, priorities, and how work might be shared very quickly.

**Sprint Goals are Still Narratives**

If you look at the Sprint Goal rows in the story map example, you can see that they still form a sub-narrative of the backbone. This allows the team to create more of an emergent experience rather than a collection of component features that will be integrated near the end of the release, postponing the overall experience.

## Developing for New Platforms

In 1996, our studio was hired by Disney to create several rides for *DisneyQuest*, a chain of indoor interactive theme parks that would feature motion-based rides and virtual reality games.

Our first attempt was a virtual reality (VR) game where one would have lightsaber battles with classic Disney villains. A few problems existed with the hardware. Back then, the $50,000 VR helmets weighed a lot and required a very powerful $250,000 mini-computer to run.

The project collapsed after Disney had us place the player on a hovercraft to fly into battle. Introducing motion to VR that had 100-millisecond motion tracking latencies resulted in half the riders getting motion sick. When so many riders got sick on $300,000 worth of hardware, the ride becomes less profitable.

Developing for new platforms has challenges in the uncertainty they bring. Like "finding the fun," the approach must be experimental, despite the promises the platform developer makes.

## Launch Title Development

In my career, I've developed many games and demos for hardware that hadn't launched yet, and I've come to learn a few things:

- The eventual device doesn't live up to its promised performance or specifications.
- Development kits are always late and rarely have decent software tools.

The situation is even more harrowing when you are developing a launch title for an entirely new class of hardware, one that may not have been used for games before, which is the case with emerging platforms such as virtual or augmented reality headsets.

Since 2015, I've worked with studios tasked with launching titles for these platforms. The challenges they face are compounded by

- Not having many examples of successful core mechanics, such as player motion
- Having an environment to play in, such as employing VR headsets on roller coasters, where each headset has to endure being worn by a hundred different riders a day
- Dealing with constantly slipping schedules for the launch
- Having critical core specifications that change almost daily, such as field of view, battery life, and peripheral design

Given the fluid state of such new hardware, doing any form of long-term design is detrimental. Such designs embed tremendous numbers of assumptions, despite the hardware development team's assurances, and when the hardware specs are updated, usually at the last minute, launch title teams have to scramble to rebuild their games, often compromising features and assets to "make it fit."

A better approach to developing launch titles is to defer decisions and minimize risk by developing parallel options based on a range of possibilities and prototyping hardware.

Here are some examples of prototyping:

- Prototyping the spaces that augmented reality (AR) will operate in that create challenges to the technology
- Prototyping UI elements and testing them in variously lit areas
- Prototyping anything that moves, such as a roller-coaster car, to explore the limits of what riders can do and tolerate and how they experience it with a headset

## Parallel Development

One of my favorite non-game project stories is about the design of the Prius. The Prius was a revolutionary car that took less than half the time from design start to production than a typical internal combustion car.

Toyota's goal was to create a car that would appeal to the "green" consumers. However, the choice of engine technology was not certain. A hyper-efficient gas engine, an electric engine, and a hybrid were all candidates. Delivering the car to market in half the time of a typical vehicle was a challenging goal.

Toyota could have chosen an engine technology upfront and focused its efforts on making it work. Most companies, faced with this tight schedule, would have done so. Instead, what Toyota did was inaugurate three research teams to study each engine technology.

Months later, the all-gas engine team found that although it could improve the efficiency of the engine, it couldn't deliver enough efficiency to attract the green market. The electric engine team found that it could achieve the efficiency, but it couldn't deliver a car with a low enough price to entice buyers. Although people want to be green, a limit exists on how much they will spend.

The hybrid engine team was able to build an engine within the mileage and cost targets, and it was chosen and refined for production.

When hearing this story, many managers are unmoved. They claimed they couldn't have teams researching multiple solutions. In response, we might ask, "How much does it cost to delay the entire project by months because the critical path was stretched out?" You can easily spend 10 times the cost on a delay for an 80+ person team than you would have been researching upfront with a much smaller one.

### Developing a Launch Title for The Magic Leap One at Weta Gameshop

"Our game studio was born out of the symbiosis between the Magic Leap and Weta Workshop[1] teams. We had two jobs:

- Create a launch game for the Magic Leap One
- Help define what the platform should be in the first place

"The idea behind the second point is that games are a great general use-case for an emerging spatial medium, with a need for great controls and input,

1. https://www.wetaworkshop.com/about-us/history/

powerful processing, graphics, high-quality audio, and so on, so using one to define the system would be an excellent shaping force.

"It was an incredibly tall order, as we started before there was any real tech at all: just a bunch of very big ideas from some very clever people. Our team was always out in front of the tech, patiently waiting for the hardware and software to come together and work as we hoped.

"That meant that for years at a time, we had to hack every solution, and it all had to be temporary and flexible, all the while focusing on the big goal of ultimately delivering a big, high-quality game with some real substance. That was an incredibly hard balancing act and required some real endurance and faith in the big vision.

"We tried lots of different ideas and tried to make informed speculations on how a game has to be to work on top of the real-world. There were no examples to work from, so we often used real-world analogs like theatre and carnivals as reference points.

"I had an analogy for new team members when they joined: We're here, on the mainland, and we're going to build a bridge out across the water to this amazing island called Magic Leap One, and we'll use bamboo and duct-tape and whatever we can find along the way, but behind us Magic Leap HQ will build a big, beautiful steel and concrete structure and we'll finish the journey on that when it catches up to us.

"We spent a lot of time on our own in the ocean.

"In the meantime, we used any bit of off-the-shelf tech that we could find that might get us a step further down the line. We set up physical test spaces, with polystyrene furniture and lightweight modular walls that we could reconfigure so that we could try and anticipate the kinds of problems we'd experience in a random player's home. We used the emerging VR tech, we acted out logic from the game in person, we built virtual room editor tools to sub in for real-time meshing. We did anything we could think of.

"And we would sit back and look at everything we had dreamed up as often as possible to guess where it might break: mainly to anticipate future pain, but also to ensure we didn't go too deep down any rabbit holes.

"Then in the last year of a six-and-a-half-year journey, we pulled together all the best ideas, put our foot on the gas, and built *Dr. Grordbort's Invaders*. We ran a sprint at the end of one tough marathon.

"The key to it all was to surround ourselves with great people, and look after one another. And don't take it all too seriously: making games is fun after all."

—Greg Broadmore, Game Director, *Dr. Grordbort's Invaders*,
and Studio Director for Weta Gameshop

## Agile and Indie Game Development

A few months before I started college, Atari released the Atari 400 home computer. It was the most detrimental thing that could have happened to my scholastic discipline.

I couldn't immediately afford the 400, so I got a job at a local computer shop that had just opened to sell the Atari. I could afford the 400, rent, and tuition, but not always food. There were a few weeks where I could only afford to purchase stale loaves of bread at the local convenience store.

But life was great! These days, one can't imagine how revolutionary it was not only to own a computer, but one that was designed for games. I ignored my classes, and with a diet of stale bread and little sleep, I created my first game: *A Defender Clone.*

My boss at the computer store let me sell my game, comprised of an audio cassette the Atari used for storage, and a few photocopied pages of instruction all packaged in a Ziploc bag. The game sold less than a dozen copies, but I was recognized as a registered developer by Atari.

Although the label didn't exist at the time, I was an indie developer.

### The Draw of Indie Development

Around 2005, there was a significant migration of developers away from AAA development to develop games independently. We lost a few talented (and well paid) developers who decided to invest their savings (and mortgages) in homemade games. Having made my own games in the past, I understood the draw. Our games had become so large in scale that the passion and engagement of making a game that I had felt decades earlier was being drained away.

Several factors created the opportunity for the indie movement:

- Digital game marketplaces, such as Steam, and digital console marketplaces offer an easier way to sell games.
- Commercial game engines, such as Unity and Unreal, lower the technical cost of entry for indie developers.
- The Internet and web tools allowed more collaborative distributed development among indie developers.

## The Challenges of Indie Development

A few years ago, I watched a documentary on Netflix, *Indie Game: The Movie*[2], with fascination. The passion the people in it had was incredible, but the emotional and physical toll the indie developers endured was stunning. Much of it was due not to the creative process, but the challenges of funding, teamwork, and a lack of disciplined development process that led to enormous wastes.

This isn't meant to characterize all indie development. Indie game developers such as Jonathan Blow (Braid and Witness) have demonstrated disciplined development practices for their games, which have met with success.

## How Agile Development Helps

An Agile approach to indie game development helps in the following ways:

- **Responding to opportunities:** The business of indie game development is very dynamic. There are many sources of potential funding that can come and go at a moment's notice. A developer might get interest for a port of his or her game to a new platform that would provide needed funding to float the project. To respond, a working build needs to be shown and a clear vision communicated to "connect the dots" for the potential stakeholder. Indie developers often need to be ready to pitch and pivot.
- **Funding:** Demonstrating an improved game every one to three weeks allows stakeholders to see real progress. With many indie game developers turning to early access programs or crowd-funding platforms to fund their game, an evolving game that shows steadily increasing value makes a better case for continued support.
- **Teamwork:** Short Sprint Goals help balance where the team needs additional or less help and establishes a vision and a target that a team of developers, often with other responsibilities and jobs, can commit to. Agile indie teams often have shorter Sprints and longer release horizons.
- **Disciplined development process:** The estimation and project management approaches described earlier in the book still apply to indie game development and can reduce wasted effort. One example I've seen is with indie teams that mix pre-production/exploration work with production work, which leads to incredible amounts of wasted efforts when a core mechanic needs to be changed and numerous character and level assets need to be rebuilt.

2. https://www.imdb.com/title/tt1942884/

**Indie Success Combos**

"When developing games independently, it is important to create success combos. Stringing together each success helps to build larger achievements to reach your goals, maintain a peace of mind, and boost your team's morale during the peaks and valleys in a development cycle."

—Justin Woodward, M.S.

**Building Community**

Indie game developers often share early versions of their games to build community and anticipation for the deployment of a version that starts to earn money. The thing that drives me crazy when I invest in an early version of a game is a lack of quality. Promising games that constantly crash, are filled with half-finished features, or have blatantly missing assets make me feel that the game will never finish[3] and shouldn't be invested in further.

3. Which is usually the case

**"Hustle Logic"**

"During the initial hustle phase of a game venture, hard work is the most valuable asset that a developer has. Strategic developers who understand this principle generate sweat equity and an understanding of their craft that can transform their game and team into valuable commodities in the future."

—Justin Woodward, M.S.

## What Good Looks Like

Just as we need to innovate what we're making, we need to innovate how we're making it. The market, technology, and people making games will never stop changing.

Studios that embrace this approach to their process are always great places to work. They are populated by developers who are passionate and whose passion is rewarded with more autonomy, mastery, and purpose in their working lives.

## Summary

This chapter contained examples of some of the emergent Agile practices and areas of development where Agile is applied. They capture the experimental nature of agility, which is necessary for success.

## Additional Reading

Keith, C., and G. Shonkwiler. 2018. *Gear Up!: 100+ ways to grow your studio culture, Second Edition.*

Patton, Jeff. 2014. *User Story Mapping: Discover the Whole Story, Build the Right Product*. Sebastopol, CA: O'Reilly Media.

# Conclusion

The practices and experiences of Agile game development are real. Most studios have adopted some form of Agile-based methods over the past decade, but most have struggled to embrace the values and principles. As new platforms and business models continue to emerge, new practices, tools, and ways for creative people to make better games less expensively will evolve. This is what makes Agile so well suited for developing games. The goal is not to find the "perfect" methodology but to embrace change.

This is a very unique and challenging time for game developers. Games are mainstream, and we are continually discovering different platforms on which to release games and new markets for them. Even "serious games" for education, health care, defense, city planning, and so on are emerging as a significant market. At the same time, massive layoffs and lawsuits over unfair working conditions threaten careers and cause talented people to leave the industry.

The overhead, drudgery, and suffering that many game developers endure to make something "fun" impacts game quality. We should share the practices that help us reduce the waste involved in making games—waste such as waiting around, losing work to crashes, spending time on unworkable solutions, and communication problems. We need only compete on the basis of our creativity and talent. Doing this, we can raise the bar for the entire market and grow it.

We need to return to the state where most of us started when making games in our spare time: We need to love making games.

# Index

## A

## D

# E

## M

## Q



## R

## S

## X



## Y-Z